# MILITARY RAILWAYS

BY

MAJ. W. D. CONNOR
CORPS OF ENGINEERS

---

Reviewed and Approved by the
Board on Engineer Troops

**Fredonia Books**
**Amsterdam, The Netherlands**

Military Railways

by
W. D. Connor

ISBN: 1-58963-878-6



Reprinted from the 1916 edition

Fredonia Books
Amsterdam, The Netherlands
http://www.fredoniabooks.com



In order to make original editions of historical works available to scholars at an economical price, this facsimile of the original edition of 1916 is reproduced from the best available copy and has been digitally enhanced to improve legibility, but the text remains unaltered to retain historical authenticity.

WAR DEPARTMENT,
OFFICE OF THE CHIEF OF STAFF,
*Washington, May 5, 1916.*

The following Manual of Military Railways, prepared by Maj. William D. Connor, Corps of Engineers, is approved and published for the information and government of the Regular Army and the Organized Militia of the United States. It is intended to supplement Part IV, Military Railways, of the Engineer Field Manual (Professional Papers No. 29, Corps of Engineers).

By order of the Secretary of War:

TASKER H. BLISS,
*Major General, Acting Chief of Staff.*

# MILITARY RAILROADS.

## COMBAT RAILWAYS.

1. The subject of military railroads as here treated will include the location, construction, operation, and maintenance of railroads in the theater of war under military auspices and for military purposes; that is, with a personnel consisting of officers, enlisted men, and civilian employees, and for the main purpose of facilitating the movements and supply of the Army.

The difference between war and peace conditions will cause a wide departure of military from civil railroad practice. Some of the conditions of military railroad service are:

(*a*) Quick results for a short period are of the first consideration.

(*b*) The mechanical possibilities of the property can not be fully developed by reason of an untrained personnel.

(*c*) Speed requirements are moderate and practically uniform for all traffic.

(*d*) The roadbed and equipment are subject to damage beyond that resulting from the operation of the road, or from the elements, or from decay. A civil road is operated on the presumption that the track is safe; a military road must be operated on the presumption that the track is unsafe.

(*e*) The property will usually be in fair but unequal condition, often hastily restored after partial demolition. The operation of the whole will depend on the condition of the worst parts.

(*f*) A military road is best operated with an ample supply of motive power and rolling stock, and a moderate speed; whereas on a civil road the tendency is to increase speed to economize rolling stock, and to increase train loads to economize motive power. The known ratios of equipment and mileage on civil roads can not be taken as sufficient for military roads.

2. Railways constructed and operated for military purposes vary from a rough, narrow-gage road on which the motive power is man or mule, to a fully equipped, modern, standard-gage road. The first would probably be used in the approaches of siegeworks or to supply an army in a winter camp or a fortified position of great extent, and the latter when an existing commercial line was taken over for military uses. Between these two extremes are many grades of railways, but each grade shades imperceptibly into the next above and below, and any considerable classification must be artificial and of little use in discussing the general subject. The only classification that seems logical is to divide them into those that are built and operated within the field of the enemy's observation and fire, and those built and operated beyond his field of observation and fire. The former are called **combat railways** and the latter **supply railways.**

3. **Combat railways** differ from permanent railways only in the degree of care taken in their construction, maintenance, and operation. The same general rules govern both, and the engineer officer must apply those rules to suit the requirements of his particular case. They will practically always be narrow gage lines, and in most cases will be made of portable track similar to that used in mines and industrial works. Rolling stock and track, while not kept on hand in large quantities, can be obtained in small amounts, and orders placed can be quickly filled.

**Requirements.**—Combat railways must be capable of transporting guns, ammunition, and other supplies, especially those of the heavier kinds, to the various siege batteries, magazines, and bombproofs, and, possibly, to the various parallels that are constructed in carrying on a siege. From the nature of the line, it must be one that can be rapidly laid and as rapidly taken up and relaid elsewhere; it must not occupy too much space in the approaches and parallels; it must be of light weight, and it must permit of very sharp curves. These various requirements demand a light, narrow gage railway.

4. **Motive power.**—The loads will be hauled either by men, animals, or gasoline motors, as a steam locomotive would indicate too clearly its position by its smoke. If the requirements of the service are great enough, **gasoline motors** of the type shown in fig. 1 can be used with advantage. These motors are made from 2 ft. to 4 ft. 8½ in. in gage, and one weighing 2 tons will haul 10 tons on a level track. Details of heavier types are shown in Table I.

TABLE I.—General dimensions and capacities of vulcan gasoline locomotives.

| Weight. | Horsepower of engine. | Diameter of drivers. | Optional speeds (miles per hour). | Rated drawbar pull. | Frictional resistance per ton. | Hauling capacity (tons of 2,000 pounds) in addition to weight of locomotive. On a level. | On a grade per mile of— 52′.8 1%. | 105′.6 2%. | 158′.4 3%. | 211′.2 4%. | 264′.0 5%. | Wheel base. | Outside dimensions. Length. | Width. | Height. |
|---|---|---|---|---|---|---|---|---|---|---|---|---|---|---|---|
| *Tons.* | | | | *Pounds.* | *Pounds.* | | | | | | | | | | |
| 4 | 25 | 16″ | 3 and 6 | 1,600 | 10 | 156 | 49 | 28 | 19 | 14 | 10 | 3′ 0″ | 10′ 0″ | 4′ 0″ | 3′ 4″ |
| | | | 4 and 8 | | 20 | 76 | 36 | 22 | 16 | 12 | 9 | | | | |
| | | | 5 and 10 | | 30 | 49 | 28 | 19 | 14 | 11 | 8 | | | | |
| | | | | | 40 | 36 | 22 | 16 | 12 | 9 | 7 | | | | |
| 6 | 35 | 18″ | 3 and 6 | 2,400 | 10 | 234 | 74 | 42 | 29 | 21 | 15 | 3′ 9″ | 11′ 0″ | 4′ 0″ | 3′ 10″ |
| | | | 4 and 8 | | 20 | 114 | 54 | 34 | 24 | 18 | 14 | | | | |
| | | | 5 and 10 | | 30 | 74 | 42 | 29 | 21 | 16 | 12 | | | | |
| | | | | | 40 | 54 | 34 | 24 | 18 | 14 | 11 | | | | |
| 8 | 45 | 22″ | 3 and 6 | 3,200 | 10 | 312 | 100 | 56 | 38 | 28 | 21 | 4′ 0″ | 12′ 0″ | 4′ 2″ | 4′ 0″ |
| | | | 4 and 8 | | 20 | 152 | 72 | 45 | 32 | 24 | 19 | | | | |
| | | | 5 and 10 | | 30 | 100 | 56 | 38 | 28 | 22 | 17 | | | | |
| | | | | | 40 | 72 | 45 | 32 | 24 | 19 | 15 | | | | |
| 10 | 55 | 22″ | 4 and 8 | 4,000 | 10 | 390 | 123 | 70 | 47 | 34 | 26 | 4′ 0″ | 12′ 6″ | 4′ 8″ | 4′ 2″ |
| | | | 5 and 10 | | 20 | 190 | 90 | 57 | 40 | 30 | 23 | | | | |
| | | | 6 and 12 | | 30 | 123 | 70 | 47 | 34 | 26 | 20 | | | | |
| | | | | | 40 | 90 | 57 | 40 | 30 | 23 | 18 | | | | |
| 12 | 75 | 24″ | 4 and 8 | 4,800 | 10 | 468 | 148 | 84 | 57 | 41 | 31 | 4′ 3″ | 13′ 0″ | 4′.8″ | 4′ 4″ |
| | | | 5 and 10 | | 20 | 228 | 108 | 68 | 48 | 36 | 28 | | | | |
| | | | 6 and 12 | | 30 | 148 | 84 | 57 | 41 | 31 | 25 | | | | |
| | | | | | 40 | 108 | 68 | 48 | 36 | 28 | 22 | | | | |
| 15 | 90 | 25″ | 4 and 8 | 6,000 | 10 | 585 | 185 | 105 | 71 | 51 | 39 | 4′ 6″ | 14′ 3″ | 5′ 0″ | 4′ 6″ |
| | | | 5 and 10 | | 20 | 285 | 135 | 85 | 60 | 45 | 35 | | | | |
| | | | 6 and 12 | | 30 | 185 | 105 | 71 | 51 | 39 | 31 | | | | |
| | | | | | 40 | 135 | 85 | 60 | 45 | 35 | 28 | | | | |

All of the above locomotives can be furnished with either one of the two-speed transmissions as listed in tables under "Optional speeds."

The **hauling capacity** is the heaviest train of cars and their loads which a locomotive can start on a straight track in addition to itself and pull at speeds specified.

**Mine cars** will usually have a frictional resistance of from 20 to 30 pounds per ton on comparatively straight track, and with sharp curves will often run as high as 40 pounds and over. To determine the maximum hauling capacity of a locomotive from the table, use the frictional resistance, together with the proper percentage of grades.

Use 10 pounds per ton frictional resistance with good cars, good track, and no curves.

Use 20 pounds per ton frictional resistance with fair cars and track and easy curves.

Use 30 pounds per ton frictional resistance with hard-running cars and track with fair curves.

FIG. 1.—FOUR-WHEEL GASOLINE LOCOMOTIVE.

This motor (fig. 1) is designed for hauling in mine, quarry, elevator, and industrial works.

SPECIFICATIONS.—Motor: Vertical type, ample power for service conditions. Gage; 24 to 56½ in. Material, metal throughout, heavy railroad construction giving ample tractive power. Control. Two speeds forward and same in reverse. Height of drawbars to suit requirements. Exhaust screened. Brakes: Standard type, applied to all four wheels.

5. The **usual motive power** will be either men or animals, and since the roadbed will ordinarily be very rough, the form of construction used should permit them to **travel outside of the track** and the cars should be supplied with corner rings for attaching the drag lines or harness. Derailments will be frequent and the rolling stock should be such that replacing loaded cars will not be a very difficult operation.

6. **Capacity.**—The portable railway used by the Japanese in Manchuria was 23.6-in. gage; that by the Russians was 30-in. gage. Both used short sections, 6.5 ft. and 5 ft. long, respectively. The Russian rails weighed 25 lbs. per yard. The Russian line had passing tracks, or sidings, at intervals of about 7 miles. They used cars weighing about 1,920 lbs., which carried a load of about 4,400 lbs. The cars were hauled by two animals, one on each side of the track. The capacity of the line was about 600 tons each way daily, equal to about the capacity of 400 escort wagons. This capacity could have been increased considerably by decreasing the interval between sidings and enormously by double tracking. Portable railway is particularly useful for laying diversion or "shoo-fly" tracks around short breaks in the line during permanent repairs.

7. **Alignment and grade.**—Within the field of observation and fire of a besieged place practically all movements must be made under artificial cover. The location of these lines of approach will be dictated by military principles, and the line of the combat railway will therefore be determined not by questions of economy or ease of construction, but by the location of the siege approaches and parallels.

For the same reason, the grade of the line is practically thrown out of the consideration, although a slight change in the direction of the approach might be made to keep the grade of the line below the limiting grade, if by such a change no military advantage were lost. This limiting grade should be kept as low as practicable, for the difficulties of moving cars under such adverse conditions are great at best, and for any slope greater than 6 or 8 ft. in a hundred the difficulties of ascent with loaded cars will be very great, even for animal traction; and above that, the cars would probably have to be moved by cable.

## TRACK.

8. **Gage.**—The word gage is used with various meanings in railroading, but its most frequent and most important use is to indicate the distance between the inner edges of the heads of the rails when newly laid. **Standard gage** is 4 ft. 8½ ins. to 4 ft. 9 ins., being adapted to running standard-gage equipment. The actual gage of any track exceeds the nominal gage by the amount of wear on the inner faces of the two rails since they were laid, and by any outward movement of either rail due to traffic. The gage of a combat railway may be determined by any of several conditions, such as the amount of portable track available, the weight of the equipment necessary, the amount of materials that must be handled on the railway, etc. The amount of narrow-gage railway stock and equipment that is kept on hand by the commercial firms of this country is very limited and for a sudden call the choice of gages would not be very great. This condition will probably be the controlling one, as at present there is no military railway equipment for our army. **A 2 ft. 6 in. gage railroad** would answer the purpose as well as, or better than, any other, and if notice can be had long enough in advance, the entire equipment for field railways might well be of this gage. Considerations of weight may require a narrower gage, and a **2-ft. gage** will give a very efficient railway. This gives lighter track sections, lighter rolling stock, and in actual siege-work requires less width of trench. Subject to these considerations, the wider the gage the better, although on the offensive a narrow-gage line will doubtless have to be used.

On the **defensive side** of a siege there is greater opportunity to use a standard gage track, and such track will be used whenever practicable, supplemented when necessary by narrow-gage lines.

9. **Roadbed.**—There will probably be no time for ballasting the roadbed, and for this reason the ties used should extend well beyond the rails and, in order to form the least possible obstruction to movements on foot in the approaches and trenches, should be as thin as practicable.

10. **Rails and connections.**—The rails may either be bought already fastened to metal ties, or the rails and ties may be ordered separately. In the former case, the sections are known as **portable track,** and usually come in 15-ft. sections (fig. 2).

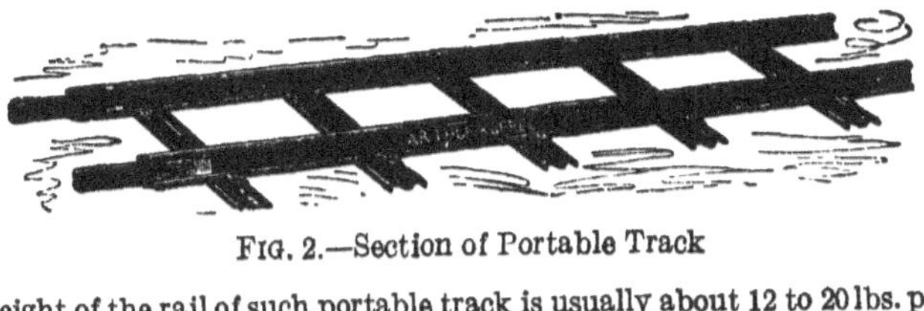

FIG. 2.—Section of Portable Track

The weight of the rail of such portable track is usually about 12 to 20 lbs. per yard, and the most common gages are 20 and 30 ins. Portable track of wider gage and heavier rails can be had by special order. The ties used are usually of the cross section shown in fig. 3, and standard sizes weigh 7 and 12 lbs. per yard. The rail is the standard T rail. The **connections** between the rails are usually the ordinary fish plates and bolts, as shown in fig. 3. **Angle bars** may be used if obtainable, though for so light a rail the **fish plate** answers every purpose.

The rails are fastened to **metal ties** with clips and bolts as shown in fig. 4.

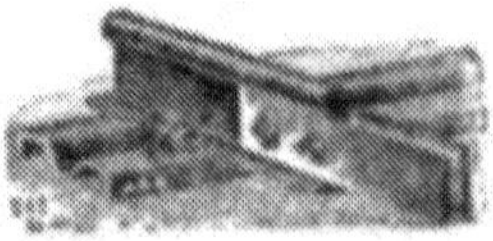

FIG. 3.—METAL TIE AND RAIL CONNECTIONS.

FIG. 4.—RAIL FASTENING TO METAL TIE.

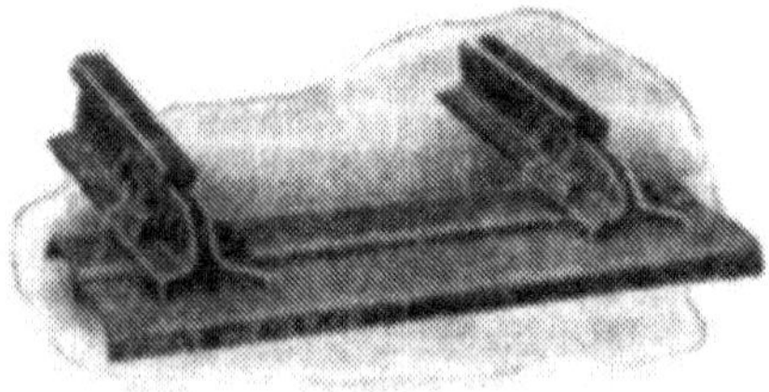

FIG. 5.—ANGLE PLATE CONNECTION WITHOUT BOLTING.

A type of connection for rapid laying, requiring no bolting, is shown in fig. 5. This is only a temporary expedient and the rails should be bolted as soon as practicable. In ordinary commercial portable track the weight of the ties is about equal to that of one rail. Hence the weight of portable track per linear foot is about equal to the weight of 1 yard of rail. Portable track can be estimated to cost about 5 cents per pound, made up at the factory.

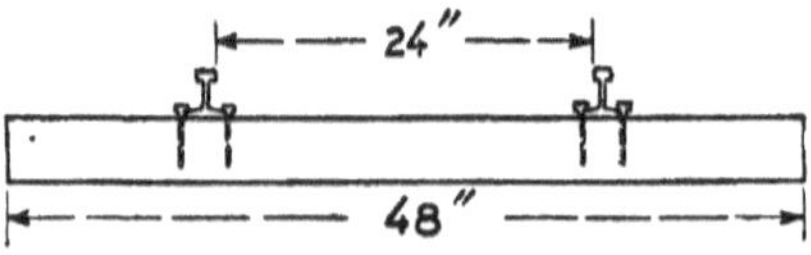


FIG. 6.

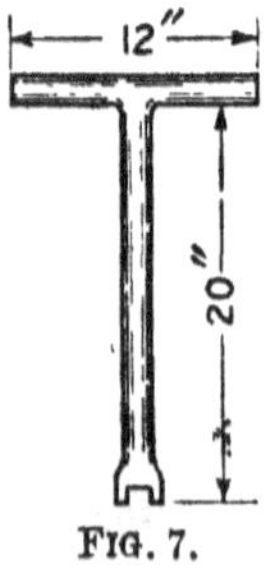


FIG. 7.

11. If the track is laid on **wooden ties,** railroad spikes will ordinarily be used to fasten the rail. However, circumstances may demand that the railroad be laid without noise, in which case **lag bolts** can be used instead of spikes (fig. 6). A wrench for lag bolts is shown in fig. 7.

12. On tracks of this sort, with a poor roadbed, it is advisable to have the rail joints opposite each other (**square**), except on curves, where they can not be so laid without cutting the rails. The joints of the rails should lie midway between two ties which are so placed that they rest under the opposite ends of the fishplates connecting the rails. This **suspended joint** has been found very satisfactory (see fig. 37).

13. **Ties.**—In case **metal ties** can be obtained, and the necessary punch for punching the bolt holes is at hand, these ties are preferable to wooden ones on account of the smaller space they occupy. Metal ties of portable track are but little longer than the gage of the track. Ties longer than those used commercially would require a special order.

In case **wooden ties** are used, 3 by 6 in. or 3 by 9 in. ties are probably the best. If ties of this size are not at hand, thicker ones may be used. If 3-in. or thicker lumber is not available, ties may be made by using inch or half-inch boards nailed and clinched to provide the necessary thickness. The distance between the ties depends upon the load and the weight of the rail. Wooden ties should be at least 2 ft. longer than the gage of the track to give good bearing.

14. **Switches.**—For a portable railway, **switch sections** are made that include the main track and turnout from the point of switch to beyond the frog. These switches are usually split switches, as illustrated in fig. 8, and can be purchased

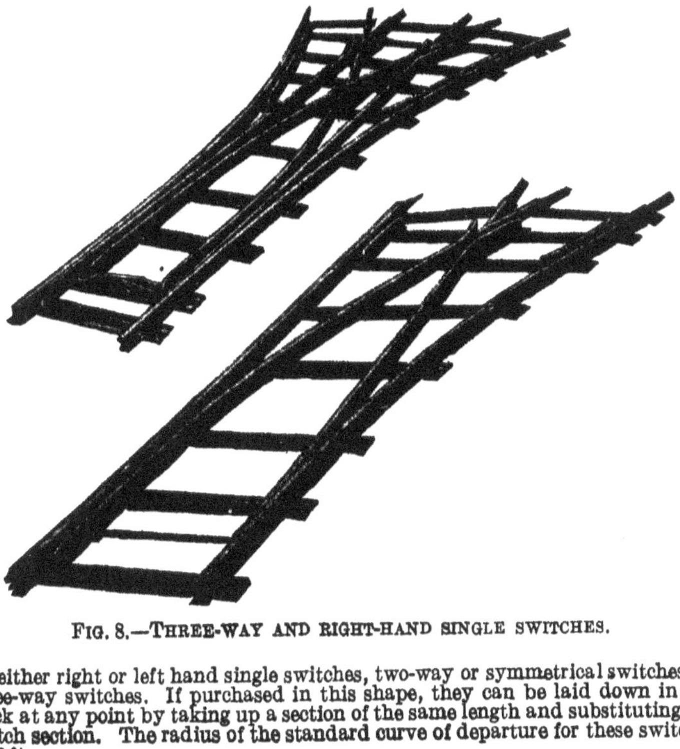

FIG. 8.—THREE-WAY AND RIGHT-HAND SINGLE SWITCHES.

for either right or left hand single switches, two-way or symmetrical switches, or three-way switches. If purchased in this shape, they can be laid down in the track at any point by taking up a section of the same length and substituting the switch section. The radius of the standard curve of departure for these switches is 30 ft.

The switch sections usually correspond in length to the sections of straight track made by the same manufacturer. **Guard rails** should be called for on all switches. (See fig. 107.)

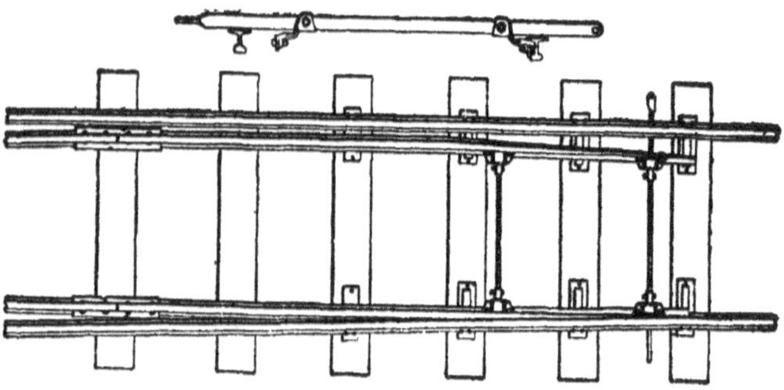

FIG. 9.—SPLIT SWITCH FOR LIGHT RAILS.

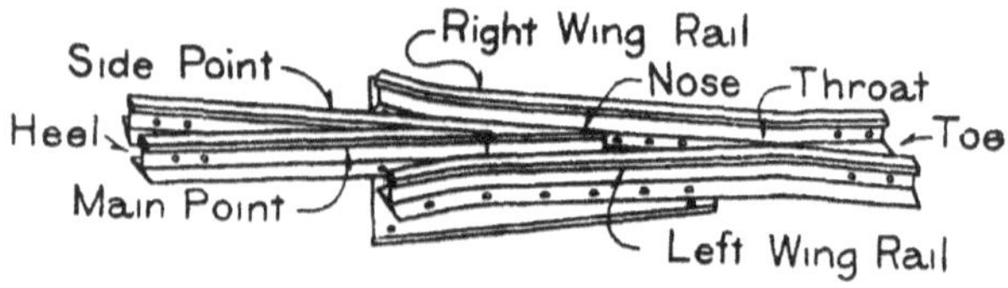


FIG. 10.—FROG.

15. The various parts for switches and turnouts for light track on wooden ties are furnished by the same dealers that furnish portable track.

The **parts of a switch** (figs. 9, 10, 11) are as follows:
- One pair switch points, with slide plates.
- The necessary connecting rods.
- One ground throw or stand.
- One frog.
- One pair guard rails.

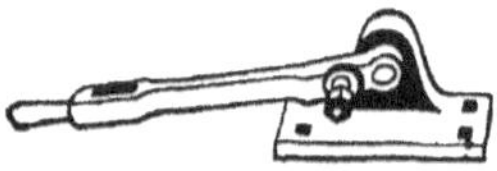

FIG. 11.—GROUND THROW SWITCH.

For the method of **putting in switches** for other than portable track, see par. 127 et seq. In cases where the point of connection changes frequently, on light track, an **inclined switch or climber,** as illustrated in fig. 12, may be used. This can be laid on a track at any point, and has been used on standard-gage roads for temporary sidings.

16. **Stub switches.**—It may happen that there are frogs on hand, but no split switches. In this case what is known as a stub switch (fig. 96) answers every purpose for a siege railway. The frog is located and the rails of the turnout and main track are laid on their regular curves until the distance between the heads of the rails is equal to the required clearance for the wheel flanges. These rails are all permanently fastened and the adjacent half of the rail on the main line is left movable, leading either to the turnout or continuing on the main line, according to the way it is set. The movable parts of these rails are connected by switch rods and slide on metal plates. (See par. 134 for fuller description of stub switches.)

17. **Curves.**—The curves used on this kind of line usually have small radii. The radius may be as small as 12 ft., although a radius of less than 30 ft. is not advisable, if avoidable. For curves with radii over 500 ft., see par. 63 et seq. Curves with

radii under 500 ft. can be laid off without the use of surveying instruments about as easily as with the use of instruments. For the portable track mentioned in par. 10, sections will be bent by the manufacturer to any desired radius. For other track, the rails must be bent and the center line of the track located in order to lay out the curve.

FIG. 12—INCLINED SWITCH OR CLIMBER.

For method of laying out curves when portable track is not used see par. 58.

18. The angles made in the trench lines of siegeworks are so sharp that curves with very short radii will be necessary. Sharp curves, even with low speed, mean derailments and the consequent trouble; and the use of "**switchbacks**" is recommended when the question of speed is a minor one, as it usually is on a siege line. ABC (fig. 13) is the change of direction of an approach; the angle is not exaggerated. A very sharp curve would be necessary to get from A to C by an auxiliary trench, F. A much better method is to extend the trench from B to D and lay the track to D. At B a switch is put in and the line continued to C. BD must be longer than the probable train length and level if possible. The train is moved onto BD, and the animals are put on the other end of the train, or the motor is run backward and the train proceeds, via BC, to the next switchback, when the operation is repeated. E makes an excellent place for storage of tools or materials, or for a dressing station.

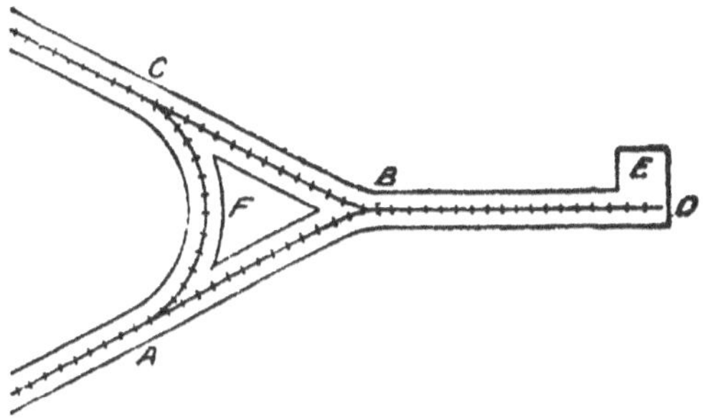


FIG 13.—SWITCHBACK.

19. **Track centers.**—Having decided upon the track to be laid, the **center line** is marked by center stakes about 100 ft. apart, on tangents, and as near together on curves as the radius of curvature requires. For portable track in siegework, very little staking out will be necessary.

20. **Track laying.**—In laying a portable railway, all sections of the track should be inspected before they are sent to the railhead, to make sure that the ties are properly bolted to the track and that the necessary fishplates are attached to one end of each section. The sections are then loaded on the cars with all fishplates pointing toward the head of the track, and the cars are hauled out to the railhead. At this point the **working party**, consisting of 2 noncommissioned officers and 24 men, unload the cars and lay the track. Two men can unload and lay a section of track in about the same time that two men can bolt the fishplates. The party can

be divided into two parts, 12 men carrying the rail sections and 12 men bolting and fastening up the joints. The cars are so light that if there is room in the trench the head cars can be lifted off the track and the remaining loaded cars run past, after which the empties can be put on the track and hauled to the rear. They will either be run singly or in trains, according to the tractive power that is used.

The track-laying party should be followed by another party, consisting of 1 noncommissioned officer and 24 men, who will level up the track, align it, and see that all ties have a good bearing. The **officer in charge** at the rear should inform himself in advance of the location, number, and kind of curved sections that will be needed, and also the location and number of switch sections, and should see that these are sent to the front in their proper order, so as to come to hand for the working party at the point where they are needed.

21. For laying combat railways on wooden ties, the rails must be loaded on the cars nearest the railhead and the ties on the cars to the rear. In every train of material sent to the railhead the proportion of ties and rails will be that of ties and rails in the completed track, so that both will be used up at the same time and allow the train to return empty and avoid unnecessary hauling of material.

The tie gang carries the ties ahead and drops them in position. One man is charged with giving ties their correct spacing and alignment; two men at the rail car fasten the fishplates to the forward end of the rail, if this has not already been done at the rear, and the rail is carried up and laid with its end between the fishplates at the head of the last preceding rail. The fishplates are bolted temporarily with one bolt, and a clip and rod (**bridle**, fig. 87) fastens the rail bases together temporarily. The construction train is then pushed ahead toward the end of the rail just laid and there halted until the next rail is laid.

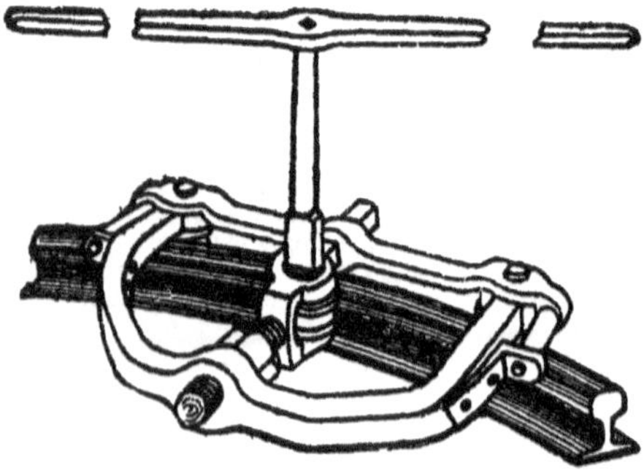

FIG. 14.—RAIL-CURVING MACHINE.

Behind the train is the bolting party that bolts the fishplates permanently to the rail the spiking party that spikes or screws the rail to the ties, and the surfacing, party that aligns and surfaces the track. This is an adaptation of the method described in pars. 118 to 125.

All the **working parties** on this work should be under an officer who has an assistant at the rear charged with getting out and forwarding all material needed. This last officer's instructions should be such that he clearly understands what material is wanted, and when and where it is wanted. As far as practicable, all rail **cutting** should be done at the rear.

It may be feasible to spike the rails to the ties and bolt on the fishplates in the rear, in which case the line is laid as described for portable track. This method would not be economical of space in loading.

22. **Curving rails.**—Before any rail is spiked to its place in a curve it must be evenly bent from end to end, so that it will assume the proper curvature when lying free. This curving may be done by hammers, but that method is slow, and a **rail-curving machine,** shown in fig. 14, is more commonly used. Two forms of **rail bender** are shown in figs. 15 and 16. These are made with either screw or hydraulic power, and are used for bending rails rather than for curving them. For many curves no rail curving is necessary, the friction between the rail and the ties being sufficient to hold the rail in position. The extent of this flexibility depends on the

weight and length of the rail, and can be found by trial; 3° and sharper curves usually require a curving of rails. Rails may be curved by fastening the machine to a tree and drawing the rails through the machine by means of a chain attached to a locomotive.

23. Knowing the radius of the curve and the length of the rail, the **middle ordinate** of the rail can be taken from Table XX. Each half of the rail, from the middle point to the ends, should also be tested for its middle ordinate to insure uniform

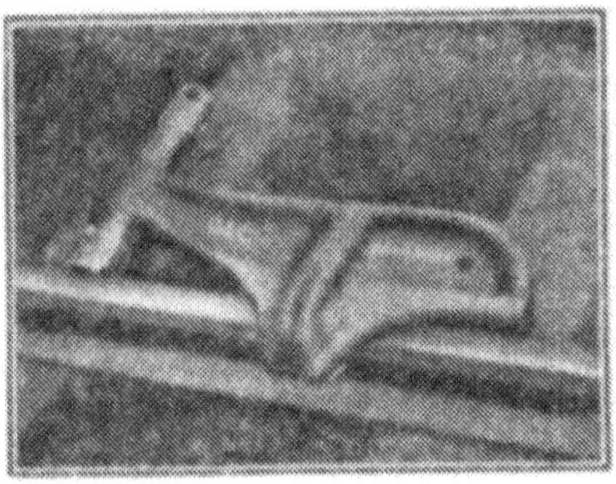

FIG 15 —Q. & C. SAMSON RAIL BENDER.

curvature. The middle ordinate of these half sections is one-fourth of the middle ordinate of the entire rail.

24. **Rail braces.**—The **outer rails** of curves are frequently braced with braces of a kind illustrated in fig. 17. An angle bar nailed to the tie and butting against the web of the rail furnishes a very good brace. (For elevation of outer rails of curves, see pars. 70, 71.) On standard-gage roads the rule seems to be about one rail brace per degree of curvature. On **very sharp curves** it is a good precaution to have the inner line of track doubled by the use of a guard rail. This will fre-

FIG. 16.—JIM CROW BENDER AND WRENCH.

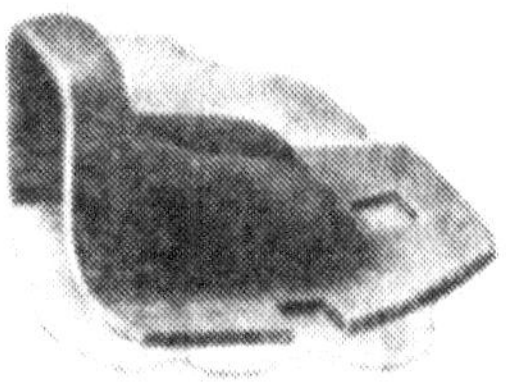

FIG. 17.—PRESSED STEEL RAIL BRACE.

quently prevent derailments and the consequent delay and trouble, and should be the invariable custom on the poorly constructed lines of combat railways.

25. **Crossings.**—For stock gages, right-angle crossings are usually kept in stock by the manufacturers (fig. 18 ) Crossings for any angle and weight of rail can be made on short notice. In ordering, state the crossing angle and the degree of curvature, the gage, and weight of rail of **each track.** The **angle of crossing** of two curves, or of a curve and a tangent, is measured by the angle between the tangents

at the point of intersection. The angle at each rail crossing can be computed in the shop. Where two roads must cross and no crossing is at hand, one track can be raised a sufficient amount to allow a movable section of rail to be put into place across the other track. When the cars have passed, the section is taken out, opening the lower track to cars.

**Crossings for vehicles** are made by nailing planks to the ties or to blocks laid in the bed of the track. To keep such crossings clean and thereby prevent cars from jumping off the track, it is a good plan to lay a rail on its side along the inside of each rail of the track, the head of such rail to lie against the web of the track rail.

FIG. 18.—CROSSING.

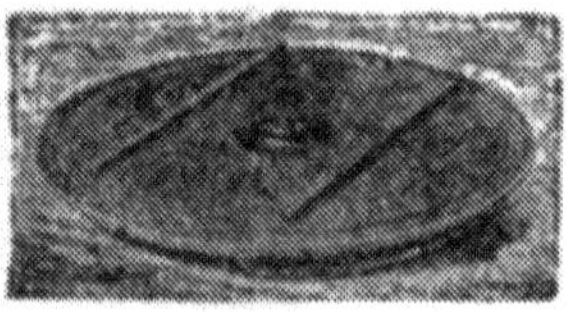

FIG. 19.—TURNTABLE.

26. **Turntables.**—For sharp turns, and for turning cars and locomotives, turntables are necessary. The commonest kind used with portable track is shown in fig. 19. These are furnished ready-made by the railway-equipment firms. (For a complete turntable see par. 168, fig. 119.)

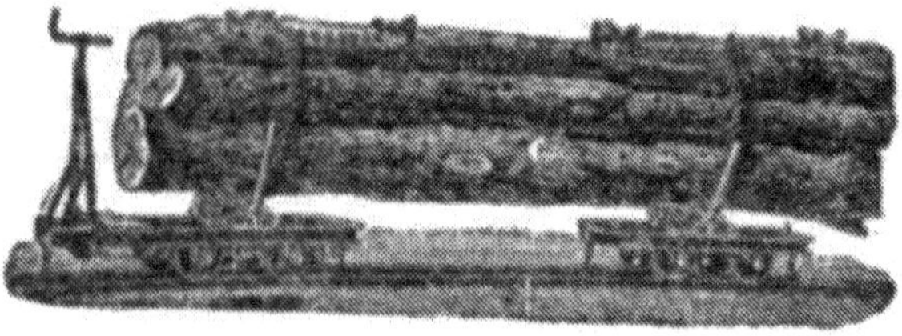

FIG. 20.

27. **Cars.**—Commercial types of narrow-gage cars are made entirely of steel, entirely of wood, or of the two combined. For certain uses the all-steel cars are very good, but for work in the field, cars with wooden bodies have been found to be much easier to repair, and a break of any sort does not throw the car out of use for a long time.

FIG. 21.

All cars should have the **coupling bars** the same height above the rail. They should have **rings** or **hooks** on each corner, by means of which they can be moved by animals walking on the *side* of the track. As far as possible all parts should be interchangeable.

Fig. 21 is a small **platform car,** with steel frame, platform of steel, of wood, or of wood lined with steel, for hand power, capacity from 2 to 3 tons, 18 to 36 in. gage, size of platform about 3 by 5 ft. to 5 by 8 ft. Other sizes made to order.

Fig. 22 shows a **flat car,** capacity from 10 to 12 tons, 12 to 20 ft. long, 3.5 to 5 ft. wide, and from 18 in. to 36 in. gage.

Fig. 23 shows a similar car with wooden end walls. The stake pockets allow sides to be put on which convert this car into a **gondola.**

FIG. 22.

28. By constructing a wooden top frame, trucks similar to those in fig. 20 can be utilized in pairs for **transporting siege guns** and other heavy armament.

The track is floored over for a sufficient distance to allow the gun to be run across the railway and moved so as to lie longitudinally along the track. By means of

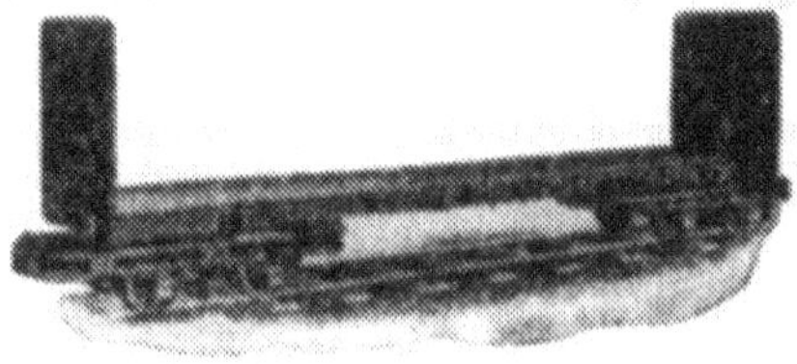

FIG. 23.

ropes, the gun and its limber are run up special ramps (outside of the rails) until they are higher than the body of the car; the wheels are then chocked and the car run under the gun. The necessary blocking is put on the car and chocks are removed, whereupon the gun and limber roll down the ramps and the gun settles on the block-

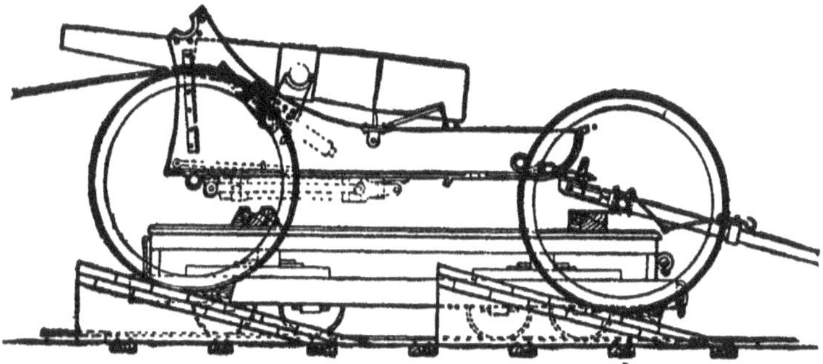

FIG. 24.—LOADING A SIEGE GUN ON TRUCK.

ing. The limber is then released and the gun is ready for movement. The gun is unloaded with similar appliances. One limber is sent on the first car to be used in unloading the guns when they arrive.

The method of mounting the armament on such a truck is illustrated in figs. 24 and 25.

29. The possibilities of combat railways for both offense and defense are very great and have never been fully utilized. Guns up to 6 in. caliber and howitzers of larger caliber can easily be fired from cars. Some blocking up may be necessary. Such use of a railway increases greatly the amount of artillery available in any sector of the defense whence it can be as rapidly moved elsewhere.

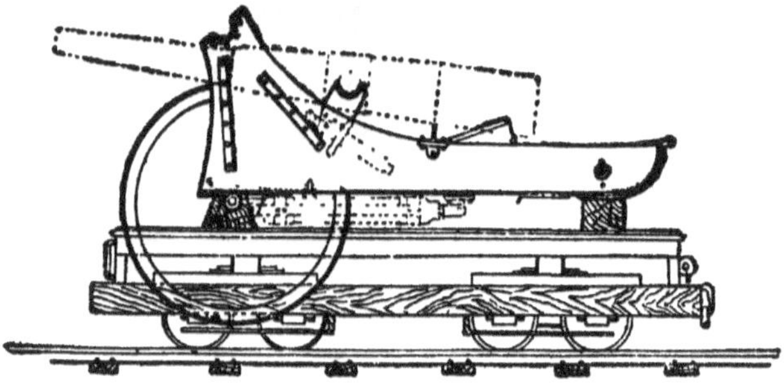

FIG. 25.—SIEGE GUN LOADED

30. **Derailments.**—Owing to the light weight of narrow-gage cars, an empty car can easily be lifted back on the track if it is derailed. With loaded cars, however, this is not always the case, and **car replacers** facilitate this replacing without unloading the cars. The one shown in Fig. 26 is a good one for heavy cars and locomotives, but for lighter cars a considerably lighter replacer would be more convenient.

FIG. 26.—BUDA LIGHT-WEIGHT REPLACER.

31. In estimating for materials for combat or other railways the following rules and tables will facilitate work:

The number of long **tons of rail per mile** of single track is found by multiplying the weight per yard by $\frac{11}{7}$. Thus, for 35 lbs. per yard, $\frac{11}{7}\times 35=55$, the number of long tons per mile.

TABLE II.—Number of crossties for 1 mile of track.

| Distance c. to c............ft.. | 1.5 | 1.75 | 2.0 | 2.25 | 2.5 | 2.75 | 3.0 |
|---|---|---|---|---|---|---|---|
| Number of ties required....... | 3,520 | 3,018 | 2,640 | 2,346 | 2,112 | 1,920 | 1,760 |

TABLE III.—Number of joints for 1 mile of track.

| Length of rail. | Number of joints. | Number of bars and bolts for each joint. |
|---|---|---|
| 30 ft........................... | 352 | 16 to 65 lb. rails have 2 angle bars and 4 bolts. |
| Standard practice (90% 30 ft., 10% short). | 357.5 | 70 to 100 lb. rails have 2 angle bars and 6 bolts. |
| 24 ft........................... | 440 | |
| 15 ft........................... | 704 | |

TABLE IV.—Number of joints to the long ton of rails.

| Weight of rail per yard. | Based on 30-ft. lengths. | Based on standard practice, 90% 30 ft., 10% shorts. | Based on 24-ft. lengths. | Based on 15-ft. lengths. | Weight of rail per yard. | Based on 30-ft. lengths. | Based on standard practice, 90% 30 ft., 10% shorts. | Based on 24-ft. lengths. | Based on 15-ft. lengths. |
|---|---|---|---|---|---|---|---|---|---|
| *Lbs.* | | | | | *Lbs.* | | | | |
| 100 | 2.24 | 2.27 | 2.80 | ........ | 50 | 4.48 | 4.55 | 5.60 | 8.96 |
| 90 | 2.49 | 2.53 | 3.11 | ........ | 40 | 5.60 | 5.69 | 7.00 | 11.20 |
| 80 | 2.80 | 2.84 | 3.50 | ........ | 30 | 7.47 | 7.58 | 9.33 | 14.94 |
| 70 | 3.20 | 3.25 | 4.00 | ........ | 20 | 11.20 | 11.37 | 14.00 | 22.40 |
| 60 | 3.73 | 3.79 | 4.67 | 7.46 | 16 | 14.00 | 14.22 | 17.50 | 28.00 |

TABLE V.—Table for 1 mile, single track.

| Rail weight per yard. | Weight of splice bars (358 prs. per mi.). | Bolts and nuts. | | | Spikes (10,560 per mi.). | | Weight of total accessories. | Weight of rail. |
|---|---|---|---|---|---|---|---|---|
| | | Size. | Number. | Weight. | Size | Weight. | | |
| *Lbs.* | *Lbs.* | *Ins.* | | *Lbs.* | *Ins.* | *Lbs.* | *Lbs.* | *Long tons.* |
| 100 | 29,642 | ¾ x 4½ | 2,148 | 1,953 | 6 x ⅝ | 7,040 | 38,635 | 157.14 |
| 95 | 27,208 | ¾ x 4½ | 2,148 | 1,953 | 5½ x 9/16 | 5,867 | 35,028 | 149.29 |
| 90 | 24,701 | ¾ x 4¼ | 2,148 | 1,867 | 5½ x 9/16 | 5,867 | 32,435 | 141.43 |
| 85 | 22,911 | ¾ x 4¼ | 2,148 | 1,867 | 5½ x 9/16 | 5,867 | 30,645 | 133.57 |
| 80 | 21,480 | ¾ x 4 | 2,148 | 1,790 | 5½ x 9/16 | 5,867 | 29,137 | 125.71 |
| 75 | 20,227 | ¾ x 4 | 2,148 | 1,790 | 5½ x 9/16 | 5,867 | 27,884 | 117.86 |
| 70 | 19,153 | ¾ x 3¾ | 2,148 | 1,753 | 5½ x 9/16 | 5,867 | 26,773 | 110.00 |
| 65 | 12,744 | ¾ x 3¾ | 1,432 | 1,169 | 5½ x 9/16 | 5,867 | 19,780 | 102.14 |
| 60 | 11,706 | ¾ x 3¾ | 1,432 | 1,169 | 5½ x 9/16 | 5,867 | 18,742 | 94.29 |
| 55 | 10,346 | ¾ x 3½ | 1,432 | 1,146 | 5½ x 9/16 | 5,867 | 17,359 | 86.43 |
| 50 | 8,628 | ¾ x 3¼ | 1,432 | 1,123 | 5½ x 9/16 | 5,867 | 15,618 | 78.57 |
| 45 | 5,942 | ¾ x 3 | 1,432 | 1,073 | 5 x ½ | 4,182 | 11,197 | 70.71 |
| 40 | 4,905 | ¾ x 3 | 1,432 | 1,073 | 5 x ½ | 4,182 | 10,160 | 62.86 |
| 35 | 4,368 | ⅝ x 2½ | 1,432 | 610 | 4 x 7/16 | 2,708 | 7,686 | 55.00 |
| 30 | 2,399 | ⅝ x 2½ | 1,432 | 610 | 4 x 7/16 | 2,708 | 5,717 | 47.14 |
| 25 | 2,041 | ⅝ x 2¼ | 1,432 | 582 | 4 x 7/16 | 2,708 | 5,331 | 39.29 |
| 20 | 1,611 | ⅝ x 2¼ | 1,432 | 582 | 3½ x ⅜ | 1,689 | 3,882 | 31.43 |
| 16 | 1,325 | ⅝ x 2 | 1,432 | 546 | 3½ x ⅜ | 1,689 | 3,560 | 25.14 |

Above table is based on standard practice for length of rails, viz, 90% to be 30 ft. and balance of 10% to be not less than 24 ft., varying by 2 ft. Ties 2 ft. c. to c.

Above number of splice bars, bolts and nuts, and spikes allow for no excess.

TABLE VI.—**Accessories** required for **10 tons of rails.**

| Rail weight per yard. | Splice bars or fish plates. | | Bolts and nuts. | | | Spikes. | | | Weight of total accessories. |
|---|---|---|---|---|---|---|---|---|---|
| | No. pairs. | Weight. | Size. | Number. | Weight. | Size. | Number. | Weight. | |
| *Lbs.* | | *Lbs.* | *Ins.* | | *Lbs.* | *Ins.* | | *Lbs.* | *Lbs.* |
| 100 | 23 | 1,904 | ¾ x 4½ | 138 | 126 | 6 x ⅝ | 672 | 448 | 2,478 |
| 95 | 24 | 1,824 | ¾ x 4½ | 144 | 131 | 5½ x $\frac{9}{16}$ | 708 | 393 | 2,348 |
| 90 | 25 | 1,725 | ¾ x 4¼ | 150 | 130 | 5½ x $\frac{9}{16}$ | 746 | 414 | 2,269 |
| 85 | 27 | 1,728 | ¾ x 4¼ | 162 | 141 | 5½ x $\frac{9}{16}$ | 790 | 440 | 2,309 |
| 80 | 28 | 1,680 | ¾ x 4 | 168 | 140 | 5½ x $\frac{9}{16}$ | 840 | 467 | 2,287 |
| 75 | 30 | 1,695 | ¾ x 4 | 180 | 150 | 5½ x $\frac{9}{16}$ | 896 | 498 | 2,343 |
| 70 | 33 | 1,766 | ¾ x 3¾ | 198 | 162 | 5½ x $\frac{9}{16}$ | 960 | 533 | 2,461 |
| 65 | 35 | 1,246 | ¾ x 3¾ | 140 | 114 | 5½ x $\frac{9}{16}$ | 1,034 | 574 | 1,934 |
| 60 | 38 | 1,243 | ¾ x 3¾ | 152 | 124 | 5½ x $\frac{9}{16}$ | 1,120 | 622 | 1,989 |
| 55 | 41 | 1,185 | ¾ x 3½ | 164 | 131 | 5½ x $\frac{9}{16}$ | 1,222 | 680 | 1,996 |
| 50 | 46 | 1,109 | ¾ x 3¼ | 184 | 144 | 5½ x $\frac{9}{16}$ | 1,344 | 747 | 2,000 |
| 45 | 51 | 847 | ¾ x 3 | 204 | 153 | 5 x ½ | 1,494 | 591 | 1,591 |
| 40 | 57 | 781 | ¾ x 3 | 228 | 171 | 5 x ½ | 1,680 | 665 | 1,617 |
| 35 | 65 | 793 | ⅝ x 2½ | 260 | 111 | 4 x $\frac{7}{16}$ | 1,920 | 492 | 1,396 |
| 30 | 76 | 509 | ⅝ x 2½ | 304 | 129 | 4 x $\frac{7}{16}$ | 2,240 | 574 | 1,212 |
| 25 | 91 | 519 | ⅝ x 2¼ | 364 | 148 | 4 x $\frac{7}{16}$ | 2,688 | 689 | 1,356 |
| 20 | 114 | 513 | ⅝ x 2¼ | 456 | 185 | 3½ x ⅜ | 3,360 | 538 | 1,236 |
| 16 | 142 | 525 | ⅝ x 2 | 568 | 216 | 3½ x ⅜ | 4,200 | 672 | 1,413 |

Above table is based on standard practice for length of rails, viz, 90% to be 30 ft. and balance of 10% to be not less than 24 ft., varying by 2 ft. Ties 2 ft. c. to c.

Above number of splice bars, bolts and nuts, and spikes allow for no excess.

TABLE VII.—Table of **steel spikes.**

| Size in inches. | Average number per keg of 200 lbs. | Number required and weight per mile, single track. | | | Rail weight per yard. |
|---|---|---|---|---|---|
| | | Based on ties 2 ft. c. to c. (10,560 per mi.). | Based on ties 2 ft. 6 ins. c. to c. (8,448 per mi.). | Based on ties 3 ft. c. to c. (7,040 per mi.). | |
| | | *Lbs.* | *Lbs.* | *Lbs.* | *Lbs.* |
| 6 x ⅝ P. R. R. | 300 | 7,040 | 5,632 | 4,693 | 75 to 100 |
| 5½ x $\frac{9}{16}$ | 360 | 5,867 | 4,693 | 3,911 | 45 to 80 |
| 5 x ½ | 505 | 4,182 | 3,345 | 2,788 | 30 to 50 |
| 4 x $\frac{7}{16}$ | 780 | 2,708 | 2,166 | 1,805 | 20 to 35 |
| 3½ x ⅜ | 1,250 | 1,689 | 1,352 | 1,126 | 16 to 25 |
| 2½ x ⅜ | 1,342 | 1,575 | 1,260 | 1,050 | 12 to 16 |

Above numbers allow for no excess.

TABLE VIII.—Table of steel bolts.

| Size, diameter by length under head. | Average number per keg of 200 lbs. | Number required and weight per mile single track for corresponding rail. Based on 30-ft. lengths. | | Based on standard practice, 90% 30 ft., 10% in lengths down to 24 ft. | | Based on 24-ft. lengths. | | Based on portable lengths averaging 15 ft. | | Rail weight per yard. |
|---|---|---|---|---|---|---|---|---|---|---|
| *Ins.* | | *No.* | *Lbs.* | *No.* | *Lbs.* | *No.* | *Lbs.* | *No.* | *Lbs.* | *Lbs.* |
| 7/8 x 4 3/4 .... | 140 | 2,112 | 3,017 | 2,148 | 3,070 | 2,640 | 3,771 | ....... | ....... | 100 |
| 3/4 x 4 1/2..... | 220 | 2,112 | 1,920 | 2,148 | 1,953 | 2,640 | 2,400 | ....... | ....... | 95 and 100 |
| 3/4 x 4 1/4..... | 230 | 2,112 | 1,837 | 2,148 | 1,867 | 2,640 | 2,296 | ....... | ....... | 85 and 90 |
| 3/4 x 4....... | 240 | 2,112 | 1,760 | 2,148 | 1,790 | 2,640 | 2,200 | ....... | ....... | 75 and 80 |
| 3/4 x 3 3/4..... | 245 | 2,112 | 1,724 | 2,148 | 1,753 | 2,640 | 2,155 | ....... | ....... | 70 |
| 3/4 x 3 3/4..... | 245 | 1,408 | 1,149 | 1,432 | 1,169 | 1,760 | 1,437 | 2,816 | 2,299 | 60 and 65 |
| 3/4 x 3 1/2..... | 250 | 1,408 | 1,126 | 1,432 | 1,146 | 1,760 | 1,408 | 2,816 | 2,253 | 55 |
| 3/4 x 3 1/4..... | 255 | 1,408 | 1,104 | 1,432 | 1,123 | 1,760 | 1,381 | 2,816 | 2,208 | 50 |
| 3/4 x 3....... | 267 | 1,408 | 1,055 | 1,432 | 1,073 | 1,760 | 1,318 | 2,816 | 2,109 | 40 and 45 |
| 5/8 x 2 1/2..... | 470 | 1,408 | 600 | 1,432 | 610 | 1,760 | 750 | 2,816 | 1,198 | 30 and 35 |
| 5/8 x 2 1/4..... | 492 | 1,408 | 572 | 1,432 | 582 | 1,760 | 715 | 2,816 | 1,145 | 20 and 25 |
| 5/8 x 2....... | 525 | 1,408 | 536 | 1,432 | 546 | 1,760 | 671 | 2,816 | 1,073 | 16 |

Threads can be either United States Manufacturer's or Whitworth's standard.
All bolts furnished with hexagon nuts unless otherwise ordered.
Above numbers allow for no excess.

TABLE IX.—**Weights and dimensions of American standard rail sections.***

| Section index. | Weight per yard. | Area. | Width of base and height. | Web. | Width of head. | Height of center of gravity above base. | Axis, $x-x$† | | |
|---|---|---|---|---|---|---|---|---|---|
| | | | | | | | Moment of inertia, I. | Section modulus, S. | Radius of gyration, r. |
| | *Lbs.* | *Sq. ins.* | *Ins.* | *Ins.* | *Ins.* | *Ins.* | | | |
| 100 A | 100 | 9 8 | 5¾ | $\frac{9}{16}$ | 2¾ | 2.8 | 43.8 | 14 6 | 2.13 |
| 90 A | 90 | 8.8 | 5⅜ | $\frac{9}{16}$ | 2⅝ | 2.5 | 34.0 | 12 0 | 1.97 |
| 80 A | 80 | 7 8 | 5 | $\frac{35}{64}$ | 2½ | 2.4 | 26.2 | 10.0 | 1.83 |
| 70 A | 70 | 6.9 | 4⅝ | $\frac{33}{64}$ | $2\frac{7}{16}$ | 2.2 | 19.6 | 8.2 | 1.70 |
| 60 A | 60 | 5 9 | 4¼ | $\frac{31}{64}$ | 2⅜ | 2.1 | 14.5 | 6.7 | 1.58 |
| 50 A | 50 | 4.9 | 3⅞ | $\frac{7}{16}$ | 2⅛ | 1.9 | 9.8 | 4.9 | 1.42 |
| 40 A | 40 | 3 9 | 3½ | $\frac{25}{64}$ | 1⅞ | 1.7 | 6 6 | 3.6 | 1.30 |
| 30 A | 30 | 3 0 | 3 | $\frac{21}{64}$ | 1⅝ | 1.4 | 3.5 | 2.3 | 1.11 |
| 20 A | 20 | 2.0 | 2½ | $\frac{17}{64}$ | 1⅜ | 1.2 | 1.7 | 1.3 | .92 |
| 16 A | 16 | 1.6 | 2¼ | $\frac{15}{64}$ | 1¼ | 1.1 | 1.1 | 0 97 | .84 |

$$\frac{M}{S}=\frac{\text{Max. bending moment}}{\text{section modulus}}=\text{stress in extreme fiber.}$$

* Am. Soc. C. E. Standard Rail Sections.
† Axis $x-x$ is perpendicular to web of rail section through center of gravity.

TABLE X.—**Maximum allowable wheel loads in pounds.**

| C. to c. of ties in ins. | Weight of rail in pounds per yard. | | | | | |
|---|---|---|---|---|---|---|
| | 16 | 20 | 25 | 30 | 40 | 45 |
| 20 | 3,550 | 4,970 | 6,390 | 8,340 | 12,780 | 14,920 |
| 24 | 2,950 | 4,140 | 5,320 | 6,950 | 10,650 | 12,420 |
| 30 | 2,360 | 3,310 | 4,260 | 5,560 | 8,520 | 9,940 |
| 36 | 1,970 | 2,760 | 3,550 | 4,630 | 7,100 | 8,280 |
| 42 | 1,690 | 2,360 | 3,040 | 3,970 | 6,080 | 7,100 |

Table IX shows the weights, dimensions, and strength of rails of standard sections, and from this table the necessary weight of a rail can be ascertained for the load to be carried. A rule given by the American Locomotive Co. is that for light rail with properly spaced ties the maximum wheel load may be 250 lbs. for each pound weight of rail per yard under 40 lbs. and 300 lbs. for rails from 40 to 60 lbs. The axle loads of the loaded cars ought to equal the axle loads of the locomotive. This rule is a rough approximation only.

Table X shows the maximum allowable wheel loads recommended by one large manufacturer of portable track.

## SUPPLY RAILWAYS.

32. Supply railways include all railways, except combat railways, that may be constructed or used for the supply of an army in the field. They may vary from a light portable track to a standard-gage railway. Their **principal uses** will be to connect the army with its base; to connect permanent camps with the nearest existing railway; to form a belt line around a besieged place outside the field of observation; to form a belt line inside the line of defense of a besieged place; for the movable gun defense, and for a general supply line to supply an army in a permanent position such as the Russian army often occupied in Manchuria. In extreme cases a railway may have to be constructed to supply an advancing army when local conditions preclude other means of transportation.

For cruder forms on which animals are used as the motive power the description already given of a combat railway will suffice. They are what are known as **tramways.** As soon as some form of mechanical traction is to be provided for the line becomes a "**railway**" in the commonly accepted meaning of the word.

33. Regardless of the gage, the same underlying principles govern the construction of all such lines, and, having a plan for the operation and maintenance of an existing line of railway, it is easy to adapt it to the requirements of a temporary line. The **principal considerations** that govern in planning for such a line are, first, the amount of army supplies, troops, and animals that must be handled; second, the time that can be permitted for its construction; and third, which applies particularly to operations beyond the sea, the amount of transportation necessary to place the railway supplies on the work. This third condition will ordinarily necessitate a narrow-gage railway for a supply railway in a country beyond the sea. Local conditions, such as a great supply of standard-gage material and rolling stock, may render advisable the building of a standard-gage railway for operations from a friendly land base; but where conditions extremely favorable to a standard-gage line do not exist, a narrow-gage railway will probably be decided upon in the general case of supply railways. The weight of the materials and rolling stock is so much smaller, the bridges can be so much lighter, and the earthwork is so much less than for a standard-gage road that the narrow-gage railway is decidedly easier and quicker to build.

34. On the Barsi Railway, built in India, a 2 ft. 6 in. gage was used. The weight of the locomotive was 58,800 lbs. in working order; it had an eight-wheel base with a four-wheel pilot truck (bogie), 13 by 18 in. cylinders, and used a working steam pressure of 150 lbs. The rigid wheel base was 8 ft. 3 ins.; total wheel base, 18 ft. 6 ins. The weight on each of the six axles was 10,000 lbs. The sharpest curve on the line has a radius of 175 ft. On a level tangent this locomotive drew 1,036 tons at 15 miles an hour; and on a 1% grade, 9½° curve, it hauled 291 tons at 8 miles an hour.

They were able to run sixteen trains a day in each direction, which, excluding the weight of the cars, carried 3,360 tons each way daily. The load on each car axle was the same as on the locomotive axle—i. e., 5 tons. The weight of rail used was 35 lbs. per yard.

35. General Sherman's army at Atlanta was composed of 100,000 men and 35,000 animals, in a hostile country. The **net train supply** to him was 1,600 tons daily, which he said was in excess of the amount necessary to supply his army. A comparison of these figures shows the great possibilities of narrow-gage railways in supplying troops in the field. However, in using them it must be remembered that the Barsi Railway was a well built and ballasted line, running under peace conditions. Estimates based thereon for war conditions should be reduced enormously to provide for the necessary passenger service and for the interruptions of traffic due to poor track conditions and to accidents incident to a state of war.

36. The **narrow-gage locomotives** built in this country give even better performances than that cited in par. 34, for an eight-wheel locomotive, 14 by 18 ins., class D. T., built by the H. K. Porter Co., of Pittsburgh, weighing in working order 60,000 lbs., is rated with a capacity of 1,875 tons on the level, 425 tons on a 1% grade, and 220 tons on a 2% grade; while class D. T. locomotive, with 11 by 14 in. cylinders, weighing 36,000 lbs., is rated at 1,075 tons on the level, 240 tons on a 1% grade, and

120 tons on a 2% grade. The **axle load** in the first case is 7½ tons; the weight of rail necessary is 30 lbs. per yard. The axle load of the second locomotive is 4½ tons and only requires a 20-lb. rail.

The **rating** of these last two engines is based on the frictional resistance of 6½ lbs. per ton. This resistance may vary from 5 lbs. to 10 lbs. for good cars and track, and may run higher for poor cars and track (see pars. 175, 176).

The **efficiency of locomotives** is being constantly increased, and a study of the latest catalogues of the prominent builders is recommended.

37. The **question of time** not only enters into the question of construction of the road, but is also an important factor as to the amount and kind of narrow-gage rolling stock that can be furnished. For a **short line,** say 10 miles in length, it is probable that the equipment and rolling stock could all be bought from stock. This would mean adapting the grade and gage to the rolling stock, supplies, etc., that the manufacturers had on hand. For a narrow-gage line of **considerable length,** say 40 to 50 miles or more, it will be absolutely necessary to have considerable notice, and the same will be especially true if the material is to be transported across the sea. Under either circumstance, the engineer will first fully acquaint himself with all the plans of the commanding general, and ascertain the general line over which the railway is to be built and the probable army that will have to be supplied. A study of the best maps available will then show him the general features of the country through which the line is to run. On over-sea expeditions the list of material may have to be made up from imperfect knowledge of existing conditions.

If a very accurate and **detailed map** is at hand, the work will be simplified; if not, a general **reconnaissance** should be made of the ground to be covered, where such a thing is at all possible. The engineer will, meantime, enter into communication with the manufacturers of railway equipment of all kinds, and he should then be able to make a bill of material for the railroad that is to be built. If necessary, pressure should be brought to bear on the manufacturers to make them rush his order through without delay and in advance of all other similar civil orders.

## SURVEYS.

38. **Routes.**—In some cases it will be possible to go over the route and locate the exact position of the whole railway before construction work commences, and in any case the general line of the road will be known although the exact location may not be determined except as the army advances. In either case, **surveying** will have to be done in order to determine the best line for the road and to locate this line on the ground. Whether this be done in peace or war makes no difference in the general principles, but the circumstances of each particular case will necessitate a judicious determination of the proper care and accuracy that must be used in that case.

39. **Surveys.**—Surveys are location surveys, and construction or final surveys. The instrumental location of a military railroad does not differ materially from that described for a new wagon road, but greater accuracy is desirable, and a much more careful adjustment of curves and grades is indispensable. As with common roads, the grade will mainly follow the natural surface, but the line must be so located as to keep these grades within the adopted limit, which will usually be 2%, though in exceptional cases and for short grades 4% is allowable.

40. **Natural drainage lines** present the most regular and easiest gradients, and in a broad sense it may be said that every railroad location follows lines of drainage. When the head or source of one drainage line is reached, the location crosses the divide to the next. With few exceptions, drainage lines have slopes not exceeding those permissible for railroad location. The first requisite in considering a railroad location is to get the lines of drainage clearly in the mind. This done, start the exploration from the initial point on a straight line for the objective. Keep on this line as long as it can be done within the prescribed limits of grade and curvature. Leave the line only when forced away from it; do not go away from it farther than is absolutely necessary, and get back to it as soon as possible.

41. Before the survey is started, the **maximum grade and degree of curvature** should be decided upon, and in surveying the line the instrument men will know what their limitations are and will locate the line accordingly. This maximum grade should be the **compensated grade.** That is, when the grade occurs on a curve, an allowance of .04% of grade should be added to the actual grade for each degree of curvature to give the compensated grade. When the level man finds the grade running steeper than the limiting grade, he will take a sufficient amount of side notes to determine the **amount of excavation** or filling that will be necessary to keep the grade within the prescribed limits; and if he finds the amount of excavation excessive, he may have to call back the transit man and have the line relocated. This should not happen frequently, as the transit man should know the maximum allowable angle of slope and should locate his line accordingly.

42. The **virtual grade** is the actual grade corrected to take advantage of the velocity head due to the speed of the train when the various grades are encountered. Its principal application is for economical construction, but even at moderate speeds it might occasionally permit the use of grades steeper than the so-called maximum.

43. A **pusher grade** is an isolated case that can not be kept down to the ruling grade nor compensated for by the velocity head. Here it is best to pass at once to nearly double the ruling grade and provide for a regular pusher engine for that special grade. They should not occur oftener than once or twice in a division.

44. It is permissible to increase the total length of the line by 1%, to reduce the ruling grade 0.1%. This is an English rule and is subject to many limitations. It would only apply to the division in which the grade lay. It does not take into account the difference between the actual profile and the virtual profile, and it does not contemplate the use of **pusher engines** on isolated heavy grades. It apparently is meant to apply where the ruling grade is used very frequently through the division.

45. The combination of notes of the transit and level parties will show the grades and the curves that will be necessary, and will thus determine the practicability of the route selected. Below the limiting grade that a lone locomotive can ascend, the **working maximum grade** for the line will be different in every case and there is no such thing as a fixed maximum. The only general rule is to keep it as low as practicable and still keep the amount of construction work within reason. Par. 175 describes the method of finding the **tractive power** of a locomotive. Knowing the available rolling stock, the amount of supplies to be transported, and the nature of the country, the maximum grade will always be a compromise between what you can get and what you would like to have. Pars. 34 and 36 show that grades above 2% are almost prohibitive. The maximum degree of curvature is not so indefinite. There is a railway in Colorado with **50 curves of 20°**, or more, in 11 miles. The Baltimore and Ohio, until recently, had a **300-ft. curve** at Harpers Ferry on its main line. The 175-ft. curve (par. 34) on the Barsi road could undoubtedly be made sharper and still be practicable. With these as limits, a road can wind in and out through almost any country. Keep in mind that **sharp curves are preferable to steep grades** if it becomes a question between the two.

46. The **maximum allowable degree of curvature** is a function of the rigid wheel base of the locomotive and the amount of clearance between the inner flanges of the rails and of the locomotive wheels. The generous use of curves to avoid heavy cuts or fills is economical of time in construction and the relation between the resistance due to curvature and that due to grade is shown by the compensation for curvature referred to in par. 41.

47. It is assumed herein that the officer in charge of the work is acquainted with the use of instruments, and so no explanation is made of the instruments nor of the methods of using them.

Upon the completion of the survey and the determination of a practical route will come the **location** of the **line of track.** This may either be done by the preparation of a map whereon are plotted the cross sections taken, or the profile may be plotted and any objectionable features, such as excessive grades, cuts, or fills, can be corrected by the necessary deviation when the engineer reaches that point in the line in the course of the actual, final location. In the first case, the centerline having been plotted, where no cross sections have been taken, it is assumed that the track may be moved 100 ft. in either direction without changing the elevation materially. Where the cross sections have been taken, the desirable center line is indicated by a series of points and the center line of the track is located to correspond approximately to these points. The line along the part not cross-sectioned is then shifted to one side or the other to correspond. Theoretically, this is the best way to locate a line of railroad; in practice, however, railroad locating engineers become expert in the location of lines on the ground, and due to inaccuracies which occur in all maps, it is usually found that the engineer will have to change the center line more or less, no matter how carefully it was located on the map.

In ordinary practice the line is actually located on the ground by the instrument men at the head of the locating pa ty, and any necessary corrections are made in the same way.

48. A **profile** will be made showing the elevations of the center line finally decided upon, and by means of pins and threads the exact elevation and grade of the line can be determined for every station. In this determination the notes taken by the transit party regarding the class of soil, rock, etc., should be considered.

49. The foregoing description of the method of location sounds cumbersome, but the actual work can be kept up so that before going to bed at night the locating engineer has determined the line and grade of his track up to the end of the day's work, or else has determined that that particular line will not satisfy the limiting conditions of the case in hand. In either case, the next morning the party is prepared to continue work, or to start afresh at some point back on the line, knowing that the work up to the point of starting has thus far determined a satisfactory location for the line.

50. In a very **rough country** it may be found advisable to use a plane table in the construction of the map for determination of the route; the advantage of this method is that a map of a certain area can thus be obtained with a great deal less labor than by the use of the transit and level. The plane table is especially useful for mapping bridge sites, but for general location has not been found as practical as the method of transit and level.

51. **Instruments** should be checked as to their **adjustment** often enough to keep the instrument man confident of their approximate adjustment. For methods of adjusting instruments, see Part I, on Reconnaissance.

52. **Sidehill work.**—In locating the line on the side of a hill the center line should be run along the surface of the ground, if this can be done by a slight movement to one side or the other. This will equalize the necessary amount of cutting and filling, and will minimize the movement of material.

53. **Estimates.**—After the location survey has been made, notes are then at hand for making an estimate on the amount of material that must be moved, the other work that must be done, and the time necessary to build the proposed line. The estimates are made, if the work is to be done by contract, to obtain a basis on which the contract shall be let and upon which payment will be made; but in the normal case of a military line the work will be done by troops, or by hired labor, and the **object of the estimate** is to determine the quantity of work to be done at different points along the line in order to so subdivide the working parties as to get the best results and the quickest return in the shape of completed line.

In case an **official report** is desired by the commanding general before he decides whether or not to construct the line, the entire survey and the estimates must be finished before this report is made. This report will be accompanied by maps and profiles showing the routes considered and the final location decided upon, and the reasons therefor. It will also show the approximate cost of material and of civilian labor, the amount and cost of rolling stock and other equipment, and will show the capacity of the line when it is completed and the time that will be necessary to complete the work as desired. In case it has been definitely decided in advance to build the line, the cost and time are only considered in that they must be kept as low as practicable, and the survey need not be completed before construction work begins.

A short section of location 4 or 5 miles in length is completed so that the working parties can be started, and thereafter it will be an easy matter for the survey parties to keep well in advance of the construction parties, since it is hardly practical for the construction party to average over 1 mile a day if conditions as to weight of track number of bridges, and amount of excavation are not peculiarly advantageous. Even under favorable conditions as to construction, and with the use of light track, probably not over 3 miles a day can be finished. The survey parties can easily make more than this and will be able to keep ahead of the construction parties. (However, see par. 115.) It took 173 days to build 190 miles of the 3 ft. 6 in. railway from Wada Halfa to Abu Hamed in 1897, on the latter part of which as much as 5,300 yards of line was built in a day. This road was built by Lieut. (now Col. Sir.) E. P. C. Girouard, R. E., British Army.

54. A line of railway is made up of curved and straight lengths; the former are called **curves** and the latter **tangents.** Railroad curves are usually arcs of circles. They may be either simple, compound, or reverse. A **simple curve** is a curve with a constant radius. A **compound curve** is one composed of two or more simple curves of different radii curving in the same direction and having a common tangent at their point of meeting. A **reverse curve** is composed of two simple curves curving in opposite directions and having a common tangent at their point of meeting. The name is also commonly applied to two simple curves curving in opposite directions, which are joined by a tangent shorter than the usual length of trains running on the line.

55. A **transition** or **easement curve** is a compound curve, or spiral, used at the ends of a sharp curve to lead gradually from the tangent to the main curve.

56. A curve with a radius of less than 500 ft. is commonly referred to by its radius; as, a curve with 150 ft. radius, or a 150-ft. curve. Curves with radii longer than 500 ft. are usually designated by the number of degrees of arc that a chord 100 ft. in length subtends from the center of the circle. Thus, a 5° curve means that a 100-ft. chord subtends an angle of five degrees (5°) from the center of the circle. There are other means used to designate curves of very short radii, but they are more or less misleading; as, for instance, $8°_{25}$, which signifies that a chord of 25 ft. on the circumference subtends an angle of 8° at the center. A **curve is measured** along its chords, and such length of chord should be assumed that the ratio of the arc to the corresponding chord is practically unity. The number of subtending chords multiplied by the length of such chords equals the length of the curve L. $L=\frac{\Delta}{D}l$, where $\Delta$=central angle, D=degree of curvature, $l$=length of chords used.

A **1° curve** is considered as the basic curve and its elements are shown in Table XIX for use in computing data for curves of other radii. Its radius is 5,729.65 ft. and a 100-ft. arc of such a curve subtends 1° at the center of the circle. The corresponding functions or elements of any two curves are proportional to their radii and therefore those for a curve of 5° are found by dividing the corresponding elements of a 1° curve for the same central angle, by 5. This rule holds good as long as the 100-ft. chord and the subtended arc are not sensibly different in length.

57. The various **parts of a curve** are shown in fig. 27. We are supposed to be moving in the direction FBH. FB is one tangent joined to BH, another tangent, by the curve ADC. The angle between FB, extended, and BH is called the **external, or central, angle** ($\Delta$). B is the **point of intersection,** usually designated P I. A is the **point of curve** (P.C.). C is the **point of tangent** (P.T.). O is the center of the arc. AC is the **long chord** (C), ED is the **middle ordinate** (M), and DB is the **external distance** (E). AB and BC are called the **tangent distances** (T). AO is the **radius** (R). The **degree of curvature** is D.

The relations between the various angles and lines can be seen from the figure. Various formulæ showing the relation of the different parts to one another are given in Table XVII.

58. **Method of laying out curves.**—These methods vary greatly, and each depends largely upon the local accidents of the terrain. A few of the simplest are given here. In running a tangent along the line FB (fig. 27), the point B is reached where the direction of the line changes to BH. The exterior angle $\Delta$ is measured, and it is desired to put in a curve connecting the tangent FB with the tangent BH. Either the radius or the degree of curvature must be assumed before the points of tangency can be located. If the ground inclosed in the triangle ABC is clear and open, practically any curve can be run between the two tangents. Sometimes, however, there is some condition that determines where the curve shall lie and consequently what the radius of curvature will be. A common condition is that the point D in the curve is fixed by some local condition, thereby fixing definitely the length of the line BD. A reference to Table XVII will show the relation of the line BD (usually referred to as E) to the other parts of the diagram, and from this table, knowing the external angle $\Delta$, and measuring E, R can be determined. $R = \frac{E}{\text{ex. sec. } \frac{1}{2}\Delta}$

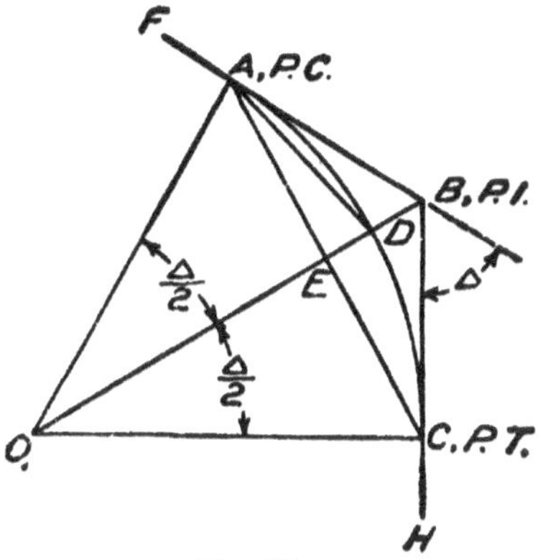


FIG. 27.

Given R, and $\Delta$, the distance AB and BC can be determined, since $T = R \tan \frac{1}{2}\Delta$.

Such a condition might arise in siege works, when the point D must lie in the bottom of a trench already dug.

Curves are usually laid out by use of the transit, but for rough work or in an emergency they may have to be laid out **without the aid of an instrument.** For such occasions the following methods are described:

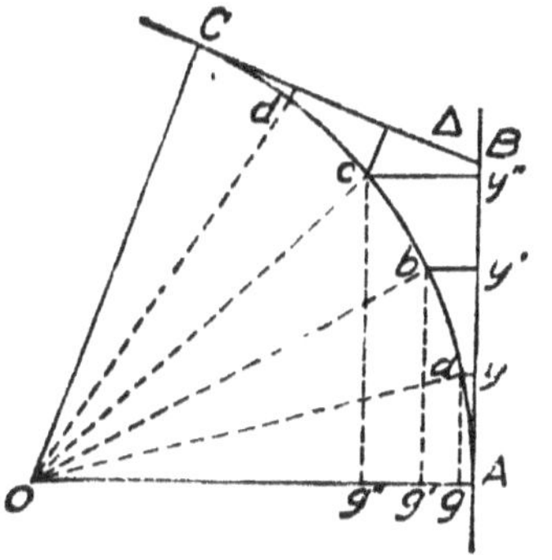


FIG. 28.

59. **The method of offsets from tangents** (see fig. 28).—Knowing the P. C., P. T., and R, make a table for tangent distances and offsets. The distances on the tangent A$y$ from the P. C. to the perpendicular offset from the extremity of any arc, A$a$, is equal to R sin D for the first station and R sin ($n$ D) for any succeeding station ($n$ being the number of the station from the P. C.); and any offset, as $ya$, from the tangent to the extremity of any arc is equal to R vers ($n$ D). Make up a two-column table, in one column of which are placed the distances to be measured along the tangent, and in the other the perpendicular offsets from the tangent to the points in the curve. Having the tangent distances corresponding to the consecutive chords for half of the curve and the offset for each, measure off the distances from the P. C. along the tangent and locate each by a peg; then at each peg lay off perpendicular to the tangent the corresponding offset from the column of offsets. This locates half of the curve. Go to the P. T. and locate the other half of the curve from that point.

60. **A simpler form** of this same method by offsets from the tangents will be found by using Table XI. This table gives the perpendicular offset for a curve with

a 1-ft. radius at points one-tenth of the radius apart, measured along the tangent from the P. C. It will readily be seen that for any other radius the table will apply if every figure in the table is multiplied by the radius of the desired curve.

TABLE XI.—Table of offsets from tangent for radius of 1 ft.

[All measurements are in decimal parts of the radius.]

| Tan. Dist., ft.... | .1 | .2 | .3 | .4 | .5 | .6 | .7 | .8 | .9 |
|---|---|---|---|---|---|---|---|---|---|
| Offset, ft......... | 0.0050 | 0.0202 | 0.0461 | 0 0835 | 0.1340 | 0.200 | 0.2859 | 0.400 | 0.5641 |

**Method of use.**—Having given the radius of desired curve, multiply each number in the table by its radius in feet and make a new table similar to the above. The figures in the lower line are then the perpendicular offsets from the tangent to the curve at points along the tangent whose distances from the P. C. are shown in the upper line.

In many cases laying out half the curve from the P. C. and the other half from the P. T. will give the best results, since the perpendicular offsets will be shorter than when all points are located from one end.

61. **To locate a curve by offsets from the chords produced.**—Having determined R, assume some length of chord, C′, equal to about 0.2 R, but less than 100 ft., and from Table XII find the corresponding offset from the tangent *t* for this length of chord. From the P. C. as a center, strike an arc across the tangent produced, using for a radius a chain whose length is C′, or A*a* in fig. 29. Find the point on this arc a perpendicular distance, *t*, from the tangent. This is the point *a* on the curve. As shown in fig. 29, produce A*a*, the distance C′ to *b*′, strike the arc *b*′*b*, with a radius C′ from *a* as a center. Strike an arc with a radius $b'b=2t$ from *b*′ as a center. The intersection of these two arcs is *b*, a new point in the curve. Produce *ab*, a distance C′, to *c*′ and strike the arc *c*′*c*, with C′ as a radius and *b* as a center. From *c*′, with $2t$ as a radius, strike an arc, and where it intersects the previous arc is *c*, a new point in the curve. Proceed in a similar manner until a point is reached where the distance to P. T. is less than C′, the chord distance used.

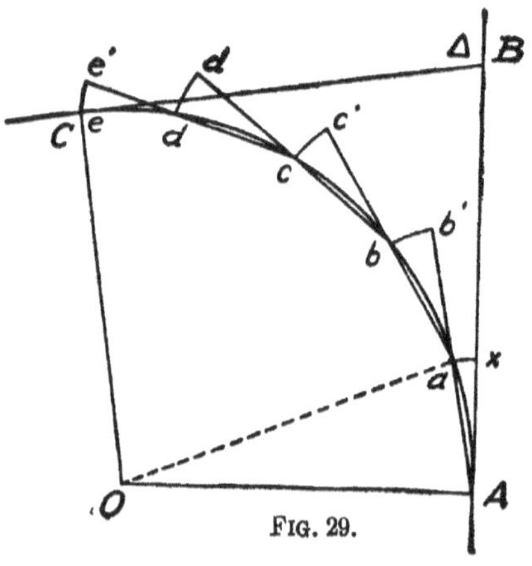

FIG. 29.

Measure or compute this remaining length of the curve and call it *x*. Establish a tangent to the curve at *d*, using $ee'=t$. Lay off $df'=x$ and locate the point *f* by the same method by which *a* was established from the tangent AB, using $ff'=\frac{x^2}{C'^2}t$. B*f* is the direction of the new tangent. If B is not visible, lay off the distance $\frac{x^2}{C'^2}t$ outward from *d* along O*d* and a line through the resulting point and *f* is the new tangent.

TABLE XII.—Table showing tangent distances and offsets therefrom for certain lengths of chord in a curve of 1′ 0″ radius. All measurements are in decimal parts of the radius.

| Length of chord... | 0.1 | 0.2 | 0.3 | 0.4 | 0.5 | 0.6 | 0 7 | 0.8 | 0.9 | 1.0 |
|---|---|---|---|---|---|---|---|---|---|---|
| Offset............ | 0.005 | 0.020 | 0.045 | 0.080 | 0.125 | 0.180 | 0.245 | 0.320 | 0.405 | 0.50 |
| Tangent distance.. | 0.100 | 0.199 | 0.2969 | 0.3912 | 0.4841 | 0.5724 | 0.6557 | 0.7332 | 0.8037 | 0.8660 |

The foregoing table is hardly necessary for the tangent offsets, which are always equal to square of the chord divided by 2R.

62. **To locate a curve by middle ordinates.**—P. C., P. T, and R being known, assume some short chord, C′, whose ratio to the corresponding arc is practically unity. From sin 1/2 D′=C′/2R, find D′, the angle that this chord subtends for the given radius. Then $\frac{\Delta}{D'}$ = N, the number of such chords in the curve to be laid out.

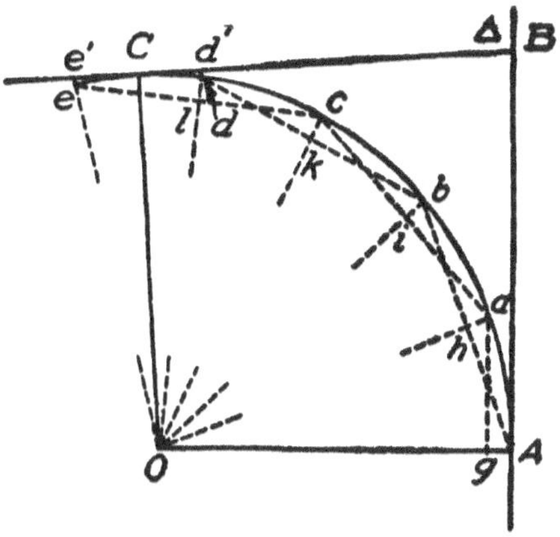


FIG. 30.

Lay off from P. C. toward center the distance A*g* (fig. 30), equal to offset *t*, corresponding to C′, taken from Table XII. Through *g* extend the line *ga* parallel to the tangent AB, and with the P. C. as a center strike an arc with a radius C′. The intersection of these two lines is a point in the curve, *a*.

From *a* lay off a distance in the direction of the center, *ah*, equal to *t*. Extend the line A*h*, and with *a* as a center strike an arc with C′ as a radius. The intersection of A*h* with this arc is at *b*, another point in the curve.

If N is a whole number, the P. T. will be one of the points found as above. If N is not a whole number, lay off the whole-numbered stations as above until a station, *e*, is located, just beyond the P. T. Measure C*d* and C*e*. From Table XII find the offset corresponding to each of these chords. From *d* and *e* lay off *dd′* and *ee′*, outward from *d* and *e* along the directions *d*O and *e*O. The line *d′e′* should coincide with the new tangent and pass through C. This method is only applicable when O can be seen from all points of the curve.

There is another method of laying off curves without the use of instruments, i. e., by **offsets from the long chord** of the curve, but it is not believed that this method would be of any practical value in the field; and if occasion arises where its use is necessary, the engineer can readily figure out the method for himself.

The foregoing methods will not always locate points on the curve a fixed distance apart, but as rapidity of location is desired rather than careful notes for future record, these methods are suited to military railways.

63. **Laying out curves with a transit.—P. I. accessible.**—Arriving at the P. I., the exterior angle is measured, and knowing either the radius, or the degree of curvature desired, the other is determined as in par. 58. Having located the P. C., the transit is set up at this point and the zeros of the plate and vernier are brought together and clamped in that position. The instrument is then sighted

along the tangent produced and an angle is turned off toward the side to which the curve is going, equal to the chord distance to the next station divided by the distance between stations, and multiplied by one-half the degree of curvature. Thus the P. C is at station 10+40; the degree of curvature is 4° R; the length of stations used is 100 ft. To locate station 11 turn off $\frac{60}{100}\times 2°$, or 1° 12′, to the right and measure 60 ft. along this line. The rear chainman holds the 40-ft. point on the P. C.; the head chainman moves to the right of the tangent until the point of his flag, held at the end of the chain, is bisected by the vertical cross hair. A stake is driven at this point and a nail is driven in the stake and the point is verified by the instrument man and the head chainman. The chainmen move out and thereafter use the full chain. The instrument man thereafter lays off 2°, that is, half the degree of curvature, for each station until the last station in the curve is reached. He then lays off the proper proportional part of the deflection angle, which should be equal to the difference between the sum of all the angles theretofore laid off and half the external angle. The line of sight should then intersect the tangent at the P. T. if the work has been correctly done, and the **length of the curve** should be $100\frac{\Delta}{D}$ ft. If either of these two conditions is not fulfilled on reaching the P. T., some mistake has been made and the work must be corrected. In turning off these angles as above, it is best to make out a table before starting that shows what the vernier should read at each point. This does away with the chance of a cumulative error that exists in turning off a small angle several times.

64. **P. I. inaccessible.**—When the P. I. is inaccessible, it may be necessary to make several changes of direction, as in fig 31. The point V would be the P. I., but it is inaccessible. The line is run along APQB, QB being the desired direction of the new tangent. The external angle is then equal to the sum of the deflection angles at P and at Q. In the triangle QPV, all the angles and the side PQ are known. Solve the triangle for QV and PV. Find the tangent distance VB and VA as in par. 58, and lay off from Q, QB equal to VB minus VQ; and from P, a distance equal to VA minus VP. The points B and A thus located are the P. T. and P. C., respectively. The curve is then laid out as heretofore described.

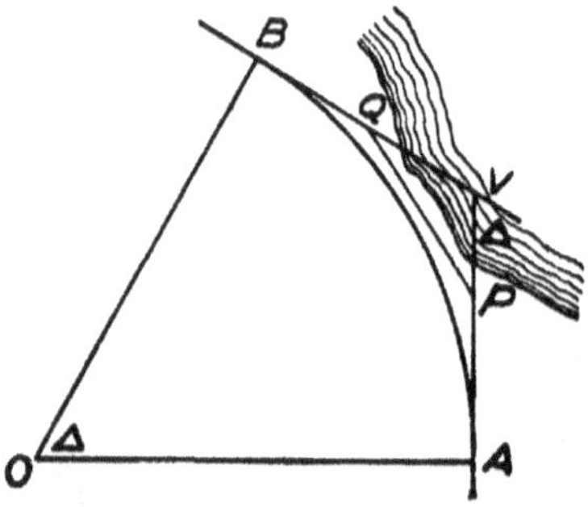


FIG. 31.

65. **A curve requiring more than one setting of the instrument.**—As errors will creep into the location of a curve if very long lines of sight are used in laying out the curve, it is customary not to lay out more than from four to six stations from one point; therefore, on curves longer than this, two or more settings of the instrument will be necessary. This is also the case when the line of sight is interfered with by some obstacle. Having located the curve as far as Q, in fig. 32, from the P. C., it is decided to use a new setting of the instrument. The instrument is moved to Q and set up over this station. The zeros having been brought together, a backsight is taken on the P. C., the telescope is plunged, and an angle is turned off to the inside of the curve equal to $\frac{D}{2}$ multiplied by the curve distance to Q, in feet, and divided by 100. This is equal to the angle VAQ. The instrument should now read the same angle that it did to locate Q, and the line of sight is tangent to the curve at this point. From Q the curve is continued in the same manner that it was from the P. C.

To be general; when the instrument is set up on any forward station of a curve, backsight to any previous station with the plates set at the originally computed deflection angle for the station sighted at. Plunge the telescope and set the plate at the angle of deflection originally computed for any forward station and the line of sight will point to that station.

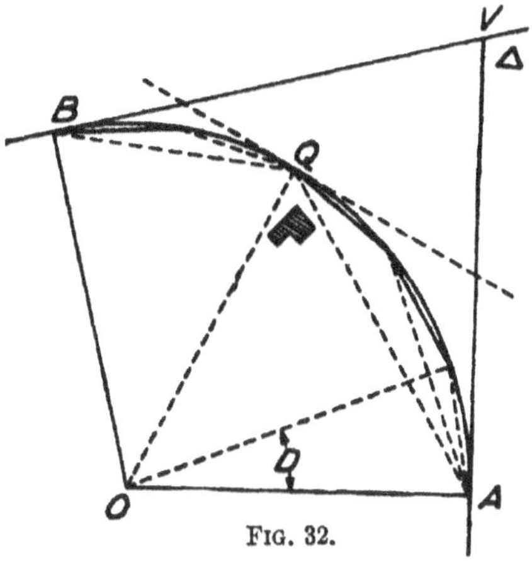

FIG. 32.

In locating curves on a line of railroad, many problems will come up for solution too numerous for description here. A knowledge of trigonometry and the use of formulæ in Table XVII will solve any problem that may arise.

66. **Reverse curves.**—A reverse curve should not be located in a line of railway unless it is impossible to avoid using it, and two curves, curving in opposite directions, should not be nearer to each other than at least the length of the longest train that it is expected to run over the line.

67. **Easement or transition curves.**—A good rule for the length of such a curve is that it shall be equal to the run-off of the superelevation of the outer rail. The transition spiral is too complicated for a full description, but its application is fairly simple. In fig. 33, ABC is the circular curve for which a transition curve, EGIB′, leading into a parallel circular curve A′B′C′, is to be substituted. The form of the **cubic parabola** is used, and is applicable wherever ED is equal to or

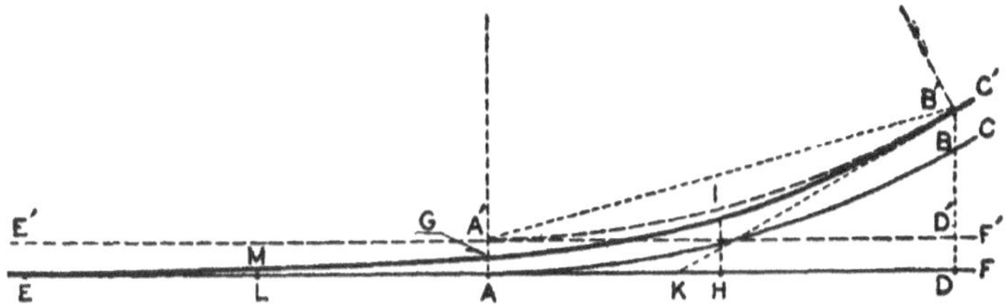

FIG. 33.—TRANSITION CURVE.

less than 0.38 R, or to be concrete up to an 11° curve, with 5-ins. elevation to the outer rail run out in 200 feet. On curves sharper than 11° a rough easement curve can be put in by applying similar methods. The curve will not be a real cubic parabola, but will be better than the sudden circular curve.

Having decided upon the elevation of the outer rail for the main curve, the length of the easement curve ED may be assumed as from 400 to 600 times the proposed elevation, and the points E and D located equidistant from A. The corresponding offset DB′ is then $(ED)^2$, divided by 6 times the radius of the curve ABC, and can be laid off perpendicular to ED.

The relation between DB′ and the perpendicular offset, HI, to any point, I, in the transition curve is then:

$$HI : DB' :: \overline{EH^3} : \overline{ED^3}; \text{ or } HI = DB' \frac{\overline{EH^3}}{\overline{ED^3}} \cdot = \overline{ED}.$$

Therefore AG, at the original PC is $\frac{1}{8}$ DB; while at the quarter points, L and H, the offsets are $\frac{1}{64}$ DB′ and $\frac{27}{64}$ DB′, respectively. A tangent to the curve at B′ cuts the line ED at a point K, such that KD=$\frac{1}{3}$ED. (The line KD in fig. 33 is distorted, because it was necessary to make ED much greater than 0.38 R to give a clear diagram.) The main curve can be continued from B′, by back-sighting either on A′ or K. From fig. 33 AA′=$\frac{1}{4}$ DB′=$\frac{1}{8}$D′B′, whence the deflection angle B′A′D′ can be determined, since R ver. sin 2 B′A′D′=D′B′.

68. **Corrections for curves of over 10°.**—It will be seen that in the foregoing curve work there is a slight error, due to the difference in length between an arc and the 100-ft. chord used in chaining. This difference is inappreciable for curves up to 10°. For curves sharper than this, there is a measurable correction to be applied, especially when subchords are used. In locating a very sharp curve, points must be located less than 100 ft. apart to properly outline the curve. In fig. 34 it is desired to use $n$ subchords, and to find the length, C′, of the subchord AB. $\frac{D}{n}$ is the angle AOB, subtended by subchord C′.

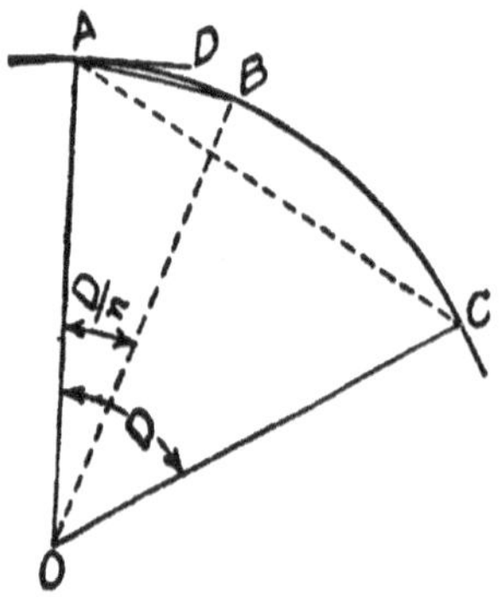


FIG. 34.

D= degree of curvature= AOC.

Then, $C' = 2R \sin \frac{D}{2n}$;

then, as $2R = \frac{100}{\sin \frac{D}{2}}$,

$$C' = \frac{100 \sin \frac{D}{2n}}{\sin \frac{D}{2}},$$

and $\sin \frac{D}{2n} = \frac{C'}{100} \sin \frac{D}{2}$.

**Example.**—Required to lay off a 36° curve with short chords so that a 100-ft. chord will subtend 36° at the center. What is the actual chord length to be used, when we wish to use three short chords?

$$\frac{D}{2n} = \frac{36°}{6} = 6° = \text{BAD}.$$

$$\frac{D}{2} = 18° \ 00'.$$

$$\therefore C' = 100 \times \frac{\sin 6°}{\sin 18°} = \frac{10.45}{.309} = 33.81 \text{ ft.}$$

The chord 33.81′ is used and 6° is turned off for each such distance.

69. **Increase in gage.**—In laying track on tangents the rails are laid with the distance from the inside of one rail to the inside of the other rail the exact gage of the track. On curves, however, it has been found better to slightly widen the gage.

This is done on account of the rigid wheel base and the consequent wear of the wheels and rails. For curves less than 3° there is no increase in the gage of the track. For curves sharper than this, the increase, according to good American practice, is shown in Table XIII. This table also shows the **distance of the guard rail from** the inner main rail. The increase in gage on a curve is dependent upon the length of the rigid wheel base and the radius of curvature. A general case can be found from the formula

$$I=\frac{3L^2}{2R} \text{ (approximately)},$$

in which L equals the length of the rigid wheel base in feet, R is the radius of the curve in feet, and I is the increase in gage in inches. This is an English rule and agrees with U. S. practice. I should never exceed about one-third of the tread. Note in Table XIII that the guard rail is a *constant* distance from the *outer* rail.

TABLE XIII.—**Increase in gage** of track on **curves.**

| Degree of curve. | Increase over standard gage. | Gage of track. | Distance of guard rail from main rail. |
|---|---|---|---|
| Less than 3° | 0 in | 4 ft. 8½ ins | 1¾ ins. |
| 3° | $\frac{1}{16}$ in | 4 ft. 8$\frac{9}{16}$ ins | 1$\frac{11}{16}$ ins. |
| 5° | ⅛ in | 4 ft. 8⅝ ins | 1⅞ ins. |
| 7° | ¼ in | 4 ft. 8¾ ins | 2 ins. |
| 9° | ⅜ in | 4 ft. 8⅞ ins | 2⅛ ins. |
| 11° | ½ in | 4 ft. 9 ins | 2¼ ins. |
| 13° | ⅝ in | 4 ft. 9⅛ ins | 2⅜ ins. |
| 15° | ¾ in | 4 ft. 9¼ ins | 2½ ins. |
| 17° | ⅞ in | 4 ft. 9⅜ ins | 2⅝ ins. |
| 19° | 1 in | 4 ft. 9½ ins | 2¾ ins. |
| 21° | 1⅛ ins | 4 ft. 9⅝ ins | 2⅞ ins. |

This table is for a first-class road. The rigid wheel base of the locomotives is about 12 to 15 ft.

70. **Elevation of the outer rail.**—The elevation of the outer rail on a curve is dependent upon the radius of the curve, the speed of the train, and the gage of the track, and can be found from the following formula:

$$E=\frac{gV^2}{15R},$$

in which E is super-elevation in feet,
$g$ is gage in feet,
R is radius in feet,
V is velocity in miles per hour.

71. In making this **correction for curvature** the inner rail may be carried along at grade and the entire elevation may be given to the outside rail, or the center line may be carried at grade and the outer rail laid one-half the elevation above the center line and the inner rail one-half the elevation below the center line. The former is considered the better practice. Whichever method is followed, the rails at the P. C. should have the full difference of elevation, and the difference of elevation is run out on the tangent at the rate of about 0.1 ft. in 60 ft. On a standard-gage military road the speed would doubtless be low, and a good rule for elevation for any curve would be ¾ in. for each degree of curvature, and the maximum elevation for any curve should not exceed 5 ins. Sharp curves and high speed do not go

together. On such curves the speed must be reduced, and the allowable speed may be found from the above formula by solving for V. A slow sign should be posted at both ends of such a curve.

72. **Lead of inside rail.**—Due to the shorter radius of the inner rail, its joints will run ahead of those of the outer rail and certain corrections must be made to keep the joints approximately square. This difference is $L-\frac{R+\frac{1}{2}g}{R-\frac{1}{2}g}L$, when R is the radius, g the gage, and L the length of rail. By using the short length rails on the curves, the joints can be kept approximately square without cutting rails. (See Table V as to specifications for rail lengths.)

73. **To find the degree of curvature.**—The middle ordinate of a 61.8-foot chord, measured in inches, gives the degree of curvature. This is only correct when the rails are properly curved, and on roughly lined curves will not give accurate results. The average of several trials is more accurate than a single measurement. **Another method** of determining the degree of curvature is shown in fig. 35, using the gage of the track, a measurement that is usually accurate, as a middle ordinate. Sight from C to A, making AC tangent to the inner rail at B. Measure AC and DB. CB should equal BA, and the point A should be relocated if measurements do not agree.

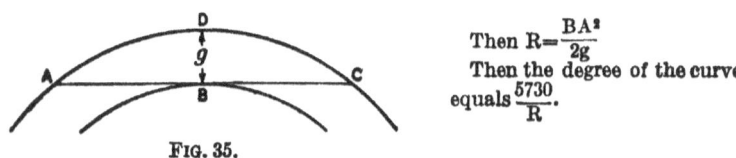

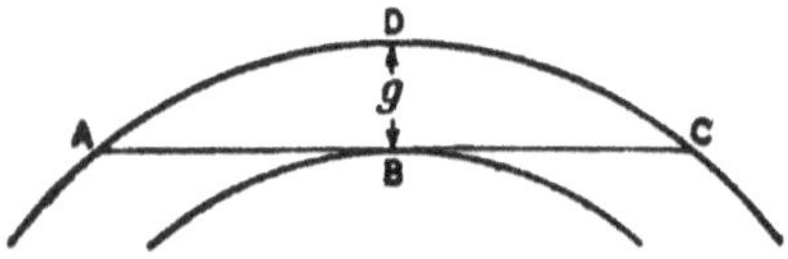


FIG. 35.

Then $R=\frac{BA^2}{2g}$

Then the degree of the curve equals $\frac{5730}{R}$.

74. **Vertical curves.**—On a line with grades as great as 1% and 2%, vertical curves will be necessary where two sharp grades come together. The curve is usually in the form of a parabola. The American Railway Engineering Association recommends that for the same change of grade the length of vertical curve in a sag should be twice what it would be for the same change on a summit, while other engineers would make them of equal length.

In fig. 36 AB is the upgrade and BC the downgrade. The stations indicated are 100-ft. stations. It is desired to run in a vertical curve on this hill and avoid the sharp change at B. Decide on the desired length of the vertical curve, and on the

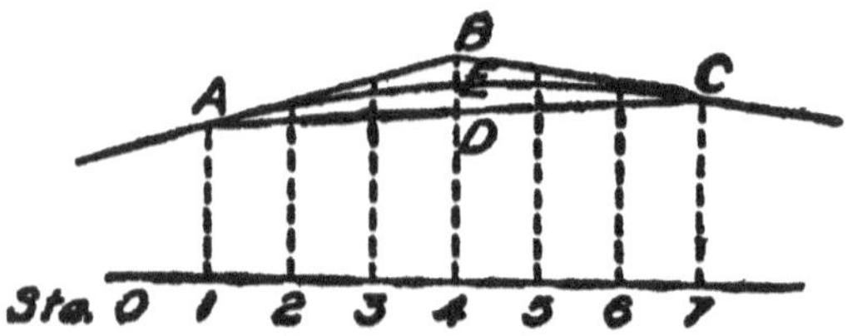


FIG. 36.—VERTICAL CURVE.

profile draw the chord AC corresponding to this length. Half the difference between the elevation of B and D is approximately the middle ordinate of the curve, and locates the elevation of the curve at the point E. Then let M be the *correction* in elevation at the point B.

$$BE=M=\frac{1}{2}\left(\frac{\text{elev. A}+\text{elev. C}}{2}-\text{elev. B}\right).$$

The correction for any other point of the vertical curve is proportional to the square of its distance from the nearest end of the curve divided by the square of the half length AB. The correction is negative when the curve is concave downward, and is positive when the curve is concave upward.

Vertical curves vary in length according to the change in grades. The A. R. E. A. rule is that the length of the vertical curve, AC, equals the change of adjacent grades (in per cents) multiplied by 1,000 ft. for summits or 2,000 ft. for sags. These lengths can safely be reduced to 250 and 500 ft., respectively. The resulting curve should extend an equal distance on each side of the apex. Improvements in couplers and brakes are decreasing the necessity of long vertical curves.

**Example.**—A +2% grade joins a −1.5% grade. How long should the vertical curve be? (2+1.5) 250=875 ft.; 437½ on each slope.

75. **Drains and culverts.**—The engineer should examine every depression crossed in the survey, and will decide whether or not water will accumulate behind the railroad bank if no culvert is put in. If there is a drainage area of any extent on the uphill side, a culvert or drain of some sort will be put through the embankment at this point to carry off the water. A blind drain will sometimes answer, but it is better to put in a box drain or leave an opening in the embankment and put in a small bridge. These drains should be perpendicular to the track. The area of the opening in square feet given by Myer's formula is:

$$A = C\sqrt{\text{drainage area in acres.}} \quad C = \begin{cases} 1, \text{ in flat country.} \\ 1\frac{1}{2}, \text{ in hilly country.} \\ 4, \text{ in rocky, mountainous country.} \end{cases}$$

76. **Tunnels.**—In a field line a tunnel is practically an impossibility on account of the difficulties of construction and the time necessary to build one. If necessary a temporary timber-lined tunnel may be constructed by an application of methods described in Part V, Field Fortification, under Mining.

CONSTRUCTION.

77. **The roadbed** is the support prepared for the track. It generally consists of the **foundation** and the **ballast.** The latter should be a material the consistency of which is not affected by water, and especially which does not become slippery when wet. Sand will do if nothing else can be had; gravel is better, and broken stone is the best of all. Cinders, shells, burnt clay, and other materials are also used. The surface of the foundation on which the ballast rests is called the **subgrade.**

Unless the natural ground is very unfavorable, it will not be necessary to use a separate material for ballast and the subgrade really disappears. Even then, the earth between and immediately under the ties which is dug into in surfacing the track is called ballast. Such roads, usually called **mud roads,** will be the rule in military practice.

78. The cross section of the roadbed must be decided upon before the level party starts on its work, in order that they may know the dimensions of the roadbed for which the stakes are to be set. Figs. 41–47 show the dimensions of standard-gage roads. For any other gage the slopes will be the same, but the shoulders outside of the ties will be slightly less. The difference will therefore be the difference in the gage of the tracks, plus twice the amount that the shoulder can be reduced in width. The dimensions of the roadbed of a 2 ft. 6 in. track would be, approximately, 11 ft. from shoulder to shoulder on a fill and 10 ft. from shoulder to shoulder in a cut. The dimensions for a track of 3-ft. gage will be about 12 ft. from shoulder to shoulder on an embankment and about 11 ft. in a cut. In excavations, plenty of depth should be allowed for **ditches** in order to insure a dry roadbed.

Wherever the grades permit, the track will be laid directly on the surface of the ground, and the necessary leveling up can be done after the track has been laid. It must be continually kept in mind that the first object desired is to get some sort of railway connection established, and that the betterments to the line in slight changes of grade, etc., can come afterward and not interfere with traffic.

79. **The track** consists of the **ties**, the **rails**, and the attachments of the latter to the former and to each other.

**Ties** for military roads will be made of the most accessible wood, and should be 8 ft. long, 6 to 7 ins. thick, and 8 to 10 ins. face, top and bottom, if hewed, and 9 ins. if sawed. They should be spaced 24 ins. c. to c., as a rule, but if the ties are broad it may be necessary to space them wider, as clear room between of 12 ins. is needed for tamping. It is usual to allot a certain number of ties (14 to 18) to a 30-ft. rail, and space them equal clear distances rather than equal center distances.

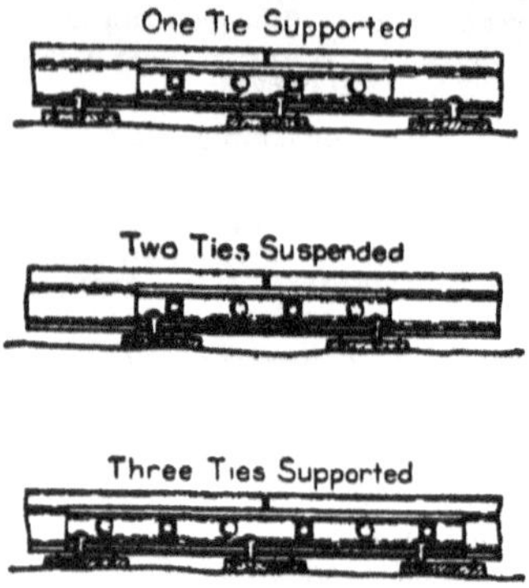


Fig. 37.—Types of rail joints and tie arrangement.

**Rails** are 30 ft. in standard length. The size of rails is reckoned by the weight per yard in lbs., and varies from 12 to 110 lbs., the former used for industrial and construction roads and the latter on a few of the highest class trunk lines. Rails for military roads will probably run from 60 to 80 lbs. The name of the mill and the weight per yard are rolled in raised letters on the web of each rail at short intervals.

80. **Rail joints.**—A rail joint consists of a pair of **fishplates**, or **angle bars**, and from four to six bolts. The length of angle bar used to-day varies from 17 to 48 ins. The bolts should alternate, one head inside and the next head outside of the track. Fig. 37 shows different classes of rail joints and tie arrangements.

Joints are either **suspended** or **supported.** The former are believed to be the most satisfactory. For size and weights of various accessories, see Tables II to VIII.

Fig. 38.

81. **Buffers.**—A buffer, or bumping post, is an arrangement placed at the end of a spur track to prevent the cars from running off the end of the track. A commercial form of the same is shown in fig. 38.

A heavy timber chained across the track answers very well for a bumping post. One of the simplest and best means of ending a spur track is to dump a **pile of cinders** across the end of the track for about half a car length from the end, about 3 ft. thick.

82. **Tie plates.**—On curves and bridges, tie plates can be used advantageously. These plates are usually of steel and prevent the rail from cutting into the tie (see fig. 39).

83. **Spikes.**—The commonest form of railway spike is shown in fig. 40. The weights of these for various sizes are shown in Table VII. The cutting edge of the spike is across the grain in crossties; if the rails are to be spiked to stringers, as occasionally on a bridge, the spikes should be "reversed" by a smith.

84. **Organization of working parties.**—The actual organization of the working parties will depend upon the manner in which it is planned to move the earth. However, there are a few cardinal principles which will apply in every case.

The work must be **laid out** far enough in advance so that no working party, either teams or men, shall be idle through lack of orders.

The men and animals must be housed and fed as well as conditions will permit. For this purpose, a quartermaster should be detailed, with a sufficient number of assistants to thoroughly handle these two important duties.

FIG. 39.—TIE PLATE.

85. The **quartermaster**, or one of his assistants, will have charge of all tools and supplies. He will be responsible for getting them to the front when wanted, and for distribution before working hours and collection afterwards. He is responsible for all camps, camp equipage, and transportation. He will be in charge of the messing and act as paymaster.

86. The **health of the men** should be looked after by a detail from the medical department, whose business it is to look after the sanitation of the camps, the proper policing of the water supply, and the general health of the men. The **health of the animals** is also important, and a proper number of veterinarians should be employed to take care of them.

87. The camps will be so located that the least possible time will be lost in getting the entire force onto the work, and the camp will be moved from time to time to fill this requirement. If necessary for the safety of the camp and the working parties, a **proper guard** will be detailed, whose commander will report to the engineer in charge of the party or parties that are to be protected. The **guard commander** of the camp will be responsible to the engineer in charge for the security and safety of the camp and working parties. He will perform his duties in the manner prescribed for the outpost commander in the Field Service Regulations, and will keep the engineer in charge fully informed as to the precautions that he has taken, and will give him timely warning of an enemy's approach.

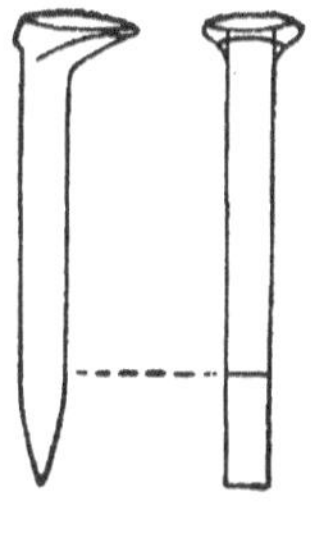

FIG. 40.—RAILROAD SPIKE.

88. **Clearing and grubbing.**—The first party sent out clears the right of way of all trees, brush, etc., and is followed by a party to grub out stumps that lie in the actual roadbed wherever the fill is not over 2 ft. Stumps up to 12 ins. in diameter can be pulled by means of a **stump puller,** which requires the use of one team and two or three men. For stumps larger than 12 ins. in diameter it is probable that dynamite will be used. To get a stump out by this means a trench is dug around the stump from 2 to 4 ft. wide and of sufficient depth to uncover the main body of the stump. A hole is bored under the stump with a 2-in. auger, and one or two ½-lb. sticks of dynamite are pushed into the hole and exploded. This small charge springs a large opening under the stump, into which the necessary amount of dynamite or powder is placed and exploded.

89. **Earth work.**—For details as to earth work, see Part III—Roads.

# ROAD BEDS.

## EARTH BALLAST.

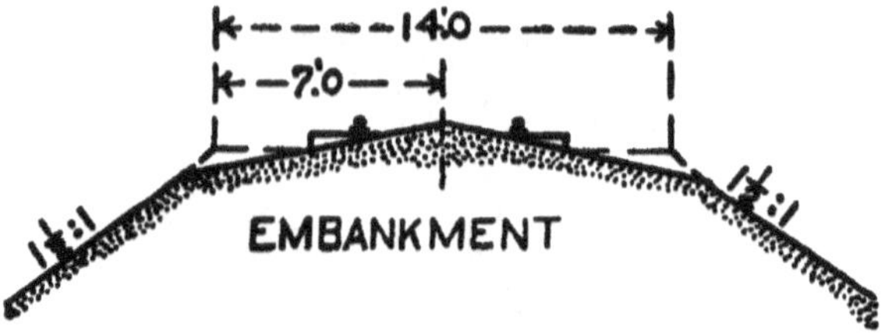


FIG. 41.

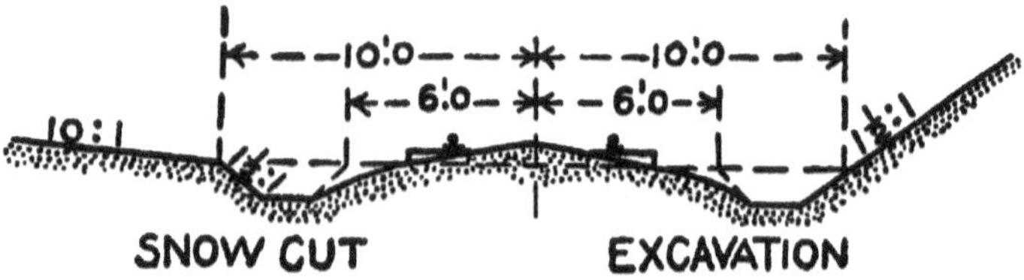


FIG. 42.—20-FT. BASE (UNDER 4 FT. IN DEPTH)

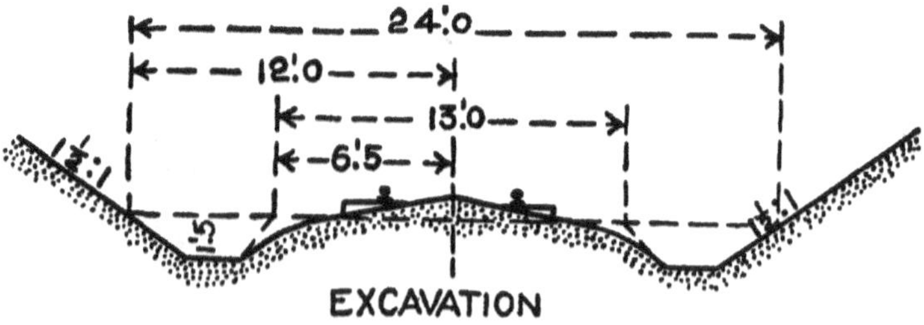


FIG. 43.—24-FT. BASE (4 FT. AND OVER IN DEPTH).

# ROAD BEDS.

## STONE OR GRAVEL BALLAST.

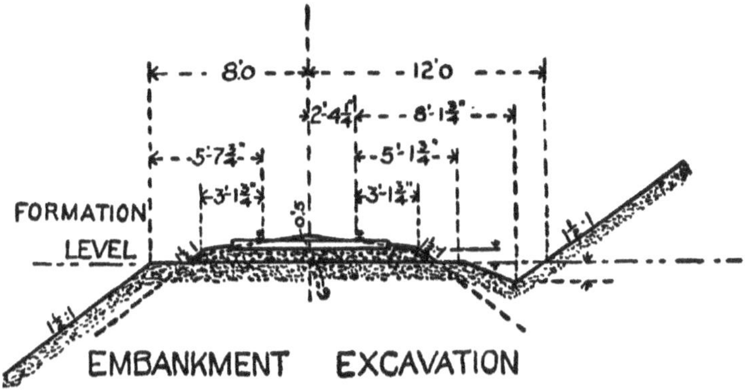


FIG. 44.—STRAIGHT LINE.

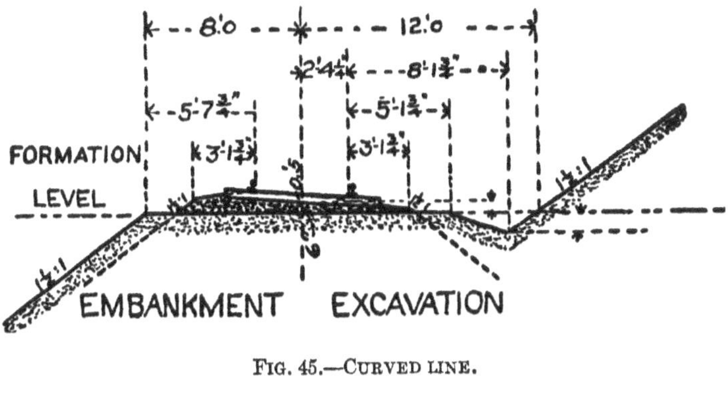


FIG. 45.—CURVED LINE.

SCALE 0 1 2 3 4 5 6 7 8 9 10 FEET

# ROAD BEDS.

## STONE OR GRAVEL BALLAST.

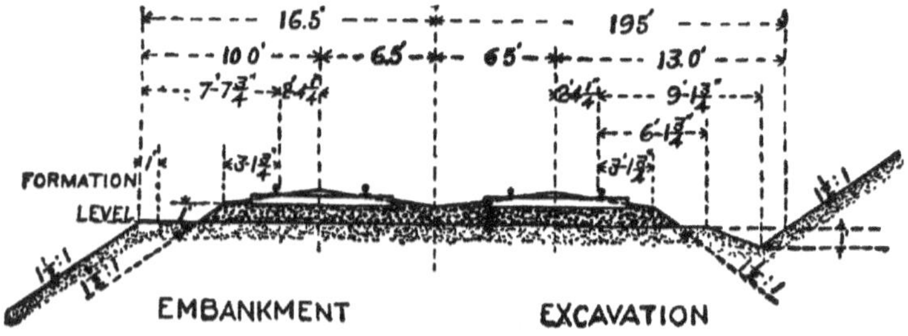


FIG. 46.—STRAIGHT LINE (DOUBLE TRACK).

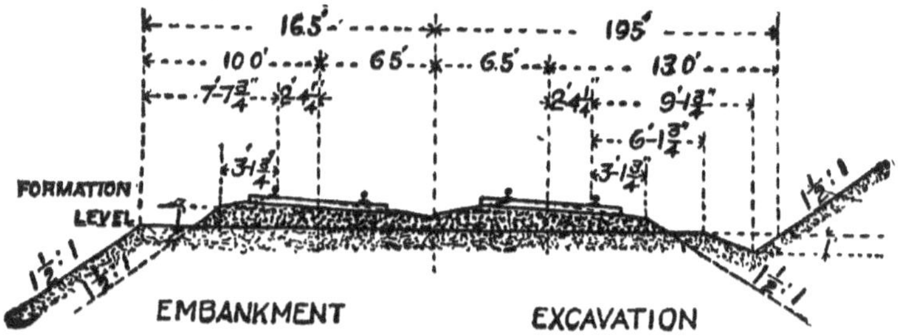


FIG. 47.—CURVED LINE (DOUBLE TRACK).

### TOOLS AND APPLIANCES.

90. Many of the tools and appliances used in railroad work are so well known that no description is given.

Figs. 48 to 71 show some of the tools and equipment that will be found in use on all railways.

Fig. 48

Fig. 49

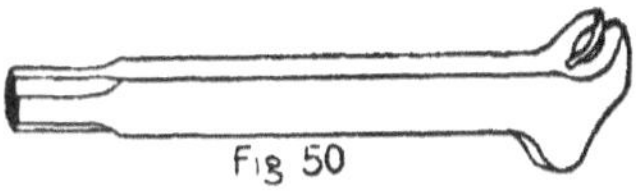
Fig 50

Fig 51

Fig 52

Fig 53

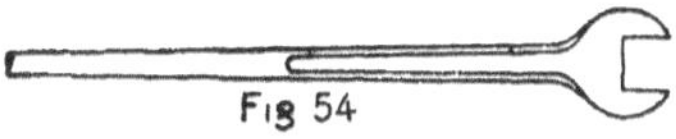
Fig 54

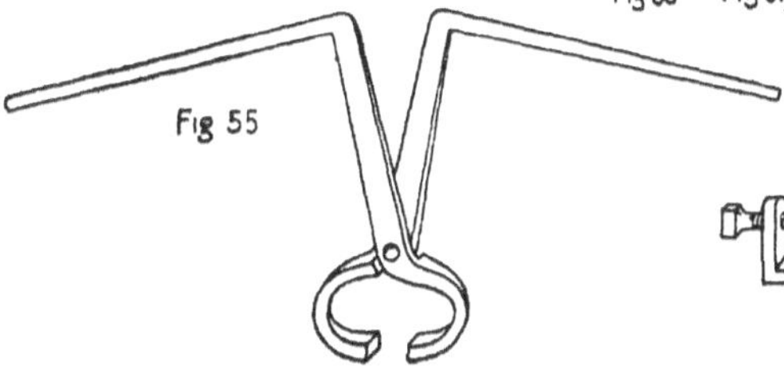
Fig 55

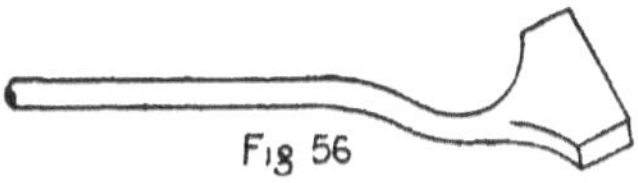
Fig 56

Fig 57

Fig 58

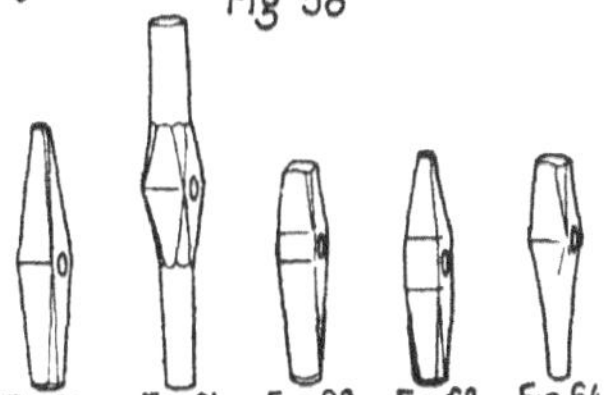
Fig 60 Fig 61 Fig 62 Fig 63 Fig 64

Fig. 59

FIG. 48.—TRACK GAUGE.
49.—TRACK LEVEL.
50.—CLAW BAR.
51.—LINING BAR.
52.—CROWBAR (PINCH POINT).
53.—CROWBAR (WEDGE POINT).
54.—TRUCK WRENCH.
55.—RAIL TONGS.
56.—TAMPING BAR.

FIG. 57.—PICKAX (CLAY PICK).
58.—TAMPING PICK.
59.—RAIL CLAMP.
60.—SPIKE MAUL.
61.—SPIKE MAUL (PITTSBURGH PATTERN).
62.—TRACK CHISEL.
63.—TRACK PUNCH.
64.—TRACK PUNCH (ROUND POINT).

FIG. 65.—RAIL SAW.

FIG. 66.—TRACK DRILL.

FIG. 67.—TRACK JACK

FIG. 68.—GASOLINE VELOCIPEDE.

FIG. 69.—HAND CAR.

91. Fig. 71 is a **Sterlingworth holding-up bar,** which will be found very useful in laying track, since the blow to the spike is transmitted directly to the rail and not to the adjacent ties, as it is when the tie being spiked is held up from the adjacent ties by pinch bars.

Fig. 70.—Portable Light.

92. A **sand blast** is an appliance that will be found useful wherever ironwork of rolling stock or bridges is to be cleaned for repainting. These sand blasts are a commercial article, and for cleaning metal work can not be equaled by any other method. The **nozzle** of a sand blast is the part that wears out quickest, and it has been found that a small piece of ¾-in. pipe pounded flat on one end and threaded at the other, for connection with the hose coupling, is as efficient as the best hardened-steel nozzles on the market.

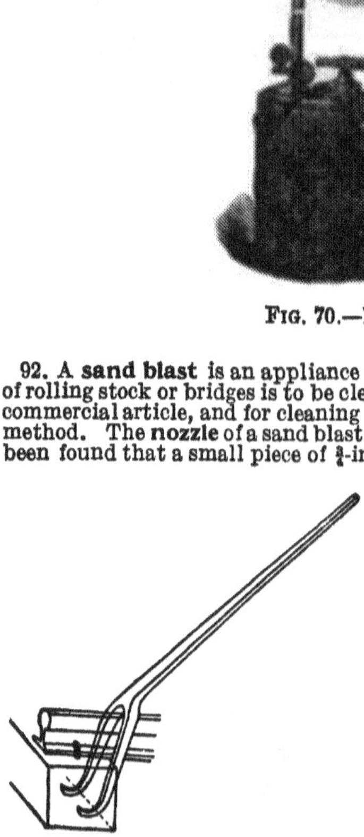

Fig. 71.—Holding-up bar.

93. With light rails the holes for track **bolts can** be punched, and a **portable rail punch** will be furnished for this purpose. Rails will be drilled when time and tools permit.

BRIDGES.

94. **Bridges.—A discussion of the stresses and strains** in bridges will **not be considered here.** The intention is **to describe certain simple** types of bridges **and to suggest a system** based on certain **openings and loadings, in** accordance with **which** the chief engineer may prepare, in advance, certain bridges or the material necessary for such bridges. If the work will be mainly reconstruction of an existing line, every effort should be made to obtain a **list of the existing bridges** and a description of each. These lists are kept by all railways. Preparation must then be made to duplicate every bridge on the first 75 or 100 miles of the line. If no such list can be obtained, or if a new line is to be constructed, certain openings shall be decided upon as standard. Knowing the maximum load, either steel or wooden stringers for these openings will be provided by the chief engineer. The

engineer in the field, on coming to an opening where a bridge is required, will plan the bridge so that the openings between abutments, or between bents of piles or trestles, shall be from the lengths previously agreed upon and for which the chief engineer is prepared to send material without delay. This classification can only apply to **single openings**, because with several spans it will be impossible to include anything general about the necessary piers.

Only in exceptional cases will openings over 50 feet be provided for. Larger spans will be subdivided into spans of less than 50 feet by temporary piers wherever possible.

The bridge material provided for the first 75 to 100 miles of the railway will probably not all be used on that part of the line. The stock of material will be increased for the next succeeding section before the end of the first section has been reached by the advancing troops.

95. In any stream the rate of the current and the amount of drift are important factors in determining the span to be used. The length of time a bridge will be in use is also important, as the river may be at such a stage that one length of span can be used, when if it were at a higher or lower stage, an entirely different one would be necessary.

96. The **strength of wooden and steel beams** is shown in the tables under "Bridges," Engineer Field Manual, and also in the various engineers' and manufacturers' handbooks. The loads to be provided for can be ascertained or decided upon beforehand. The locomotive loads are the maximum loads and can easily be found for any standard locomotive.

97. On arriving at a bridge that has been destroyed, the first consideration is to get some sort of a line across to connect with the road on the other side. This can frequently be done by making a **deviation** which will carry the roadbed into the river bottom and up the other bank, necessitating only a very short, low bridge. This work is done by the advance party, and a second party follows and constructs the permanent bridge at the grade of the permanent track. Sharp curves on this diversion line should be avoided, since steep grades will be inevitable, and the combination may cause frequent derailments.

98. **Piers and abutments.**—Before the beams or trusses for the necessary spans can be decided upon, it is necessary to decide upon the location of the piers and abutments. The local conditions as to the banks and the bottom of the stream will, in general, determine the location and kind of abutments and piers that are to be used. In general terms, they will be either of piles, cribs, or trestles. A description of the methods and conditions that govern the use of these three, and their method of construction, is given in the chapter on Bridges.

99. Unless the bottom is very muddy, a crib or trestle bridge can be built quicker than a pile bridge; and on this account, unless a pile bridge is necessary, one of the other two kinds will be used. The question whether **cribwork or trestles** will be built will depend upon the amount and kind of material at hand. Cribs can be built in a shorter time with unskilled labor than can trestles, but the amount of

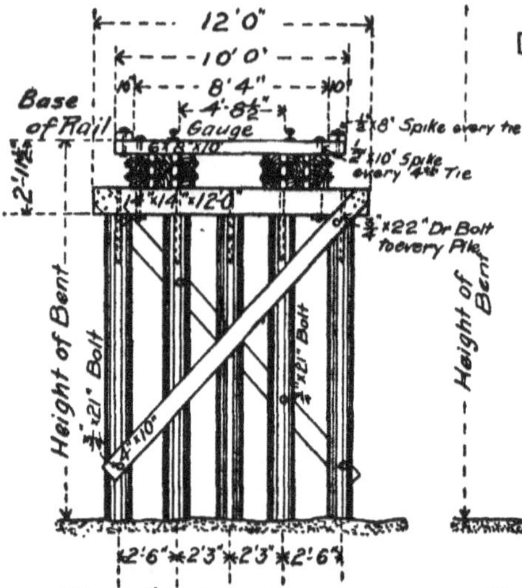


To 20' in height

FIG. 72.

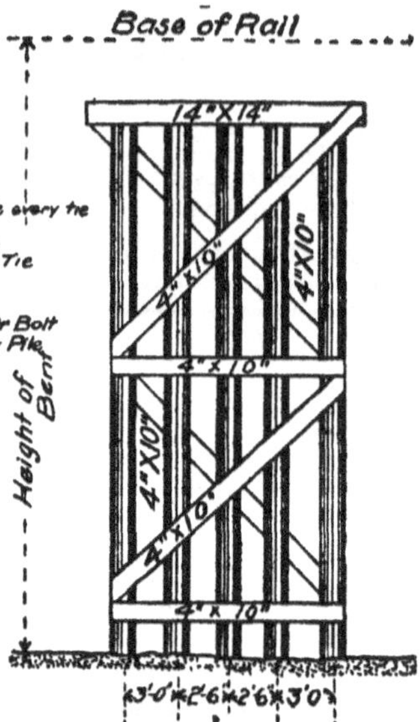


From 20' to 30' in height

FIG. 73.

NOTE.—No bracing on bents up to 9 ft. high. Double bracing on bents over 18 ft. high and up to 28 ft.

material in cribwork is greatly in excess of that in trestles. Cribwork occupies so much of the waterway that it is more exposed to washouts and accumulation of drift than are trestle or pile bridges.

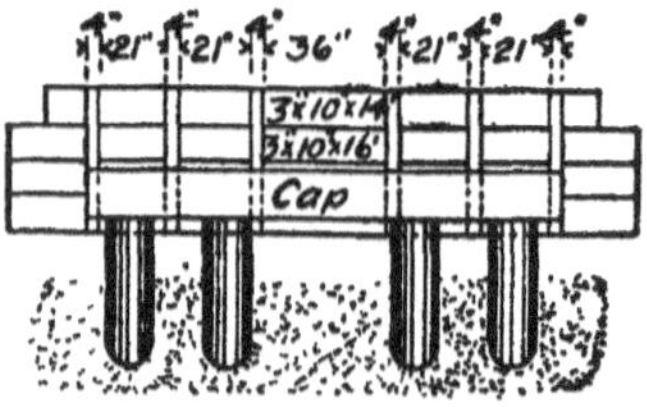


FIG. 74.—ABUTMENT WALL.

100. Up to a height of 18 ft., crib piers can be built more rapidly than trestles if the material is at hand. Above this height, the advantage of the crib over the trestle rapidly decreases; and above 25 ft. the trestle has the advantage. (Experience in South Africa.)

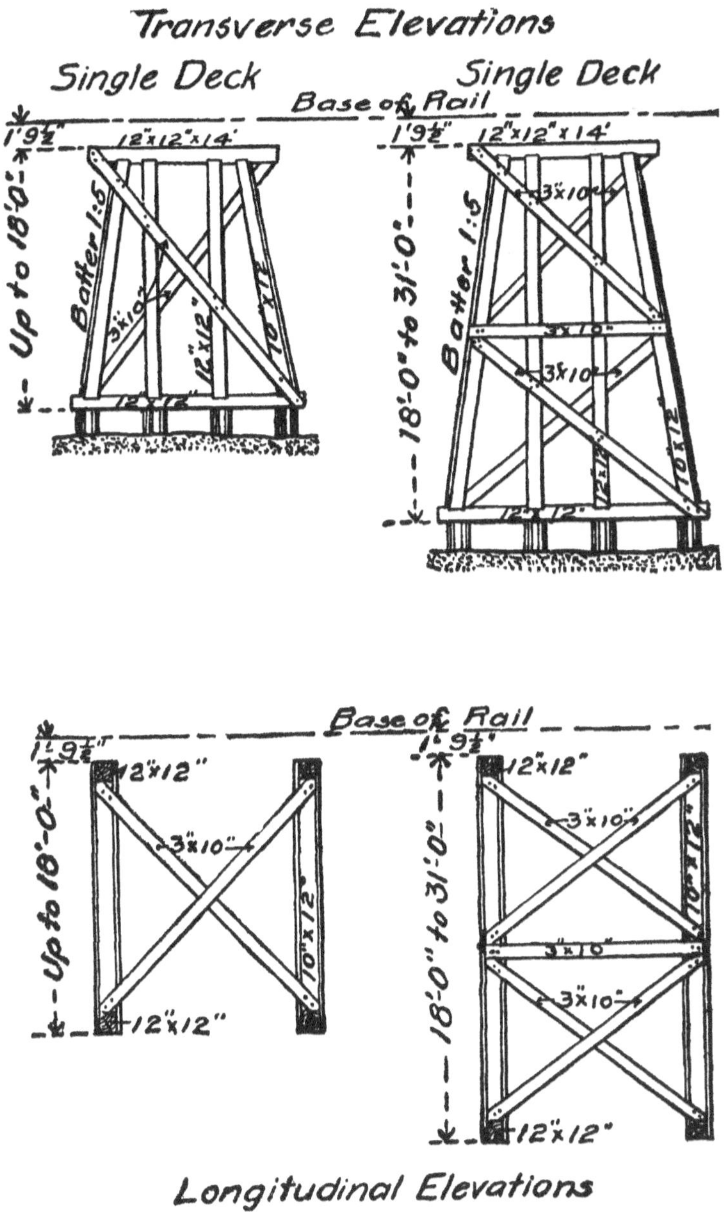
Transverse Elevations
Single Deck
Single Deck
Base of Rail
1'9½"
12"x12"x14'
Up to 18'0"
Batter 1:5
3"x10"
12"x12"
10"x12"
12"x12"
1'9½"
12"x12"x14'
3"x10"
18'0" to 31'0"
Batter 1:5
3"x10"
3"x10"
12"x12"
10"x12"
12"x12"
Base of Rail
1'9½"
12"x12"
3"x10"
Up to 18'-0"
10"x12"
12"x12"
1'9½"
12"x12"
3"x10"
18'0" to 31'0"
10"x12"
3"x10"
3"x10"
12"x12"
Longitudinal Elevations

FIG. 75.

101. In trestlework it is frequently advisable to fasten the uprights to the caps and mudsills by means of **dogs or side plates,** instead of by **driftbolts,** on account of the difficulty of drawing driftbolts out of the timber in case the trestle is dismantled for future use.

102. On a **rocky bottom,** little difficulty is encountered in the foundations, as the bottom can be leveled off, either by cutting or by the use of concrete in bags. On a sandy bottom, two or three layers of ties make a very good foundation. Care should be taken to prevent any scouring under the foundation of the trestles.

103. **Types of pile bents** are shown in figs, 72, 73, 74. Table XXI gives a complete list of material required for any number of 16-ft. spans of pile bridge. It includes everything except rails and rail fasteners. It may be impracticable to obtain the wooden stringers shown in the table. In such a case steel I beams may be obtainable, and if so, a new table can be made incorporating such changes as the substitution of steel stringers requires.

104. **Beams.**—Knowing standard size of openings and the loading, and having decided upon the location and number of spans necessary, the corresponding floor system can be taken from the material previously prepared, or the superstructure can be ordered from the base storehouse by a very short telegram. Work can be immediately begun on the piers and abutments, and knowing the height of rail and dimensions of ties and stringers, the piers and abutments can frequently be ready for the floor system when it arrives.

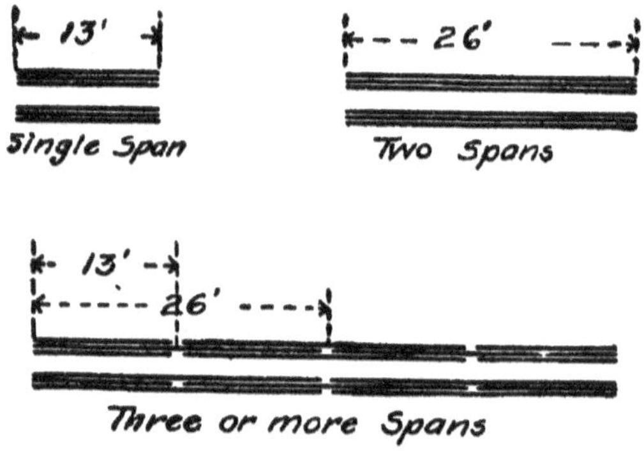


FIG. 76.—ARRANGEMENT OF STRINGERS.

Wherever practicable, the stringers of the floor system should be lapped as shown in fig. 76, but in ordering a **floor system,** care should be taken not to ask impossible things. For instance, to ask for double lengths for a 15-ft. span would require timber 30 ft. in length, which is about the limit of length that can be supplied from the ordinary market; and if a longer span than 15 ft. were contemplated, it would not do to ask for double lengths unless it were known positively that such lengths could readily be obtained.

105. **Trestles.**—Figs. 75 and 77 show the form of construction for trestles of various heights and show the necessary bracings. From these figures and from fig. 78 bills of material for trestle bridges can easily be made up to suit any particular case.

106. The various methods of **erecting the trusses** or beams are fully described in the chapter on bridges. The ends of beams or trusses should be securely fastened to the caps by driftbolts or by some other method that will keep them from sliding sidewise or lengthwise. Adjacent beams should be separated by blocks of wood, or by C. I. spools.

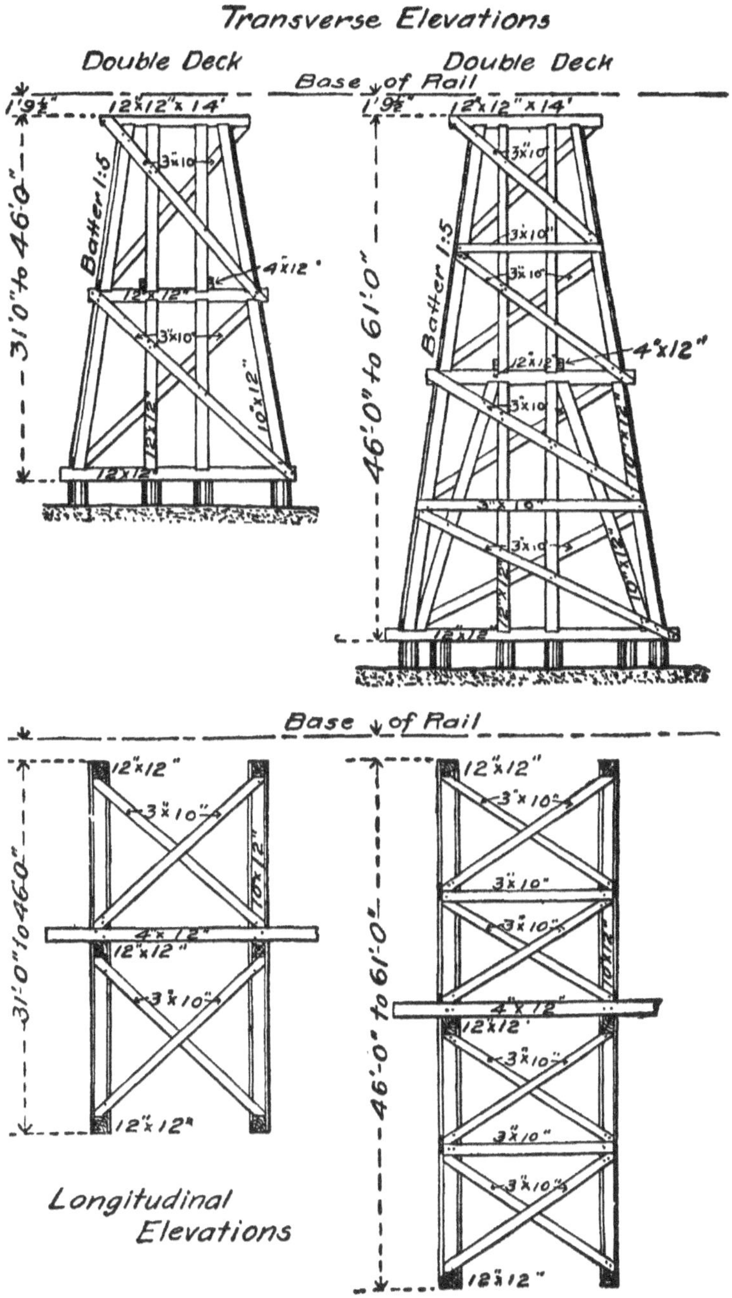
Transverse Elevations
Double Deck
Double Deck
Base of Rail
1'9½"
12"x12"x14'
Batter 1:5
3"x10"
4"x12"
12"x12"
10"x12"
12"x12"
31'0" to 46'0"
46'0" to 61'0"
Base of Rail
Longitudinal Elevations
4"x12"
3"x10"
12"x12"

FIG. 77.

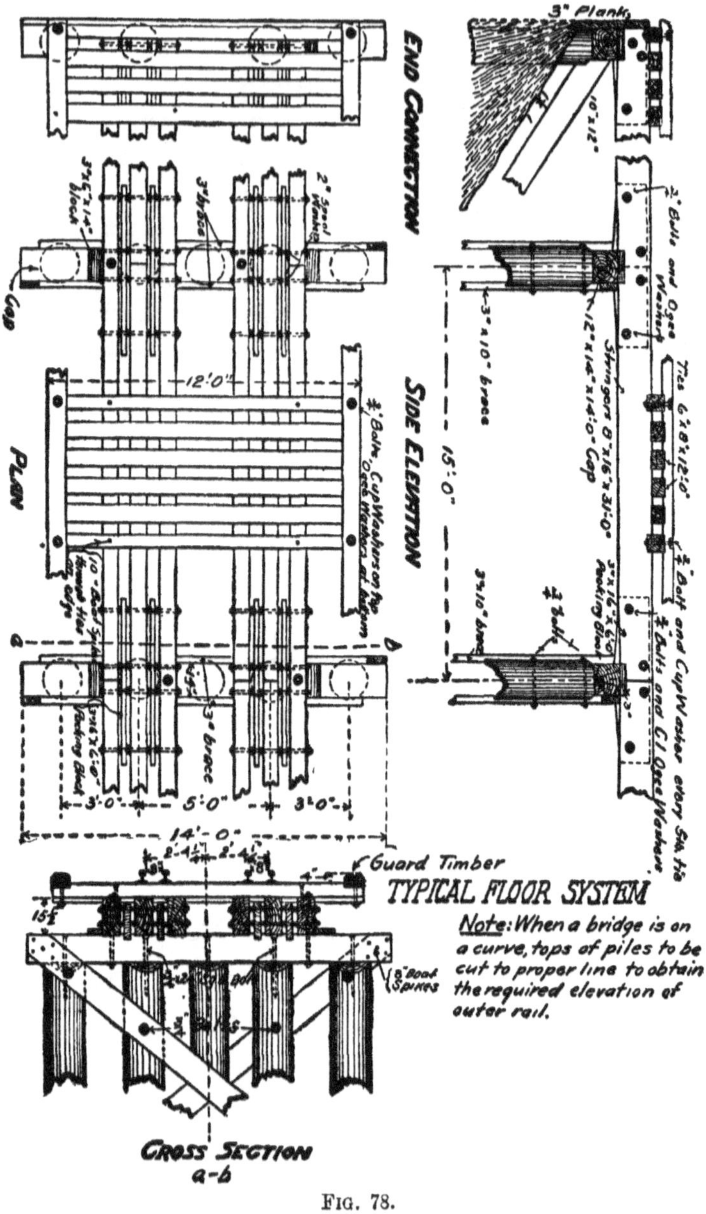
End Connection
Plan
Side Elevation
Gross Section
a-b
Guard Timber
TYPICAL FLOOR SYSTEM
Note: When a bridge is on a curve, tops of piles to be cut to proper line to obtain the required elevation of outer rail.
3" Plank
12'0"
14'-0"
5'0"
15'0"
3"x10" brace
Cap

FIG. 78.

107. **Cross bracing.**—Whether trusses or beams are used, some system of floor bracing must be used that will make the bridge rigid under side pressure from wind or other causes, and will prevent lateral movement from vibration due to moving loads.

108. **Floor system.**—The part of a pile or trestle bridge above the caps is known as the floor system. A standard floor system is illustrated in fig. 78, where the various parts are designated by name. The strength is varied by changing the number of stringers.

109. **Creeping.**—The ties of a railway bridge should be spaced from 4 to 6 ins. apart, and about every sixth tie should be fastened to the stringers, either by letting the tie into the stringer or by nailing a block to the stringer that completely fills the space between that tie and the next. This prevents creeping of the track on the bridge. When I beams are used for stringers, the track is prevented from moving sideways by fastening the ties to the flanges with lag bolts. Creeping is prevented by clips that clamp the rail to the flange, or end, of the I beams.

110. **Guard rails** and **guard timbers** are necessary to prevent trains running off the bridges in case of derailment while crossing a bridge. On a single-track bridge, the guard rails extend the full length of the bridge on both sides and are brought together at both ends after leaving the bridge. On a double track bridge, they are brought together at the end from which traffic comes and are left open beyond the other end of the bridge (see fig. 79). Guard rails should be from 8 to 12 ins. inside the main rails. Guard timbers are bolted to the ends of the ties on both sides of the track, the full length of the bridge. They are usually from 4 by 10 to 5 by 8 ins. and lie about 3 ft. outside of the rails.

NOTE.—No guard rails to be used on bridges having a clear span under coping of less than 20 ft.

Guard timbers to be placed at proper distance outside of rails on all bridges except those with solid floor and ballast.

111. **Trusses.**—For spans greater than 50 ft. suitable girders or beams could not practically be carried in stock in the storehouse. Such openings must be spanned by trusses built on the site. As far as practicable, all the materials are framed at the rear and sent to the site ready for erection.

The chief engineer will have on file in his office complete bills of material for trusses of various standard lengths. He will keep on hand a supply of all **standard bridge materials,** and can thus supply the necessary material for any of these trusses.

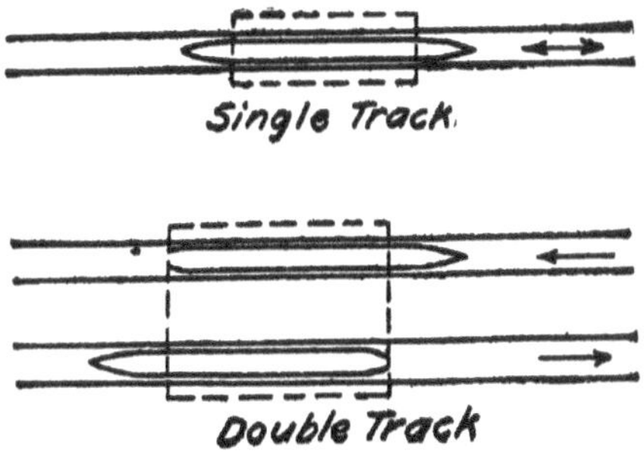


FIG. 79.—GUARD RAILS.

112. **Cableways.**—In some places an overhead cableway can be used to great advantage in erecting or building a bridge, or in transporting supplies across a stream that vehicles can not cross. There are two classes, the **ordinary cableway** (fig. 80) and the **balanced cable crane** (fig. 81). The first form can be quickly rigged if large trees are close to the bank, and is very convenient when the load does not have to come in to the very foot of the supports. If towers must be used to support the cable, they are difficult to erect and the material is too heavy to carry in a field equipment. A considerably longer span is always necessary than the actual width of the stream, and the load must be pulled uphill over one-half of its journey and is only stable at the lowest point in the catenary. The balanced cable crane, on the other hand, can carry loads farther inshore than its points of support; the stress in the cable is constant whatever the position of the load, and only sufficient force to over-

come friction is required to move the load along the cable. The key to the construction of this cableway is that the length of the cable must be such that **both** counterweights can not rest on the ground at the same time. The automatic rising and falling of the counterweights as the position of the load on the cableway changes keeps the angles of the cable at the load symmetrical with the action line of gravity, and hence the load is stable at any point on the cable.

One end only need oscillate; the other can be rigidly anchored. The counterweights are the only excessively heavy parts of this cableway. They will probably be bags of sand filled on the spot. The amount of material to be transported is comparatively small, and much of it will have other uses.

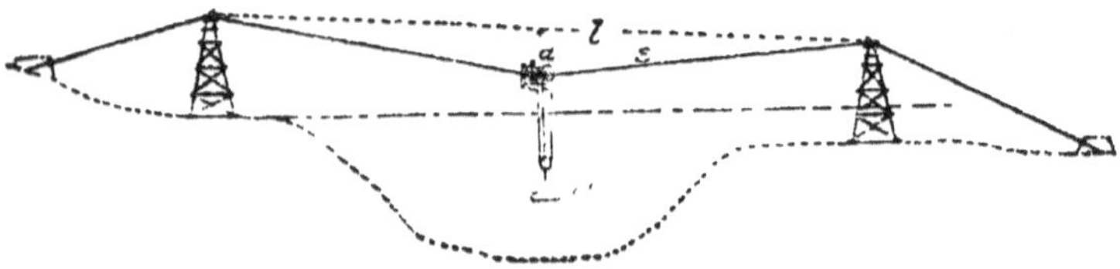


FIG. 80.—ORDINARY CABLEWAY.

For efficient hand operation, the cable of either class must have both ends at approximately the same elevation.

In reconstruction work, the use of cableways will be found to facilitate the erection of bridges very greatly; and in cases where a ferry is not practicable, a cableway may be constructed for the transportation of supplies.

Light cableways with a capacity of about 60 tons per hour for spans up to 400 ft. are commercial articles, and from 25 to 30 tons per hour can be carried over a span of 1,000 ft. on a comparatively light cableway.

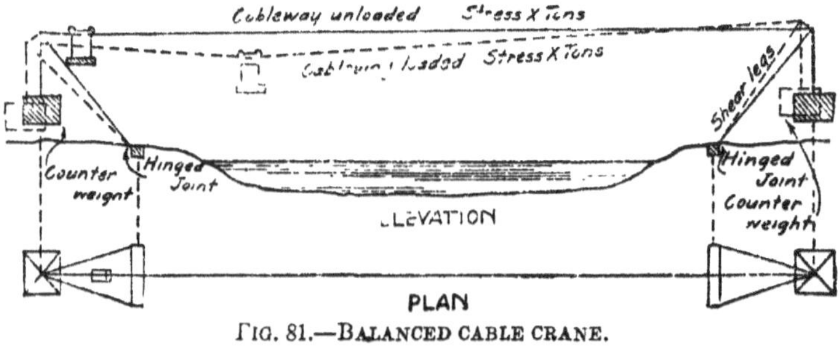


FIG. 81.—BALANCED CABLE CRANE.

TRACK LAYING.

113. **Final center line.**—As soon as the roadbed is completed, the transit party runs over the line and sets center stakes 100 ft. apart on tangents and 50 ft. apart on curves, and re-marks the center of the track by tacks in the head of the stakes. The road is then ready for the track-laying gang. This center line must be accurate, for bridge and track work will begin simultaneously.

114. **Track laying.**—The track-laying party now follows, and the plans for all preceding work should be such that the track laying can go on continuously. The **rapidity of track laying** is governed by the rate of supply of material at the working point. This can be accelerated on sidetracks and on double-track work by unloading ties, rails, and other material directly from the cars alongside of the

existing track, and work under these conditions is simple and rapid, for the material can be easily distributed.

On **new work,** however, the rails, ties, and all other materials must be either distributed along the line by the **use of wagons** or must be carried on a **train** and the track built ahead of the train; ties, rails, etc., being unloaded and placed in position by laborers.

115. On ground that is fairly level and free from streams the first method, that of distributing material from **wagons,** is the most rapid. The following example gives the working force and distribution of labor used in laying an average of 4.27 miles of track per day of 10 hours during the month of August, 1887, between Minot, N. Dak., and Great Falls, Mont. The force was distributed as follows:

| | *Men* | *Horses.* |
|---|---|---|
| Hauling ties | 75 | 150 |
| Loading ties | 28 | .... |
| Distributing ties | 10 | .... |
| Spacing ties | 4 | .... |
| Lining ties | 2 | .... |
| Marking and placing joint ties | 4 | .... |
| Unloading flats and loading iron cars | 24 | .... |
| Unloading iron cars and placing rails | 13 | .... |
| Hauling rails | 3 | 6 |
| Spikers | 38 | .... |
| Nippers | 19 | .... |
| Strappers | 12 | .... |
| Distributing spikes | 2 | .... |
| Lining track | 8 | .... |
| Total | 242 | 156 |

Six rail cars were used, and as soon as each car was unloaded at the front it was run back behind the spikers and taken off the track. When the last of the six cars had been unloaded, the other five were again placed on the track and the supply train moved ahead. The best record made was 8 01 miles of track in 11½ hours. This is supposed to be the best day's work of track laying on record.

The ties were unloaded from the construction train, placed in wagons, and hauled to the front, and then thrown into place, lined, and spaced by the first 123 men in the above list. The rails were unloaded from the construction train onto small rail cars, hauled to the front, and unloaded from these cars and placed on the ties by the next 40 men of the table. Rails were spiked to the ties, the bolts put in, and the track lined by the remainder of the crew.

The method just described is the most rapid that can be followed but is more expensive than other methods to be described later and therefore is not generally followed in commercial lines. On a military road, labor is plentiful and cost, often is not a deterrent. Where the adjacent country is rough or swampy the use of wagons becomes impracticable and the track must be built from the roadbed itself.

116. In the second case all the track material is carried **on a train** and distributed ahead of that train. The ties, rails, etc., can be carried **by hand** from the cars to their place on the roadbed, or use can be made of what is commonly called a **track laying machine.**

When the track material is **distributed by hand,** a crew of 3 foremen, 64 men, and 2 teams ought to lay about 1 mile of track in 10 hours under average conditions. The following distribution of the crew is suggested:

| | | | |
|---|---|---|---|
| Tie carriers | 21 | Nippers | 6 |
| Tie placers | 6 | Spike distributors | 1 |
| Rail placers | 8 | Bolt distributors | 1 |
| Head strappers | 2 | Water boy | 1 |
| Back strappers | 4 | Teamsters | 2 |
| Spikers | 12 | | |

This table is based on the use of push cars for both rails and ties and allows but one man to carry a tie. Two men to a tie would probably have to be used.

The **Meru Charjui** section of the **Trans Caspian Railway** was laid by this method in 1885 at the rate of 38 5 miles per month. The **Sibi Railway,** in India, 133 miles long, was laid at the rate of 40 miles per month.

117. **Tools for laying track.**—Allowing for breakage and for changing men from some kinds of work to other kinds at times, the following tools will be needed for a track-laying crew of 64 men:

26 spike hammers.
18 pinch bars.
12 track wrenches.
16 picks.
4 pinch bars 3½ ft. long.
2 water buckets, 4 dippers.
72 track shovels.
3 adzes.
4 chopping axes.
2 hand axes.
4 rail forks
6 rail tongs.
2 ratchet drills and bits.
50 expansion shims, ¼ in.
100 expansion shims, ⅛ in.
200 expansion shims, $\frac{1}{16}$ in.
1 grindstone.
3 sixteen-pound sledges.
3 adz handles (extra).
48 spike hammer handles (extra).
12 pick handles (extra).
4 ax handles (extra).
2 track jacks.
2 tie-spacing poles.
1 drawshave.
4 claw bars.
1 push car.
3 rail cars.
1 hand car.
1 keg 10d. wire nails.
1 keg 20d. wire nails.
1 keg 40d. wire nails.
1 keg 60d. wire nails.
3 oilers.
4 gallons black oil.
4 white lanterns.
2 red lanterns, 2 red flags.
Extra white and red lantern globes.
3 monkey wrenches, 6, 8, and 12 in.
2 nail claw hammers.
1 steel tape 100 ft. long.
1 linen tape 50 ft. long.
6 track gages.
2 crosscut saws.
2 hand saws.
4 water barrels.
2 tie squares.
1 rail curver.
1 rail bender (jim-crow).
2 curving hooks.
2 track levers.
1 tie line, 1,000 ft. long.
Flat, round, quarter-round, eighth-round, and three-cornered files, three or four sizes of each.
4 horses or mules, with harness for hitching double, single, or in tandem.
2 lumber wagons
2 large tool boxes.
2 thermometers.
1 rail car clamp gage.
24 track chisels.
3 1-inch ropes for rail cars, ring and hook on each.
1 chalk line.
1 track level
6 cold chisels.
6 switch locks.
4 doz. torpedoes.
1 tool car.
1 brace and 6 bits.
1 2-inch auger.

In case it is intended to turn the crew to surfacing and ballasting, in addition to the above, there would be needed 1 level board, 2 track jacks, and 32 tamping picks where broken or crushed stone ballast is used.

118. **The organization and plant** required for rapid track laying by means of **a track-laying machine** will bear description, and apply not only to new work but also to the repair of breaks where a roadbed has been torn up by the enemy.

The party consists of 1 foreman, 3 subforemen, and from 80 to 100 laborers. The materials are carried on cars that are *pushed* to the railhead by a locomotive. Fig. 82 illustrates the arrangement of such a train, loaded with about 1 mile of railway material. The amount of material in such a train depends directly upon the weight of the rail and the size of the ties. On a standard-gage road a 40-ft. flat will carry about 1,100 ties or 125 to 150 rails (70-lb ). These loads are in excess of the rated carrying capacity of the cars, but the train moves very slowly, and the loads can be safely carried.

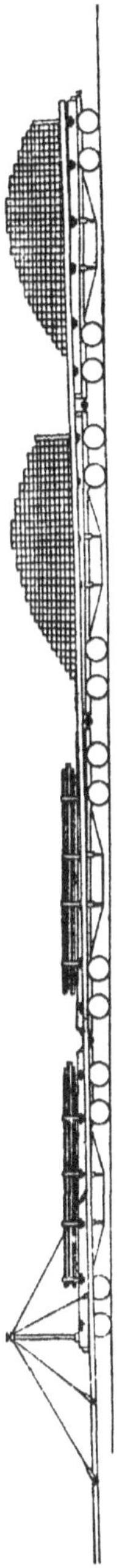

FIG. 82.

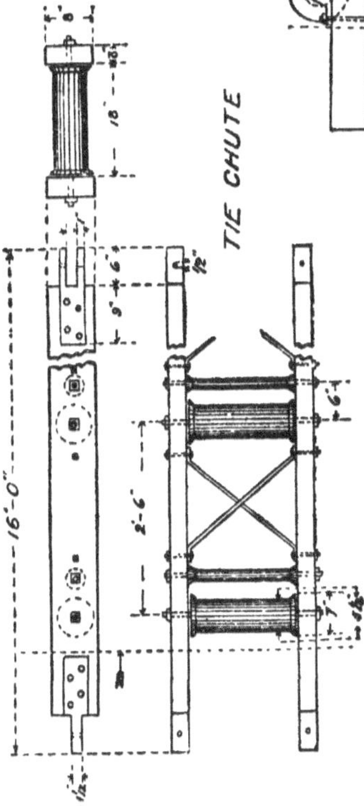


FIG. 83.

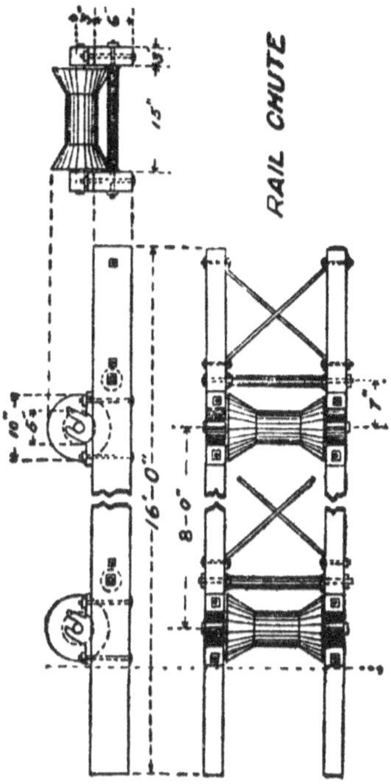


FIG. 84.

119. A train should be made up to carry either a half day's or a whole day's supply of material, in order that no time shall be lost in going to the rear for new material during working hours. The first two cars are loaded with rails and the necessary angle bars, or fisnplates, and bolts. The next two cars are loaded with ties. There will be one or two cars for the transportation of the working gang and for storing tools, spikes, and other supplies.

120. The ties and rails are supplied to the front by means of chutes that extend along the sides of the train. The dimensions and details of these chutes are shown in figs. 83, 84. They are supported by iron brackets, shown in figs. 85, 86, which are

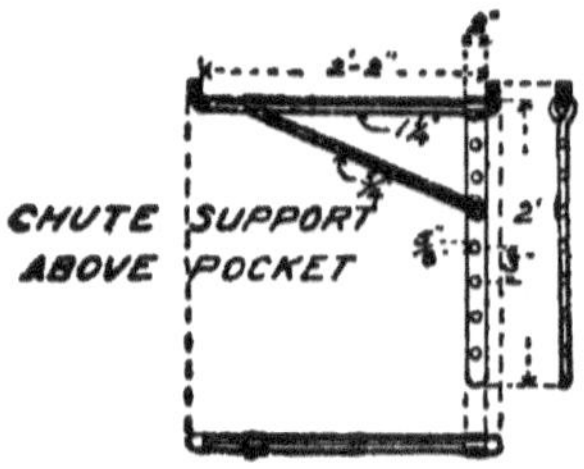


FIG. 85.

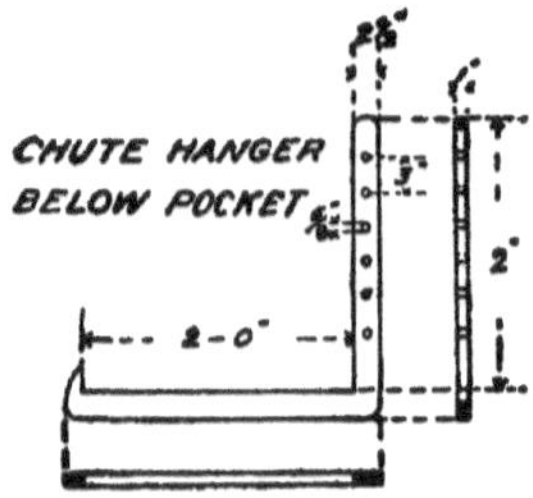


FIG. 86.

set in the pockets along the sides of the flat cars. These brackets are adjustable, and are set at such an elevation as to give the chutes a slope of about 6 ins. in each car length. The ties come down the left-hand side and the rails down the right-hand side of the train. The tie chute extends about 30 ft. in front of the forward car and is supported by guy ropes, as shown in fig. 82. The ties are thrown onto the chute by four men on the front tie cars, and they are pulled along the chute by means of boat hooks (fig. 88). After the ties are in the chute, one man per car

FIG. 87.

can keep them moving to the front. The ties are received at the end of the chute by a gang of nine laborers, who place the ties on the roadbed one rail length in advance of the chute. Two men see to the proper centering and spacing of the ties. For each 30-ft. rail, on a standard-gage road, 18 ties will be used.

121. In the meantime, the necessary fishplates, or angle bars, have been bolted to the forward ends of two rails, and these rails have been dumped into the rail chute. As soon as a rail length of ties has been placed on the ground, the rails are pulled out of the chute and are placed in position on the ties, the rear ends going between the angle bars at the ends of the last rails laid. The rear rail man on each rail takes

FIG. 88.

a track bolt and nut and wrench from the box on the head of the rail car and loosely bolts up one track bolt at each joint. Meantime the track is temporarily spaced with four **bridles** of the kind shown in fig. 87. These bridles are put in place and

FIG. 89.

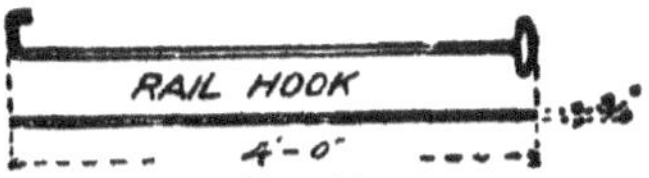


FIG. 90.

fastened by the rail men after depositing the rail on the ties, and are brought up after the construction train passes over them, to be used again.

The train then moves forward one rail length, that is, till the head of the forward car is within a few feet of the railhead. Then the operation is repeated.

122. A **derrick** sometimes is rigged on the forward end of certain track-laying machines, and when the rails reach the end of the rail chute, which in this case extends a half rail length beyond the end of the car, a clamp is fastened to the middle of the rail and the rail is swung by means of the derrick to its place on the ties. The advantage of this machine is that it decreases the number of laborers necessary to handle the rails, and this reduces the number of men working at the immediate head of the train. The tools used by the men on the rail car are shown in figs. 89, 90. These tools facilitate handling the rails and prevent the men from injuring their hands. With a machine like the one described, about 2 miles of track can be laid in a day of 10 hours.

123. The **composition of the party** ahead of the train on this work is about as follows, for 70-lb. rail, standard-gage ties: For handling ties, 18 men (4 on tie cars, 2 moving ties in chute, 2 spacing and centering, 9 carrying, and 1 subforeman); handling rails, 24 men (3 on rail car, 12 rail carriers, 4 clip carriers, 4 spike and angle carriers, and 1 foreman). In addition to these, there is 1 conductor, 1 brakeman, 1 engineman, 1 fireman, and 1 head foreman of the gang, making a total of 47 men.

124. **Behind the train** is a gang that spikes the rails to the ties and tightens all the track bolts. Following this gang is a gang that aligns the track to the stakes previously set. In the rear of these is another gang that surfaces the track.

These last three gangs are in charge of one subforeman, and are made up as follows: Bolting gang, back strappers, 4 men; spiking gang, 4 spacers, 10 strikers, and 8 bar men; aligning gang, 8 men. The number of men in the surfacing gang will depend entirely upon the amount of work to be done in leveling the track, throwing in the earth ballast, and tamping the same.

125. In order to lay track rapidly by this last method, the joints must be opposite each other (square), or practically so; and on a temporary line this is the best method of laying track, as with earth ballast the joints will be pounded down by the traffic, and there is less danger where the low joints are opposite each other than there is with the low joints on one side opposite the middle of the rail on the other.

Rails are usually bought under specifications that 90% of the rails shall be 30 ft. long and the other 10% may vary by 2-ft. lengths from 24 ft. to 30 ft. These short rails can be used on curves, and thus keep the rail joints nearly opposite each other.

126. **Expansion.**—In laying track, allowance must be made for expansion. A 30-ft. rail changes its length 0.252 in. for 100° change in temperature. Knowing the maximum and minimum temperatures of the place, thin plates, called expansion shims, can be made for use when laying steel at the various temperatures. For track laying before 10 a. m., use expansion shim for 10° lower than indicated by thermometer. From 10 a. m. to 4 p. m. use same shim as indicated by thermometer. After 4 p. m. use shim for 10° higher than indicated by thermometer. The thermometer should have the same exposure to the sun that the rail has.

## TURNOUTS AND CROSSOVERS.

127. **Turnouts and crossovers.**—A turnout is a curved track by means of which cars are moved from one track to another. The special parts of a turnout are the frog (fig. 9) and the switch (fig. 10), and the guard rails. The term "switch" is frequently applied to the part of a turnout from the point of switch to include the frog. The **switch proper** may be either a stub or a split switch. The latter is the form now generally used. Stub switches are only used on unimportant lines or in yards. In a stub switch, EAD, fig. 91, is a single rail, free to move from A to D, but spiked to ties from E to A. The same is true of the rail BH. The switch rails are fastened together by connecting rods between point and heel. The **headblock** and **switch stand** are at the free end, D, of the switch rails. The arrangement of the switch rails of a split switch is shown in fig. 95.

The point, B, fig. 91, is the **theoretical point of switch,** but is not the actual point on account of the extreme thinness that would be necessary at the end of the switch rail and the great length of switch rail that would be required. The **toe of the switch** is the free end of the switch rail. The **heel of the switch** is the fixed end of the switch rail. The **throw** or **clearance** is the distance D K. For stub switches, this throw is the distance between gage lines at the toe. For split switches it is the distance between the adjacent faces of the switch rail and the main rail.

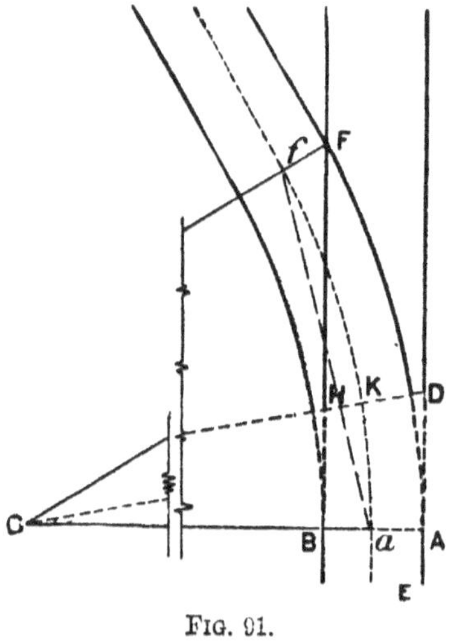


FIG. 91.

Reference to Tables XIV and XV will show that the length of switch rail required for a frog above No. 7 is over 20 ft. Twenty feet is about the greatest length of rail that can safely be left free from the ties, and for each frog number above 6 a certain length of switch rail, called the "point," is usually prescribed on each road. The point of sufficient clearance, H, is fixed, and then the P. C. of the switch falls wherever the arbitrary length of the "point" requires. See columns 5 and 6, table, fig. 97, for the practice on the Chicago and Northwestern Railway.

**Frogs** are usually designated by number, and this number, $n$, equals $\frac{1}{2}\cot\frac{1}{2}$ F. Sometimes **special frogs** are referred to by the frog angle in degrees and minutes. Tables XIV and XV give all the data necessary to lay out various standard turnouts from a tangent, for the gage, and clearance, indicated at the head of each table. For other gage, or clearance, the engineer can readily construct a similar table to meet his case.

The distance from the actual toe of the switch to the point of frog is sometimes called the **practical lead.** The distance, in inches, from the theoretical to the real nose of the frog is 0.5 $n$.

H or D is {Toe of stub switch. / Heel of split switch.}
B or A is {Heel of stub switch. / Toe of split switch.}

DK is the throw of the switch.
BF is the theoretical lead or "total lead."
HF is the practical lead or "lead" for a stub switch.
BF and AF are the lead rails.

In the following discussion the **general case** is assumed to be the turnout from a curve whose radius is greater than the radius of the turnout, both centers lying on the same side. On this assumption there are **three other cases** which may be considered special: First, when the radius of a turnout curve is greater than the radius of the mainline curve, but its center is on the same side of the main line as the center of the main-line curve; second, when the center of the turnout curve is on the opposite side to that of the main-line curve; and third, when the main line is a tangent, i. e., its radius is infinite.

128. Fig. 92 illustrates the general case considered.

$R = Oa =$ radius of the main-line curve.
$r = Ca =$ radius of turnout.
$\theta =$ angle of main-line curve subtended by BF.
$F = CFO =$ angle of frog.

$$n = \text{No. of frog} = \frac{1}{2}\cot\frac{1}{2}F.$$

At the point G, the line AF, produced, cuts the other rail of the main line.

$$\text{Then, } \tan\frac{1}{2}\theta = \frac{g}{2R}\cot\frac{1}{2}F = \frac{gn}{R},$$

$$r + \frac{1}{2}g = \left(R - \frac{1}{2}g\right)\frac{\sin\theta}{\sin(F+\theta)},$$

$$\text{and } BF = 2\left(R - \frac{1}{2}g\right)\sin\frac{1}{2}\theta,$$

$$\text{and } af = 2r\sin\frac{1}{2}(F+\theta).$$

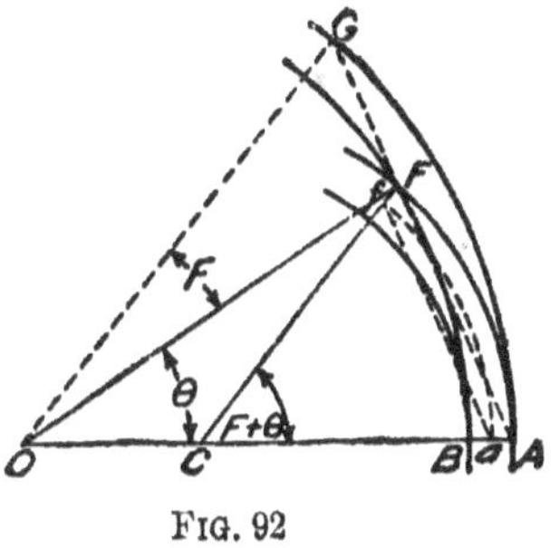

FIG. 92

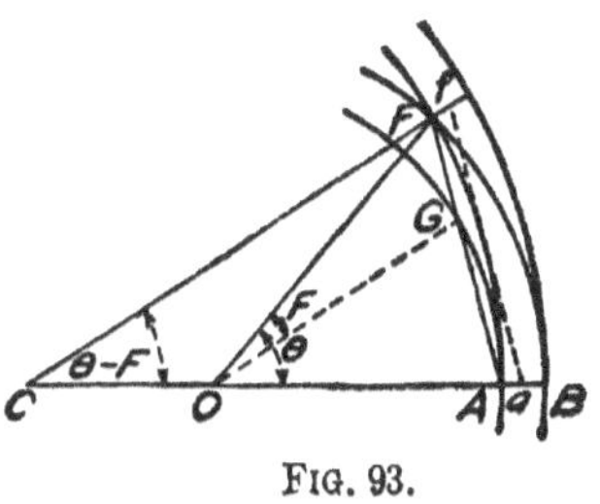

FIG. 93.

When R is greater than 500 ft. and $n$ is a standard frog number, the degree of curvature of the turnout will be equal to the sum of the degree of curvature of the main track and the degree of curvature for the turnout from a tangent corresponding to $n$ in Table XVIII or XIX.

$AD=\sqrt{\frac{10000\ DK}{t-t'}}$ (approx.), fig. 91, $t$ and $t'$ are the offsets from the tangent for 100 ft. on curves with R and $r$, respectively, as radii (see par. 61). Therefore, knowing radius of curvature of main line and of turnout and the throw of the switch, the switch length, AD, can readily be found.

In deducing the foregoing formulæ, R, $r$, $\theta$, $t'$, and F have been considered positive.

129. **First special case.**—$R<r$, $t'$ positive, and F negative (fig. 93).

$$\text{Then, } BF=2\left(R+\tfrac{1}{2}g\right)\sin\tfrac{1}{2}\theta \text{ (sign not considered).}$$

$$af=2r\sin\tfrac{1}{2}(\theta-F) \text{ (numerically).}$$

$$AD=\sqrt{\frac{10000\ DK}{t-t'}}.$$

$$r-\frac{1}{2}g=\left(R+\frac{1}{2}g\right)\frac{\sin\theta.}{\sin(\theta-F)}.$$

130. **Second special case.**—$\theta$ and F opposite signs, $t'$ negative (fig. 94).

$$\theta=FOA;\ F=FOG;\ F-\theta=FCA.$$

$$\text{Then, } BF=2\left(R+\tfrac{1}{2}g\right)\sin\tfrac{1}{2}\theta \text{ (sign not considered).}$$

$$af=2r\sin\tfrac{1}{2}(F-\theta) \text{ (sign not considered).}$$

$$AD=\sqrt{\frac{10000\ DK}{t+t'}}.$$

$$r+\frac{1}{2}g=\left(R+\frac{1}{2}g\right)\frac{\sin\theta}{\sin(F-\theta)} \text{ (sign not considered).}$$

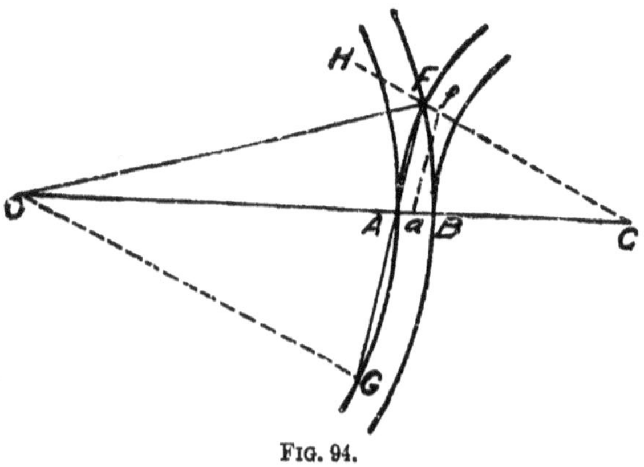


FIG. 94.

131. **Third special case.**—R=infinity, $\theta=0, t=0$ (fig. 91).

Then, $BF=g \cot \frac{1}{2} F= 2gn.$

$af=2r \sin \frac{1}{2} F.$

$$AD=\sqrt{\frac{10000\ DK}{t}}.$$

$$AD=100\sqrt{\frac{DK}{t}}=BF\sqrt{\frac{DK}{AB}}=\sqrt{2rDK}.$$

$$r+\frac{1}{2}g=\frac{g}{\text{vers } F}.$$

132. **To lay out a turnout.**—In laying out a turnout, the first thing to be determined is the point from which the turnout is to start, or else the location of the point of frog (P. F.). Having decided on one of these, and upon the number of the frog, the other may be found by laying off the distance BF (Table XIV).

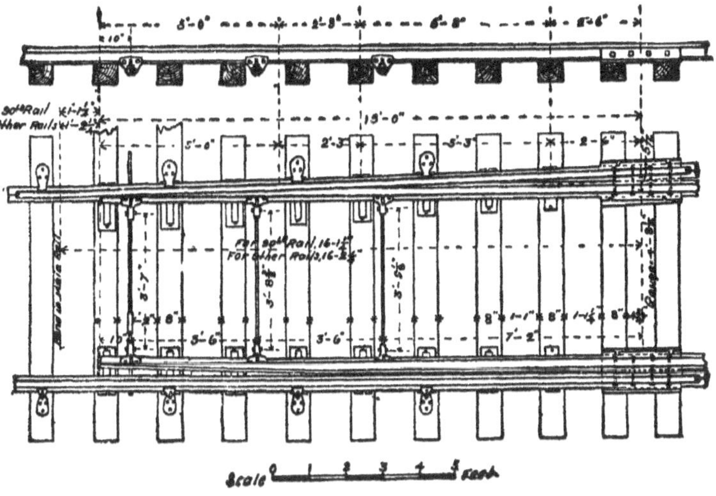

FIG. 95.—STANDARD SPLIT SWITCH.

133. **For a split switch,** locate F so that the end of the main point of the frog will be at a rail joint and lay off the distance to H, equal to (BF—AD), (Table XIV). From H lay off a distance equal to the length of the switch point (15 to 20 feet) plus about 1.25 ft. (see fig. 95). This is the actual P. C. of the switch where the rail begins to bend. From F and B, *a* and *f* can be located and the center line of the switch laid out. A quicker way is to locate the quarter points of the theoretical lead BF from F along the main rail; call these quarter points 1, 2, and 3, respectively, from F and mark them on the rail. The lead rail, AF, having been curved by use of the ordinates of Table XX, can then be laid, the inner side of the head of the rail being $\frac{7g}{16}$, $\frac{12g}{16}$, and (g—DK—width of rail head), from points 1, 2, and H, respectively. These gage distances must be measured very carefully. The head block and switch stand should be about 1 ft. from the toe of the switch, toward F. Remember that F is not the actual nose of the frog.

134. **For a stub switch,** fix H at a rail joint, then locate F by measuring a distance (BF−AD) from H. Then mark the quarter points and proceed as for a split switch. If the joints are square, this saves cutting one rail. If the joints are not square, either H or F may be located first. The head block and switch stand should be about 1 ft. from the toe of the switch away from F. In case the throw of the switch is not that shown in the tables, the length of AD can readily be figured from the formulæ and will not affect the method. Be sure to leave room at HD for **expansion of rails.**

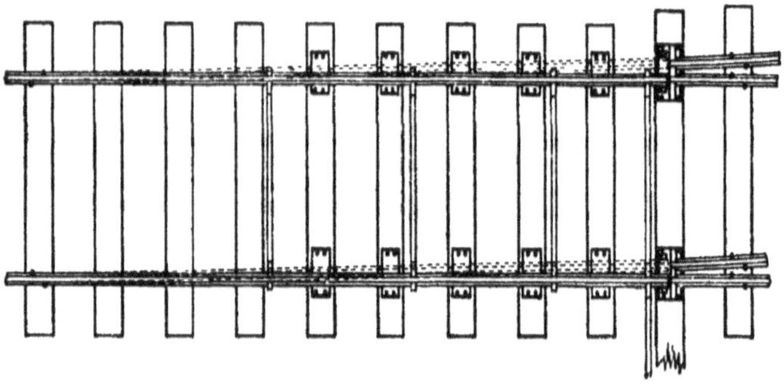

FIG. 96.—STUB SWITCH.

TABLE XIV.—**Switch leads and distances** (circular throughout).

Gage, 4 ft. 8½ ins.=4.708 ft. Throw, 5 ins.=0.417 ft.

| No., *n*. | Angle, F. | | | Distance, BF. | Chord, *af*. | Switch, AD. | Radius, *r*. | Degree of curve. | | |
|---|---|---|---|---|---|---|---|---|---|---|
| | ° | ′ | ″ | | | | | ° | ′ | ″ |
| 4 | 14 | 15 | 00 | 37.664 | 37.373 | 11.209 | 150.656 | 38 | 45 | 57 |
| 4½ | 12 | 40 | 49 | 42.372 | 42.113 | 12.610 | 190.674 | 30 | 24 | 09 |
| 5 | 11 | 25 | 16 | 47.080 | 46.846 | 14.012 | 235.400 | 24 | 31 | 36 |
| 5½ | 10 | 23 | 20 | 51.788 | 51.575 | 15.413 | 284.834 | 20 | 13 | 13 |
| 6 | 9 | 31 | 39 | 56.496 | 56.301 | 16.814 | 338.976 | 16 | 57 | 52 |
| 6½ | 8 | 47 | 51 | 61.204 | 61.024 | 18.215 | 397.826 | 14 | 26 | 25 |
| 7 | 8 | 10 | 16 | 65.912 | 65.744 | 19.616 | 461.384 | 12 | 26 | 34 |
| 7½ | 7 | 37 | 41 | 70.620 | 70.464 | 21.017 | 529.650 | 10 | 50 | 02 |
| 8 | 7 | 09 | 10 | 75.328 | 75.181 | 22.418 | 602.624 | 9 | 31 | 07 |
| 8½ | 6 | 43 | 59 | 80.036 | 79.898 | 23.820 | 680.306 | 8 | 25 | 47 |
| 9 | 6 | 21 | 35 | 84.744 | 84.613 | 25.221 | 762.696 | 7 | 31 | 04 |
| 9½ | 6 | 01 | 32 | 89.452 | 89.328 | 26.622 | 849.794 | 6 | 44 | 46 |
| 10 | 5 | 43 | 29 | 94.160 | 94.043 | 28.023 | 941.600 | 6 | 05 | 16 |
| 10½ | 5 | 27 | 09 | 98.868 | 98.756 | 29.424 | 1,038.114 | 5 | 31 | 17 |
| 11 | 5 | 12 | 18 | 103.576 | 103.469 | 30.825 | 1,139.336 | 5 | 01 | 50 |
| 11½ | 4 | 58 | 45 | 108.284 | 108.182 | 32.227 | 1,245.266 | 4 | 36 | 08 |
| 12 | 4 | 46 | 19 | 112.992 | 112.894 | 33.628 | 1,355.904 | 4 | 13 | 36 |

Gage, 3 ft. Throw, 4 ins.=0.333 ft.

| No., *n*. | Angle, F. ° | ′ | ″ | Distance, BF. | Chord, *af*. | Switch, AD. | Radius, *r*. | Degree of curve. ° | ′ | ″ |
|---|---|---|---|---|---|---|---|---|---|---|
| 4 | 14 | 15 | 00 | 24 | 23.815 | 8 | 96.0 | 62 | 46 | 34 |
| 4½ | 12 | 40 | 49 | 27 | 26.835 | 9 | 121.5 | 48 | 36 | 04 |
| 5 | 11 | 25 | 16 | 30 | 29.851 | 10 | 150.0 | 38 | 56 | 33 |
| 5½ | 10 | 23 | 20 | 33 | 32.865 | 11 | 181.5 | 31 | 58 | 55 |
| 6 | 9 | 31 | 39 | 36 | 35.876 | 12 | 216.0 | 26 | 46 | 07 |
| 6½ | 8 | 47 | 51 | 39 | 38 885 | 13 | 253.5 | 22 | 45 | 04 |
| 7 | 8 | 10 | 16 | 42 | 41.893 | 14 | 294.0 | 19 | 35 | 01 |
| 7½ | 7 | 37 | 41 | 45 | 44 900 | 15 | 337.5 | 17 | 02 | 21 |
| 8 | 7 | 09 | 10 | 48 | 47.906 | 16 | 384.0 | 14 | 57 | 48 |
| 8½ | 6 | 43 | 59 | 51 | 50 912 | 17 | 433.5 | 13 | 14 | 47 |
| 9 | 6 | 21 | 35 | 54 | 53 917 | 18 | 486.0 | 11 | 48 | 37 |
| 9½ | 6 | 01 | 32 | 57 | 56.921 | 19 | 541.5 | 10 | 35 | 46 |
| 10 | 5 | 43 | 29 | 60 | 59.925 | 20 | 600.0 | 9 | 33 | 38 |
| 10½ | 5 | 27 | 09 | 63 | 62 929 | 21 | 661.5 | 8 | 40 | 12 |
| 11 | 5 | 12 | 18 | 66 | 65.932 | 22 | 726.0 | 7 | 53 | 54 |
| 11½ | 4 | 58 | 45 | 69 | 68.935 | 23 | 793.5 | 7 | 13 | 32 |
| 12 | 4 | 46 | 19 | 72 | 71.938 | 24 | 864.0 | 6 | 38 | 60 |

Angle and distance of middle frog, F″.

| No., *n*. | No., *n*″. | Angle, F″. ° ′ ″ | Distance, *a*F″. Gage, 4 ft. 8½ ins. | Distance, *a*F″. Gage, 3 ft. | No., *n*. | No., *n*″. | Angle, F″. ° ′ ″ | Distance, *a*F″. Gage, 4 ft. 8½ ins. | Distance, *a*F″. Gage, 3 ft. |
|---|---|---|---|---|---|---|---|---|---|
| 4 | 2.817 | 20 07 36 | 26.736 | 17.037 | 8½ | 6.005 | 9 31 08 | 56.643 | 36.094 |
| 4½ | 3.172 | 17 54 52 | 30.054 | 19.151 | 9 | 6.359 | 8 59 30 | 59.969 | 38.213 |
| 5 | 3.527 | 16 08 19 | 33.374 | 21.266 | 9½ | 6.713 | 8 31 10 | 63.296 | 40.333 |
| 5½ | 3.881 | 14 40 58 | 36.695 | 23.383 | 10 | 7.067 | 8 05 40 | 66.623 | 42.453 |
| 6 | 4.235 | 13 27 57 | 40.018 | 25.500 | 10½ | 7.420 | 7 42 35 | 69.950 | 44.573 |
| 6½ | 4.589 | 12 26 07 | 43.342 | 27.618 | 11 | 7.774 | 7 21 36 | 73.277 | 46.693 |
| 7 | 4.943 | 11 33 04 | 46.666 | 29.736 | 11½ | 8.128 | 7 02 26 | 76.605 | 48.813 |
| 7½ | 5.297 | 10 47 02 | 49.991 | 31.855 | 12 | 8.482 | 6 44 51 | 79.932 | 50.934 |
| 8 | 5.651 | 10 06 44 | 53.317 | 33.974 | | | | | |

TABLE XV.—**Switch leads and distances** (circular throughout).

Gage, 2 ft. 6 ins. Throw, 4 ins.=0.333 ft.

| Frog No. | Frog angle. | | | Distance, BF. | Chord, *af*. | Switch length. | Radius. | Logarithm. | Degree of curve. | | |
|---|---|---|---|---|---|---|---|---|---|---|---|
| | ° | ′ | ″ | *Ft.* | *Ft.* | *Ft.* | *Ft.* | | ° | ′ | ″ |
| 4 | 14 | 15 | 00 | 20.0 | 19.85 | 7.30 | 80.00 | 1.90309 | 77 | 20 | 00 |
| 4½ | 12 | 40 | 49 | 22.5 | 22.35 | 8.21 | 101.25 | 2.00539 | 59 | 11 | 12 |
| 5 | 11 | 25 | 16 | 25.0 | 24.88 | 9.12 | 125.00 | 2.09691 | 47 | 09 | 28 |
| 5½ | 10 | 23 | 20 | 27.5 | 27.38 | 10.03 | 151.25 | 2.18256 | 38 | 20 | 38 |
| 6 | 9 | 31 | 39 | 30.0 | 29.89 | 10.94 | 180.00 | 2.25527 | 32 | 15 | 20 |
| 6½ | 8 | 47 | 51 | 32.5 | 32 40 | 11.86 | 211.25 | 2.32480 | 27 | 21 | 56 |
| 7 | 8 | 10 | 16 | 35.0 | 34.91 | 12.77 | 245.00 | 2.38917 | 23 | 33 | 06 |
| 7½ | 7 | 37 | 41 | 37.5 | 37.42 | 13.68 | 281.25 | 2.44910 | 20 | 28 | 48 |
| 8 | 7 | 09 | 10 | 40.0 | 39.92 | 14.59 | 320.00 | 2.50515 | 17 | 48 | 44 |
| 8½ | 6 | 43 | 59 | 42.5 | 42.43 | 15.50 | 361.25 | 2.55781 | 15 | 54 | 40 |
| 9 | 6 | 21 | 35 | 45.0 | 44.93 | 16.42 | 405.00 | 2.60746 | 14 | 11 | 00 |
| 9½ | 6 | 01 | 32 | 47.5 | 47.43 | 17.33 | 451.25 | 2.65442 | 12 | 43 | 22 |
| 10 | 5 | 43 | 29 | 50.0 | 49.94 | 18.24 | 500.00 | 2.69897 | 11 | 28 | 42 |
| 10½ | 5 | 27 | 09 | 52.5 | 52.44 | 19.16 | 551.25 | 2.74135 | 10 | 24 | 28 |
| 11 | 5 | 12 | 18 | 55.0 | 54 94 | 20.07 | 605 00 | 2.78176 | 9 | 28 | 52 |
| 11½ | 4 | 58 | 45 | 57.5 | 57.44 | 20.99 | 661.25 | 2 82037 | 8 | 40 | 24 |
| 12 | 4 | 46 | 19 | 60.0 | 59.94 | 21.90 | 720.00 | 2.85733 | 7 | 57 | 50 |

135. **On curves,** where R and *r* are both over 500 ft., very little error is made in taking BF and AD from the corresponding table for tangents; but where they are both under 500 ft. there will be considerable error and the values should be computed from the formulæ. These formulæ are also given on account of the great variety of existing gages in tracks in various parts of the world, and the impracticability of making up a table for every such gage, or throw. Turnouts to the inside of sharp curves should be avoided.

136. Having located the point of frog and point of switch, the center of the turnout opposite each of these points may also be fixed by laying off ½ *g* along the radius *r*. This locates the points *f* and *a*, fig. 91. Having located these two points, **the center line of the turnout** can be located by laying off from the middle of *af*, a distance equal to ¼ *g*, perpendicular to *af*, and from the quarter points of *af* a distance equal to $\frac{3}{16}$ *g*. The distance AD, taken from Table XIV or XV, is laid off, locating the point D. At this point the distance from center to center of rails must be equal to *d*, the throw. Having located this point, and knowing the dimensions of the frog to be used, the rails will be cut, the frog put in, the remaining fixed rails spiked in place, and the switch proper is then put in. The first method, described in par. 133, is the better of the two. The **guard rails** are located well in advance of the point of frog so as to protect it from the wheels, the flanges of the rails being cut away, if necessary, to place them close enough together.

137. For each special case, the turnout should be so located as to require the **least amount of rail cutting.** Fig. 97 shows the dimensions of certain **standard frogs** used on the Chicago & North Western Railway. These are built to such dimensions that standard lengths of rail, as shown in the last column of the table in the figure, can be kept on hand, and thus a turnout can be put in without cutting rails at the time.

A similar table should be prepared for any military railroad and a stock of specially cut rails kept on hand.

| Designation | Angle | CURVE Degree | CURVE Radius | P.C. to P.F. | H.B. to P.F. |
|---|---|---|---|---|---|
| 1 in 5 | 11°25'16" | 24°31'36" | 235.4 | 47.08 | |
| 1 in 6 | 9°31'39" | 16°57'52" | 338.97 | 56.5 | |
| 9° SPECIAL | (For Double Slip). | | | | |
| 9° (1 in 6.353) | 9°00' | 15°07' | 380.05 | 59.85 | 56.75 1-30' Rail, 15' Point, 11.75 Wing |
| 1 in 7 | 8°10'16" | 12°27' | 461.1 | 65.92 | 61.14 1-28', 1-14.89 Rails, 15' Point, 3.25 Wing |
| 1 in 8 | 7°09'10" | 9°30' | 603.8 | 75.33 | 67.75 2-24' Rails, 15' Point, 4.75 Wing |
| 1 in 10 | 5°43'30" | 6°05' | 942.3 | 94.16 | 81.50 2-30' Rails, 15' Point, 6.5 Wing |
| 1 in 14 | 4°05'26" | 3°06' | 1848.5 | 131.8 | 117.27 3-30' Rails, 20 Point, 7 3/4" Wing |

| Rail | Height | Head | Base |
|---|---|---|---|
| 60 lb. | 4 1/4 in. | 2 5/16 in | 4 3/16 in |
| 65 " | 4 3/8 " | 2 5/16" 2 13/32" | 4 7/16 " |
| 72 " | 4 3/4 " | 2 3/8 in | 4 3/4 " |
| 80 " | 5 " | 2 1/2 " | 5 " |
| 90 " | 5 3/8 " | 2 5/8 " | 5 3/8 " |

No. 10-72 lb. same as No. 10-80 lb. excepting 6" bet. theoretical and actual Points.

9°-60 lb. (17 ft. Frog) same as 9° 72 lb.

Present Width of Flangeways adopted 1895

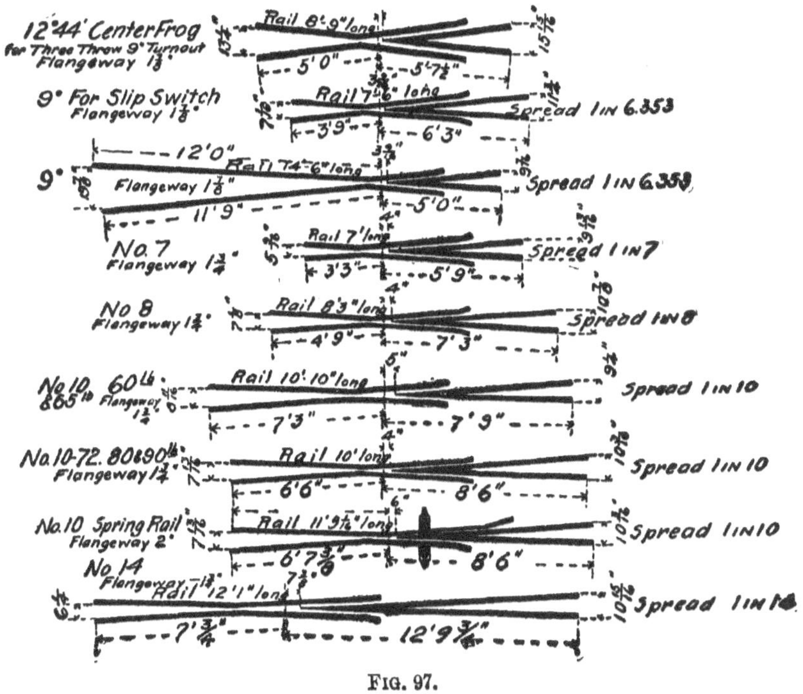


Fig. 97.

138. The main-line rail, on the side toward which the turnout leads, is not curved from the theoretical point of switch, but the bend begins at a point slightly in front of the toe of switch as determined by the length of the switch rail from the point D (see figs. 91 and 95). The actual turnout as laid out will not be the theoretical one herein described, since the switch rail is straight and is usually fixed at 15 ft. in length, and the frog rail is also straight. This discussion will, however, answer for all military purposes. Most turnouts, in fact, are laid out as herein described and from tables similar to Tables XIV and XV.

139. After passing the frog, the turnout will be located just as any other line is located, but sometimes certain conditions are placed upon a turnout, as in fig. 98. The condition here is that the turnout shall run parallel to the main line at a distance $p$ from center to center. Such a siding is then composed of the curve lead, a short tangent, and another curve in the opposite direction leading into the tangent of the siding. (The short tangent $fm$ is sometimes omitted.)

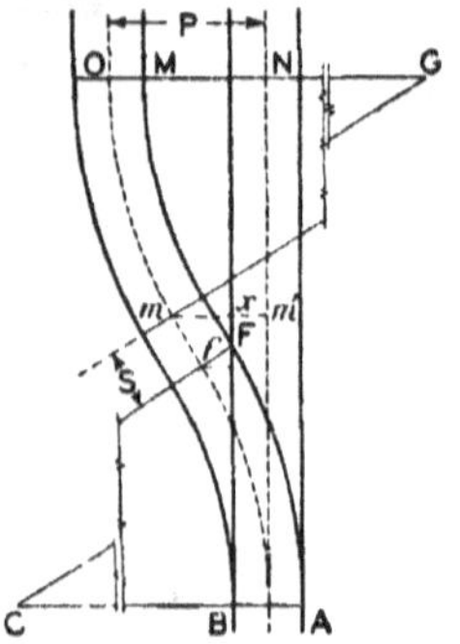


FIG. 98.

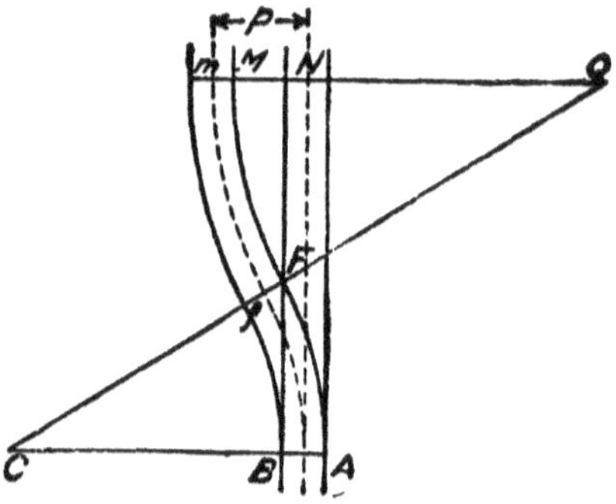


FIG. 99.

140. As a general rule, the second curve of this reverse curve is similar, but opposite in direction, to the first curve, although this is not necessary.

The **length of the tangent** S, fig. 98, is $\frac{p-g}{\sin F}-\frac{g}{\tan F}$, and F$x$, on the main line, is $(p-g)\cot F-\frac{g}{\sin F}$. Lay off this distance, S, from $f$, fig. 98, to $m$, making an angle, F, with the main line. This point, $m$, lies a distance $(p-g)$ from the center of the main line, and a distance $g$ from the center of the proposed siding. This point $m$, can be located without an instrument by laying off F$x$ from the P. F. along the center of main line to $m'$, and at $m'$, laying off $(p-g)$ perpendicular to the main line to $m$.

From $m'$ lay off a distance $m'$ N on the main line equal to BF, fig. 98, and from N lay off a distance $p$ from the center of the main line and perpendicular to it. This locates the point, $o$, which is the P. T. of the curve leading to the siding.

The line $mo$ corresponds to the line $af$, fig. 91, and the center line of the curve can be laid out in the same manner that the first curve lead was laid out.

141. The short tangent S may be omitted and the siding and main line may be connected by a **reverse curve** (fig. 99), $r'$ being the radius of the second curve.

$$\text{Then, } p-g=\left(r'-\frac{1}{2}\right)\text{vers F, or } r'-\frac{1}{2}g=\frac{p-g}{\text{vers F}},$$

$$\text{and FN}=\left(r'-\frac{g}{2}\right)\sin F.$$

142. Another **special case** is where the turnout leads into another track. This is called a **crossover** (fig. 100). In case the lines to be connected are parallel, and $p$ is the distance from center to center, the length of the tangent joining the two curve leads is found, as in par. 140.

The point in the siding opposite to point N is the P. F. of the turnout of the second track.

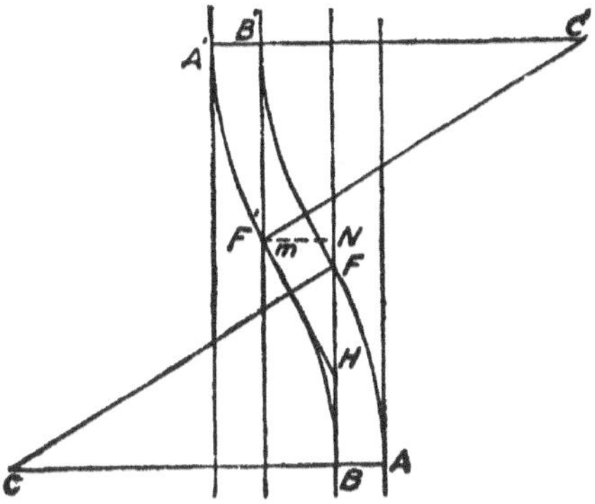


FIG. 100.

143. As in the case of a siding (par. 141), the tangent S may be replaced by a **reverse curve** (fig. 101), in which case, **if both frogs are alike,**

$$\cos C = 1 - \frac{p}{2r}.$$

$$PL = r \sin C = PL'.$$

The **distance** between points of frog measured along the main line is FN.

$$FN = 2\,(PL - BF)$$

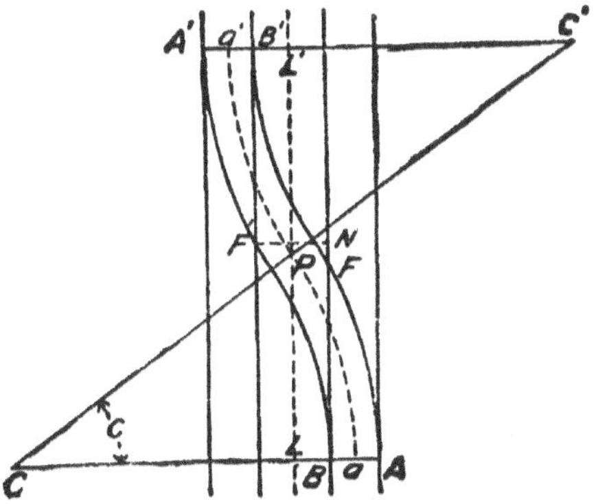


FIG. 101.

If the **frogs are different,** vers $C = \frac{p}{(r+r')}$, and $LL'L' = (r+r') \sin C$.

144. **To connect two parallel curved lines.**—It will be seen from fig. 102, in which O is the center of the main-line curve, C and C′ the centers of the reverse curves of the crossover, that the three sides of the triangle COC′ are known and that the solution depends upon the value of the angle COC′.

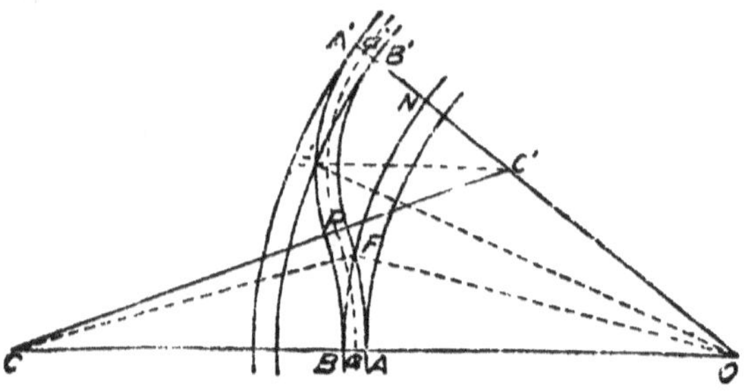


FIG. 102.

Let $r$=radius $a$C,
$r'$=radius $a'$ C′,
$p$=distance between track centers,
R=radius $a$O,
$\alpha$=COC′.

$$\text{Then, vers } \alpha = \frac{p(r+r'-\frac{1}{2}p)}{(R+r)(R+p-r')}.$$

The arc $BN = 100\frac{\alpha}{D}$ ft., in which D=degree of curvature of the main line.

$$\text{vers C}'\text{ CO} = \frac{p(R-r'+\frac{1}{2}p)}{(R+r')(r+r')}.$$

The angle CC′A′=$\alpha$+C′ CO.

Knowing C′CO and CC′A′, the lengths of the arcs $a$P and P$a'$ can be found as BN was found above.

Knowing the frogs to be used, $r$ and $r'$ can be found from pars 130 and 128 respectively, as can also BF and B′F′, remembering that the R of this paragraph must be increased by $p$ when used in par. 128.

145. Another special case is found in **laying out a yard** where one distributing track leads from the main line and branches into several parallel sidetracks (see fig. 103). This is called a **yard lead, or a ladder track.** In this figure the distance $p$ and the angle $\varphi$ between the sidings and the distributing track determine the distance between points of frogs on the distributing track where the same numbered frogs are used throughout.

$$FF' = F'F'' = \frac{p}{\sin \varphi}.$$

This distance FF′ must be greater than the half length of the frog used plus the length of curve lead (BF, fig. 91).

146. **"Y."**—Fig. 104 shows the layout for a **Y**. This form is most economical of space, though one side of the Y is frequently a tangent (fig. 105). A Y consists of a combination of turnout and curves, and from the figures can be laid out by an application of the principles heretofore given for curves and turnouts. Figs. 1 4 and 105 are two of the simplest forms. There are several other combinations, but all of them present simple trigonometrical problems.

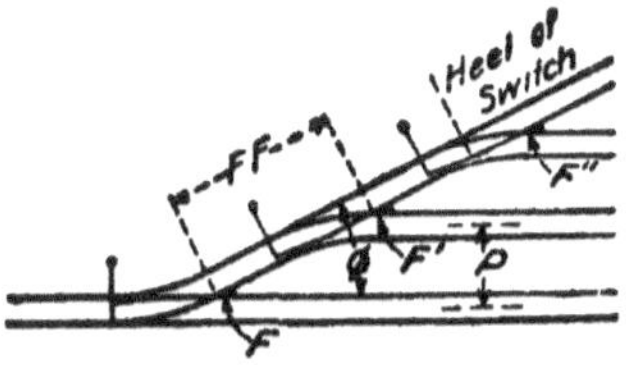


FIG. 103.—LADDER TRACK.

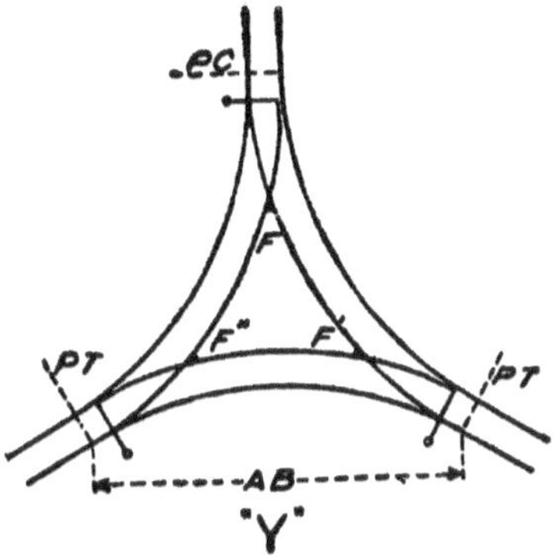


FIG. 104.

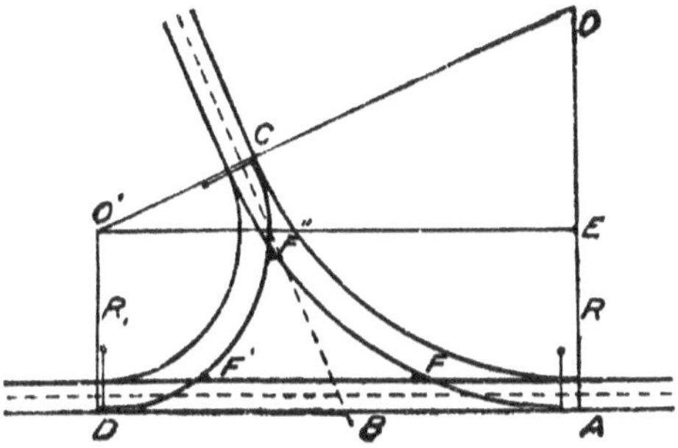


FIG. 105.

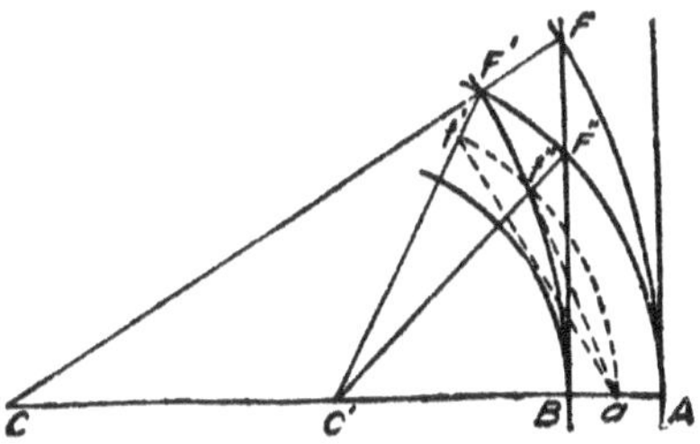


FIG. 106.

147. **A double turnout** is one where two tracks diverge from the main line, either on the same side or on opposite sides (see figs. 106, 107, 108). In fig. 106 the various distances for the first turnout are figured as in par. 131.

Ordinarily the frog F′ will be the same as F, and opposite to it. From the figure, then,

$$r' = C'a;\ r = Ca.$$

$$2r' = r - \tfrac{1}{2}g$$

$$\text{vers } F'' = \frac{g}{r' + \tfrac{1}{2}g}.$$

$$BF'' = (r' + \tfrac{1}{2}g) \sin F'' = 2gn'' - g \cot \tfrac{1}{2} F''.$$

$$n'' = \sqrt{\frac{r'}{2g}}$$

$$af'' = 2r' \sin \tfrac{1}{2} F'' = \frac{2r'}{\sqrt{1 + 4n''^2}}$$

$$af' = 2r' \sin F.$$

The **throw of the second switch** is double that of the first.

148. When the turnouts are on **opposite sides of the tangent,** as before, E usually equals F′. Then, from fig. 108,

$$\text{vers} \frac{1}{2} F'' = \frac{g}{2\left(r + \frac{g}{2}\right)},$$

$$\text{and } aF'' = \left(r + \frac{g}{2}\right) \sin \tfrac{1}{2} F'';$$

$$\text{also, } aF'' = r \tan \tfrac{1}{2} F'' - \frac{r}{2n''}.$$

$$n'' = \frac{n}{\sqrt{2}} = 0\ 7071n \text{ (approx.)}$$

For $n''$ use nearest numbered frog, Table XIV or XV.

Switches for double turnouts are commonly called **"three throw switches."**

149. The data in regard to **three throw switches** apply mainly to stub switches. Owing to the sharp change in direction due to the large throw of the second switch and the short straight switch point, three throw switches usually occur only where the turnouts are on opposite sides of the main line.

Strictly speaking, there is no such thing as a three throw split switch. The name is applied when the points of two split switches are only a few feet apart. Each has its own head block and switch stand. They should be avoided if possible. A rough rule for determining $n''$ is to divide $n + n'$ by three, using the nearest whole number.

150. Comparing the two values of F″ as found in pars. 147 and 148, it is seen, by assuming the vers ½ F″ = ¼ vers F″, which is practically true for ordinary values of F″, "that a set of frogs (F = F′, and F″) which is adapted to a double turnout in opposite directions from a straight line (as in fig. 108) is also adaptable to a double turnout on one side (fig. 106), the curves being simple curves in both cases. This being true, the set is also adapted to a double turnout in opposite directions from any curved track, the radius of which is not less than $r$ as given for F, since any such

case is intermediate between the two cases named."* Therefore, having adopted a frog number, $n$, for general use in double turnouts, another frog number, $n''$, should be adopted equal to $0.7071n$ for use as a secondary frog, F'', known as the **crotch frog.**

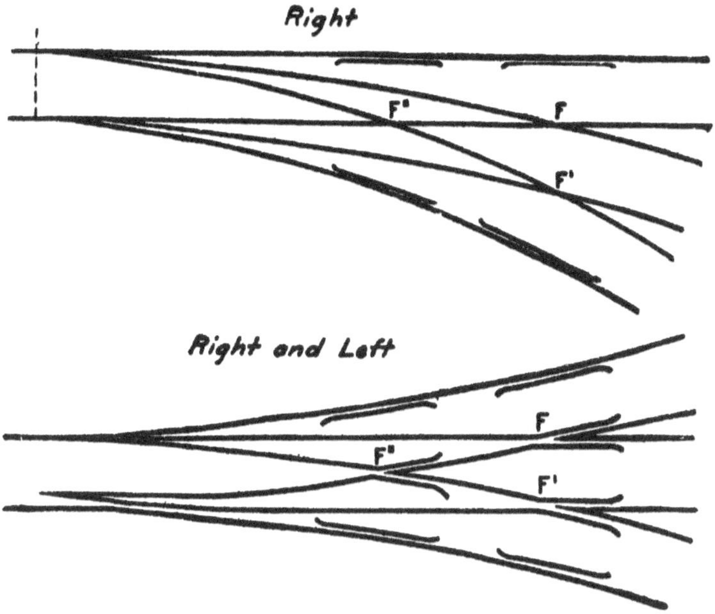


FIG. 107.—DOUBLE TURNOUTS, SHOWING FROGS AND GUARDRAILS.

151. **Frogs.**—The frog in general use for a crossover on standard-gage double track is No. 10. The frogs commonly used for leads to yards are Nos. 6, 7, and 8.

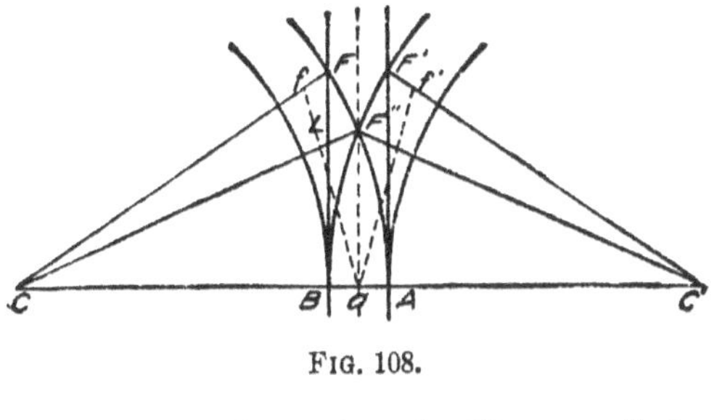


FIG. 108.

The V's in a frog and the openings at the ends of the wing rails should have blocks of wood driven into them. If left without such blocks, they are a great source of danger to switchmen running to throw a switch.

* Searle's Field Engineering, p. 155.

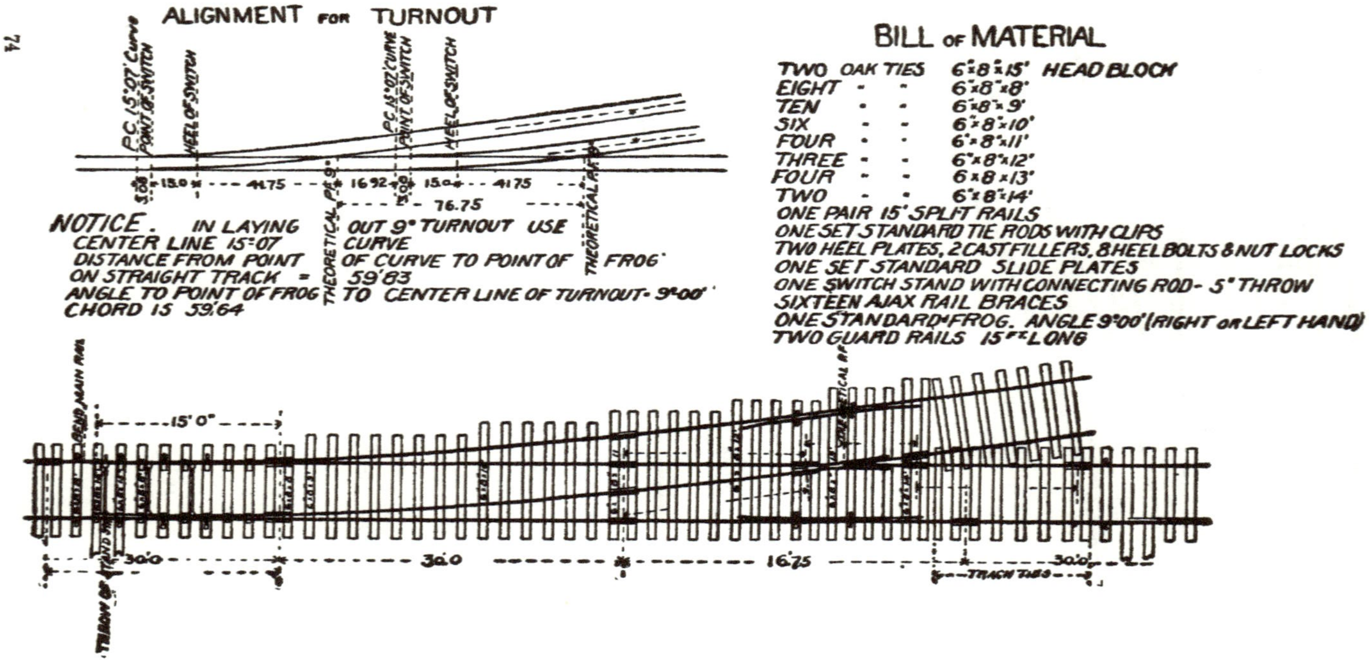


FIG. 109.—ARRANGEMENT OF TIES IN A TURNOUT.

152. **Rigid frogs** can be used for a turnout either to the right or left. When **spring rail frogs** are used, care should be taken to state in the requisition to which side the turnout leads.

153. **Location of turnouts.**—It has been stated in various places that in turnouts from curves having a large radius, the dimensions given in Tables XIV and XV for turnouts from a tangent can be used with little error. However, in a turnout from a curve, the curvature of the turnout for a given frog is different from the curve of turnout from a tangent, and is equal to the curve of the main line plus the curve of the turnout from a tangent for a corresponding frog. The lengths of rail would not be exactly the same on the turnout from a curve as they would be on a turnout from a tangent. On account of this, and because of the desirability of having a number of turnouts ready for use at any time, it is best to locate all turnouts on tangents, where practicable. These ready-made turnouts should include all material for the turnout, as shown in bill of material, in fig. 109, so that by leaving out an exact number of 30-ft. rails the track laying can be continued; and when the turnout is put in place the opening left will be exactly filled. **Frogs and switches** can either be bought outright from equipment companies or can be made in the shops.

154. **Compound curved turnouts.**—The curves used in laying out turnouts and crossovers are ordinarily arcs of circles and are usually simple curves. It may happen that no frog is at hand, in laying out a double turnout, that will permit a simple curve to be run from the heel of the switch to beyond the farthest frog. In this case, use the frog that will require the sharpest curve as the crotch frog, allowing the flatter curve to lie between the two frogs. F″ must not be greater than 2 F.

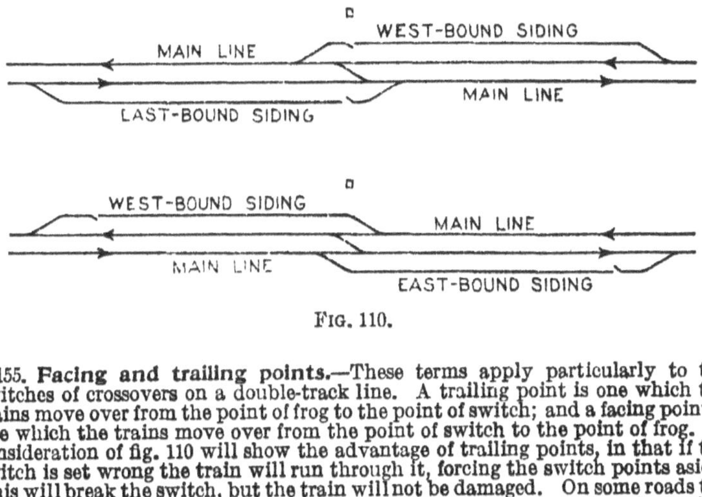


FIG. 110.

155. **Facing and trailing points.**—These terms apply particularly to the switches of crossovers on a double-track line. A trailing point is one which the trains move over from the point of frog to the point of switch; and a facing point is one which the trains move over from the point of switch to the point of frog. A consideration of fig. 110 will show the advantage of trailing points, in that if the switch is set wrong the train will run through it, forcing the switch points aside. This will break the switch, but the train will not be damaged. On some roads the policy is to have all main-line switches trailing points, and although this requires a little more time in switching cars or going into a siding, it is safer.

156. **Switch stands.**—A switch stand is a mechanism by means of which the switch points are moved. Types of these are shown in figs. 111, 112. The largest kind is more readily seen than the smallest one, and would be used in cases where the engineman must be able to note a missetting of the switch. The smallest kind is the kind used in the interlocking plant, where it is next to impossible for a switch to be set wrong and the engineman not be notified of it long before he reaches the switch. The middle type is one that is commonly used in yards. Economy of space and weight might dictate the use of the smallest switch in all cases on a supply

road. For **stub switches** these stands should be on the engineman's side approaching in a facing direction. For **split switches** they should be on the side of the turnout. Fig. 113 shows a simple form of a **three-throw, ground-lever switch stand.**

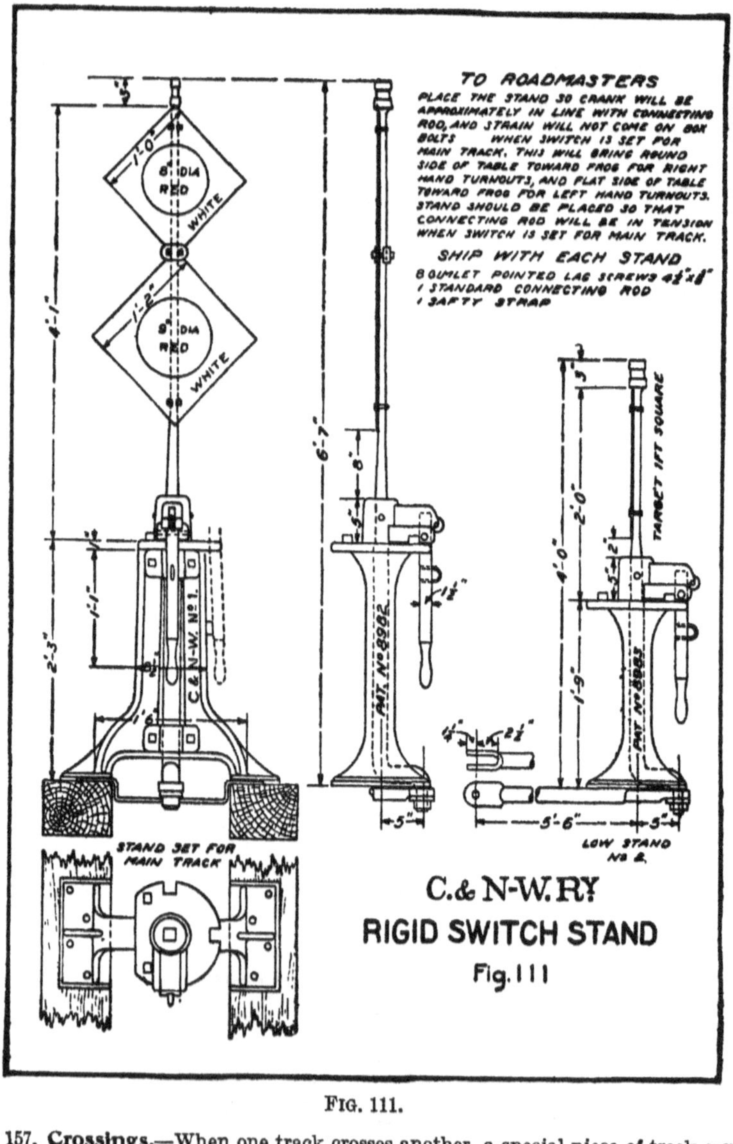


FIG. 111.

157. **Crossings.**—When one track crosses another, a special piece of track construction, called a crossing, is put in. The best results are obtained when both tracks of the crossing and the rails for a foot or so on each side are in one piece,

rigidly fastened together. This lessens the settlement, and what settlement there may be will be the same for the whole crossing. (For methods of measuring the angle of crossing, etc., see par. 25.)

158. When a crossing is very oblique, it is sometimes called a **diamond crossing.** When one or two turnouts connect the tracks at this point and each entire turnout

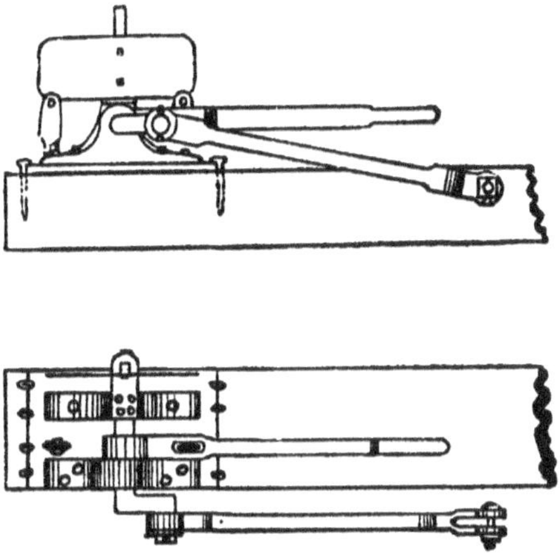

FIG. 112.

lies within the limits of the longer axis of the diamond, it is called a **single, or double, slip switch** (see fig. 114). The latter is sometimes referred to as a puzzle switch. The switch rods for throwing these switch rails are quite complicated and are not shown in the figure.

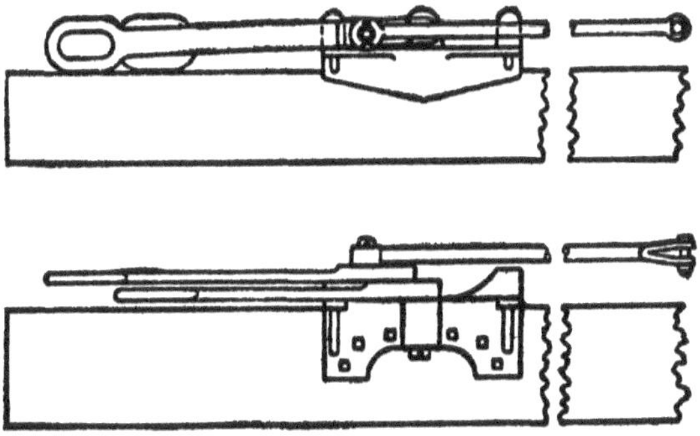

FIG. 113.—GROUND-THROW STAND FOR THREE-THROW STUB SWITCH.

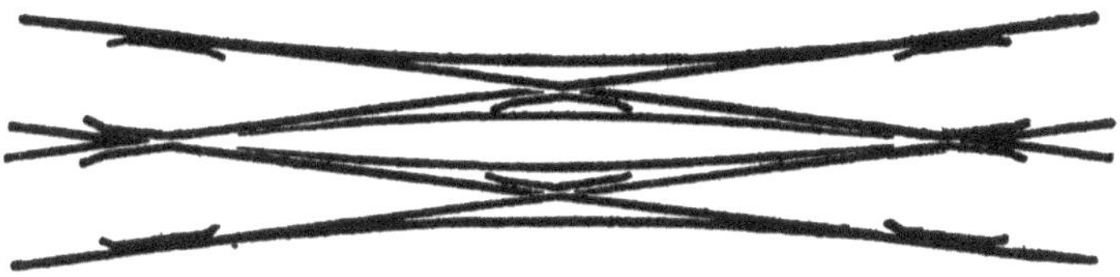

FIG. 114.—DOUBLE SLIP SWITCH.

159. When a turnout from one of two adjacent tracks must cross the other track, the line of the turnout is run until it crosses the center line of the second track. The common point of center is found and the angle of the crossing is determined as heretofore described.

## STATIONS AND STRUCTURES.

160. **Mileposts.**—Every mile along the track should be marked with a conspicuous milepost, showing the distance to and from the division terminals or other important points. These are valuable in definitely locating points along the line, in making reports of engagements, accidents, etc. **Telegraph poles** should be similarly numbered, showing mile and pole number.

161. **Stations.** The number of stations, or sidings, that will be necessary depends upon the number of trains that must be run to supply the army and the speed at which such trains can move. This distance between stations will vary according to the grades, but having the profile in hand and knowing the speed of the locomotives in miles per hour for certain grades and loads the distance apart of sidings can be determined, approximately, as follows: N is the total number of trains necessary to pass over the line in a day; T is the time in hours necessary for a train to pass from any station to the next one, and return; if $\frac{24}{T}$ is less than N for any two stations some measure must be taken to decrease this maximum value of T. This can be done by putting in an intermediate siding or by installing a pusher service. On civil railroads, the next alternative is double tracking. Stations should be spaced so that the time required for a train to cover the interval both ways between all adjacent stations will be approximately equal.

Four miles is about the minimum allowable distance between stations, except under rare special conditions.

The amount of construction work that must be done at any station depends upon the location of the station, the number of buildings, and the length of auxiliary track that will be needed at that station to suit the local conditions. The questions of **water supply** and **storage room** at a station must be especially considered and are taken up later.

The **location of stations** may be determined by any number of military causes beyond the control of the locating engineer, but where such conditions do not fix the station, and the geography of the ground does not compel the location at any certain point, a study of the grades will be made as indicated in pars. 175, 176, and the stations located as above. The amount of siding, or passing tracks, that will be necessary at a station will have to be figured in each special case, and the minimum amount should be about two and one-half times the maximum train length contemplated on that division. The passing tracks are usually parallel to the main line (see par. 172, **Lap sidings**).

The **station sites** should be as level as practicable, and if possible, located so that the yards can be seen by trains approaching from either direction.

An **open space** should be left near the tracks to facilitate the loading and unloading of troops, by allowing a systematic and orderly arrangement of the troops and their baggage in the immediate neighborhood of the station.

162. **Storage tracks.**—The number and length of these tracks depend upon the importance of the station, the number of troops that will be stationed there, the number of depot storehouses that may be located at that point, etc. A study of these items shows that each must be dealt with as it arises, and as it is impossible to tell how important a station may become at any future time, available track room will be left for additional loading platforms and storage tracks. In locating the storage tracks room should be left between the various tracks so that at least one and preferably two li es of wagons can drive in and receive freight from cars on the storage tracks.

163. **Water supply.**—The question of a good water supply is important for the troops that will be located at the station, as well as for railway purposes. This water supply will be obtained by means of hand pumps, steam pumps, or windmills.

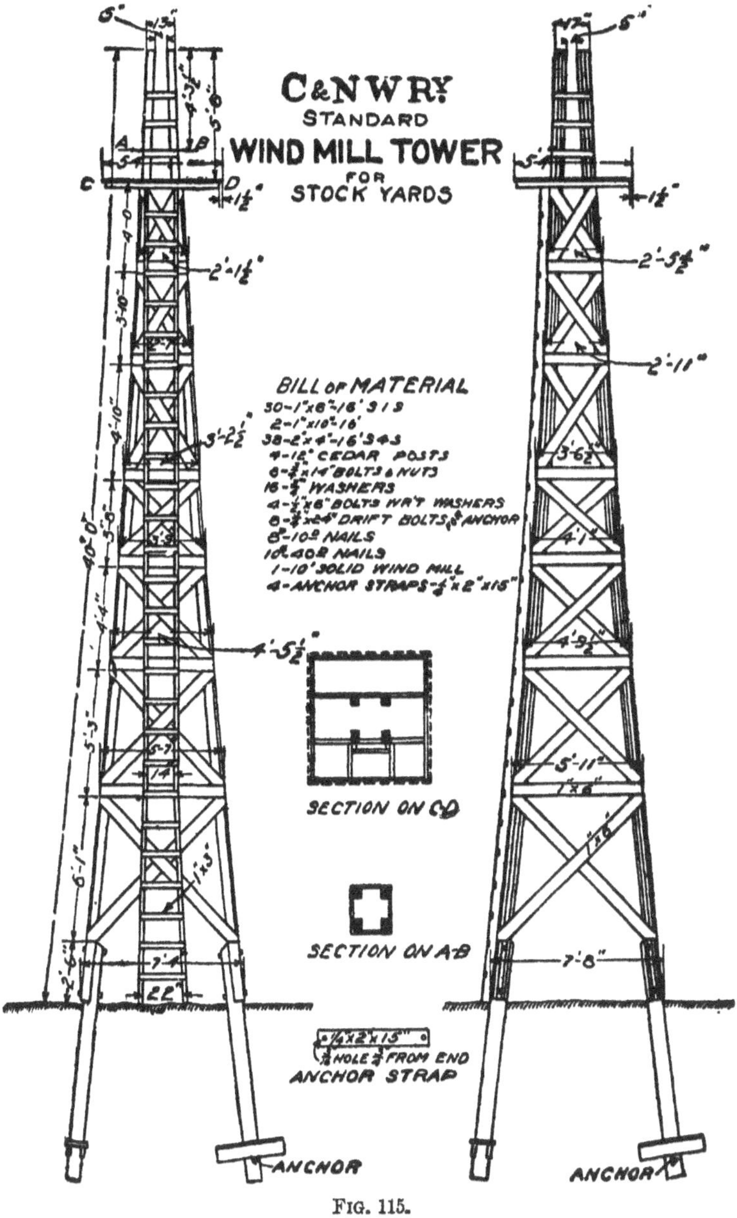
C&NWRY
STANDARD
WIND MILL TOWER
FOR
STOCK YARDS
BILL OF MATERIAL
30-1"x6"-16' S1S
2-1"x10"-16'
38-2"x4"-16' S4S
4-12" CEDAR POSTS
8-5/8"x14" BOLTS & NUTS
16-5/8" WASHERS
4-1/2"x6" BOLTS WR'T WASHERS
8-3/4"x24" DRIFT BOLTS FOR ANCHOR
8#-10d NAILS
10#-40d NAILS
1-10' SOLID WIND MILL
4-ANCHOR STRAPS-1/4"x2"x15"
SECTION ON C-D
SECTION ON A-B
1/4x2x15
ANCHOR STRAP
ANCHOR
ANCHOR
40'0"

FIG. 115.

These pumps of various kinds are commercial articles, and their pumping capacity can be obtained from the various manufacturers.

A steam pump which apparently has great possibilities for field use is the **pulsometer**, and by means of it the locomotives can water themselves from streams, where the water can be used direct from the stream without having to allow it to settle.

The **amount of water required** for railway purposes varies too widely under different conditions to permit any general rule. Locomotive tanks carry from 3,000 to 7,000 gallons. The amount of water used per mile depends on the loads, grades, and condition of track and rolling stock. On down grades it may be nothing, while on steep ascents it may run as high as 150 gallons per mile, although 75 gallons is a more usual figure. To allow for accidents there should be a water

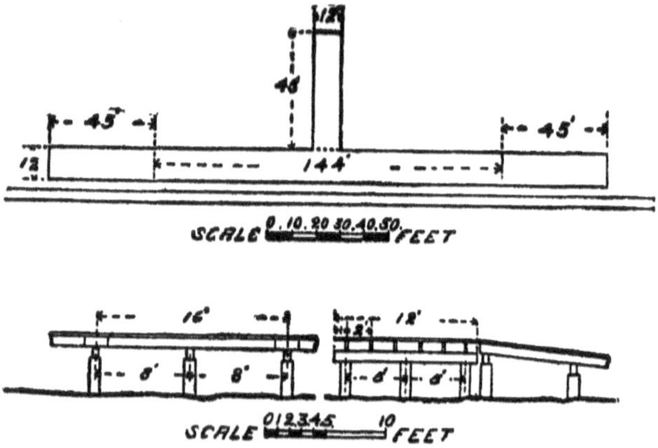


BILL OF MATERIAL

| FOR 16' PANEL | | TOTAL | |
|---|---|---|---|
| Pieces | Dimen. | Pieces | Dimen. |
| 2 | 6"x10"x12' | 32 | 6"x10"x12' |
| 2 | 10"x10"x10' | 20 | 10"x10"x10' |
| 6 | 2"x10"x18' | 108 | 2"x10"x18' |
| 20 | 2"x10"x12' | 345 | 2"x10"x12' |

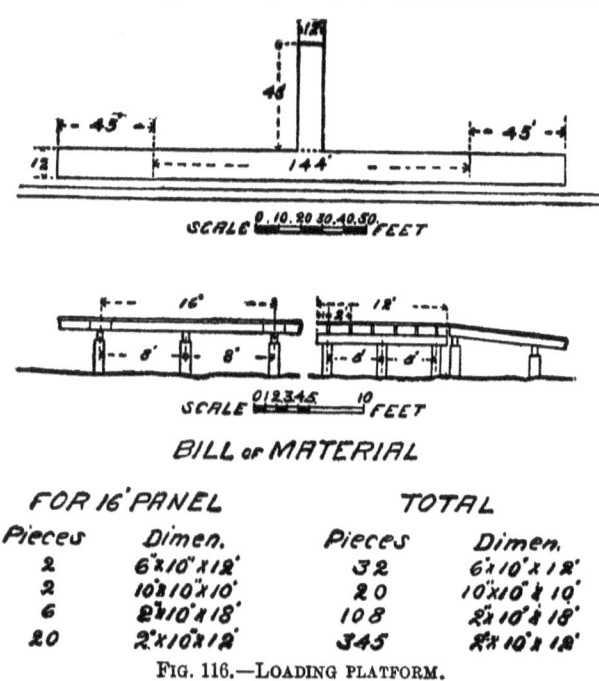

FIG. 116.—LOADING PLATFORM.

supply for each 10 miles of track. Wooden and metal tanks are commercial articles readily obtainable. They are shipped knocked down and can quickly be assembled when needed. There should always be one day's supply in the tank if practicable. A very common size tank is 24 ft. in diameter, 16 ft. high, holding 50,000 gallons. The bottom of the tank should be 12 ft. above the rails.

For a movable water supply, **tank cars**, such as are used for the shipment of oil in this country, can be taken with the locomotive. This applies particularly to construction trains.

164. A bill of materials for a **windmill tower** is given in fig. 115. This is made up of small stock material and, on account of the lightness of the material, the tower can be easily built. Such a tower would be useful as a signal tower or observation station.

165. **Platforms.**—On every train length of siding there should be a platform at least 12 ft. wide and long enough to load three or four standard cars at one time. The tops of these platforms should be on a level with the bottoms of the car floors, and the platforms should have ramps leading to the ground at both ends and one

in the middle, if the other tracks permit. These platforms are particularly useful in loading and unloading animals and vehicles and facilitate the handling of freight. Fig. 116 shows the platform and gives bills of materials for the whole platform and for each extra length of 16 ft.

166. **Stockyards.**—At each station a stockyard should be constructed, and this should be connected with the side ramp of one of the loading platforms by a

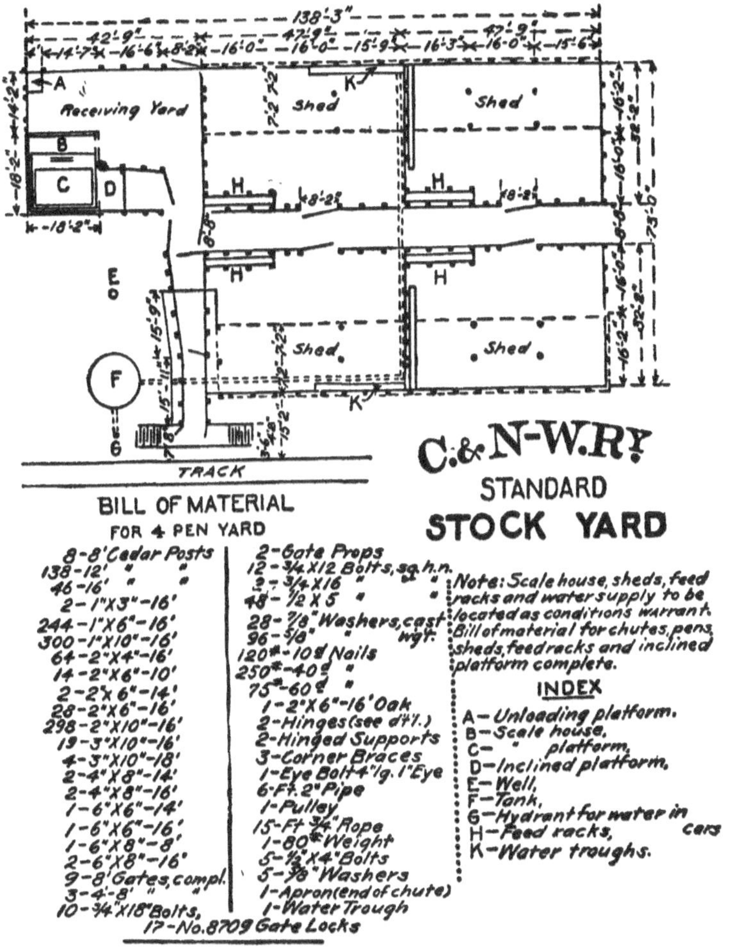


Fig. 117.

movable fence that can be thrown out of the way when the platform is desired for other purposes (fig. 117).

167. **Coal stations.**—The rapid and easy coaling of locomotives requires a gravity supply. This is obtained by raising the coal either by hoisting it into pockets or by running the coal cars up an incline and dumping the coal into bins. One coal station should be located in about each 60 to 70 miles of track and t division terminals.

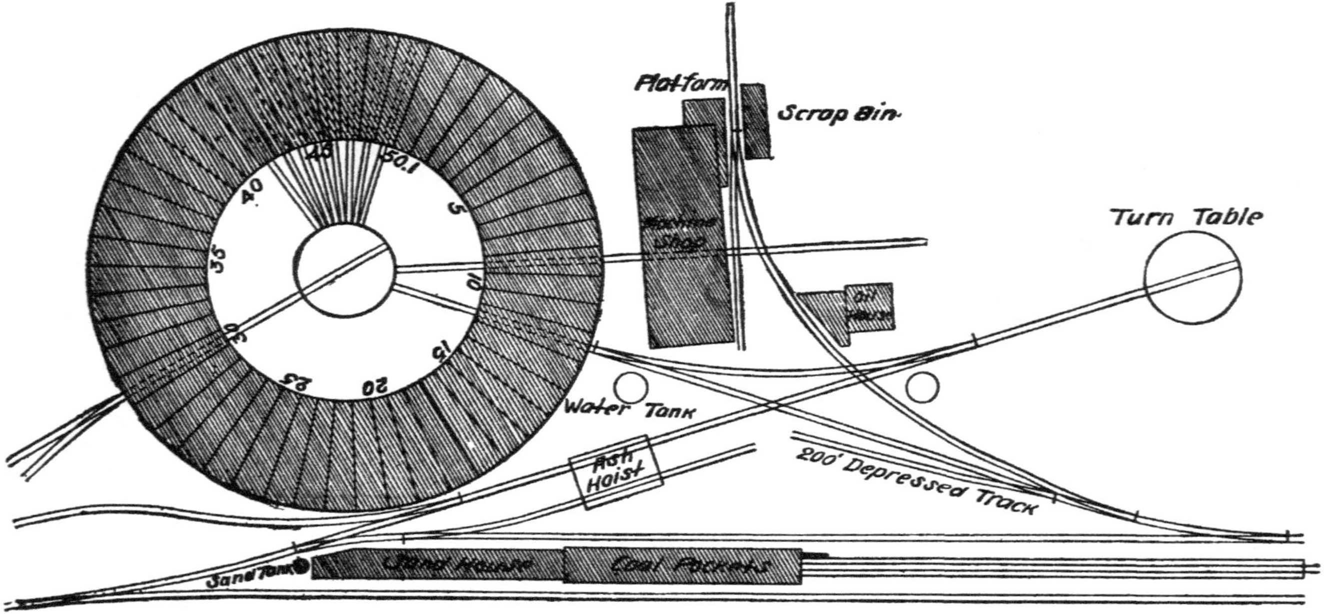


FIG. 118.—ROUNDHOUSE AND TRACKS.

**Coal consumption.**—The amount of coal required is dependent upon the same factors that determine that of water supply. On the average about 1 lb. of coal is consumed on a locomotive in evaporating 6 to 9 lbs. of water (U. S. gallon, 8.3 lbs.; English gallon, 10 lbs.). Each locomotive carries from 5 to 10 tons of coal.

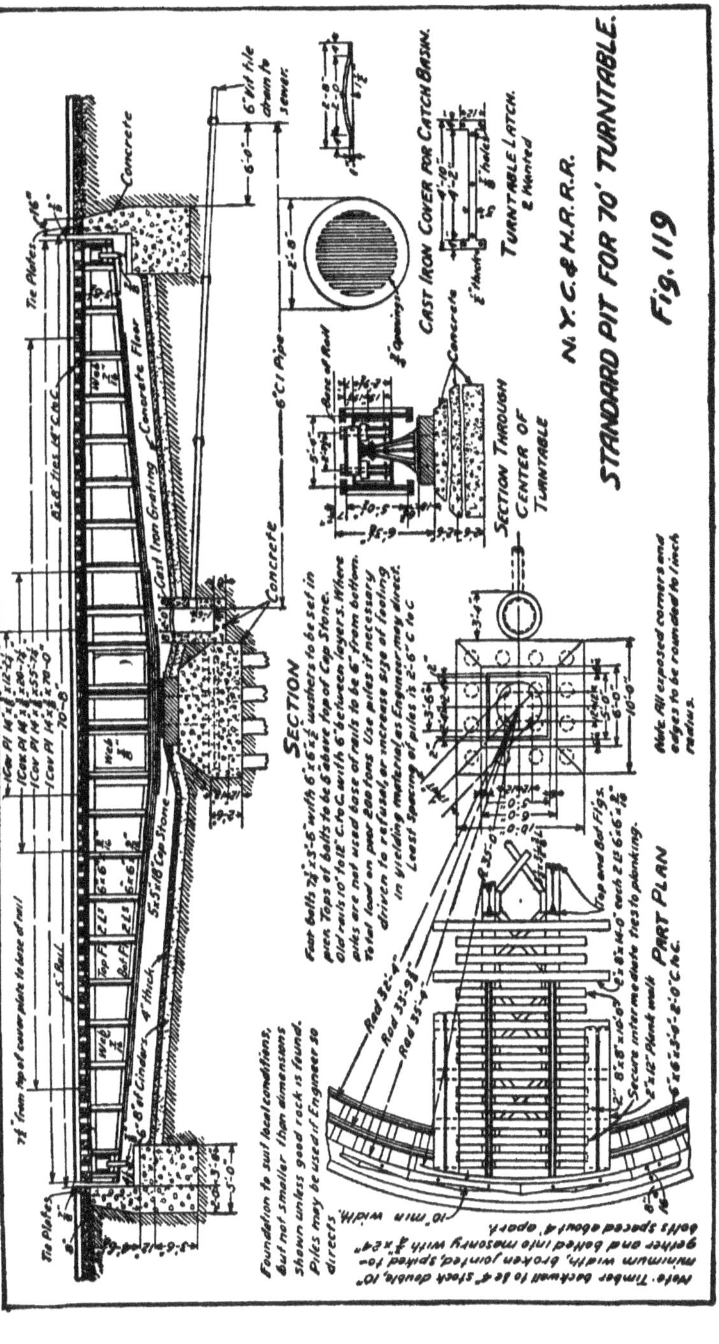


STANDARD PIT FOR 70' TURNTABLE.

Fig. 119

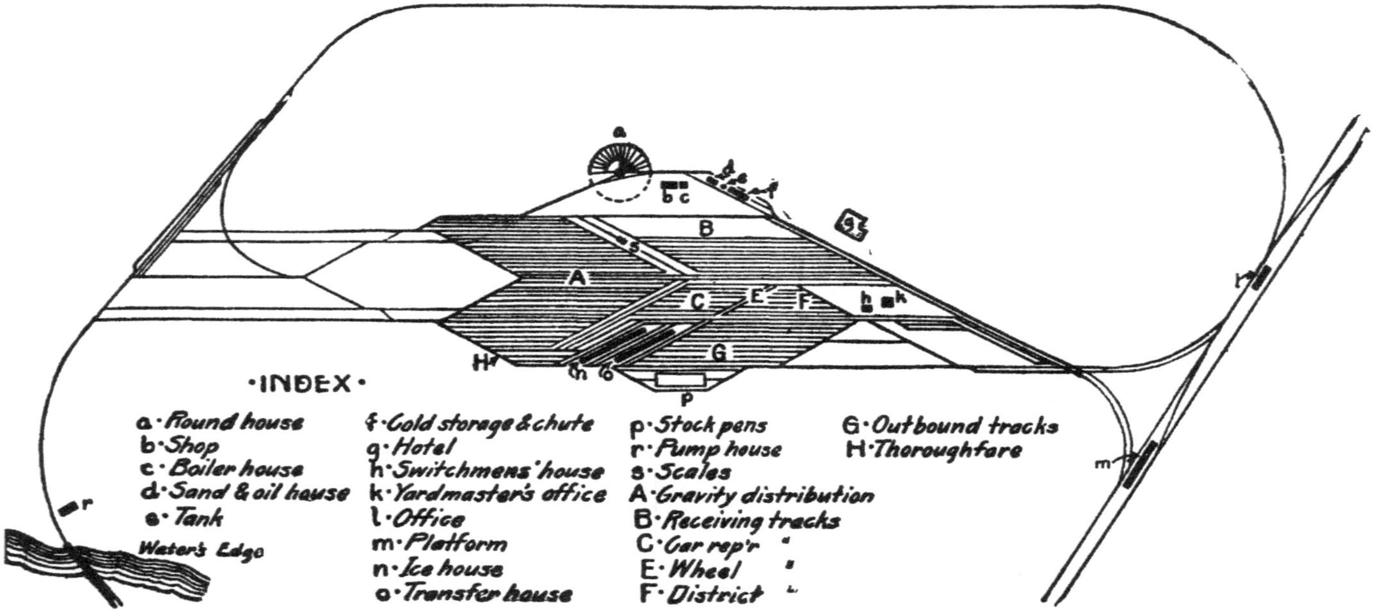


FIG. 120.—TERMINAL YARD.

168. **Buildings.**—The buildings at the stations may be constructed after the line has been finished. Tents can be used temporarily and will answer nearly every purpose.

The railway staff officer in charge of each station must see that there is sufficient storage room for all railway purposes, so that under the most adverse circumstances there will be **no excuse for leaving material stored in cars.** Tents should be supplied for this purpose when buildings are not available or convenient.

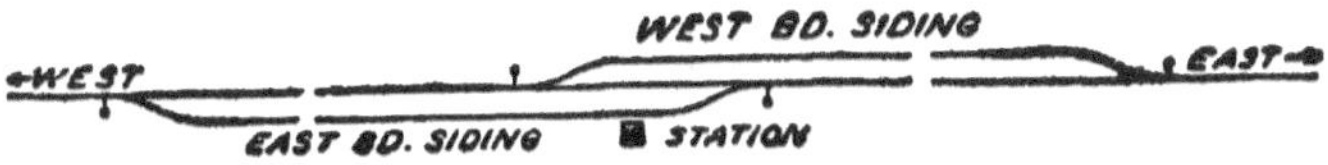


FIG. 121.—PLAIN LAP SIDING ON STRAIGHT TRACK.

**Roundhouses.**—At division terminals temporary roundhouses will be constructed, or storage tracks will be laid, for the proper cleaning and repairing of engines. The plan of such a roundhouse is shown in fig. 118. A **turntable** (fig. 119) is desirable at such points, but if the number of engines is not great, and no roundhouse is available, a few parallel tracks and a Y (fig. 104) for turning engines will answer the purpose of a roundhouse with a turntable. Simplifications of the

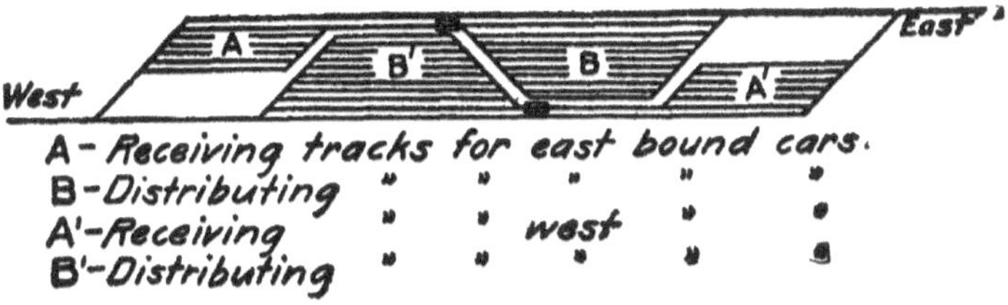


FIG. 122.—DIVISIONAL TERMINAL YARD.

elaborate turntable shown in fig. 119 will suggest themselves to the engineer, but a good turntable for heavy locomotives must be a very permanent structure.

169. **Shops.**—At these same terminals would be located machine shops large enough to keep in repair all the locomotives that would be stabled in the roundhouse, and car repair shops large enough to make all necessary repairs to cars damaged on that division.

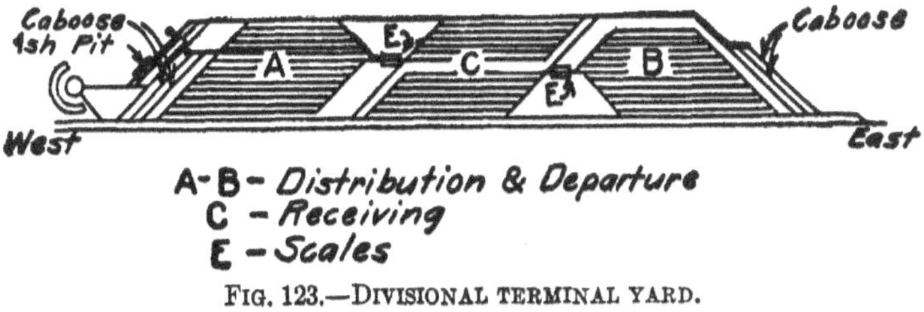


FIG. 123.—DIVISIONAL TERMINAL YARD.

170. **Yards and terminals.**—At division terminals and at other large stations yards must be constructed large enough to receive all the cars entering the station and still allow room for the switching that is necessary in making up trains and in moving cars to and from the storage tracks. In addition, there will be the necessary number of passing tracks.

**A yard** is a number of sidings and spurs, usually parallel to each other, although often not parallel to the main track. These auxiliary tracks must be sufficient in number to permit the convenient and rapid breaking up of trains, classification of cars by contents, destination, or otherwise, and making them up into new trains in accordance with the new requirements. Yard tracks are divided into groups, according to their purpose. A certain number near the main line at one end of the yard are called **receiving tracks,** and trains arriving pull in on them. In convenient proximity is a **caboose track,** where cabooses are stored when not in trains. A group of **repair tracks** are convenient to the shops, and the **engine track** leads to the engine house, near which should be the coaling and watering stations and the ash pit.

The train on the receiving track is broken up and its cars switched onto the **distribution tracks,** selected so that those on each of these tracks will belong in the same outgoing train. There should be enough distribution tracks to permit the convenient classification of freight cars according to their contents and destination, and of passenger cars according to character, as baggage, express, coaches, tourist and standard sleepers. In most cases, outgoing trains are completed on the distribution tracks and pulled from them onto the main track, when authorized by order to do so. It is better, when possible, to have a third group of tracks at the other end of the yard, which may be called the **departure tracks.** When a train is completed on a distribution track it may be pulled out onto a departure track, where a caboose and engine are added, the designated crew takes charge, and the train is ready, on the receipt of orders, to pull out on the main line without delay, and without crossing or interfering with any of the yard traffic. Departure tracks permit the distributing tracks to be fewer and somewhat shorter. If there are departure tracks, they and the receiving tracks should be divided into two groups designated for traffic in opposite directions. Trains which go through or return without change go direct from the receiving tracks to a distribution or departure track, the returning trains through a loop or Y to turn them around.

All yard tracks, except repair and team tracks, should be open at both ends, so that all traffic over them may be in the same direction. This permits all traffic through the yard to be in one direction, which saves much confusion and delay. The standard method of arranging yard tracks for greatest convenience and compactness is by the use of **ladder tracks,** fig. 103, which are oblique tracks at the proper distance apart to accommodate the other tracks between them. Each receiving, distribution, and departure track connects with a ladder track at each end by the ordinary switch. The dead end of each spur track should be provided with an obstacle, to prevent cars running off.

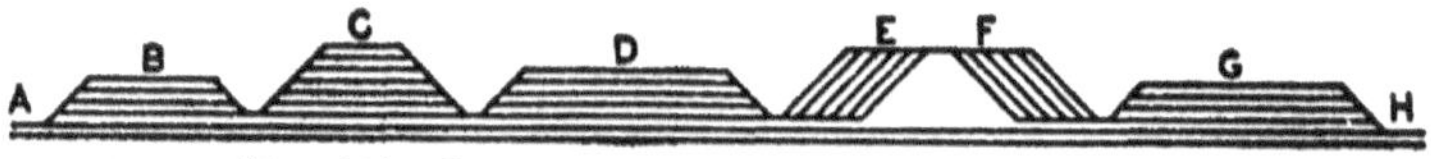


FIG. 124.—CONVENTIONALIZED TERMINAL LAYOUT.

171. **Gravity or "Hump" yards** will not be considered since there is no chance of having to construct them on a military railway. They are simply yards on a down grade in which the cars are started by a locomotive and then run by force of gravity to their desired position. Theoretically the movement of all cars through a yard should be forward, but this condition would require a layout somewhat like fig. 124. The lead "A" runs into a receiving yard "B." The train is broken up and cars are classified as to destination, etc., on the tracks of the yard, C. The cars are grouped into trains in yard D. The train is sorted and arranged in station order, or as required by regulations in yards E and F and is then run out into yard G ready to proceed. Such a yard layout is not practical, but an understanding of the uses of each part of this layout may assist in planning other yards. Yards at intermediate stations can readily be elaborated from the passing tracks shown in figs. 110 and 121.

172. **Permanent yards** seldom form a part of military construction. For **field terminals,** which are temporary, the arrangement of auxiliary tracks will be much less regular and more open. Sidings will be provided wherever it is necessary to

unload cars. Stores consigned to organizations present will ordinarily not pass through storehouses, but will be unloaded from the trains onto the ground, or, so far as possible, directly into wagons.

Stores consigned to the supply departments will usually go into storehouses or into compact piles at designated points for temporary cover, pending issue. **Platforms** will be used to the degree to which time and materials at hand permit, but the **main reliance for discharging** cars will be **ramps** of suitable form to lead from the car floor to the ground, which should be provided in profusion and so distributed that it will be next to impossible to set out a car at a time or place where a ramp can not be procured within easy carrying distance.

Figs. 141 and 142 show convenient forms of ramps, which may be carried on the car or used otherwise.

**Storehouses** should be narrow and long enough to permit all the cars of a train to discharge simultaneously. If there are no houses, the ground occupied by the supply departments for storage should be of similar shape for the same purposes.

A very complete type of **terminal yard** is shown in fig. 120. Types of **division terminal yards** are shown in figs. 122, 123.

Local conditions will govern the exact location of yards and special tracks, and only general rules can be made in reference thereto.

A good and convenient form of siding, known as a **"lap siding,"** is shown in fig. 121. When two sidings are necessary and the space is available, this form is an excellent one; whichever train is waiting, or if two are waiting, the locomotives are both within a few steps of the station. Signals are given, and orders are transmitted with more convenience and certainty and less time is lost than if the two sidings were adjacent.

## ROLLING STOCK.

173. **Rolling stock.**—The rolling stock of a road consists of the locomotives and cars. Unless notice is given in advance of the proposed construction of a railroad, the rolling stock then on the market or procurable from other railroads will have to be used, and whatever disadvantages are met with will have to be overcome in the best manner possible. If due notice be given, however, of the proposed construction of a road, an equipment can be ordered that will be suited to the local conditions.

If the plans contemplate the use of a railway in a hostile country, plans should be made, well in advance, to obtain a sufficient supplv of rolling stock suited to the road, since it will not be safe to count on capturing rolling stock in usable condition rom the enemy.

A study of the grades and the working time tables will permit an estimate of the necessary amount of rolling stock that will be required. A large allowance for accidents should be made.

174. **Composition and distribution of traffic from bases.**—The amount of traffic originating from the base of an army can be roughly calculated from the following data: From October 1, 1899, to October 31, 1900, there were transported from the three ports, Cape Town, East London, and Port Elizabeth, South Africa, approximatelv 200,000 men; for **each thousand of these men,** during this time, there were also transported 41 officers, 765 animals, 2 guns, 15 vehicles, and 1,406 long tons of stores and supplies.

A compilation for a longer length of time shows that from October, 1899, until June, 1901, from the same three ports, 287,571 men were moved, and that for **each thousand men** there were also transported 44 officers, 672 animals, 1.5 guns, 14.5 wagons, and 1,960 long tons of supplies and stores. From the port of Durban, 89,399 men were transported to the front from September 20, 1899, to June 30, 1901; for **each thousand of these men,** during this time, there were also transported 34.7 officers, 855 animals, 1.9 guns, 7.8 vehicles, and 3,624 long tons of stores and supplies. In addition to this and to the civil traffic that was permitted, from November, 1899, until June, 1901, the railroads moved 941,764 soldiers, 346,965 animals,

10,494 vehicles, and 380,066 long tons of stores and supplies, for which no average length of haul is given. The **percentages of carloads** of the various supplies originating at the bases were as follows: Supplies, 48.5%; ordnance and engineers' stores, 9%; troops, including animals and baggage, 25%; railway stores and labor, 1.5%; remounts, 14.5%; hospital trains and stores, 1.5%.

Based on very scanty data, an estimate of the desired **train tonnage for the supply of an army** seems to be about 35 to 50 lbs per day per man plus the passenger service plus the service to care for the necessary civil traffic. This includes supplies for animals, guns, etc.

175. **Locomotives.**—On supply lines, the sharpest curve allowed would determine, in a measure, the gage to be used, as sharper curves can be used on a narrow-gage road than on a standard or broad-gage road, probably because the rigid wheel base is shorter on the lighter locomotive, since the maximum curvature is theoretically dependent only on the length of the rigid wheel base.

Having decided upon the gage to be used, the first thing to be considered is the **tractive power** desired in the locomotives. A reference to the catalogues of the various firms that build locomotives will give all the data in reference to the ones built by those firms. The tractive power, T, is usually given in pounds and represents the pulling power of the locomotives on a clean, level track. Other conditions being equal, the tractive power of locomotives varies directly with the working steam pressure, the area of the piston, the length of the stroke, and inversely as the circumference of the drivers. It is limited to about $\frac{1}{5}$ of the weight on the drivers, under favorable conditions, and to as low as $^1/_7$ of that weight on slippery track.

$$T = \frac{(\text{diam. piston})^2 \times \text{ave. steam pressure} \times \text{stroke}}{\text{diameter of drivers}} \text{ (ins. and lbs.).}$$

Not more than 80% of the theoretical tractive power should be counted upon in working a locomotive, as it has been found in railway practice that this is about the economical percentage to be used. The length of the rigid wheel base and the shape of the wheel should be noted to make sure that the engine can take the maximum curve of the road. The maximum weight on a single axle will determine the lightest rail that can be used for that locomotive (Table IX or X).

The average steam pressure, or mean effective pressure in the formula falls off rapidly with the speed of piston travel. It is about 85% of the boiler pressure up to a piston speed of 250 feet per minute, and falls off, at practically a uniform rate, to 42.5% at a piston speed of 750 ft. per min.; at higher speeds the rate of decrease in mean effective pressure slowly decrease to 30% at 1,075 ft. per min. and 22% at 1,500 ft. per min.

The kind of grate will depend on whether wood or coal is to be used as fuel; only in exceptional circumstances would a wood burner be counted upon at the present day.

All locomotives should be equipped with the modern air brake.

Where the locomotives are to be built to order, the specifications should require that the boiler, water tank, cab, and other vulnerable parts should be **bullet-proof.**

The **speed of the locomotive,** under certain loads and grades, must be computed, and a **freight locomotive** should be required to have an average speed of about 15 miles per hour when hauling 80% of its maximum load. The speed of a locomotive and the hauling capacity should be considered together, for it is evident that a locomotive that will move 500 tons at 15 miles per hour can handle more freight than a locomotive that moves 600 tons at 10 miles per hour on the same grade.

For **passenger service** a locomotive with larger driving wheels and higher speed should be used.

176. With good cars and a good track 1 ton (2,000 lbs.) can be moved by about 6½ lbs. pull. It is probable that on a supply railway the **tractive resistance** per ton, F, would be considerably more than this; probably from 10 to 15 lbs. per ton.

This, however, would depend upon the condition of the track and the condition of the rolling stock, and is given approximately by the following formulæ:

Engineering News formula, $F=2+\frac{V}{4}$,

American Locomotive Co. formula
Baldwin Locomotive Co. formula } $F=3+\frac{V}{6}$,

in which F=tractive resistance in pounds per ton at a speed of V miles per hour on a straight level track.

Up to 40 miles an hour the average of these two formulæ is a conservative estimate.

The hauling capacity of a locomotive is rapidly cut down by grades, and on this account the ruling grade should be kept as small as the conditions of construction will permit.

The **total force,** T, in pounds required to move W tons up a grade where the **grade resistance** is G lbs. per ton, and the force required to move 1 ton on the same track on the level is F lbs. per ton, is given by the formula

$$T=W\,(G+F)\ \text{(G is not affected by speed)},$$

in which $G=2000 \tan \theta$, when $\theta$=angle of compensated slope (see par. 41). (Practically, G=20 times the percentage of grade.) The weight of locomotive must be included in the train load in above formula. Inertia and wind resistance are not included in T.

Having decided upon the locomotives to be purchased, a table should be made showing their hauling capacity on various grades, and from this table and the division profiles can be determined what is known as the **tonnage rating** of the locomotive; that is, the number of tons that the locomotive will haul over the grades on the division where it is to be used. If different types of locomotives are used on the same division, the tonnage rating of each class should be determined and given to the chief dispatcher, in order that he may know the maximum load that should be required with each locomotive.

177. The tonnage rating depends upon the **train resistance** and the **tractive power** of the locomotive. The train resistance increases with the speed while the tractive power decreases and a consideration of these two factors for each speed fixes the allowable tonnage for that speed. A further consideration of tonnage and speed gives the comparative number of **ton miles** for the different speeds. The maximum seems to correspond to a speed of from 12 to 15 miles per hour.

178. Due to the various other car resistances than those produced by weight alone a locomotive can not haul the same tonnage in empty or half loaded cars that it can in cars loaded to their full capacity.

This gives rise to what is known as **adjusted weight** in trains and **adjusted tonnage rating** in locomotives.

Suppose that it is found that a locomotive will haul, under exactly the same condition except as to train, 20 loaded cars weighing 1,200 tons or 50 empty cars weighing 1,020 tons. The difference is 30 cars and 180 tons. Then the resistances, other than those due to weight, amount for each car to the resistance produced by a weight of 6 tons. Add this adjusted weight to each car of each train and we have 1,320 tons in each case.

$$(50\times6)+1020=1320$$
$$(20\times6)+1200=1320$$

The adjusted weight of the two trains is therefore equal. For any other case for this same rolling stock, use this **adjusted tonnage** as the tonnage rating of the locomotive. Suppose that the yardmaster finds that he has about 35 cars loaded and empty actually weighing 1,050 tons to send in a train using this same locomotive. Then (35×6)+1,050=1,260 is the adjusted tonnage of the train. One more car weighing 54 tons can be added to the train, making the adjusted tonnage 1,320 tons. The adjusted weight for cars can be found by a similar experiment on any line.

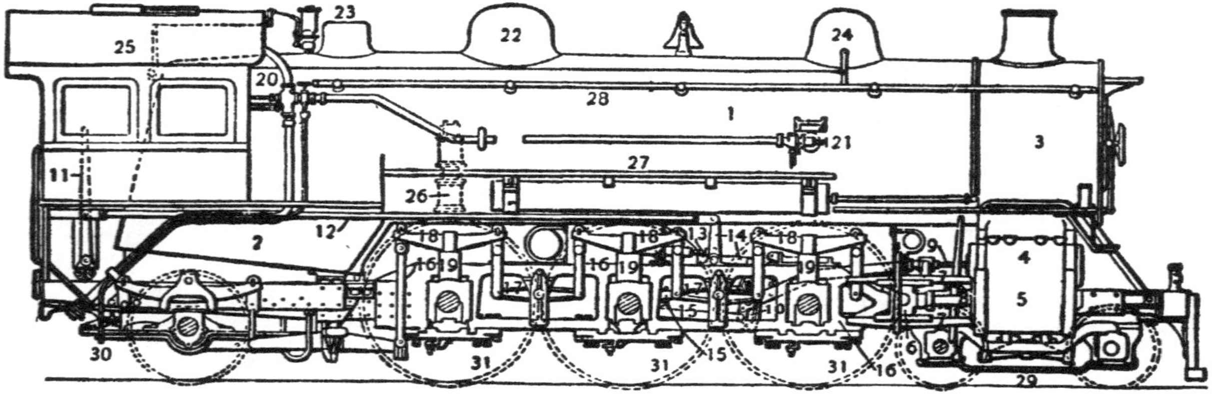


FIG. 125.

NOMENCLATURE OF PARTS OF LOCOMOTIVE.

1. Boiler.
2. Fire box.
3. Smoke box.
4. Steam chest.
5. Cylinder.
6. Crosshead.
7. Guides.
8. Piston rod.
9. Valve stem.
10. Link.
11. Reverse lever.
12. Reach rod.
13. Tumbling shaft.
14. Rocker arm.
15. Eccentric rod.
16. Frame.
17. Equalizing bars.
18. Springs.
19. Pedestals.
20. Injector.
21. Boiler check.
22. Steam drum.
23. Filling funnel.
24. Sand box.
25. Cab.
26. Air pump.
27. Footboard.
28. Handrail.
29. Pilot truck.
30. Trailing truck.
31. Drivers.
32. Main rod.
33. Side rods.

179. **Tenders.**—The capacity of the tender in fuel and water is determined by the local conditions, and since the establishment of pumping and coaling plants entails considerable time and labor, the tender should carry more fuel and water than would be desirable under commercial conditions.

On standard gage railways, tenders usually carry from 3,000 to 7,000 gallons of water and from 5 to 10 tons of coal.

180. **Number of locomotives.**—Knowing the amount of supplies to be carried by the railroad and the amount that can be handled in one train, the **number of locomotives** can be easily computed; but in providing locomotives provision must be made for a great many accidents, and the number of locomotives ordered should be about one and one-half times the number that it is expected to use at one time, thus allowing one-third of the whole number to be in the repair shop at one time.

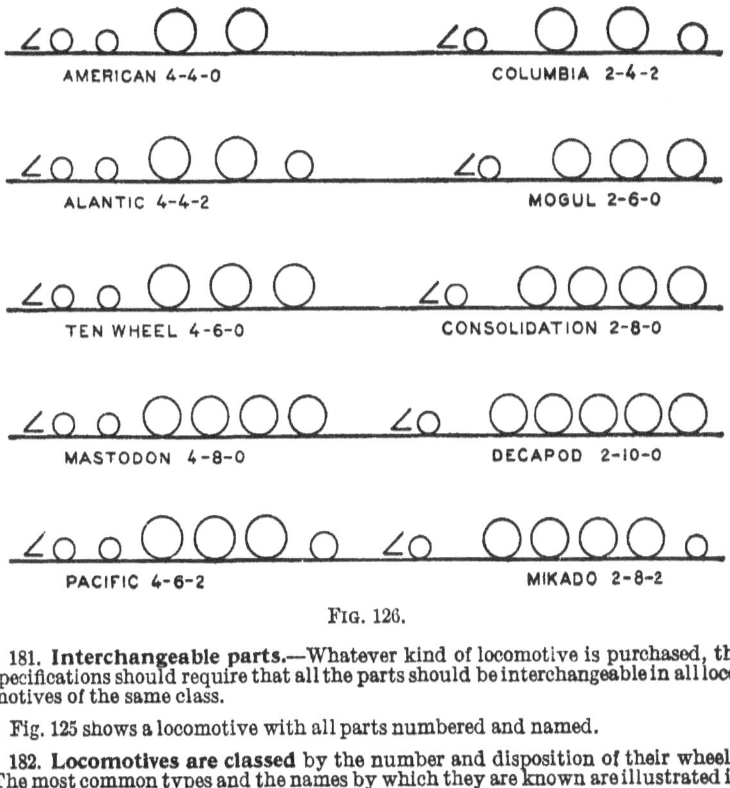


FIG. 126.

181. **Interchangeable parts.**—Whatever kind of locomotive is purchased, the specifications should require that all the parts should be interchangeable in all locomotives of the same class.

Fig. 125 shows a locomotive with all parts numbered and named.

182. **Locomotives are classed** by the number and disposition of their wheels. The most common types and the names by which they are known are illustrated in Fig. 126, in which the larger circles represent drivers and the smaller ones truck wheels, the direction of forward motion being indicated by the cowcatcher.

**A better system,** rapidly coming into use, is to describe the running gear by giving the no. of wheels in the three following groups in the order named: (1) **Forward non-drivers,** (2) **drivers,** and (3) **rear non-drivers.** Thus an engine with 2 forward truck wheels, 4 drivers, and 2 rear truck wheels is indicated by 2—4—2, etc.

By this system the Atlantic type becomes 4—4—2; the Columbia, 2—4—2, etc.

Locomotives are also classed as passenger and freight, the former having large drivers and other proportions adapted to high speed.

183. **Cars.**—In deciding upon the cars to be used on a supply railway, the gage of the track will almost entirely govern the kind of cars to be used. There is one rule that should be followed in purchasing or designing an equipment for such a road; that is, to have the **axle load** for loaded cars the same as that for locomotives whenever practicable. This will not be difficult for narrow-gage equipment, but on standard-gage roads the weight of some of the engines is so great that it is not economical to have the axle load of the cars equal to the axle load of the locomotives. If all axle loads were the same, there would be considerable economy in cars, and the track would then be utilized to its greatest working value by every wheel that went over it.

184. **Passenger equipment.**—Passenger cars may be divided into day coaches, standard sleepers, tourist sleepers, dining cars, baggage cars, and kitchen cars. It will be impossible to obtain a narrow-gage passenger equipment in this country, except by special order with plenty of time for building the new equipment.

The narrow-gage equipment of the Barsi Railway in India is for a 2 ft. 6 in. gage. These cars are compartment cars with side entrances. Their length is 40 ft. 6 ins.; width, 6 ft. 2 ins. inside; weight, about 20 tons.

The second-class cars will carry, crowded, 64 passengers; the first-class cars will carry about 24 passengers. One train on this road carried comfortably 30 first-class and 736 second-class passengers in 13 cars. (Distance not stated, but less than 21 miles.)

The baggage cars would not differ materially, except in size, from the standard baggage car.

Passenger equipment for a standard-gage road would not be difficult to obtain from the various roads in this country, and in a foreign country such cars could be shipped from this country, or purchased from some neutral, or captured from the enemy.

185. **Day coaches.**—A standard day coach will carry about 60 persons, seating two in a seat. Unless there were an emergency, only three men would be put in a double seat, leaving the remaining room for the soldiers' equipment. About 45 men per car can be counted on by this arrangement. Whatever kind of coach is decided upon, the toilet arrangements and drinking supply should be ample for the car when fully loaded.

In an emergency about 30 persons can stand in the aisles. By running a detail on the seats, 90 persons per car can be carried for a daylight trip with no hardships.

186. **Sleeping cars.**—A standard sleeper has about 15 sections counting the drawing room, and will carry, crowded, about 45 people. A tourist sleeper is similar to a standard sleeper, except in its appointments, and will carry about the same number of people. The remarks as to water supply and toilet arrangements with reference to coaches apply equally to sleepers.

187. **Baggage cars.**—Baggage cars carry about 2,500 cu. ft. of baggage. This gives about 150 lbs. in 13 cu. ft. for about 193 passengers. This will allow for rations for the men, as well as for their luggage. These cars should have end doors for communication while the train is in motion. **Kitchen cars** are baggage cars equipped for cooking.

188. **Freight equipment.**—The freight equipment of a road is of first importance, and in an emergency the troops can be moved in the freight equipment by arranging benches in the box cars, stock cars, and flat cars.

189. **Box cars** for narrow-gage roads would be similar in construction to, but smaller in dimensions than, those for a standard-gage road. Box cars on a 2 ft. 6 in. railway can be built to carry 15 tons, and the carrying capacity varies from this up to 40 tons for a good standard-gage box car (see fig. 127).

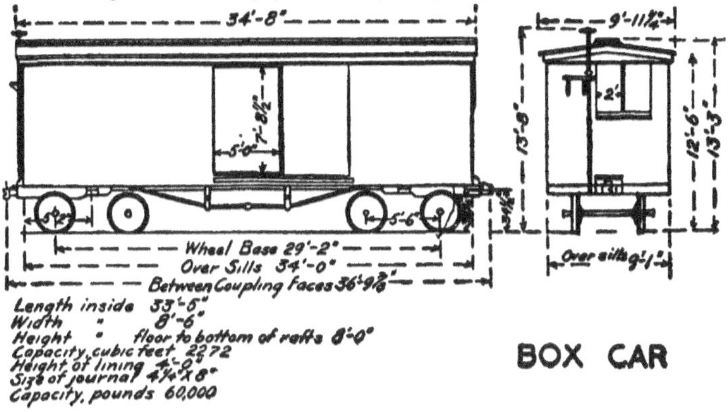


FIG. 127.

190. **Stock cars** on a narrow-gage road would have to be built to carry the animals lengthwise of the car. A 34-ft. car 7 ft. wide would carry from 8 to 12 horses Padded **cross gates** would have to be put in to keep them from being injured by the

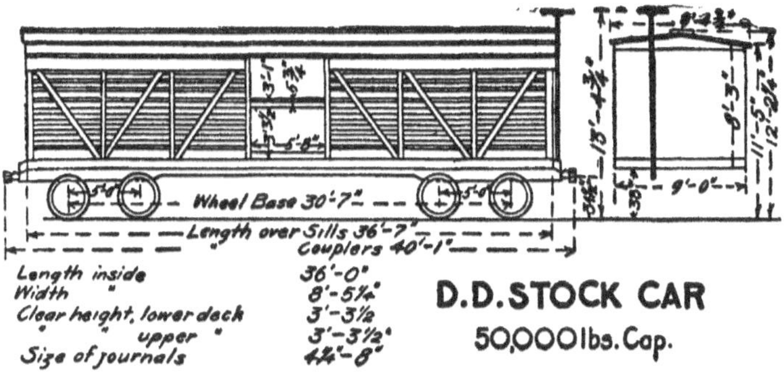


FIG. 128.—DOUBLE-DECK STOCK CAR.

movement of the train. Standard-gage stock cars carry from 16 to 20 animals. Some stock cars are fitted for feeding and watering en route, but the ordinary ones have no feeding arrangements, except for hay (see fig. 128).

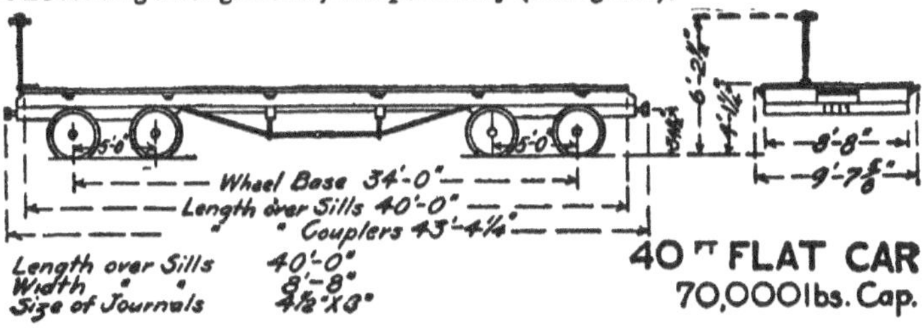


FIG. 129.

191. **Flat cars** are used for carrying heavy and bulky articles that will not be injured by exposure to the weather. The capacity of these cars varies from 15 or 20 tons on a 2 ft. 6 in. road to 50 tons on a standard-gage road. The average capacity of a standard-gage flat car is about 70,000 lbs. (see fig. 129).

By means of the platforms or ramps, guns and vehicles can easily be loaded on these cars. By removing the tongues and chocking the wheels, the vehicle is ready for shipment. Empty wagons and other vehicles should have both wheels and

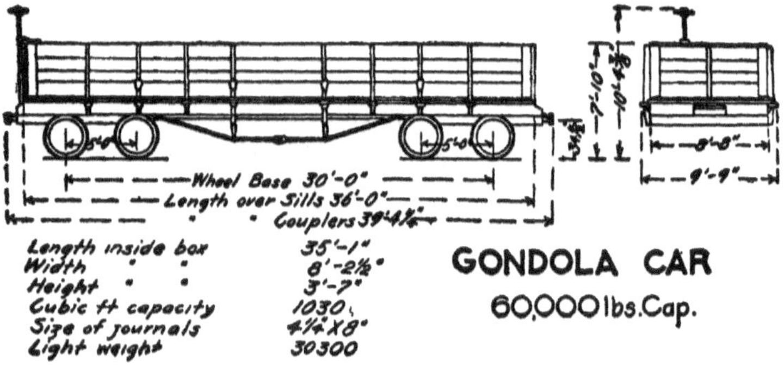


FIG. 130.

tongues removed for shipment in order to allow a greater number to be shipped on one car.

192. **Gondolas.**—A gondola is a flat car with sides and ends from 2 ft. to 3 ft. 6 ins. in height. The remarks about flat cars apply to gondolas (see fig. 130).

193. **Cabooses** or **way cars** are cars for use with freight trains for the accommodation of the train crew (see fig. 131).

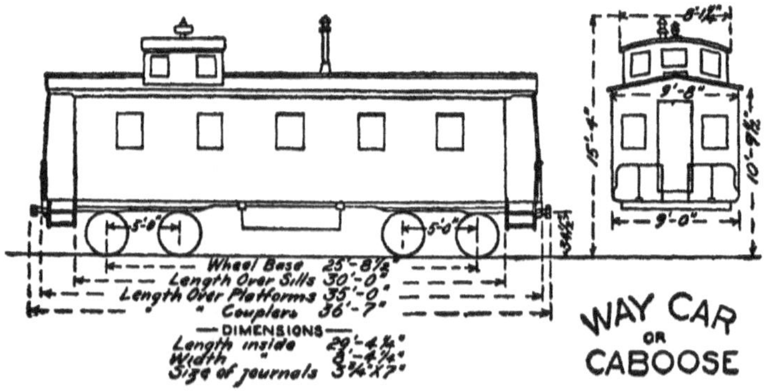


FIG. 131.

In addition to the freight equipment mentioned above, there are **refrigerator** cars, **furniture** cars, **vehicle** cars, and **special ballast** cars, all of which would be made use of under special conditions.

Refrigerator cars would be especially useful in the supply of an army, and should form a part of the original equipment.

Furniture cars and vehicle cars are extra large box cars for carrying freight of the names specified. They will be useful for hay, camp equipage, and other light, bulky freight.

194. **Interchangeable parts.**—Whatever equipment is purchased, care should be taken to have wheels, trucks, and all other parts the same, as far as is practicable, for all kinds of cars. This facilitates repairs both in time and money.

195. In addition to the cars above referred to, there are certain smaller cars used for maintenance and **inspection purposes.** These are the **velocipede motor car,** and **hand car,** which are illustrated in figs. 68, 70. All of these cars are now made equipped with gasoline motors, and for speed are preferable to the old type. Special cars for transportation and service of heavy field artillery will doubtless be provided in the future.

196. **Track capacity.**—In figuring on the length of sidings, the length of the cars and locomotives must be known. These lengths for a 2 ft. 6 in. gage may be taken about as follows:

Locomotives, 50 ft.
Box cars, 30 ft.
Flat cars, 30 ft.
Passenger equipment, 45 ft.
Stock cars, 34 ft.

The length for a standard-gage road may be taken about as follows:

Locomotives, 65 ft.
Day coach, 60 ft.
Sleepers, 75 ft.
Baggage cars, 50 ft.
Box cars, 37 ft.
Furniture cars, 50 ft.
Flat cars, 44 ft.
Gondolas, 40 ft.
Refrigerator cars, 40 ft.
Cabooses, 40 ft.
Stock cars, 40 ft.

Certain special cars will be longer than these lengths given; but in the general run of a train, taking all cars as they come, these lengths will give a fair estimate of the length of a train. (See Table XVI for exact data.)

197. **Capacity of a 36-ft. open car.**

Heavy bridge equipage:
1 ponton or trestle wagon loaded, or
2 chess wagons, or 2 company tool wagons, or 2 field wagons.

Light bridge equipage:
1 ponton or trestle wagon, loaded, or
2 company tool wagons, or 2 chess wagons.

Light artillery and horse artillery material:
1 gun and limber and 2 caissons and limbers, or
2 caissons and limbers and 1 store or battery wagon, or
2 field wagons, or 3 reel carts.

4.7″ gun matériel:
1 4.7″ gun, carriage and limber; 2 4.7″ limbers, and 1 4.7″ caisson.
A 4.7″ gun, battery wagon and forge limber, or its store wagon and store limber takes same space as the 4.7″ gun carriage limber.

4.7″ howitzer matériel:
1 4.7″ howitzer and carriage, 2 4.7″ howitzer caissons, 2 4.7″ howitzer limbers, and 1 4.7″ howitzer carriage limber, or
1 4.7″ howitzer battery wagon and 1 forge limber, and 2 4.7″ howitzer caissons, and 2 4.7″ howitzer limbers.
A 4.7″ howitzer store wagon and store limber require the same space as a battery wagon and forge limber.

6″ howitzer matériel:
Same as for a 4.7″ gun battery, substituting 6″ howitzer for 4.7″ gun.

Signal Corps matériel:
2 instrument wagons and 1 kit wagon; or
4 wire carts, or 2 field wagons; or
1 repair and 2 telephone or telegraph wagons.

198. **Capacity of a 40-ft. open car.**

**Heavy bridge equipage:**
1 ponton or trestle wagon, loaded, and 1 chess, or company tool, or field wagon; or 3 chess, company tool, or field wagons.

**Light bridge equipage:**
2 ponton or trestle wagons, loaded; or
3 company tool or chess wagons.

**Light artillery and horse artillery matériel:**
1 gun and limber and 3 caissons with limbers, or
2 caissons and limbers and 1 store or battery wagon; or
3 field wagons or reel carts.

**4.7" gun, 4.7" howitzer, and 6" howitzer matériel:**
Same as for a 36-ft. car, but one more limber or one more caisson can be added.

**Signal Corps matériel:**
3 field wagons, or 2 instrument and 1 kit wagons; or
2 lance trucks and 1 field or repair wagon.

OPERATION AND MAINTENANCE.

(For general regulations concerning the Service of Military Railways, see Army Regulations and Field Service Regulations.)

199. Whether a road is constructed or merely taken over for military purposes makes no difference in the operation and maintenance of the line.

The **unit of organization** is the **division**; such a division is a section of line from 150 to 300 miles in length, and is self-contained. As to operation and maintenance, the general principles and rules are laid down by the higher authorities, but the details are left to the Division Superintendent to work out as he thinks best. The results show in the economy and efficiency of his division, which are the tests of the soundness of his methods.

200. **Organization and duties.**—The persons in charge of a military railway can be divided into two classes: **Military controlling staff** and **civilian officials.** The military controlling staff will be chosen from engineer officers and others who have had railway experience, and their function is to make known the military desires and to see that the roads are operated so as to attain these ends. Having given their instructions, they allow the civilian officials and employees to work out the technical details in the manner dictated by their railway experience; the military staff will only interfere in cases where they believe that the civil officials are not endeavoring to carry out the military plans, or are not succeeding in doing so.

The organization and **line of responsibility** are shown in fig. 132.

The relation of the military controlling staff to the civilian officials is shown in that figure.

The presence of civilian employees on a military railroad, particularly in the lower grades, is likely to prove a source of friction with the personnel of the service of defense, with the railroad troops, and with troops of all kinds traveling on the line. Furthermore, the lack of military discipline is prone to cause difficulty in strikes, disagreements as to pay and promotion, and individual insubordination and desertion. It will seldom if ever be practicable in the United States to secure a purely military organization, but in the case of railroads operated in occupied foreign territory effort should be made to secure a military organization with fixed military rank, pay, and allowances for all employees, if possible, and in any case for all train crews, dispatchers, yard operatives, and the higher officials. It will seldom be practicable to include laborers or mechanics of construction and repair gangs or those employed in shops, roundhouses, warehouses, etc.

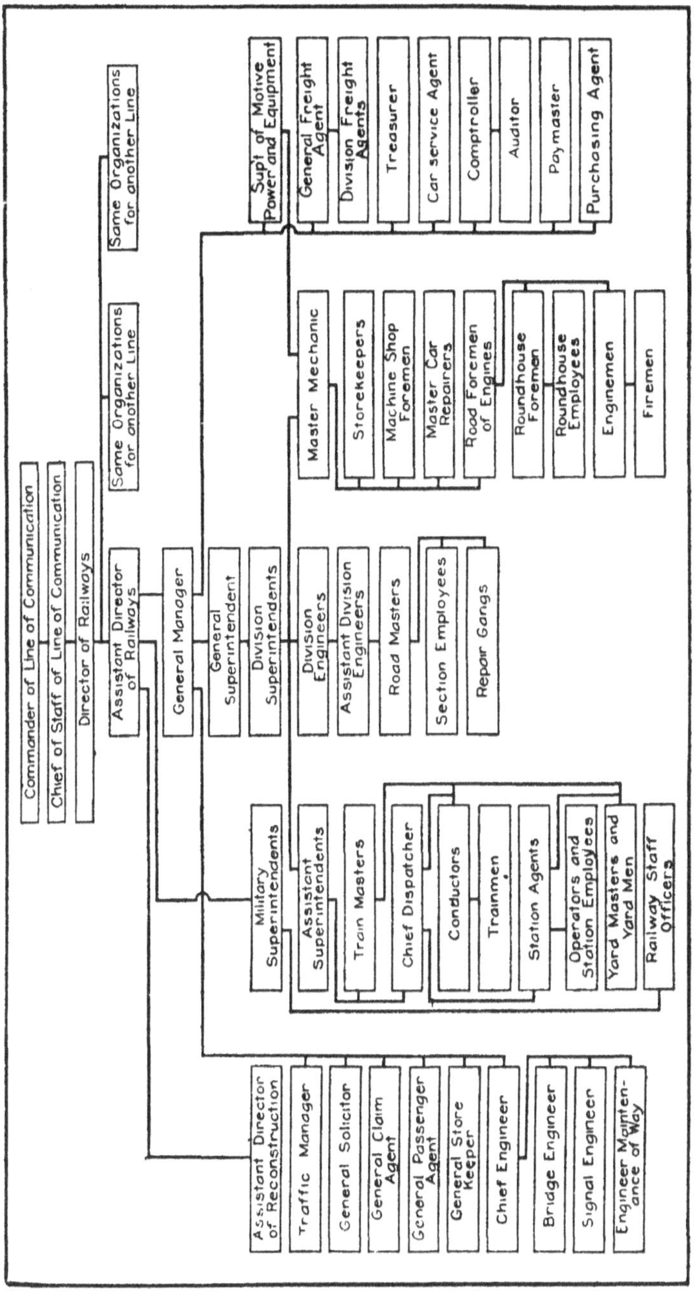
Commander of Line of Communication
Chief of Staff of Line of Communication
Director of Railways
Assistant Director of Railways
Same Organizations for another Line
Same Organizations for another Line
General Manager
General Superintendent
Division Superintendents
Military Superintendents
Assistant Director of Reconstruction
Supt. of Motive Power and Equipment
General Freight Agent
Division Freight Agents
Treasurer
Car service Agent
Comptroller
Auditor
Paymaster
Purchasing Agent
Master Mechanic
Storekeepers
Machine Shop Foremen
Master Car Repairers
Road Foremen of Engines
Roundhouse Foremen
Roundhouse Employees
Enginemen
Firemen
Division Engineers
Assistant Division Engineers
Road Masters
Section Employees
Repair Gangs
Assistant Superintendents
Train Masters
Chief Dispatcher
Conductors
Trainmen
Station Agents
Operators and Station Employees
Yard Masters and Yard Men
Railway Staff Officers
Traffic Manager
General Solicitor
General Claim Agent
General Passenger Agent
General Store Keeper
Chief Engineer
Bridge Engineer
Signal Engineer
Engineer Maintenance of Way

FIG. 132.

No organization has been provided for railway troops in the United States Army. The war organization of the pioneer regiment, which is outlined below, may be adapted to railway troops, special designations, such as wagoner, being maintained in order to facilitate rating as to pay and allowances.

## REGIMENT OF ENGINEER TROOPS.

Commissioned:
- 1 colonel.
- 1 lieutenant colonel.
- 1 captain, adjutant.
- 1 captain, quartermaster.
- 1 captain, engineer.

Enlisted:
- 4 master engineers, senior grade.
- 1 sergeant major.
- 2 supply sergeants.
- 2 color sergeants.
- 1 sergeant bugler.
- 2 sergeants.
- 1 cook.
- 25 wagoners.

And two battalions.
Total: 33 commissioned; 1,036 enlisted.

## BATTALION OF ENGINEER TROOPS.

Commissioned:
- 1 major.
- 1 captain, adjutant.

Enlisted:
- 1 sergeant major.
- 6 master engineers, junior grade.

And three companies.
Total: 14 commissioned; 499 enlisted.

## COMPANY OF ENGINEER TROOPS.

Commissioned:
- 1 captain.
- 2 first lieutenants.
- 1 second lieutenant.

Enlisted:
- 1 first sergeant.
- 3 sergeants, first class.
- 1 mess sergeant.
- 1 supply sergeant.
- 1 stable sergeant.
- 8 sergeants.
- 18 corporals.
- 1 horseshoer.
- 2 buglers.
- 1 saddler.
- 3 cooks.
- 31 privates, first class.
- 93 privates.

Total: 4 commissioned; 164 enlisted.

A regiment of railway troops if organized in time of war from volunteer troops should secure a personnel as follows:

Colonel and three other officers from the Corps of Engineers of the Regular Army; remaining officers should be appointed from men actively engaged in railway work and holding some of the higher positions; e. g., general manager, general superintendent, division superintendent, assistant superintendent, chief engineer, division engineer, signal engineer, engineer maintenance of way, superintendent motive power and rolling stock, master mechanic, general freight agent, general passenger agent, road foreman of engines, train master, road master, superintendent bridges and buildings, car service agent, general storekeeper.

The noncommissioned staff, regimental and battalion, should be selected from such positions as chief clerk, storekeeper, and special foreman. For the enlisted personnel of companies the following classes and approximate numbers of men are suggested as advisable in so far as practicable:

| | | | |
|---|---|---|---|
| Conductors | 8 | Electricians | 4 |
| Brakemen | 14 | Gas enginemen | 2 |
| Enginemen (locomotive) | 10 | Stenographers | 2 |
| Enginemen (stationary) | 4 | Draftsmen | 2 |
| Foremen | 10 | Surveyors | 2 |
| Switchmen | 10 | Car repairers | 4 |
| Oilers | 3 | Clerks | 2 |
| Machinists | 10 | Storekeepers | 3 |
| Operators | 4 | Carpenters | 10 |
| Station agents | 4 | Masons | 3 |
| Freight agents | 4 | Pile-drivermen | 3 |
| Dispatchers | 4 | Plumbers | 2 |
| Yardmasters | 2 | Horseshoer | 1 |
| Trackmen | 8 | Farrier | 1 |
| Bridge carpenters | 10 | Cooks | 4 |
| Bridge builders (steel) | 8 | | |
| Pumpmen | 3 | Total | 164 |
| Linemen | 3 | | |

This organization contains 108 men who may easily be utilized as laborers; if more are required they may be obtained by additional enlistment of laborers enlarging the company, or by detail of troops from other branches.

The transportation and equipment of railway troops should be that provided for an engineer regiment in so far as relates to supply, shelter, and administration; technical equipment with its necessary transportation will be furnished as deemed necessary from the base by the director of railways. Sanitary personnel and equipment should be the same as provided for an engineer regiment.

201. **Duties of the director of railways and his staff.**—The duties of the director of railways of an army and his staff are, to operate the railroads so as to promote the plans of the commanding general, to supply the military knowledge not possessed by the technical railway staff, and to shield the railway operatives and officials from unauthorized **military interference.**

In any large theater of operations there will be one or more independent lines of railway. For military purposes all such lines should be operated as a single system under the director of railways. If only one line exists, the director of railways will act as the military executive of the line. If more than one line exists, he will act as military executor of the system composed of all the lines, and assign an assistant director of railways to each separate line to act as military executive of that line. In the description of duties, etc., that follows it will be assumed that more than one line of railway exists. If two or more lines of communications exist in one theater of operations, they might be operated as separate systems under separate heads **if they were entirely separate lines physically;** but if at any point they come together, they should be operated under a single director of railways. Such a case would be out of the ordinary, but if it did occur, the director of railways should be on the staff of the commanding general of the field forces, and the assistant director of railways in each line of communications would be on the staff of the general commanding the line of communications.

202. **Duties of the director of railways.**—This officer is responsible to his commanding officer for the successful operation and cooperation of all the railroads in his charge. He receives his orders from the chief of staff, and takes the necessary steps to have them executed by his subordinates. He must keep in close touch with his assistant directors and with the higher civil officials of all his railroads. He must make arrangements at home for the prompt and accurate filling of requisitions. He keeps in close touch with the general defense and the armored-train defense of the railways, but the direct control of that defense is under the commander of the district of the line of communications in which the armored trains are operating. He will have such assistants, both military and civil, as efficient operation and maintenance require.

The work on each line will usually be divided into two classes, the **reconstruction** of the line in rear of the army and the **operation and maintenance** of the reconstructed line.

The reconstruction work at the head of each line of railway will be in charge of an assistant director of railways of reconstruction, who is immediately responsible to the assistant director of railways in charge of that particular line of railway, or to the director of railways if only one line exists. Reconstructed line will be turned over to the operating department as rapidly as it is made fit for trains. The reconstruction work will be more or less of a temporary character, suited to passing a few trains at low speed, and will be done by railway troops with such civil or other military assistance as may be available. The more permanent work of reconstruction will be done by the maintenance department in the zone of the line of communications, using such labor, civil or military, as conditions require.

No organization has yet been provided in the United States service for railroad troops. If sudden need for their organization arises, models mav be taken from the organization of foreign armies. In any case they should be armed and equipped as infantry, and lacking other means of raising such troops, infantry companies may be detailed for the duty, transferring thereto as many officers and men who are familiar with railroad work as may be available.

203. **The assistant director of railways** may be called the **military manager** of the road to which he is assigned, the **civil manager** being his close adviser, and the person through whom he controls his civil employees. He is charged with the efficient operation of the line to which he is assigned, including its operation, maintenance, and supply, and he advises the director of railways as to its requirements for defense. He has charge of the **special railway police** on his line.

The **military controlling staff** will decide what affairs will be left entirely to the civilian officials and what ones must be referred to the coordinate military officer for final decision. The assistant director of railways will decide the above points usually after consultation with his military and civilian assistants.

As regards his own immediate line, his duties are similar to those of the director of railways for the entire system, being limited only by the questions that he must submit to the director of railways for decision.

204. **Civil traffic.**—The assistant director of railways of each line, after consultation with his assistants and with the approval of the director of railways, will recommend such civil traffic on his line as will not interfere unduly with the military traffic. Regulations governing such civil traffic will be issued for the different lines by the commander of line of communications and only such traffic will be allowed as the orders permit.

205. **Military assistants** may be assigned to one or more divisions of the line, depending upon the road, and they may be termed the **military superintendents** of such divisions. The **civil superintendents** are their close advisers. They are responsible to the assistant director of railways for the efficient handling of their divisions. They supervise the personnel of their divisions, and must be thoroughly conversant with the possibilities and needs of such divisions. They must keep track, through the car distributor, of all rolling stock, and if cars are not promptly unloaded and released, will call the proper persons at the detaining station to account for it. They must correct all weaknesses in their divisions, or call upon higher authority to do so. They are responsible for the maintenance and the regular military police of their divisions, and for the transportation of troops and supplies within the limits of their divisions. They are responsible that the various stations have the proper sidings, platforms, ramps, stockyards, and watering facilities to fill the military requirements.

206. **Railway staff officers.**—At each **important station** there will be detailed a railway staff officer who will be independent of the commanding officer of any troops that may be stationed at that point and will be on the staff of the military superintendent.

The railway staff officers of stations look after the loading and unloading of troops and supplies at their stations. They keep the military superintendent fully informed as to all the **station requirements.** They are in charge of all railway employees while at that station, and will execute such authority, as a general rule, through the local station agent. They issue, on proper authority, **all transportation** from their stations, and forward with their indorsement **all communica-**

tions from the local officers to the railway officials. They are responsible that all cars are promptly unloaded and released, and that no empty cars are asked to be sent to their stations before the cargo will be ready for loading. They make arrangements for **food and hot coffee** for troops en route through their station, upon notification from proper authority.

The railway staff officer reports daily, to the military superintendent of his division, the organizations or parts of organizations that depart from or arrive at his station, and includes the following data: Destination, or starting point; the number of officers, men, guns, horses, vehicles, and the amount of supplies in each train; the number of the train, and the time of its departure or arrival.

The military superintendent consolidates all these reports for each week, and renders this **consolidated report** to the assistant director of railways, with such other information with reference to the movements as may be desired.

At the base the duties of this officer become very great and important because the greater part of all shipments originate or end at that place. The railway staff officer at the destination should always be promptly notified of the probable arrival of troops or animals in any large numbers or supplies in large quantities.

The railway staff officer is responsible that no **railway buildings** or **property** are used by the troops at the station, when necessary for railway use; and before permission is given for such military use, authority will be obtained from the military superintendent.

Upon the **arrival of troop trains**, the railway staff officer will be present and give the commanding officer on the train all information and proper assistance that he is able to give.

The railway staff officer will pay particular attention to the daily telegraphic car reports. (See par. 234.)

207. **Civil officials.**—On a road operated for military purposes, the head official is the **general manager.** The president, vice president, etc., are temporarily replaced by the higher military officers. The **general manager** is responsible for the entire working of the road and for all maintenance and construction thereon. He has the number of assistants necessary to relieve him of all minor details and leave him free to keep a keen oversight of the entire working of the road.

Fig. 132 shows the various other officials who report to him. Their duties are explained in the following paragraphs:

208. The **general solicitor** of the road is the legal adviser of the general manager, and even in time of war there would be many occasions on which this official would be necessary. He has the necessary number of assistants, and all **local attorneys** for the road report to him.

209. The **general claim agent** has charge of all **claims** made against the road for damages. He investigates all such claims, procures all available information and witnesses to defend the case, and recommends the action to be taken. His function will be very important on a commercial line taken for military purposes, as claims against the Government will arise and agreement as to facts at the time of occurrence will save litigation at a later period.

210. The **general passenger agent** in time of peace is charged with the duty of procuring all passenger business that he can for the road. **In time of war** this duty would lapse, but he would be utilized in connection with the shipment of troops and the handling of passenger traffic generally.

211. The **general storekeeper** has charge of and issues all stores from the central storehouse. He keeps a supply of stores that will meet all possible needs of the road. The storekeepers at various points on the railroad make requisitions on him through the general manager and render their returns to him.

212. The **chief engineer** of the road is the engineer adviser to the general manager. He plans and has charge of all new construction, and he keeps a general oversight of the division engineers and the signal engineer. He has no control over the assistant director of railways of reconstruction

213. The **superintendent of motive power and equipment** has charge of all the rolling stock belonging to the road. He is charged with all repairs to locomotives, machinery, cars, and other equipment. He investigates all **failures of engines.** He keeps complete **records of performances** of locomotives and cars. He has charge of the discipline of all his employees, except enginemen and firemen who may violate operating department rules while on the road.

214. The **purchasing agent** of the road buys all supplies, equipment, etc., that may be used on the road, upon authorization of the general manager.

The **treasurer** is responsible for all funds received for operating the road and for the disbursement ol all moneys.

215. The **comptroller** has the final decision as to the correctness of expenditures and accounts, and he allows or disallows accounts according to their merits and the rules of the road. The treasurer and comptroller would be used to keep the account between the railway and the Government while the road is under military control.

216. The **general freight agent** of the road in time of war would have few of the duties that this official has in time of peace, but he will be useful to the general manager in the **handling of military freight.**

217. The **signal engineer** is under the chief engineer. He has charge of construction and maintenance of all **signals and telegraphs** and other work requiring electrical knowledge.

218. The **car-service agent** is charged with the proper distribution of rolling stock to the various parts of the road. He keeps track of all cars sent to foreign roads, the mileage of all cars on the road, and the length of time that foreign cars are held on the road.

219. In the operating department, the next official in rank to the general manager and his assistants is the **general superintendent,** who has charge of the operation, maintenance, and discipline of the road, the arrangement of time schedules, the distribution of motive power, and such other duties as may be assigned to him by the general manager. He has such assistants as may be necessary. The officials that report to him are shown in fig. 132. His control is through the various division superintendents.

220. **Duties of division superintendents.**—The road will be divided into divisions, and each division is in general charge of a **division superintendent.** These superintendents are directly under the general superintendent and his assistants. They have complete charge of their divisions, and are responsible to the general superintendent and general manager for the proper operation and maintenance of their divisions. **Matters of construction** that come under the division engineer are not under the division superintendent, and the subject of **repairs to rolling stock and equipment** is handled by the master mechanic direct with the superintendent of motive power and equipment and is not under the division superintendent.

While a division, from an operating standpoint, should be from 150 to 300 miles in length, the economic length of run with a single train crew for freight trains is from 90 to 140 miles, and for passenger trains about 150 to 200 miles. The length is largely fixed by the time consumed by the trains in running over it. Long divisions must therefore be subdivided into lesser units for train crews, but the division is the smallest self-contained unit on a railway.

The division superintendent is assisted in his work by one or more **assistant superintendents, division engineers, and master mechanics.**

221. Each **assistant superintendent** is charged witn such duties as the superintendent may assign to him. In general, the division will be divided and each assistant superintendent will nave charge of one such subdivision. He handles all train movements and has charge of trainmen, agents and operators. He is charged with the **discipline** of these men and with that of employees in the master mechanic's department for the violation of operating-department rules.

222. Each **division engineer** is charged with all maintenance and construction work on his division. For **maintenance** he is responsible to the superintendent, and for **construction work** to the chief engineer of the road.

The division engineer has the necessary number of assistants, and in general, the work under his office will be subdivided into **bridges and buildings, track work, masonry work, and water supply.** Each of these departments will be under a competent foreman, who will have charge of the tools and supplies necessary to carry out his work on the division. A fuller description of his department will be found under "Maintenance of Way," par. 494 et seq.

223. Each **master mechanic** is charged with the **inspection and repair** of all rolling stock. In all matters aside from the operating-department rules, the enginemen and firemen are directly under him. He has charge of the inspection department and of all roundhouses, machine shops, car shops, storehouses, etc., and the employees therein are under his orders. For all subjects that arise in his department on the road, he is responsible to the superintendent. Aside from this, he is under the direct supervision of the superintendent of motive power and equipment. He is responsible that all locomotives are in condition to haul their **tonnage rating** (par. 175).

The master mechanic is assisted in his work by one or more **traveling engineers, or road foremen of engines,** who look after the proper handling of the locomotives on his division and investigate accidents and failures that occur on the road.

Each roundhouse and shop is in charge of a foreman, who is responsible for the discipline of the shop and the employment of the necessary workmen, etc.

224. The **storekeepers** at various points are under the master mechanic. They issue supplies on requisitions signed by any division officer, and in an emergency will issue supplies direct, without the necessary approval, taking the proper receipts for the same.

225. The **assistant superintendents** are assisted by the necessary number of **train masters** and **dispatchers.** The **train masters** travel over their divisions and look after the movement of trains and the actions of trainmen and yardmen. They accompany all important shipments or movements of freight or troops over their divisions, and see that the movements take place promptly and properly. They recommend any discipline that may be necessary, and can issue orders for trains when they think necessary. They are directly under the assistant superintendent, but can receive orders from any higher officials. They give special attention to the prompt and regular movement of traffic and see that the full number of cars are moved by each locomotive, and that no more trains are run than are necessary. They inspect and report on the cleanliness of the passenger trains, and investigate delays in trains, as well as delays in loading and unloading of cars. In **case of an accident,** they proceed to the scene of the accident and take general charge in clearing up the road and protecting the wrecked property. They perform such other duties as may be assigned to them by the proper authority.

226. The **chief dispatcher** has entire charge of the movement of trains over his division, unless the train master interferes for some special reason. He distributes the cars and motive power; he places and displaces operators and subordinate dispatchers, subject to the approval of the division superintendent and of the signal engineer. He has charge of all telegraph matters and movement of trains by telegraph over his division. He sees that all train orders are issued according to prescribed forms, and gives special attention to the condition of the telegraph equipment on his division. He sees that only one person issues train orders over any territory at one time. He is responsible that all locomotives are worked up to their full tonnage rating.

227. **Train dispatchers** receive their instructions from the chief train dispatcher. They are assigned to certain subdivisions and issue orders governing the movement of trains over such subdivisions. They see that such orders are properly transmitted and recorded. They keep a record of the movement of all trains, or locomotives, over their subdivisions. They order the necessary number of locomotives in time to be ready to move when the train is made up. **Train orders** and **locomotive orders** are kept separate. One dispatcher keeps a book showing the

**telegraphic address** of every official and lineman that may be out of his office working along the division, so that they may be found if needed. On **double-track work,** the dispatcher's main duty is to see that the trains are kept moving and that no unnecessary delays occur. On **single-track work,** the position of train dispatcher is much more important than on double-track work, on account of the constant danger from collision in case of carelessness. He arranges the proper **meeting** and **passing** places for all trains, and in case one train is late, changes the meeting places to correspond. On going off duty, he makes a transfer of all orders that have not been fully executed, and sees that such orders are understood by his successor.

228. **Car distributor.**—One operator in the chief dispatcher's office is assigned the duty of distributing cars. He receives the **daily telegraph report** from each station (par. 234), and arranges the information for the chief dispatcher for use as described in par. 452. In this distribution of cars, due attention should be given to empties; otherwise a car famine may exist at one point on the line, while the road may be blocked with empties at another point. To avoid this and keep the entire line properly provided with the kind of cars needed, the chief dispatcher makes a daily report to the car-service agent at headquarters, similar to the one described in par. 234. Car-service agents at headquarters, on receiving these telegraph reports from the various chief dispatchers, distribute cars over the entire line just as the chief dispatcher distributes cars over his division. This report includes passenger as well as freight equipment.

229. **Station agents** are directly under the assistant superintendent and train masters. They have general charge of all station work. They are responsible for the condition of the station, the prompt placing of cars for loading and unloading, and for the proper arrangements for safety and comfort at the stations. They see that the ticket office is kept open at the proper time and that **tickets** are issued only on proper authority and to proper persons. They are responsible that the necessary **signals** are displayed. They are responsible that the track within the limits of their station is in good condition and that the proper switch signals are set. They see that the correct time, time-tables, and official notices are displayed in the depot. They inspect loaded cars, and when satisfied that they are loaded as indicated, they seal the car for shipment. They see that cars are not **overloaded** and that they are **properly loaded.** When cars are received, they promptly notify the persons to whom they are billed, and see that the cars are **promptly placed for unloading.** They will not allow any unauthorized persons to hang about the station, nor near the telegraph office, and they will see that all station employees do their duty properly. They will comply with all instructions from the railway staff officer of the station.

230. Where there is no railway staff officer, the **station agent** performs the railway duties of that officer, and the **commanding officer** of the troops at that station performs his military duties. At **larger stations,** the station agent is assisted by a station master in charge of the station and grounds, and by a ticket agent and such other employees as may be necessary.

231. At **terminals** and at **large stations** the **yard work** is in charge of a **yard-master.** Yardmasters are directly responsible to the station agents and to the train master. They have charge of the employment of yardmen, the movement of trains and engines, and the distribution of cars in the yard under their charge. They see that all trainmen are called for duty on time, and that they report in condition for work. They have charge of the making up of all trains and the distribution of cars in the yards to facilitate the making up of trains. They are responsible that the trains leave on time and that the proper slips, or waybills, accompany each car. They see that all cars are properly secured and keep a record of the **car seals.** They keep a record of the cars received and delivered to other lines, they see that cars are properly placed for loading and unloading, and that all cars needing repairs are sent to the repair tracks or to the shops.

232. **Duties of subordinate employees.**—The duties of employees subordinate to those heretofore mentioned are covered very minutely in the rules and regulations of the operating department issued by all roads. The set issued by the particular road under military operation will probably be found best suited to its requirements. They will be changed when necessary to meet the military require-

ments or where a better rule can be substituted. The Standard Code of Train Rules of the American Railway Association are used by practically all railways in the United States and form a standard for any necessary changes. Changes in the standard code should be made with caution.

233. **Proportions of operatives.**—Based upon 1,017,653 employees on about 190,000 miles of railway in the United States involving the movement of about 140,000 ton-miles per employee, the following table shows the proportional distribution of employees in 18 different classes. (U. S. Dept. Labor Bulletin 37–1901.)

*Classified employees on railways of the United States.*

| Class. | Number per 100 miles of line. | Per cent. | Class. | Number per 100 miles of line. | Per cent. |
|---|---|---|---|---|---|
| General officers | 3 | 0.5 | Section foremen | 17 | 3.3 |
| Other officers | 2 | .4 | Other trackmen | 118 | 22.0 |
| General office clerks | 17 | 3.2 | Switchmen, flagmen, and watchmen | 26 | 5.0 |
| Station agents | 16 | 3.1 | Telegraph operators and dispatchers | 13 | 2.5 |
| Other station men | 47 | 9.0 | Employees on floating plant | 4 | .7 |
| Enginemen | 22 | 4.3 | Other employees and laborers | 65 | 12.4 |
| Firemen | 23 | 4.4 | Total | 529 | 100 |
| Conductors | 16 | 3.1 | | | |
| Other trainmen | 39 | 7.4 | | | |
| Machinists | 17 | 3.2 | | | |
| Carpenters | 24 | 4.6 | | | |
| Other shopmen | 60 | 11.0 | | | |

The foregoing table gives an idea of the number of men in different grades and classes necessary to operate a railway under peace conditions. The proportions would not hold on a line that had to be reconstructed after destruction by an enemy, but as a guide for preliminary preparation it has a certain value. In France the number of employees per 100 miles is about 2.5 times that shown for the United States; in Germany it is about 3.5 times as many.

234. **Daily telegraphic car report.**—Before 8 o'clock in the morning the agent at each station shall report, daily, to the chief dispatcher the following information with reference to freight equipment:

**Local cars:**

(1) *Number of empties wanted during next 24 hours.* State kind and size, destination, loading, and when wanted.
(2) *Number of empties on hand.* State kind and size.
(3) *Cars to unload.* State kind and size (O. H. 24 hours or less).
(4) *Cars to unload.* State kind and size (O. H. 24 to 48 hours).
(Special report for all cars O. H. loaded over 48 hours.)

**Foreign cars:**

(1) *Number of cars wanted.* State kind, size, destination, and when wanted.
(2) *Number of empties on hand.* State kind, initials, number, and size.
(3) *Cars to unload.* State kind, initials, number and size (O. H. 24 hours or less).
(4) *Cars to unload.* State kind, initials, number, and size (O. H. 24 to 48 hours).
(Special report for any car O. H. loaded over 48 hours.)

**Cars ready to move:**

(1) *State number of loads and empties.*
(2) *Cars ready to move over 24 hours.* State number of loads and empties.

The weather report, amount of water in tank, and coal report will be sent in at the same time.

This daily telegraphic car report will be formed into a large blank. The various headings and subheadings across the top will be numbered or lettered, so as to form a code that the operators can use in making this report.

An alphabetic code necessitates the use of only two letters, and hence is quicker. The list of stations is printed down the side of the blank.

On receipt of this information from all points on his division, the chief dispatcher is able to distribute the required empties and arrange to pick up all loaded cars.

A summary of the consolidated report showing the car situation on each division is promptly telegraphed to the car-service agent, who distributes cars among the divisions.

235. **Detaining cars.**—The history of the **Civil War** and the war in **South Africa** both emphasize strongly the necessity for the most stringent orders with reference to the **prompt unloading of cars.** The R. S. O. is authorized to call on the C. O. of the station for the necessary details to unload the cars immediately upon their arrival. If for any reason he can not get such details, or can not unload the cars inside of 24 hours, he will report the facts to the military superintendent by telegraph.

236. **Troop movements.**—When an order for the movement of troops from any station is received at the station, the R. S. O. will immediately find out the following points with reference to the proposed movement from his station:

(1) The number of men and officers.
(2) The number of animals.
(3) The number of wagons, guns, etc.
(4) The amount of supplies that will be carried with the troops.
(5) The destination of such troops.
(6) The time of departure.

He will immediately forward this information by telegraph to the military superintendent with such other information with reference to the movement as he may think necessary.

237. **Inspection of rolling stock.**—The inspection department is directly under the master mechanic; and is divided into two parts—inspection of cars and inspection of locomotives. Certain points along the line are indicated as **inspection points for cars,** and all cars entering such stations are inspected to see that all parts are in proper condition. The wheels are tested by a blow with a hammer to discover defects. At these inspection points cars are marked "O. K." if in good shape, and "B. O." if in bad order, and the initials of the inspector are written below to show who made the inspection. "Bad-order" cars are forwarded to the nearest car-repair station, if practicable; if not, they are set out (their loads may be transferred) and car repairers sent to repair them at that point.

These car inspectors are usually also oilers, and they see that the boxes are properly filled with waste and properly oiled.

In **oiling cars,** the oiler should be careful to get the waste packed well under the journal and in contact with the bottom of the journal. They must not get the boxes too full, as this is a fruitful source of **hot boxes.**

238. **Locomotives are inspected** on their arrival at the roundhouse by regular locomotive inspectors. They go over the locomotive thoroughly and submit a separate report on each. This report is **compared** with the report made by the engineman on the completion of his run, and each is held responsible for a defect reported by the other that is not shown in his report.

This method of inspection of locomotives is especially necessary when the power is pooled. **Power is** known as "**pooled**" when no certain locomotive is assigned to one engineman, but the locomotives are run out of the roundhouse in the order of their coming in. An engineman needs from eight to ten hours' rest after a run, whereas a locomotive, if in good order, can be made ready for another run inside of a couple of hours. In addition to this saving of power, it has been found that the locomotives are in better shape on account of the report required by the engineman and the **check report** made by the locomotive inspector. This pooling of power brings bad results except when used in connection with a double inspection and separate reports.

Any defect reported on a locomotive by either engineman or inspector is promptly repaired in the roundhouse if possible; if not, the locomotive is sent to the shops

**Power** is known as **assigned** when each locomotive is assigned to a single engineman and used by him alone. The advantage of this method is that the engineman takes special pride in his own locomotive and may give it greater care than he will if the locomotive will be out under several other enginemen before he again has occasion to run it. The disadvantage is that the locomotive must lie up unnecessarily long waiting for the crew to rest.

**A combination** of the two methods combines the advantages of both and practically eliminates the disadvantages. This is attained by assigning two locomotives to three crews; under this method, as under the pooling method, cross-inspection by enginemen and locomotive inspectors is imperative for good results.

239. Operators and dispatchers are authorized to use the following **calls and abbreviations:**

1......Wait a minute.
3......Give me correct time.
4......Where shall I repeat from?
5......Close your key; you are breaking.
7......I have business; are you ready?
8......Busy on other wire.
9......To clear the line for train orders, and for operators to ask for train orders; on division, wire will have preference over all signals excepting "21."
12......Do you acknowledge receipt of this order, and do you fully understand it?
13......I hereby acknowledge the receipt of order, and state that I fully understand and will execute the same.
14......What is the weather?
15......Have you any orders?
16......Dispatcher's freight report.
17......Daily weather report.
18......What is the matter?
19......Train order, as provided in par. 334; or call for same.
21......Extreme emergency; on division wire this must have preference over all other business; on through wire will have preference over signals "25" and "34."
23......The following is for you and others.
24......Repeat this back.
25......Time reports of passenger and troop trains to general superintendent (used on through wire); preference of circuit over ordinary and "34" business.
28......Do you get my writing?
29......This is private and must be delivered in sealed envelopes.
31......Train order as provided in par. 334; or call for same.
34......This message is of great importance.
39......This must have preference over all other business on all wires, and will be used *only* by the G. C. and C. of S. of army or of L. of C., the D. R., D. D. R., and A. D. R.
41......This will have preference over all calls on through wires except 39, and will be used only by general manager, general superintendent, and chief engineer.
92......This message should be copied in ink.

Operators must not make use of any signals for business other than that to which such signals are assigned. In other words, signals must **not be given falsely**; as, for instance, making use of "39" for "34" business in order to obtain the wir.

C. & E..Conductor and engineman.
X.......I have displayed my train order signal, and train will be held until ordere is made complete.
H. R....I wish to hold the circuit.
S. D.....Stop displayed.
Usual abbreviations for months and stations.
Initials for signatures of division officials, office calls, and other signals authorized by chief dispatcher.

240. **Signals.**—On every road a system of signals is used to convey certain fixed orders or information. The following, while not universal, are in very common use. Flags of the prescribed color are used by day and lanterns or lamps at night.

241. **Color signals.**

| Color. | Indication. |
|---|---|
| (*a*) Red | Stop. |
| (*b*) Green | Proceed, and for other uses prescribed by the rules. |
| (*c*) Green and red | Proceed with caution, and for other uses prescribed by the rules. |
| (*d*) Green and white | Flag stop (see par. 263), and for other uses prescribed by the rules. |
| (*e*) Blue | Men working under or about cars on that track. |

If the light system of a road taken over for military use **differs from above**, these rules must be changed to correspond to adopted system.

A **fusee** on or near the track **burning red** must not be passed until burned out.

242. **Hand, flag, and lamp signals.**

| Manner of using. | Indication. |
|---|---|
| (*a*) Swung across the track | Stop. |
| (*b*) Raised and lowered vertically | Proceed. |
| (*c*) Swung vertically in a small circle across the track when the train is standing. | Back. |
| (*d*) Swung vertically in a circle at arm's length across the track when the train is running. | Train has parted. |
| (*e*) Swung horizontally back and forth above the head when the train is standing. | Apply air brakes. |
| (*f*) Held at arm's length above the head when the train is standing. | Release air brakes. |

**Any object waved violently** by anyone on or near the track is a signal to stop, unless the engineer has reason to believe it to be a **ruse** to induce him to stop the train, when he will proceed with caution.

### Audible signals.

243. **Locomotive whistle signals** ("○" indicates short blast; "——" indicates long blast).

| Sound. | Indication. |
|---|---|
| (*a*) ○ | Stop. Apply brakes. |
| (*b*) —— —— | Release brakes. |
| (*c*) —— ○○○ | Flagman go back and protect rear of train. |
| (*d*) — — — — | Flagman return from west or south. |
| (*e*) — — — — — | Flagman return from east or north. |
| (*f*) — — — | When running, train parted; to be repeated until answered by the signal prescribed by par. 242 (*d*). Answer to signal prescribed in par. 242 (*d*). |
| (*g*) ○○ | Answer to any signal not otherwise provided for. |
| (*h*) ○○○ | When train is standing, back. Answer to signal prescribed in pars. 242 (*c*) and 247 (*c*). |
| (*j*) ○○○○ | Call for signals. |
| (*k*) — ○○ | To call the attention of trains of the same or inferior class to signals displayed for a following section. |
| (*l*) —— —— ○○ | Approaching public crossings at grade. |
| (*m*) —————— | Approaching stations, junctions, and railroad crossings at grade. |

244. Should a train fail to answer signal 243 (*k*), the train displaying the signals **must stop at once** and not proceed until they are acknowledged. On double track, signal (*k*) will only be used when passing trains.

245. **A succession of short sounds** of the whistle is an alarm for persons or cattle on the track, and calls the attention of trainmen to danger ahead.

246. The **explosion of one torpedo** is a signal to **stop**; the explosion of **two** not more than 200 ft. apart is a signal to **reduce speed** and look out for a stop signal.

**Torpedoes must not be placed** near stations or road crossings where persons are liable to be injured by them.

247. **Air-whistle or bell-cord signals.**

| Sound. | Indication. |
|---|---|
| (*a*) Two | When train is standing, start. |
| (*b*) Two | When train is running, stop at once. |
| (*c*) Three | When train is standing, back the train. |
| (*d*) Three | When train is running, stop at next station. To be answered as per par. 243 (*g*). |
| (*e*) Four | When train is standing, apply or release air brakes. |
| (*f*) Four | When train is running, reduce speed. |
| (*g*) Five | When train is standing, call in flagman. |
| (*h*) Five | When train is running, increase speed. |
| (*j*) Six | When train is running, increase steam heat. |

248. The **headlight will be displayed** to the front of every train by night, but **must be concealed** when a train turns out to meet another and has stopped clear of main track, or is standing to meet trains at end of double track or at junction.

249. **Yard locomotives** will display the headlight to the front and rear by night. When not provided with a headlight at the rear, two white lights must be displayed with a red light between them. Yard locomotives will not display markers.

250. **The following signals** will be displayed, one on each side of the rear of every train, as **markers,** to indicate the rear of the train: By day, a green flag; by night, a green light to the front and side and a red light to the rear, except when the train turns out to be passed by another, and is clear of main track, when a green light must be displayed to the side and rear.

251. **By night,** passenger and freight trains, while upon main track, will display a red light to the rear **in addition to the markers,** and freight trains, when practicable, will display a white light to the front from the top of caboose.

252. **All sections of a train,** except the last, will display two green flags, and in addition two green lights by night, in the places provided for that purpose on the front of the engine.

253. **Extra trains** will display two white flags, and in addition two white lights by night, in the places provided for that purpose on the front of the engine.

254. **When two or more locomotives** are coupled to the head of a train, the leading one only shall display the signals prescribed by pars. 252 and 253.

255. **When cars are pushed** by a locomotive (except when shifting or making up trains in yards), a white light must be displayed on the front of the leading car by night.

256. Each car on a passenger train must be connected with the locomotive by a **communicating signal appliance.**

257. A **blue flag** by day and a **blue light** by night displayed at one or both ends of a locomotive, car, or train, indicates that workmen are under or about it. When thus protected it must not be coupled to or moved. Workmen will display the blue signals and the same workmen are alone authorized to remove them. Other cars must not be placed on the same track so as to intercept the view of the blue signals, without first notifying the workmen.

258. A **green and red flag** by day, and in addition a **green and red light** by night, placed beside the track on the engineman's side, indicates that the track 3,000 ft. distant is in condition for speed of but **6 miles per hour** and the speed of a train will be controlled accordingly.

259. A **green flag** by day, and in addition a **green light** by night, placed on the engineman's side at a point beyond the slow track, indicates that **full speed** may be resumed.

260. **Main-track switch targets** will show **green** when the switch is set for the main track, and **red** when set for sidings, crossings, or junction tracks. All other switch targets will show white or green.

261. A **slow board** placed alongside the track, reading "Reduce speed to —— miles per hour," will indicate the rate of speed at which the track may be used at a point 3,000 ft. distant from such slow board. The rate of speed indicated on the slow board must not be exceeded. Beyond the point to be protected will be placed a sign reading "Resume full speed." **A green and red light** and a **green light,** respectively, will be suspended from these boards at night.

262. A signal **imperfectly displayed,** or the absence of a signal at a place where a signal is usually shown, must be regarded as a stop signal and the fact reported to the assistant superintendent.

263. The **combined green and white** signal is to be used to stop a train only at the flag stations indicated on the schedule of that train. When it is necessary to stop a train at a point that is not a flag station for that train, a red signal must be used.

TIME.

264. Trains will be operated on **standard time**, when standard time is available. Otherwise, a certain clock will be used, and its time used as a standard.

The clocks and watches used in the operation of the road must conform to the adopted time.

The time will be **sent over the road** at least once daily.

265. **All watches** of employees **will be examined** and certified to by some officer or watch inspector, who will certify to the condition and kind of watch carried by each employee.

OPERATIONS OF TRAINS

266. Trains are operated so as to keep them a certain distance apart for safety. This distance is measured either by a **time interval** or a **space interval.** The various systems receive their names from the kind of interval used and the method of maintaining them. The following are the best-known systems:

Time interval { Telegraphic orders.
Telephonic orders.

Space interval, i. e., block system { Absolute.
Permissive.

- Manual block system.
  - Simple manual block system.
  - Controlled manual block system.
    - Lock and block form.
      - Simple communication between stations.
      - Communication between stations and partial electrical track protection.
      - Communication between stations and complete electrical track protection.
    - Staff form.
      - Single staff.
      - Half and half.
- Automatic block system.

267. **Time interval.**—Operating trains upon this method involves train dispatching and is usually known as the **train order method.** These orders govern the train movement from one station to another where orders for further movement are received. The meeting and passing points are given for other trains. The train can be stopped at any intermediate point by directing the operator at that station to display his train order signal. Trains are held a certain distance apart forming the time interval. The system is inadequate and unsafe under fast and heavy traffic conditions. The orders are issued by telegraph or telephone. The former is the older and was universal until a few years ago, but the telephone has to-day largely displaced the telegraph owing to the greater facility and speed and safety in the transmission of orders. This system has become efficient through the selective method of signaling to one or more operators whereby there is no time lost in ringing up the one or more persons desired. The same forms of train orders are used with both the telephone and telegraph .

To obviate the issuance of train orders for trains which run regularly every day, a time table is made up covering the regular movements. A train included therein will operate habitually on this schedule and hence require train orders only to assist it when it or others can not meet the schedule conditions or to provide for movements of other trains not included in the time table.

268. **Space interval.**—As the name implies, the interval between trains in this method of operation is measured by distance instead of time. The road is divided into sections or blocks, into which only one train is allowed full rights at a time Others may be admitted going in the same direction, but they are limited by the presence of the other trains in front of them.

The method is applicable to both single and double track lines and for trains going in the same direction there are two methods, the **absolute** and the **permis-**

**sive** systems. In the former only one train is allowed in a block at one time; in the latter, one or more trains, with certain time intervals, may be allowed in the same block under a **caution card** or **clearance card** warning them of the other train ahead in the block. The length of the blocks varies from one mile to five or six miles.

269. **Simple manual block system.**—In this system the operator at station C ascertains if the block CD is clear, and if so, he admits the train into CD, notifying operator at D that he is doing so. D ascertains if DE is clear, and if so, lowers his signal and allows the train to pass. If not clear, he holds his signal against the train, which can not proceed until the block is clear. The method is controlled by telegraph or telephone communication. There is no lock system. The system is only a step in the right direction.

270. **Controlled manual block system—Lock and block.**—In this system there is electrical communication between the block signals at stations B and C and at C and D, as well as between the operators. By agreement between C and D, operator C opens his block and allows the train to pass C; the block at C then automatically locks at danger and remains there until the train passes the block at D. Permissive blocking will allow another train to follow, with a caution card, after a certain time interval.

271. **Staff system.**—In its simplest form this consists in the operator at C giving a staff to the conductor of one train, who carries it to the next station, D, turns it over to the operator there, who delivers it to the next train in the opposite direction, as authority to proceed back to C. The objections and delay in this are obvious. The electrical staff system consists of instruments at each station, each electrically connected to the next station on each side. When a train at C desires to go to D, the operator at C, by agreement with the one at D and mutual action, is able to remove a staff from his instrument. He gives this to the conductor, who proceeds to D. Meantime the staff instruments at both C and D are locked, and no staff can be taken out until the staff is delivered at D and placed in that instrument. Either one of the operators can then again release the other's instrument for another train movement.

A jointed staff of two parts for both conductor and engineman is a guard against the dangers arising from a train breaking in two. A many-jointed staff is used in the permissive blocking, a part being given to each train in the block. The blocks at C and D remain locked until the complete rejointed staff has been returned to the instrument at D. An adaptation permits the staff to be received or delivered while the train is in motion as trains catch mail sacks.

272. **Automatic block system.**—This system is especially applicable to a double-track line but can be applied to single track also. The towers of the signals carrying the arms are at convenient distances apart. As soon as the rails are cross connected beyond the tower the arm is moved to the danger position and stays there till the last wheels leave that block. Usually they also affect the second signal in rear, moving its arm to the caution position. This system is necessarily a permissive one as a signal may be out of order and a train can proceed with caution after waiting a prescribed time for the signal to clear the line. On a single-track line this system must protect the train from the front as well as from the rear and must also give that protection at the next siding so that an opposing train can take the siding and get out of the way. This system is not usual on single-track lines, but by using automatic blocks between stations with the manual system at stations the capacity of a single-track line has been estimated to have increased 30%.

273. **Movements of trains.**—Freight and passenger trains are usually divided into classes, and each class has certain rights over inferior classes; one direction is also made superior to the other.

Trains of any class going in the superior direction are superior to trains of the same class going in the inferior direction.

First-class trains are usually regular passenger trains; second-class trains are usually quick-dispatch, or time, freights, third-class trains are usually dead freights, empties, or local freights. Extra trains will be given such rights, by train orders, as the chief dispatcher or his superiors may direct. Some of the more general regulations governing train movements are given in the following paragraphs.

Complete sets can readily be prepared from those now in use by any of two or three of the leading railways. They all follow very closely the American Railway Associations Standard Code previously referred to.

274. A train must not leave its initial station on any division (or district), or a junction, or pass from double to single track, until it has been ascertained whether all trains due, which are superior or of the same class, have arrived or left.

275. A train leaving its initial station on each division, when a train of the same class in the same direction is **overdue,** will proceed on its own schedule and the overdue train will follow at least **10 minutes later.**

276. **An inferior train** must keep out of the way of a superior train by the amount of time indicated in the time-table. A train failing to clear the main track in the time required in the time-table must **protect itself** by a flagman, who will go back a sufficient distance to insure protection. When recalled, he will return to his train, first complying with par. 322 when the conditions require it.

277. When a train **stops or is delayed on the main line,** similar precaution will be taken; and if danger exists from the front, a flagman will be sent out in that direction.

278. At **meeting points of trains** of the same class, the inferior train must clear the main track 5 minutes before the leaving time of the superior train. If necessary to back into siding, it will protect itself as hereinbefore provided.

279. **When extra trains meet,** the train of the superior direction will hold the main line unless otherwise directed. The train holding the main line will adjust the switch for the opposing train. At meeting points between trains of **different classes,** the inferior train must take the siding and clear the main line at least **5 minutes** ahead of the other's time.

280. **An inferior train** must keep at least **10 minutes** off the time of a superior train in the same direction.

281. **Trains must stop** at schedule meeting or passing stations if the train to be met or passed is of the same class, unless the switches are right and the track clear.

282. Trains should stop **clear of the switch** used by the train to be met, or passed, in going on the siding.

283. When the expected train of the same class is not found at the schedule meeting or passing station, the **superior train** must approach all sidings prepared to stop until the expected train is met or passed.

284. When trains meet by special order or time-table regulation, the conductors and enginemen will inform each other what train they are by word of mouth.

285. Unless some form of block signal is used, trains in the same direction must keep at least **10 minutes apart,** except in closing up at stations.

286. A train must not arrive at nor leave a station in **advance of its scheduled time.** At schedule passing stations between trains of the same class, the train to be passed, unless otherwise directed by special order, will remain at that point until the expected train has passed.

287. A train which **overtakes a superior train,** or train of the same class, so **disabled** that it can not proceed, will pass it if practicable, and if necessary will assume the schedule and take the train orders of the disabled train, proceed to the next open telegraph office, and there report to the assistant superintendent. The **disabled train** will assume the schedule and take the train orders of the last train with which it has exchanged, and will, when able, proceed to and report from the next open telegraph office.

288. A train must not display signals for a following section nor an extra train be run without orders from the chief dispatcher.

289. Trains must approach the end of the double track, junctions, railroad crossings at grade, and drawbridges prepared to stop, unless the switches and signals are right and the track is clear.

290. **All trains must stop** not less than 200 ft. nor more than 800 ft. before crossing any railroad at grade, except where **interlocking signals** are in use.

291. **Both engineman and fireman** must see signals at block stations, railroad crossings, drawbridges, and junctions, and communicate with each other the position of the signals.

292. When a train is to **back out of a siding,** the flagman must go a sufficient distance to the rear to insure full protection.

293. Before a train crosses over to or obstructs another main track, unless otherwise provided, it must be protected on that track.

294. **When a flagman goes back** to protect the rear of a train, the conductor can assign any one of the trainmen to perform his duties until he returns.

295. In case a **passenger train is due** within 10 minutes, or an approaching train is within sight or hearing, the flagman must remain out until it arrives.

296. **If a train should part** while in motion, trainmen must, if possible, prevent damage to the detached portions. The signals prescribed by pars. 242(*d*) and 243(*f*) must be given, and the front portion of the train kept in motion until the detached portion is stopped.

297. The **front portion** will then go back to recover the detached portion, running with caution and following a flagman. The **detached portion** must not be moved or passed until the front portion comes back.

298 **Messages or orders** respecting the movement of trains or the condition of track or bridges must be in writing and in train-order form.

299. Switches must be left set and locked for the main track after having been used.

300. Conductors are responsible for the position of the switches used by them and their trainmen, except where switch tenders are stationed.

301. A switch must not be left open for a following train, unless in charge of a trainman of such train.

302. **When a train backs** in on a siding to meet or be passed by another train, the engineman, when his locomotive is in the clear, must also see that the switch is properly set for the main track.

303. Enginemen must know that switches are properly set before they pull into or out of sidings or other tracks.

304. Trainmen or other employees **must not unlock** main-track switches, nor stand within 20 ft. of such switch on the approach of or during the passing of any train, and when practicable, on single track, he will stand on the **opposite side of the track** from the switch lever.

305. No attempt should be made to close the switch until the last wheels are off the switch rails. The person who locks the switch must grasp the chain and pull the lock to see that it is securely fastened, and after having done so, must look at the switch rails and know that they are in their proper position.

306. Both switches to a crossover between main tracks must be locked for the main tracks during the passing of any train on the opposite track, and must not be unlocked or opened until the train is ready to use the crossover.

307. If any switch upon the main track is found **to be defective,** or to have a **defective lock,** the switch must be secured and reported at once by telegraph to the assistant superintendent by the conductor, engineman, or other person who may have discovered it.

308. Both conductor and engineman are responsible for the safety of their trains, and under conditions not provided for by the rules, must take every precaution for their protection.

309. **In all cases of doubt or uncertainty, the safe course must be taken.**

310. Where **yard limits** are defined by limit boards, no locomotive or train is permitted to occupy main line in the time of regular trains without protection. At such points extra trains must approach at reduced speed, prepared to stop within their vision.

311. It must be understood that a train is **officially due to arrive** at a station upon its schedule departing time from the preceding station.

312. **When signals** displayed for a section **are taken down** at any point before that section arrives, the conductor will, if there be no other provision, notify the operator or agent in writing, who will immediately display the train-order signal and keep it in danger position for the benefit of opposing trains until the arrival of the train so flagged, and he must personally see that opposing trains are fully notified.

313. If the signals displayed for a section are taken down where there is no operator or agent, a flagman must be left for the purpose of notifying all opposing trains of the same or inferior class leaving such points that the section for which the signals were displayed has not arrived.

314. Conductors and enginemen taking down signals for a following section, as above, must not rely solely on notice being given at said station, but must themselves notify other trains met until they arrive and register at the next registering station.

315. **Work extras** will be assigned **working limits** by train order daily. In case orders should be given to a point outside of the working limits for water, fuel, or any other cause, the "working order" is thereby canceled, unless the subsequent order expressly states the contrary.

316. **Conductors of work extras** must know that all trains due have arrived before they start out with the work train. They must also leave a memorandum every evening with the nearest telegraph operator, stating where the train will be at work during the following day, and this memorandum must be forwarded by telegraph to the chief dispatcher.

317. **Work extras** will be assigned working limits, and when operating upon **double track** must move, within these limits, with the current of traffic, unless train orders otherwise direct.

318. No freight train shall pass an open telegraph office not controlled by telegraph block system, except as provided by division time-tables, whether or not train-order signal be displayed, until the conductor and engineman have received orders from the train dispatcher, or a **release** or **clearance**, as the case may require, from the operator. Conductors and enginemen of passenger trains will observe the same rule at such telegraph offices as are regular stops for their trains. Extra freight trains will observe the same rule as regular freight trains, but extra passenger trains are not required to make stops solely for this purpose. They will be governed in this respect the same as regular passenger trains. This does not relieve operators from promptly displaying red signals whenever they have orders, or making other necessary efforts to stop trains.

319. A **"clearance"** (see par. 385) will be properly filled out and given, in duplicate, to the conductor and engineman of the train in all cases where the rules governing the movement of trains require conductors to ask for orders, provided the train-order signal is not displayed and no orders have been received for their train.

A clearance should be given in cases where trainmen are required to ask for orders and the train-order signal is not displayed, except as may be provided for by division time-tables.

320. If the train-order signal be displayed, but for another train, a **release** must be given instead of a clearance.

321. A "**release**" (see par. 383) will be properly filled out and given, in duplicate, to the conductor and engineman of a train when held by the train-order signal, in case no order has been received for their train, except as provided for by division time-tables.

322. **In case of stoppage between stations,** the flagman must immediately go back with not less than two torpedoes, and a red flag by day or a red and a white lantern and two red fusees by night, and at night place a lighted red fusee in the center of the track 500 ft. behind the rear of the train, proceeding by day or night to a point not less than ¾ mile distant from rear of train until he reaches a point where the danger signal can be seen not less than ¼ mile by the engineman of any approaching train. The **flagman will at once** place one torpedo on the rail on the engineman's side, and will remain at such point until the train has arrived, or until he is recalled. The engineman of approaching train, on seeing the flagman's signal, will immediately call for brakes, as evidence that the signal has been seen. When the flagman has been recalled, and no approaching train has arrived, he will place a second torpedo on the rail 200 ft. nearer his train than the first and return with all possible dispatch to his train. On exploding one torpedo, only, the approaching train will be brought to a full stop, and thereafter proceed with extreme caution, expecting to find some obstruction on the track. When a second torpedo is exploded, the engineman will know that the flagman has been recalled, and will proceed cautiously, keeping a sharp lookout for the train ahead. Immediately on the sound of the whistle recalling flagman, if there is not a clear view to the rear for ¼ mile from the rear of train, the train should be moved ahead at a speed of not less than 6 miles per hour until a point is reached where the track is straight for ¼ mile in the rear of train, always bearing in mind that the time of the flagman's return is the **period of greatest risk.** When the character of the road or weather makes it necessary, the flagman shall go a greater distance with the signals, so as to insure absolute safety. It must be distinctly understood that the conductor of the train, or the engineman of a locomotive running light, is held responsible for the safety of his train or locomotive. **When any train has been stopped** by a preceding train in the manner above mentioned, the conductor of the last train must use the same precautions with regard to any following trains as those heretofore described. When it is necessary to protect the front of a train, the same precaution shall be observed by the front brakeman or fireman. Conductors are held responsible for the proper protection of their trains under all circumstances.

323. A train must **not** be allowed to **stand on a curve** between stations, if practicable to avoid it.

324. **In addition to the above protection,** a red fusee will be considered an extra precaution, and will be used under circumstances requiring the same. Should a train, for any cause, be required to reduce its speed between stations, or at unusual points, a red fusee must be lighted and placed upon the track as an additional protection for the following trains, to insure a time limit between trains of not less than 5 minutes.

325. If a conductor or engineman discovers anything **wrong with the track,** bridges, or culverts which would be likely to cause an accident to a following train, he must leave a flagman, call the section men, and notify the train dispatcher by wire.

### RULES FOR TRAIN MOVEMENT BY ORDERS.

326. If all trains run on a division were regular trains, and all such trains were always on time, trains could be run on the time-table without any assistance or intervention of the train dispatcher. This is manifestly impossible, and a system **of telegraphic control** is used on all roads to control the movement of trains. Any train movement not covered by the time-table or by some rule of the road must be ordered by the train dispatcher. Each train leaves the terminal with orders to go to a certain point, where further orders will be received. The train proceeds to that point, unless sooner stopped by signal at some intervening point for different orders. Upon reaching the designated station, or if stopped (by signal) at some intermediate point, it receives orders that cover its move over another short section of line.

Whenever a regular train is late and can not run on its schedule, other trains are helped along by train orders which change the meeting or passing points of the respective trains for that particular trip.

327. Trains **meet** each other when moving in opposite directions, and they **pass** each other when moving in the same direction.

328. For movements not provided for by time-table, train orders will be issued by authority, and over the signature, of the chief train dispatcher. They must be **brief and clear,** in the **prescribed form** when applicable, and without erasure, alteration, or interlineation.

329. Each train order must be given in the **same words** to all persons or trains addressed.

330. Train orders will be numbered consecutively each day, beginning at midnight.

331. Train orders must be addressed to those who are to execute them, naming the place at which each is to receive his copy. Those for a train must be addressed to the conductor and engineman, and also to anyone who acts as pilot. A copy for each person addressed must be supplied by the operator.

332. Each train order must be written in full in a book provided for the purpose at the office of the chief train dispatcher, and with it recorded the names of those who have signed for the order, the time and the signals which show when and from what offices the order was repeated and the responses transmitted, and the train dispatcher's initials. These records must be made at once, and never from memory or memoranda.

333. Regular trains will be designated in train orders by their train numbers (written in words *and* figures), engine numbers, and conductors' names, as "*2d No. Ten 10 Eng. 504, Smith;*" extra trains, by engine numbers and conductors' names, as "*Extra 798, White,*" with the direction as *North, South, East,* or *West.* **Time in body of the orders** must be written in words and duplicated in figures. Figures must not be surrounded by brackets, circles, or other characters, but appear plainly without accompanying marks.

334. **To transmit a train order,** the signal "31" or "19" must be given to each office addressed, the number of copies being stated, thus: "31 copy 5;" "19 copy 2." A "31" order is not completed until after signed by conductor and operator. A "19" order is completed on signature of operator.

335. A train order to be sent to two or more offices must be **transmitted simultaneously** to as many of them as practicable. The several addresses must be in the order of superiority of trains, each office taking its proper address. When not sent simultaneously to all the order must be sent first to the superior train.

336. When a meeting point is to be made between two trains at a certain station, the order, when practicable, should be sent for said trains to stations at either side of the actual meeting point; also to the operator at the actual meeting point, if a telegraph office.

337. Operators receiving train orders must write them in manifold during transmission, and if they can not at one writing make the requisite number of copies, **must trace others** from one of the copies first made.

Operators required to make new or additional copies of an order will, in every instance, repeat these copies the same as the original order.

338. When a train order has been transmitted, operators must **first set their signals,** then give "X" response (see par. 239), and (unless otherwise directed) repeat it at once from the manifold copy in the succession in which the several offices have been addressed, and then write the time of repetition on the order.

339. Each operator receiving the order should observe whether the others repeat correctly.

340. Those to whom the **"31" order** is addressed, except enginemen, **must read it aloud**, then sign it, and the operator will send their signatures, preceded by the number of the order, to the train dispatcher. The response "O. K." and the time, with his initials, will then be given by the train dispatcher. Each operator receiving this response will then write on each copy "O. K.," the time, train dispatcher's initials, and his own last name in full, and then deliver a copy to each person addressed, except enginemen. The copy for each engineman must be delivered to him personally by the conductor, and the engineman must read it aloud to the conductor before proceeding.

341. When a **"19" order** is received at actual meeting point as per last clause of par. 336 the operator will set his signal, give "X" response, repeat the order, sign his name, and receive "O. K." to same, and after receiving the signature of the conductor will deliver two copies of the order to the conductor of the train first arriving. This rule applies to time and positive meet orders. On a single-track road **a "19" order** is used only to **confer a right** upon a train, and **not to restrict the rights** or the superiority of a train.

Some roads do not use the "19" order form. The safe use of this form requires a highly trained personnel and, in view of this fact, it is probable that form "31" would be the only form used on a military railway.

342. Conductors must **show their orders** to rear brakeman or flagman, and the engineman to the fireman, and (in case of a freight train) to the head brakeman, who are required to read them.

343. A **train order must be acknowledged** by the operator responding: "X; (*number of train order*) to (*train number*)," with the operator's initials and office signal. The operator must then write on the order his initials and the time.

344. **"O. K." must not be given** to a train order for delivery to an inferior train until the "X" response has been sent by the operator who receives the order for the superior train.

345. When the "X" response is given to a train order and before the "O. K." has been received, an order must be treated as a **holding order** for the train addressed, and must not be delivered until it has been repeated and the "O. K." has been given.

346. If the **line fails** before an office has sent the "X" response, the order at that office is of no effect and must be there treated as if it had not been sent.

347. The operator who receives and delivers a train order must preserve the **lowest copy.**

348. For train orders delivered by the train dispatcher, the requirements as to the record and delivery are the same as at other points.

Such orders shall be first written in manifold so as to leave an impression in the record book, from which transmission shall be made.

349. A **train order** to be delivered to a train at a **point not a telegraph station,** or at one at which the telegraph office is closed, must be addressed to:

"*C & E. ...... at ......, care of ......,*" and forwarded and delivered by the conductor or other person in whose care it is addressed. In such cases the "O. K." will be given upon the signature of the person by whom the order is to be delivered, who must be supplied with copies for the conductor and engineman addressed, and a copy upon which he shall take their signatures. This copy he must deliver to the first operator accessible, who must preserve it and at once transmit the signatures of the conductor and engineman to the train dispatcher.

Orders so delivered must be acted on as if "O. K." had been given in the usual way.

For orders which are sent in the manner herein provided, to a train, the superiority of which is thereby restricted, "O. K." must not be given to an inferior train until the signature of the conductor and engineman of the superior train has been received by the train dispatcher.

350. When a train is named in a train order, **all its sections** are included unless particular sections are specified, and each section included must have copies addressed and delivered to it.

351. An operator **must not give the "X"** response to a train order for a train the locomotive of which has passed his train-order signal, until he has ascertained that the conductor and engineman have been notified that he has orders for them.

352. **Train orders once in effect** continue so until fulfilled, superseded, or annulled. Any part of an order specifying a particular movement may be either superseded or annulled.

353. When a conductor or engineman relieves another before completion of a trip, they exchange orders, and before proceeding conductor must compare orders with the new engineman.

354. A train must not leave a terminal without a clearance, release, or train order.

355. A fixed signal must be used at each train-order office, which shall indicate "stop" when trains are to be stopped for train orders. When there are no orders, the signal must indicate "proceed," except when used to keep trains a required distance apart.

356. When an operator **receives an order** for a train, before acknowledging by the "X" response to the train dispatcher the receipt of same he will display his train-order signal at "stop" position; and until the orders have been delivered or annulled, the signal must not be restored to "proceed "

While "stop" is indicated, trains must not proceed without a release (par. 383).

357. Operators must have the proper appliances for hand signaling ready for immediate use if the fixed signal should fail to work properly.

358. If a signal is not displayed at a night office, even a train which has not been notified must stop and ascertain the cause, and report the facts to the train dispatcher from the next open telegraph office.

359. When a semaphore is used, the arm indicates **"stop" when horizontal,** and **"proceed" when in an inclined position.**

360. Operators will promptly record and report to the train dispatcher the time of departure of all trains and the direction of extra trains. They will record the time of arrival of trains and report it when so directed.

### FORMS OF TRAIN ORDERS.

361. The following are the **standard forms** prescribed by the **American Railway Association.** They are applicable to military railway conditions and should be **followed literally.**

362. **Form A.—Fixing meeting points for opposing trains:**

(1) ...... will meet ...... at .......

(2) ...... will meet ...... at ......, ...... at ...... (and so on).

**Examples.**

(1) *No. Three 3 Eng. 96, Jones, will meet Second No. Four 4 Eng. 105, Lane, at Siam.*

(1) *No. Five 5 Eng. 176, White, will meet Extra 95 West, Phillips, at Hongkong.*

(1) *Extra 652 North, Williams, will meet Extra 231 South, Yates, at Yokohama.*

(2) *No. One 1 Eng. 80, King, will meet No. Two 2 Eng. 100, Vilas, at Bombay Second No. Four 4 Eng. 65, Peat, at Siam, and Extra 95 West, Phillips, at Hongkong.*

Trains receiving these orders will run with respect to each other to the designated points, and there meet, in the manner provided by the rules.

363. **Form B.—Directing a train to pass or run ahead of another train:**

(1) ...... will pass ...... at .......

(2) ...... will run ahead of ..... ...... to ......

(3) ...... will pass ...... at ...... and run ahead of ..... ...... to .......

**Examples.**

(1) *No. One 1 Eng. 67, Palmer, will pass No. Three 3 Eng. 105, Seton, at Khartoum.*

(2) *Extra 594 East, Potter, will run ahead of No. Six 6 Eng. 1015, King, Bengal to Madras.*

(3) *No. One 1 Eng. 67, Palmer, will pass No. Three 3 Eng. 105, Seton, at Khartoum and run ahead of No. Seven 7 Eng. 415, Asker, Madras to Bengal.*

When under (1) a train is to pass another, both trains will run according to rule to the designated point and there arrange for the **rear train to pass promptly.**

Under (2) the second-named train must not exceed the speed of the first-named train between the points designated.

364. **Form C.—Giving a train the right over an opposing train:**

(1) ...... has right over ......, ...... to .......

**Examples.**

(1) *No. One 1 Eng. 67, Palmer, has right over No. Two 2 Eng. 85, Bates, Mecca to Mirbat.*

(2) *Extra 37 South, Engle, has right over No. Three 3 Eng. 105, Seton, Natal to Ratlam.*

This order gives the train first named the right over the other train between the points named.

If the trains meet at either of the designated points, the **first-named train** must take the siding, unless the order otherwise prescribes.

365. Under (1), if the second-named train reaches the point last named before the other arrives, it may proceed, keeping clear of the opposing train as many minutes as such train was before required to clear it under the rules.

If the second-named train, before meeting, reaches a point within or beyond the limits named in the order, the conductor must stop the other train where it is met and inform it of his arrival.

Under (2), the regular train must not go beyond the point last named until the extra train has arrived.

When the extra has reached the point last named, the order is fulfilled.

366. The following modification of this form of order will be applicable for giving a work extra the right over all trains in case of emergency:

(3) Work extra ...... has right over all trains between ...... and ...... from ...... m. to ...... m.

**Example.**

*Work extra 275, Smith, has right over all trains between Manila and Honolulu from Seven 7 p. m. to Twelve 12 midnight.*

This gives the work extra the exclusive right between the points designated between the times named.

367. **Form E.—Time orders:**

(1) ...... will run ...... late ...... to ......
(2) ...... will run ...... late ...... to ...... and ...... late ...... to ......, etc.
(3) ...... will wait at ...... until ...... for ......

**Examples.**

(1) *No. One 1 Eng. 67, Palmer, will run twenty 20 mins. late, Joppa to Mainz.*

(2) *No. One 1 Eng. 67, Palmer, will run twenty 20 mins. late, Joppa to Mainz, and fifteen 15 mins. late, Mainz to Muscat, etc.*

(3) *No. One 1 Eng. 67, Palmer, will wait at Muscat until Ten 10 a. m. for No. Two 2 Eng. 89, Willits.*

368. (1) and (2) make the schedule time of the train named, between the points mentioned, as much later as stated in the order, and any other train receiving the order is required to run with respect to this later time as before required to run with respect to the regular schedule time. The time in order should be such as can be easily added to the schedule time.

Under (3) the train first named must not pass the designated point before the time given unless the other train has arrived. The train last named is required to run with respect to the time specified as before required to run with respect to the regular schedule time of the train first named.

369. **Form F.—For sections:**

(1) ...... will display signals ...... to ...... for ......

**Examples.**

*Eng. 20, Smith, will display signals and run as First No. One 1 London to Paris.*

*No. One 1 Eng. 67, Palmer, will display signals London to Dover for Eng. 85, King.*

*Second No. One 1 Eng. 105, King, will display signals London to Dover for Eng. 90, Roberts.*

370. This form may be modified as follows:

*Engs. 70, Creighton, 85, King, and 90, Knox, will run London to Dover as First, Second, and Third No. One 1 respectively.*

Under these examples, the engine last named will not display signals.

371. **To annul a section** for which signals have been displayed over a division or any part thereof when no train is to follow the signals, Form K must be used.

372. **Form G.—Extra trains:**

(1) Eng. ...... will run extra ...... to ...... .
(2) Eng. ...... will run extra ...... to ...... and return to ...... .

**Examples.**

(1) *Eng. 99, Jones, will run extra Berber to Gaza.*

(2) *Eng. 99, Jones, will run extra Berber to Gaza and return to Cabul.*

A train receiving this order is not required to protect itself against opposing extras unless directed by order to do so, but must keep clear of all regular trains as required by rule.

(3) Eng. ...... will run extra leaving ...... on ......, as follows, with right over all trains:

Leave ...... .
Leave ...... .
Arrive ...... .

### Example.

(3) *Eng. 77, Wilson, will run extra leaving Turin on Thursday, February 17, as follows, with right over all trains:*

*Leave Turin Eleven thirty 11.30 p. m.*
*Leave Pekin Twelve twenty-five 12.25 a. m.*
*Leave Canton One forty-seven 1.47 a. m.*
*Arrive Rome Two twenty-two 2.22 a. m.*

This order may be varied by specifying the kind of extra and the particular trains over which the extra shall not have the right. Trains over which the extra is given the right must clear the time of the extra 10 minutes. The train dispatcher may increase the clearance time at his discretion.

373. **Form H.—Work extra:**

(1) Work extra......will work......until......between......and.......

### Examples.

(1) *Work Extra 292, Smith, will work Seven 7 a. m. until Six 6 p. m. between Berne and Turin.*

374. The working limits should be as short as practicable, to be changed as the progress of the work may require. The above may be combined thus:

(a) *Work Extra 292, Smith, will run Berne to Turin and work Seven 7 a. m. until Six 6 p. m. between Turin and Rome.*

When an order has been issued to "work" between designated points, no other extra shall be authorized to run over that part of the track without a definite meeting order with the work extra.

When it is anticipated that a work extra may be where it can not be reached for orders, it will be directed to report for orders at a given time and place, and a meeting order issued with other extra.

375. To enable a work extra to work upon the time of a regular train, the following form may be used:

(b) *No. Fifty-five 55 Eng. 342, Jones, will wait at Berne until Six 6 p. m., for Work Extra 292, King.*

A work extra receiving this order will work upon the time of the train mentioned in the order as per par. 279.

A train receiving this order must not pass the designated point before the time given unless the work extra has arrived.

376. **Form J.—Holding order:**

(1) Hold............

### Examples.

(1) *Hold No. Two 2 Eng. 481, Palmer.*
(2) Hold all eastbound trains.

This order will be addressed to the operator, and acknowledged in the usual manner. It must be respected by conductors and enginemen of trains thereby directed to be held as if addressed to them.

377. When a train has been so held, it must not proceed until the order to hold is annulled, or an order given to the operator in the form:

"*......may go.*"

Form J will only be used when necessary to hold trains until orders can be given, or in case of emergency.

378. **Form K.—Annulling a regular train; or section:**

(1) ......of......is annulled......to.......
(2) ......due to leave...... ......, is annulled......to.......

**Examples.**

(1) *No. One 1 Eng. 392, Smith, of Feb. 29, is annulled Alaska to Halifax.*
(2) *No. Three 3 Eng. 768, Wilson, due to leave Naples Saturday, Feb. 29, is annulled Alaska to Halifax.*

The train annulled loses both right and class between the points named, and must not be restored under its original number between those points.

379. **Form L.—Annulling an order:**

(1) Order No....... is annulled.
(2) Order No.......to......at....is annulled.

If an order which is to be annulled has not been delivered to a train, the annulling order will be addressed to the operator, who will destroy all copies of the order annulled but his own, and write on that:

*Annulled by Order No........*

**Examples.**

(1) *Order No. Ten 10 is annulled.*
(2) *Order No. Ten 10 to C. & E. No. Two 2, at Alaska, is annulled.*

An order that has been annulled must not be reissued under its original number.

380. In the address of an order annulling another order, the train first named must be that to which right was given by the order annulled, and when the order is not transmitted simultaneously to all concerned, it must be **first sent** to the point at which that train is to receive it, and the required response received, before the order is sent for other trains.

381. **Form M.—Annulling part of an order:**

(1) That part of Order No. ...... reading ...... is annulled.

**Example.**

*That part of Order No. Ten 10 reading No. One 1 Eng. 67, Palmer, will meet No. Two 2 Eng. 58, King, at Sparta is annulled.*

In the address of an order annulling a part of an order, the train first named must be that to which right was given by the part annulled, and when the order is not transmitted simultaneously to all concerned, it must be first sent to the point at which that train is to receive it, and the required response received, before the order is sent for other trains.

382. **Form P.—Suspending an order or a part of an order:** This order will be given by adding to prescribed forms the words "instead of ......."

(1) ...... will meet ...... at ...... instead of .......
(2) ...... has right over ...... ...... to ...... instead of .......
(3) ...... will display signals for ...... ...... to ...... instead of .......

**Examples.**

(1) *No. One 1 Eng. 765, King, will meet No. Two 2 Eng. 642, Palmer, at Hongkong instead of Bombay.*
(2) *No. One 1 Eng. 765, King, has right over No. Two 2 Eng. 642, Palmer, Mecca to Medina instead of Mirbat.*
(3) *No. One 1 Eng. 765, King, will display signals for Eng. 85, Smith, Astrakhan to Teheran instead of Cabul.*

An order that has been suspended must not be reissued under its original number.

In the address of a superseding order, the train first named must be that to which right was given by the order superseded, and when the order is not transmitted simultaneously to all concerned, it must be **first sent** to the point at which that train is to receive it, and the required response received, before the order is sent for other trains.

383. **Release:**

(*a*) From Train Order Signal, but not from Block, unless stamped "BLOCK IS CLEAR:"

......................, 19..

C. & E., No. .......

My train-order signal is displayed for ...........................

I have no orders for ......................

Last train ahead left at .......

......................, Signalman.

Or, signalmen will fill out the following release:

(*b*) From train order *and* block signal:

Signal is displayed for ...... and ...... to meet or pass at ............

Except as above block is clear.

Issued at ...... m.

Last train ahead left at ...... m.

......................, Signalman.

NOTE.—When a block signal is at diagonal it only indicates that block is clear to the first switch reached at the next block station.

Should any train have orders not to pass a station *without orders*, the receipt of this blank does not release it, but in such cases regular train orders must be obtained.

384. **Caution card:**

To C. & E., Train ......

Block is not clear. You may proceed with caution, prepared to stop within your vision.

................., Signalman.

385. **Clearance:**

................., 19

C. & E., No. ......

No orders have been received at ................... station for train No. ......., due at said station at ...... m., .........., 19

Last train ahead left at ...... m.

..............., Operator.

NOTE.—Should any train have orders not to pass any station *without orders*, the reception of this blank does not release it, but in such cases regular orders must be obtained.

386. **Standard train-order blank for "31" order:**

Form 31. Form 31.

UNITED STATES MILITARY RAILWAY.

TRAIN ORDER NO. *10.*

*March 27, 1906.*

To *C. & E., No. 2.* At *Joppa.*

To ..................... .....................

X *J. D. B* Opr. *1.45 a.* m.

Train ahead left at *12.30 a.* m.

*No. One 1 Eng. 765, King, has right over No. Two 2 Eng. 642, Palmer, Mecca to Medina instead of Mirbat.*

*"12" P. G. C.*

Conductor and engineman must both have a copy of this order.

Repeated at *2.20 a.* m.

| CONDUCTOR. | TRAIN. | MADE. | TIME. | OPR. |
|---|---|---|---|---|
| *Palmer* | *2* | *Complete* | *2.20 a.* m. | *Black* |
| | | | | |
| | | | | |
| | | | | |
| | | | | |
| | | | | |

387. **Standard train-order blank for "19" order:**

| Form 19. | | Form 19. |
|---|---|---|
| UNITED STATES MILITARY RAILWAY. | | |
| TRAIN ORDER No. *10.* | | |
| | | *March 27, 1906.* |
| To *C. & E., No. 1.* | At *Teheran.* | |
| X ............, Opr. | | *1.45 a.* m. |
| *No. One 1 Eng. 765, King, will meet No. Two 2 Eng. 85, Smith, at Astrakhan instead of Cabul.* *"12" P. G. C.* Conductor and engineman must both have a copy of this order. | | |
| Made *complete* | time *1.50 a.* m. | *Black*, Opr. |

CONTROL OF TRAINS BY BLOCK SIGNALS.

388. The telegraphic train-dispatching system is so dependent upon the dispatcher and so many accidents occur through negligence or incompetence, that a system of control known as the block system is used on all first-class roads. For this system each division is divided into blocks, i. e., into lengths of track of defined limits the use of which by trains is controlled by block signals.

389. A **block signal** is usually a semaphore or a disk, placed on a pole so as to be conspicuous to trains whose movements are governed by it. The **normal position** of all block signals is at **danger** or **stop.**

390. A **home block signal** is a fixed signal at the entrance of a block, to control trains in entering and using said block.

391. A **distant signal** is a fixed signal, used in connection with a home signal to indicate that the home signal may be at "stop" when the distant signal is at "caution," or that the home signal is clear when the distant signal is clear.

392. An **advance block signal** is a fixed signal, used in connection with a home block signal to subdivide the block in advance.

393. A **block station** is an open station where there is a block signal.

An **intermediate siding**, as used in block-signal rules, is a siding between block stations, or a siding where the block station is closed.

394. The **telegraph block system, or manual block system,** is the one that would lend itself most readily to military use. The other systems require apparatus that would undoubtedly be destroyed on a road captured from the enemy, and that could easily be disarranged by a few active spies, or partisans, who knew enough about the system to know how to disable it most seriously.

The block stations will either be connected by telegraph or telephone, and one wire on each division must be allotted for the use of this block system. At all block stations at least a home signal, and if practicable both a home and distant signal, will be erected, bearing lights and arms as shown in figs. 133, 134.

It has been found that about 5 miles is the length of block that gives the best results for this system.

395. The movement of trains is regulated by block signals between limits designated by the time-table or by special instructions.

396. Block signals control the use of the blocks but, unless otherwise provided, do not affect the movements of trains under the time-table or train rules nor dispense with the use or observance of other signals whenever or wherever they may be required.

397. Where the semaphore is used, the governing arm is displayed to the right of the signal mast, as seen from the approaching train, and the indications are given by position; the arm in a horizontal position, and in addition at night a red light, when the block is not clear or there are train orders, will indicate **stop**, and will be referred to as a **stop signal.** The arm inclined downward, and in addition at night a green light, when the block is clear or there are no train orders, will indicate **proceed,** the block is clear to the first switch reached at the next block station, and will be referred to as **clear signal**.

398. Block signals are to be used to control movements of trains upon main track, and must *not* be accepted by trains on sidetracks.

399. **Proper authority** must be obtained from signalmen before proceeding, by trains arriving at a block station where signal is at "stop," by trains occupying sidetracks, or by trains starting from terminal stations.

"Proper authority" consists of:

(*a*) A caution card and a release.
(*b*) A release stamped "Block is clear."
(*c*) Train order stamped "Block is clear."
(*d*) Train orders and a caution card.

Trains will be governed as per instructions on caution card par. 384. This does not relieve the preceding train from compliance with par. 322.

400. Upon the arrival of a train the signalman will first execute any train orders or block orders he may have, then ascertain from his block register if block is clear, but will not clear his signal until all orders concerning such trains are satisfied and block in advance is clear, and he has received the "13" response, as per code, from next block station in advance.

401. In moving trains in established direction the signalman will, on approach of a train, ascertain from his block register if block is clear, and will not clear his signal until all orders concerning such train are satisfied and block in advance is unoccupied.

402. When there are no train orders and the block ahead is clear for an approaching train, the signal will be changed to "clear" so that the train may enter without reducing speed; and when the train has passed the block signal and the signalman has seen the markers, he must display the stop signal; and when the rear of the train has passed 300 ft. beyond the block signal, he must give train number and the time to the next block station in the rear.

403. Should a train pass a block station in **two or more parts,** the signalman must notify the signalman at the next block station in advance. A signalman having received this notice must stop any train running in the opposite direction. The stop signal must not be displayed to the engineman of the divided train if the block in advance is clear, but the **train-parted** signal must be given. Should a train going in the opposite direction be stopped, it may be permitted to proceed when it is known that its track is not obstructed.

404. **A caution card** is used when trains are permitted to enter a block under notice that such block is not clear. This may be used as follows:

**First.**—By direction of the train dispatcher, in which event he will send an order of the following form:

"Signalman at ......, issue caution card No. ......, to ......, O. K. ......."

Dispatchers must not authorize operators to issue caution card to any train or engine to enter a block occupied by a passenger train except in case of accident.

**Second.**—If from the failure of telegraph line or other cause a signalman be unable to communicate with the next block station in advance, he must stop every train approaching in that direction. Should no cause for detaining the train be known, it may then be permitted to proceed, provided 10 minutes have elapsed since the passage of the last preceding train, using caution card, par. 384.

When a train is allowed to enter a block under caution card because communication with the signalman in advance can not be had, positive orders will be given by notation on the caution card, directing train and enginemen to stop at next station and ascertain the trouble.

405. Should a portion of a train **run back** in the wrong direction, the signalman must notify the next block station toward which the portion of the train is running. The signalman receiving this notice must stop any train running on the same track in the opposite direction, and take such other protective measures as may be practicable.

406. A signalman informed of **any obstruction in a block** must display the stop signal and notify the signalman at the other end of that block. The signalman at the other end of that block must immediately display the stop signal. The clear signal for that block must not be displayed until the obstruction is removed.

AUTOMATIC BLOCK SYSTEM.

407. **Explanation of signals.**—The signals used are either the **semaphore** or the **inclosed disk.**

The signal indications are given by not more than two positions of an arm or a disk, and, in addition, at night by lights of prescribed color.

The apparatus is so constructed that the failure of any part directly controlling a signal will cause it to give the normal indication, i. e., danger.

408. The signals, if practicable, are either over or upon the right of and adjoining the track to which they refer. On double track the high signals will be located on the left of and adjoining the track to which they refer. For less than three tracks, the signals for trains in each direction may be attached to the same signal mast.

409. When main running tracks are operated in the same established direction and the space between tracks will not permit of signal masts being located adjoining the track to which they refer, the masts will be located either on a signal bridge or a bracket post.

410. On a bracket post signals on the right-hand mast refer to the main running track farthest to the right; the signals on the next mast to the left refer to the main running track to the left of the first-mentioned track, and so on for each main running track operated in the same established direction.

411. Semaphore arms that govern are displayed to the right of the signal mast as seen from an approaching train.

412. Switches in the main track are so connected with the block signals that the home block signal in the direction of approaching trains will indicate **stop** when the switch is not set for the main track.

413. Distant block signals are connected with the corresponding home block signals and so constructed that a train between the distant and home signals, or a switch not set for the main track within the same limits, or the failure of any part controlling the signal, shall cause it to indicate **caution.**

414. Where indicators are placed at the main-track switches, the indicator disk will be visible (through the front opening of the case) when the head of an approaching train has reached a point not less than 1,000 ft. in advance of the block signal protecting the switch.

415. The indications for the main running track are given by a high home signal.

416. Automatic block signals are numbered to indicate the established direction of the running track for which the signal is given, and lettered to denote the district in which they are located.

417. Even-numbered signals govern train movements upon the southbound or eastbound track, and odd-numbered signals upon the northbound or westbound track.

418. Where the semaphore is used, the governing arm is displayed to the right of the signal mast as seen from an approaching train, and the indications are given by two positions of the arm, and, in addition, at night by lights of prescribed color.

419. Where a single disk is used, the two indications are given by the position of a red or green disk, and, in addition, at night by lights of prescribed color.

420. A **home semaphore signal** (see fig. 133) will display an arm in the horizontal position, and in addition at night a **red** light, when the block is not clear. This will indicate **stop**, and will be referred to as a **stop signal.** Or, it will display an arm inclined diagonally downward from the horizontal, and in addition at night a **green** light, when the block is clear. This will indicate **proceed,** and will be referred to as a **clear signal.**

Where two signals are displayed from the same mast, the upper one is the home block signal for the block in advance, and the lower one the distant signal for the second block in advance (see fig. 135).

421. A **distant semaphore signal** (see fig. 134) will display a forked arm in a horizontal position, and in addition at night a **red and green** light, when the home signal with which it is used is at **stop** or the track obstructed between home and distant signal. This will indicate **proceed with caution to the home signal,** and will be referred to as a **caution signal;** or, it will display a forked arm inclined diagonally downward from the horizontal, and in addition at night a **green** light, when the home signal with which it is used is at "clear" and the track unobstructed between home and distant signal. This will indicate **proceed,** and will be referred to as a **clear signal.**

422. A **home disk signal** (see fig. 136) will display a red disk, and, in addition, at night a **red** light, when the block is not clear. This will indicate **stop,** and will be referred to as a **stop signal:** or, the red disk will be withdrawn from view and, in addition, at night a **green** light will be displayed, when the block is clear. This will indicate **proceed,** and will be referred to as a **clear signal.** The face of a home signal case is painted black and the back yellow.

423. A **distant disk signal** (see fig. 137) will display a **green** disk with a **white cross** on its face, and in addition at night a **red and green** light, when the home signal with which it is used is at **stop** or the track obstructed between home and distant signal. This will indicate **proceed with caution to the home signal,** and will be referred to as a **caution signal.**

Or, the disk will be withdrawn from view, and, in addition, at night a **green** light will be displayed, when the home signal with which it is used is "clear" and the track unobstructed between the distant signal and the home signal. This will indicate **proceed,** and will be referred to as a **clear signal.**

The face of a distant signal case is painted white and the back yellow.

424. Block signals control the use of blocks, but, unless otherwise provided, do not affect the movements of trains under the time-table or train rules, nor dispense with the use or the observance of other signals whenever and wherever they may be required.

425. Block signals apply only to trains running in the **established direction.**

426. When a train is stopped by a block signal, it may proceed when the signal is cleared, or after waiting one minute and then running under caution to the next clear signal.

427. When a signal is out of service, the fact will be indicated by a white rectangular shield hung over the number. Trains finding a signal out of service must, unless otherwise directed, proceed with caution to the next signal.

428. When a train is stopped by a signal which is evidently **out of order,** and not so indicated, the fact must be reported to the division superintendent.

429. A signal **imperfectly displayed,** or the absence of one at a place where a signal is usually shown, must be regarded as a danger signal and the fact reported to the division superintendent.

430. The home signal will indicate "**stop**" when the block is occupied, when a switch is set for a siding or a crossover, when a car on a siding fouls the main-line track, when the track circuit is broken, or when the signal is out of order.

431. The **crossover switches** between the main running tracks are so connected with the block signals that the home block signals in the direction of approaching trains will indicate **stop** when either switch of the crossover is not set for the main running track.

432. A switch must not be opened to permit a train movement **to** the main track when the red disk is visible in the indicator box at that switch.

433. A switch may be opened to permit a train movement **from** the main track when the red disk is visible in the indicator box at that switch.

INTERLOCKING PLANTS.

434. A **high signal** is a signal supported on a mast at a height of at least 20 ft. above the track; it may be a home signal or a distant signal.

A **mast** is an upright to which the signals are directly attached.

A **home signal** is a fixed signal at the point at which trains are required to stop when the route is not clear.

A **distant signal** means the same as the block-signal term.

**Dwarf signal.** A low home signal.

435. The following are the general principles on which interlocking signals are located and applied:

The **signal** used is the semaphore.

The **indications** are given by not more than two positions of an arm, and in addition at night by lights of prescribed color.

The apparatus is so constructed that the failure of any part directly controlling a signal will cause it to give the normal indication.

436. The signals, if practicable, are either over or upon the right of and adjoining the track to which they refer. On double track the high signals will be located on the left of and adjoining the track to which they refer.

437. The normal indication of a home signal is **stop,** and of a distant signal is **caution.**

The semaphore arms that govern are displayed to the right of the signal mast, as seen from an approaching train.

The apparatus is so constructed that the failure of any part directly controlling a switch or lock will prevent the display of the clear signal.

438. When main running tracks are operated in the same established direction and the space between tracks will not permit of the signal masts being located adjoining the track to which they refer, the masts will be located either on a signal bridge or bracket post.

On a bracket post, signals on the right-hand mast refer to the main running track farthest to the right; the signals on the next mast to the left refer to the main running track to the left of the first-mentioned track, and so on for each main running track operated in the same established direction.

439. When the train service on one main running track is superior to that on another, the signals for that track will be placed 6½ ft. higher on its mast than those for the track of inferior service.

440. The indication for a main running-track movement in the established direction will be given by a high home signal (see fig. 133).

441. The indication for a main running-track movement in the established diverging direction at a junction will be given by one of two signals, located one above the other on the same mast; the topmost signal will govern the superior route and the lower signal that of the secondary or inferior route (fig. 138).

442. The indication for a diverging movement from the main running track in the established direction to a secondary or side track will be given by a dwarf signal located on the right of and adjoining the track to which it refers and either at the foot of or opposite the high home signal. The light on the dwarf signal corresponding to the stop indication will be shielded off, the high home signal giving the **stop** indication, and the dwarf signal the **proceed** indication for the diverging movement.

443. The indication for **reverse movement** from the established direction on or from a main running track, or for a movement on a side track in either direction, or from a sidetrack to the main running track, will be given by a dwarf signal.

444. The semaphore arms that govern are displayed to the right of the signal mast as seen from an approaching train.

445. **Interlocking signals**, unless otherwise provided, do not affect the movements of trains under the time-table or train rules, nor dispense with the use or the observance of other signals whenever and wherever they may be required.

446. **Trains.**—The number of regular passenger trains to be run daily will be specially determined in each case, and will not provide for larger troop movements than parts of companies. Where one company or more is to be moved, extra cars will be added to the regular passenger train, or extra trains will be run. These extra trains can, by train orders of the train dispatcher or his superior, be given any rights on the road that are necessary. **Quick dispatch** is freight that must be rushed through without delay in the fastest time practicable. Speed is essential.

447. **Time freight** is freight that must be delivered within a certain time, and must be forwarded without delay. Regularity of movement is essential.

448. **Dead freight** is freight that need not be hurried and that delay can not harm. Military conditions will sometimes change the classification from dead freight to time freight. A hurried shipment of ammunition illustrates the case in point.

449. **Local freight** is freight shipped from one point on a division to another point on the same division, or to a point on an adjacent division. On a military road, the number of regular time freights, or other freights, will depend entirely upon the local conditions. On any division at least one local freight will be run each way daily. These locals deliver freight from the division terminals to various points along the division, distribute empties where they may be required, and pick up loads at the intermediate stations and carry such loads to the other division terminal, where they are either placed in through trains for their ultimate destination or are forwarded on another local if their destination is on the next division.

Time freights may stop at intermediate stations to pick up an important car, or such a car may be forwarded by a local freight train to the nearest large station, or division terminal, before it is placed in a through freight train.

450. When a shipment of through freight **requiring an extra train is received** on a division, the train dispatcher of that division promptly notifies the **train dispatcher of the next division** of the number of cars of such shipment, together with the class and probable time of arriving on the next division. This permits the next train dispatcher to arrange his power and train crews to take care of such extra shipment.

451. **Number of trains daily.**—The only general statement that can be made in regard to the capacity of a line is the number of trains that can be run over a line in 24 hours. Mr. M. Kirkman, of the C. & N. W. Ry., cites a case where, for a period of two weeks, a single-track line handled 25 trains per day, 4 passenger and 21 freight, in each direction. This is probably a maximum for single track, and will be attainable only under the most favorable conditions and the most efficient operation.

On double-track line the distance apart of trains is only dependent upon considerations of safety and ability to handle the trains at the terminals.

452. The **ordinary accumulation** of cars that collect at division terminals are arranged into the **regular** trains by the yardmaster, who notifies the roundhouse foreman of the locomotive needed, and the train crew to run the train. When the total accumulation of cars can not be run in the regular trains, he notifies the chief dispatcher, who orders out **extras** enough to move the cars. As soon as a train is made up and ready to move, the conductor of the train makes up **a consist, or detail sheet,** showing the composition of his train. This sheet shows the date, train number, time of leaving, number of locomotive, names of engineer and conductor, and gives the contents and destination of each load, and will state when carded, or specify time freight. For **time freight,** they will give the junction point through which it is routed. For **empties** in their train, they give the initials, destination, size and kind of each car. This consist is telegraphed to the chief dispatcher, who thus knows the contents of each train. He has at hand the local car sheet, described in par. 234, and thus can arrange to **keep the train full,** distributing empties where needed and picking up loads at intermediate stations on the line, and he issues telegraphic orders to accomplish this result. In case the train is late, the consist enables him to order certain cars of unimportant freight set out to lighten the train and thus increase the speed.

453. If all the cars in the train are loaded to their full capacity the weights will be given in the consist; otherwise, the chief dispatcher estimates the weight of the train from a list that he keeps showing the approximate weight of the different kinds of empties and of the same cars normally loaded, and from which he can form a correct estimate of the tonnage in each train. The chief dispatcher must endeavor to keep each locomotive loaded to its **tonnage rating** over each section of the division. Standing instructions should be issued that when trains are not filled to the tonnage rating of the engine this opportunity will be taken to deliver coal along the line.

454. Agents will report daily the amount of **coal on hand,** so as to give timely notice for a new shipment.

## TIME-TABLES.

455. After the military controlling staff has decided on the number of trains that must be run for military purposes, the places at which such trains must stop to fulfill requirements, and the amount of civil traffic that will be permitted, they turn this data over to the railway officials to work up into a time-table.

The conditions laid down have determined the number of regular trains of the various classes that must be run, and the time of starting from the initial station will be fixed so as best to meet the military requirements.

The speed of the trains will depend upon the condition of the roadbed, the maximum grade, power of the engine, loads to be hauled, etc., as laid down in pars. 175, 176.

456. A time-table is first made out in **graphic form** (see fig. 139). A rectangle is laid out, and is divided by perpendicular parallel lines into equal divisions representing the 24 hours of the day, subdivided into 5-minute intervals. It is divided by horizontal parallel lines whose distances apart represent the distances between

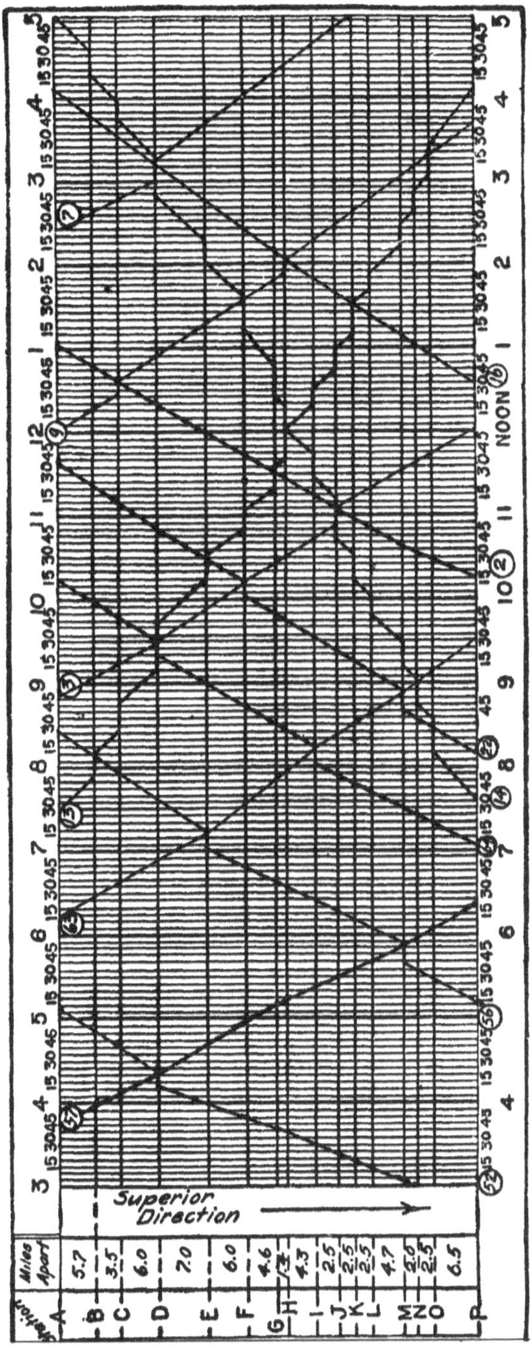


FIG. 139.—PART OF GRAPHIC TIME-TABLE.

corresponding stations for the scale assumed. This drawing is then fastened to a large drawing board.

Having determined the speed for each class of train, the movement of the train can be indicated on the graphic table by a right line, if the speed between stops is assumed to be uniform. At stations where there is a stop of over 2 minutes, the train movement will be indicated by a horizontal line at that station. Fig. 139 is a type of time-table for a single-track road. On a single-track road all trains meet and pass at stations, therefore all lines representing train movements must intersect on the horizontal lines indicating stations.

Having determined on the speed for the various trains, the trains will be arranged so as to least interfere with one another. Slow trains must take the sidetrack for fast trains; and if a slow train starts just ahead of two or three superior trains, it may be laid out on sidings for 2 or 3 hours while waiting for such fast trains to pass it. It is wise, therefore, to group the trains, and to start the slow trains immediately after the group of fast trains has left the terminal. By this means it is often possible to get the fleet of slow trains across a division with only one or two delays on account of stops for superior trains.

457. **The fewer classes of trains** as regards speed and rights the better and more efficient will be the working of the line.

A rough diagram will readily show the advantages of the following points:

(*a*) The equal time spacing of sidings.
(*b*) The proper starting time of different classes of trains.
(*c*) The fewest possible classes of trains.

458. The train movements (fig. 139) are represented by threads, and, for the sake of clearness on the board, threads of different colors represent different classes of trains. Each thread is tagged at the upper and lower end, and by this means it is easy to follow every train across the board.

Where speed changes, or a train stops, the change in direction of the thread is made by driving a pin into the board at such points of change.

When a new train is put on, having the time of departure and the speed of the train, it is easy to thread this train onto the time-table board, making such corrections in the other threads as may be necessary.

On a **double-track road** the manner of making a time-table is similar to that just described, but is simpler, since all trains go in one direction on each track, and there is no need of working out meeting points for trains from opposite directions.

459. Having completed the graphic time-table, the **working time-table** is made up by taking the times from the board and inserting them in their proper places in the printed time-table. Such time-tables will show the distances between stations, the capacity of passing tracks in each direction, the stations at which all trains stop, watering stations, coaling stations, etc. Any **special rules** that change the time that one train must clear the time of another will be published therein, as will also a list of registering stations, railway grade crossings, junction points, and overhead obstructions. A list of railway officers, officials, and surgeons, with their addresses, will be printed on the time-table. This time-table corresponds to the employees' time-tables of civil railroads which contain much information not found in time-tables for the use of passengers. The time-table will show the **tonnage rating** of locomotives of different classes over different sections of the division for fast freights and for slow freights, together with empty weights of the various kinds of cars used.

460. Each time-table, from the moment it takes effect, supersedes the preceding time-table. A train of the preceding time-table shall retain its train orders and take the schedule of the train of the same number on the new time-table.

461. A train of the new time-table which has not the same number on the preceding time-table shall not run on any division (or district) until it is due to start from its initial station on that division (or district) after the new time-table takes effect.

462. The explanation in the time-table will state the direction that is **superior** on different parts of the line. Trains to the front will usually be superior to those going to the rear.

463. The trains of the time-table will be arranged in classes. Trains of the **first class** are superior to those of the second, trains of the **second class** to those of the third, and so on.

464. **Extra trains** are inferior to regular trains. All trains in the **superior direction,** as specified in the time-table, are superior to trains of the same class in the opposite direction.

465. **Regular trains** 12 hours behind their schedule lose both right and class, and can thereafter proceed only on train orders.

466. The time-table will give special instructions regarding the sidetrack to be taken, and any special rules that may be necessary to facilitate movement over the division for which the time-table is issued.

467. A list of **registering stations** will be indicated in the time-table, at which stations conductors of passenger and freight trains will register.

468. When one time is given in the time-table, unless otherwise specified, it is the leaving time. When two are given, they are the arriving and leaving times. **Schedule meeting or passing stations** have the time indicated in full-faced type. When more than one train is to be met at a station, a small number between the time of leaving and arriving indicates the number of trains to be met.

469. The time-tables will indicate by reference marks the points where trains stop, meals are taken, and any other information necessary to clearly explain the time-table. They will also indicate the length of time that inferior trains will allow in **clearing the time** of superior trains at special points where pars. 279 and 280 do not apply for some local reason.

FREIGHT.

470. All supplies must be shipped on **shipping bills** or receipts for freight received. One copy is sent by mail to the consignee and one copy is held by the station agent where the freight was received. In loading supplies, endeavor should be made to load each car to its full capacity, if this can be done and not mix shipments to too great an extent. Hay and hard-tack are examples of supplies that utilize only about two-thirds of the actual capacity of a flat car or gondola, whereas if loaded into a box car they utilize about 90% of the actual capacity. Other supplies, such as grain, flour, sugar, etc., must be loaded in box cars, and easily load the car to its full capacity without occupying all the space. For **important shipments** a copy of the receipt may be sent to the agent at the destination so that he may be ready to care for the shipment on its arrival.

471. All freight to be shipped on a military railway will be delivered to the agent in exchange for a receipt for goods shipped. This receipt will be of the simplest form, indicating the date of shipment, name of consignor and consignee, and address of each, the serial number of the receipt, a list of the packages, with weight, marks, and contents of each. The agent or clerk will keep a duplicate of the receipt and will ship the freight on a waybill. The original receipt is delivered to the consignor to be sent to the consignee (pars. 470 and 473).

472. The **waybill** will be given the conductor of the train carrying the goods, and will indicate the routing desired in addition to the information contained in the receipt.

473. The conductor who first receives the waybill turns it over to the yardmaster at the end of his run. The latter delivers the waybill to the conductor who next takes the car. This is continued to the destination of the car, and the waybill and freight are there delivered to the receiving agent, who takes a list of the door seals, checks the freight against the waybill, and delivers the freight to the consignee, taking up the original receipt for goods shipped, or taking an **informal receipt** if the original has not been received by the consignee and the latter is known by the agent to be responsible.

474. Quick dispatch, time, slow, and local freight should be shipped on **differently-colored waybills,** so that the character of shipment will appear at a glance.

475. **Stock.**—In moving live stock over a railroad, it is necessary at intervals to unload them for feed and water and then forward them. This plan will necessitate stockyards at such stations. A plan and bill of material for a **four-pen stockyard** is given in fig. 117. The laws usually require that stock shall not be kept aboard cars longer than 24 consecutive hours, and at the end of that period they shall be unloaded for feeding and watering. Stock should be packed tightly to prevent them from lying down or being thrown down by the movement of the train.

476. **Overs and shorts.**—If any packages indicated on the waybill are not found when the shipment is received, a list of such "**shorts**" is taken. If there are any packages in the car not accounted for on the waybill, a similar list of "**overs**" is made. This list of "overs" and "shorts" must be immediately reported to the division superintendent, giving the number of car that such "overs" or "shorts" occurred in, a list of the transfer stations, the shipping point, consignee, and such other notes from the waybill as will give a history of the journey that the car has made. In the office of the division superintendent there is a clerk who immediately takes the matter up. This clerk looks through his list of overs and shorts received from all other agents on the division, and is frequently able to locate lost packages from such list and to send extra ones to the proper destinations. For all packages that can not be found, or whose destination can not be determined, an investigation is immediately started, beginning with the original shipping agent and following through the various persons who had charge of the shipment en route and at the same time a division list of "overs" and "shorts" is sent to the general superintendent, in whose office a similar investigation is made from the combined reports of "overs" and "shorts" received from the various division superintendents.

477. In investigating for overs and shorts it will be found advantageous to make out a printed list of numbered questions, such as follows:

SUPERINTENDENT'S OFFICE, .................... DIVISION,

.......... .........., 19..

Agent, Condr. ...................., File ......

Please see papers attached and comply with request No. ......

1. Examine your warehouse, platform, billing, etc., and advise if loaded as billed.
2. If you find not loaded as billed, give full explanation.
3. Was freight checked when loaded and by whom? How long after loaded before car was sealed?
4. For what stations did you load similar freight?
5. Into what car might this freight have been loaded in error and for what points?
6. Who had car ...... out of your station, and on what date?
7. Are you still short the within-mentioned packages?
8. Car ...... into your station ....... Were you over, and was car made empty? If not, give disposition.
9. Car ...... delivered to your division at ......, date ....... Please trace to an empty and advise if over.
10. Trace through to destination and advise if freight has been received and from what source.
11. Has shortage been filled? If so, give waybill reference on which received.
12. Give your transfer record, disposition of original car if not empty. Did you transfer similar freight, and for what points? How do you account for this shortage?
13. See short report attached. Are you over?
14. You had car ...... in train ...... date ....... Where did you leave it? Are you positive freight was not in car? Can you account for shortage? Did you unload similar freight? If so, at what stations? Give all around seals when taken and when left and say at what stations opened.
15. See over report attached. Are you short, and on what billing?
16. Give record of car passing. Show train, date, conductor, seal record, and advise if you check over.
17. See over report attached. Did you handle similar freight on your train this date? Can you give disposition?
18. Who had car ...... to you and under what seals?

19. Please show delivery to the ...... division.
20. See over report. Can you furnish billing to cover?
21. See attached over report. Will this fill your shortage?
22. First agent note and forward consecutively as shown above, last-named agent forwarding papers to this office.

**Please return papers promptly to this office.**

...................., Division Superintendent.

Make a list of the persons to be questioned, and opposite each name set the numbers of the above questions that it is desired to have each answer. Send this list to first person and direct him to answer his questions and then forward all the papers to No. 2, etc. Thus this list of questions is sent to the original shipping agent with the request that he answer questions 1 to 6, inclusive, and then forward papers to first conductor to answer question 14. This conductor answers his question and forwards the papers to second conductor, etc. If nothing develops from the investigation of conductors, the papers may then be sent back to the receiving freight agent with request that he answer question 7, or to any agent who opened the car en route, for answer to question 8. The various questions suggest the persons to whom the paper should be sent in the investigation. A prompt investigation of all overs and shorts is especially necessary on a military railway.

478. **In loading freight**, the agent will always check all articles received before giving the waybill; and when such freight is loaded into the cars, some system must be adopted which will make sure that the freight is placed in the proper car and that all the freight on the bill is properly loaded and indicated on the waybills and that all packages are shipped in proper form to insure their safe carriage.

479. At large terminal stations this question of loading becomes a very important factor in the satisfactory operation of the road. A system of loading must be devised so that there will be a cross check on the loading. A suggestion of a scheme is as follows:

Freight is loaded into cars from receiving platforms by truckers, and checked by a loading clerk.

Freight will be received at different doors for different parts of the line.

Each trucker will call out destination and mark of each package as he places it on his truck.

The clerk has blank forms for each trucker, as below; and when the destination is called he writes the number of car and track on the card, records the identification mark, and makes a check after "No." on the blank. No truck will carry packages for more than one car at a time.

| Trucker *3*. | |
|---|---|
| Car *6*. | Track *4*. |
| Marks *A. B. C.* | No..... |
| Marks *C. D. E.* | No..... |
| Marks *F. G.* | No..... |

This card is given to the trucker when his truck is loaded, and he leaves the card in a box in the car in which he leaves the packages. These cards are afterwards collected by an inspector and checked back against the waybill. One clerk can card for about four to six truckers. Large signs will be hung in each car, giving car and track numbers, and points for which that car will be loaded, thus:

| Car No. 6.<br>Track No. 4. | Way stations.<br>N. Y. City<br>to<br>Albany. |
|---|---|

Fig. 140 indicates position of tracks for loading at a large station. The cars are run onto the parallel tracks and so "spotted" that the side doors of cars on all six tracks shall be in line, perpendicular to the loading platform. The platform is con-

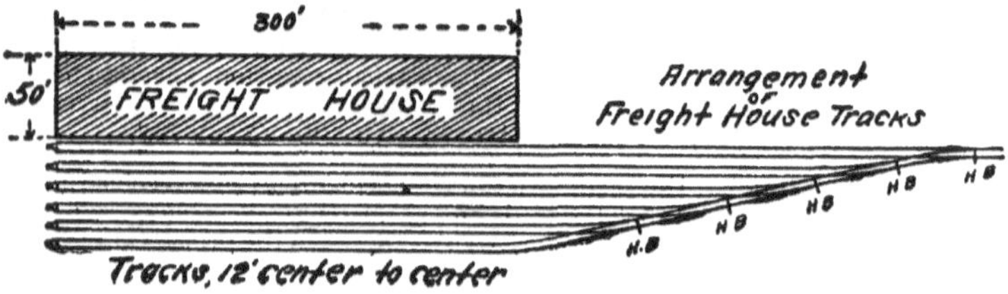


FIG. 140.

nected with the nearest car, and each car thereafter is connected through the side doors with the corresponding car on the next track by a wide plate of steel, over which the trucks run.

TROOP MOVEMENTS.

480. **Entraining of troops.**—As soon as a railroad is taken under military control, a bulletin for railway use should be published, giving the capacity of cars, and the maximum number of cars, loaded and empty, to be run in trains, where the whole tonnage rating of the engines can not be utilized. The carrying capacity of coaches and other cars should be given for both **normal transportation** and **hurried transportation**; the normal transportation will be used unless the other be specifically stated, in which case trains will be made to carry every available man that safety will permit.

481. **Rations** for the men on the train will be carried in the baggage cars, or kitchen cars if provided. Where an entire unit can not be carried on one train, battalions can be broken up and certain companies assigned to one train, while the remainder follow in another. The **assignment of troops** to trains will rest with the railway officials. Where regiments carry tentage and camp equipage, these will normally be sent ahead of the troops in one train and will not be divided up amongst the trains carrying the troops. The baggage of the companies traveling on different trains will be kept separate so that the baggage of each company can be shipped in the train with the company. All **company baggage** will be **plainly marked,** indicating the company and regiment. In Infantry regiments, the officers' horses will be shipped ahead in the train with the camp equipage.

482. In **mounted regiments,** the first trains will carry the horses, with men to look after them. The picket lines and a proper amount of forage will be carried on the horse trains. Guns, caissons, and wagons will follow on trains in the rear of the regiments to which they belong.

483. In loading artillery wagons on trains, they will be loaded on the cars from a platform or from portable ramps (fig. 141). They will be loaded on one car and run by hand or horse power to the car on which they are to be carried. The openings between cars will be covered by plates of iron, or wooden runways, over which the vehicles may run. As soon as a vehicle is on the car, a rope with a hook will be attached to the wagon; a team of horses on the ground, moving parallel to the train, will pull the vehicle while it is guided by men on the tongue. By this means, loading of heavy vehicles will be greatly facilitated.

484. **Unloading of troops and animals** at or near the railhead must be expedited in every possible way. Platforms and portable ramps must be supplied at all unloading points. A type of platform and bill of material for same is shown in fig. 116. A portable ramp for vehicles is shown in fig. 141. The method of unloading is just the converse of the method of loading, as described in par. 483. A portable ramp for unloading animals is shown in fig. 142. These can easily be lashed on the truss rods of the cars.

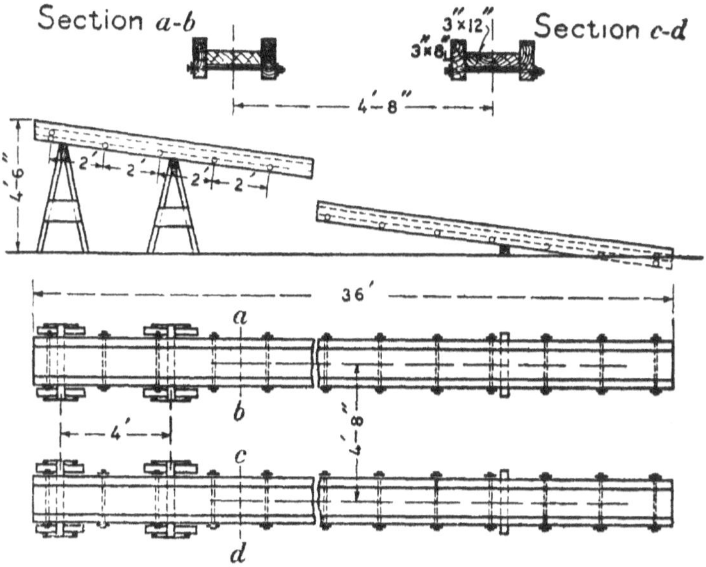


FIG. 141.—PORTABLE RAMPS FOR VEHICLES.

For troop movements on a military railway, each stock car should be supplied with one such ramp. It can be carried on the truss rods or otherwise fastened to the car.

485. No officer, soldier, or civilian can travel on the military railway except he be provided with the **proper transportation.** Such transportation will not be issued except upon the presentation of an order authorizing the journey, or granting a leave; and in the case of a civilian, an order from headquarters authorizing him to travel on the military railway.

486. When trains are running through a district **infested by the enemy,** all officers and men traveling by such trains must go **properly armed.** The senior officer on the train is responsible that order is kept on the train and that the regulations are obeyed; and in case of attack, he assumes command during the attack. **In case of disorder** on the train he can call any other officer or soldier to his assistance in maintaining discipline.

## WRECKING OUTFITS.

487. The organization and equipment of the **wrecking outfits** on a military road must be complete in every particular. These wrecking outfits will be assigned to certain sections of the line and will be stationed at or near the center of the territory to which they belong. The wrecking outfit proper is composed of a crane car equipped with a 50-ton derrick and engine, the number of flat cars necessary to carry the heavy equipment, such as extra trucks, rails, ties, etc., a certain number of box cars that are arranged inside as storerooms for the lighter material, and one or two cars fitted up as living quarters for the wrecking crew, and as a hospital car to take care of the injured that may be found in the wrecks.

One locomotive will be kept under steam at all times so that the wrecking outfit can be started to the scene of wreck on a few minutes' notice.

The wrecking train is equipped with medicines, instruments, bedding, etc., and the commissary is always ready to care for the crew for at least two days. The crew must always be where they can be rapidly collected on notification of a wreck.

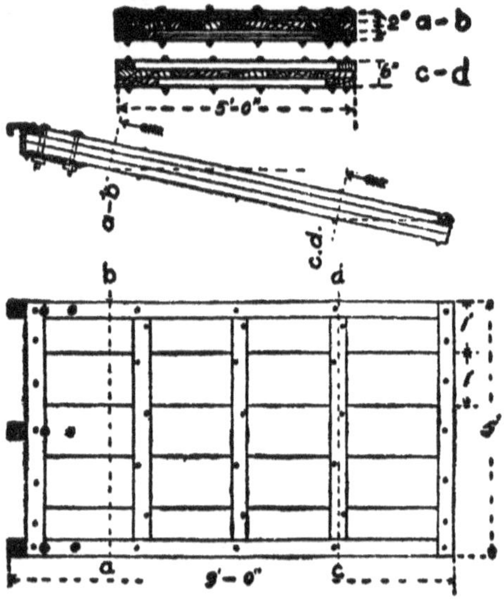


FIG. 142.—PORTABLE ANIMAL RAMP.

The crew will consist of one wrecking master and an assistant, one cranesman and an assistant, and five men, one of whom shall be a cook, and the other four expert car or locomotive repairers. This crew will be employed in the shops when not on wrecking work. Laborers will be obtained from maintenance, or section, crews near scene of wreck.

488. On receipt of information of a wreck, the wrecking crew, together with the necessary train crew, will be immediately notified, and the wrecking train should ordinarily be under way, with good management, within 15 minutes, in daytime, and within from 20 to 25 minutes at nighttime, after the receipt of call for tne wrecking train.

489. The **wrecking master** is responsible that the train is at all times fully equipped as to tools, supplies, and commissary stores. The surgeon who accompanies the wrecking outfit is responsible that the proper hospital supplies, instruments, medicines, etc., are in the hospital car. The surgeon is notified at the same time the train crew is.

490. A list of the railway tools and equipment for a wrecking outfit on a standard-gage road is given below:

2 pairs Tilden rerailing frogs for proper rail
2 pairs Fewings rerailing frogs.
2 35-ton 31-in. Norton jacks, with hooks.
2 30-ton hydraulic wrecking jacks, with claw (Watson & Stillman 18-in. runout).
2 20-ton hydraulic wrecking jacks, with claws (Watson & Stillman 18-in. runout).
2 track jacks (Barrett).
4 16-in. triple blocks. Two of these blocks, together with one rope, constitute block and fall ready for use, the remaining blocks and rope being held separately as a reserve.
4 18-in. double blocks and 2 manila ropes, 2 in. in diameter, each 400 ft. long, rove as 2 blocks and falls.
4 12-in. triple blocks, and 2 manila ropes, 1¼ in. in diameter, each 400 ft. long, rove as 2 blocks and falls.
1 2-in. manila rope 200 ft. long.
1 1¼-in. manila rope 200 ft. long.
2 30-in. snatch blocks.
2 18-in. snatch blocks.
2 12-in. snatch blocks.
1 1-in. crucible cast-steel cable 100 ft. long.
1 manila dragrope 6 in. in diameter, 50 ft. long, with hook on one end and link on the other.
2 4-in. manila dragrope 50 ft. long, with hook on one end and link on the other.
2 3-in. manila dragrope 50 ft. long, with hook on one end and link on the other.
2 crucible, cast-steel, 1¾-in dragrope 40 ft. long, with hook on one end and link on the other. This is intended for special use where large engines have to be handled.
10 bumper chains.
4 ½-in. chains 22 ft. long, with rings on each end, one ring to pass through the other; tested to 70,000 lbs.
6 Crosby cable clamps.
2 crab links for 1½-in. chain.
2 crab links for 1¼-in chain.
2 crab links for 1-in. chain
2 crab hooks for 1½-in chain.
2 crab hooks for 1¼-in chain.
2 crab hooks for 1-in. chain.
4 heavy hooks and links.
2 hauling links.
4 anchor shackles and pins, 1½-in. iron.
2 S hooks.
2 splice links.
1 singletree cable and L hooks for steam crane only.
Assortment of oval and round thimbles for ropes.
1 16-ft. ladder.
Signal oil and cans, waste, and car oil.
4 gallons alcohol for jacks.
6 pairs rail tongs.
12 track chisels.
6 claw bars.
10 lining bars.
2 hand hammers.
3 18-in. screw wrenches.
3 track wrenches.
2 hand axes.
6 chopping axes.
2 handsaws.
3 crosscut saws.
6 clay picks.
2 sledges and handles.

List of the railway tools and equipment for a wrecking outfit.—*Continued.*

12 fire extinguishers.
1 pair pole climbers.
4 pairs rubber boots.
2 pieces medium weight canvas, 20 by 30 ft., for protection of perishable freight removed from cars in stormy weather.
2 kegs of track spikes.
1 keg of track bolts of the sizes used on the division.
1,000 nut locks.
50 lbs. 8-in. boat spikes.
½ keg assorted nails.
200 ft. rail.
80 ties.
6 picks.
1 headlight at base of boom of steam crane.
1 crane push pole.
220 pieces, wedges, etc., for blocking; assorted sizes specified, but omitted here. It is also required that about twice this amount be kept on hand to replenish car (very important).
2 Pierson jacks and 2 Jeremiah truck levers.
2 long punches for driving out kingbolts.
1 stretcher.
12 hand torches.
6 wrecking torches.
8 white lanterns.
3 Dressel station lights.
2 Sherry lights.
4 cant hooks and handles.
6 grappling hooks and handles.
10 short-handled, round-pointed shovels.
6 scoop shovels.
6 spike mauls.
4 adzes.
1 track gage.
4 pairs extra car trucks.
1 locomotive truck.
1 tank truck.
4 extra car knuckles.
1 extra switch (in some cases).
1 extra frog.
2 extra center plates.
6 kingbolts.
An assortment of wedges and brasses.
6 extra air hoses.
6 coupling links and pins.
2 long, crooked pins.
4 fire buckets.
1 wheel gage.
1 complete outfit for cutting in a telegraph station at scene of the wreck.
Hospital equipment as directed by surgeon in charge.

**One such wrecking outfit** will be supplied for every 100 to 200 miles of line, depending upon the condition of the roadway and the activity of the enemy.

A **track-repair gang** will follow the wrecking train to the scene of the accident as soon as they can be collected, and a bridge-building crew will also be sent out in case a bridge was damaged in the accident.

An assistant superintendent or train master immediately repairs to the scene of the wreck and takes charge of operations.

### RAILWAY POLICE.

491. In addition to the troops employed to protect the line of railway, there will be need of a force of railway police. Certain of these policemen, or detectives, will be directly under the A. D. R., and others will be under the division superintendents. The number employed will depend upon the necessities. They will be detailed to this service by the head of the police of the line of communications.

The **duties of railway police** are to detect theft from cars, issuance or sale of bogus transportation, interference with the operation of the railway, or destruction of railway property. They will assist in the detection of spies, of employees who illegally transport liquors, or of mail that may have been forbidden by the censor.

### ARMY LABOR BUREAU.

492. This bureau will have entire charge of the employment of all labor used by the different departments of the Army, and the bureau should be organized as soon as the Army takes the field. There must be absolutely no competition between the different departments if satisfactory labor conditions are to prevail.

493. Any officer requiring laborers should **apply direct to the bureau,** stating the number and kind desired. The laborers employed by the bureau will be divided into gangs of from 25 to 30 men each, under a foreman. Employment of labor outside the bureau, except in cases of emergency, will be forbidden, and **in no case** should the pay or allowances be more than that paid by the bureau.

### MAINTENANCE OF WAY.

494. In a theater of war, with an active enemy, the number of breaks in a railway will be very large. The repairs thus necessitated must be rapidly and effectively accomplished. The **maintenance of way department** must be so organized that it is prepared to repair any break of whatever nature that may occur. This department can not be an economical one from a money standpoint. A large maintenance force must be kept on each division at all times, and during intervals between breaks it may not be possible to utilize the services of these men. The maintenance of way department behind Sherman's army was at times larger than all the other departments of the railway combined.

495. This department on each division will be under the **division engineer,** and for a division of from 100 to 200 miles in length the department must be self-sustaining. For this reason, the division engineer on maintenance and repair matters is directly under the supervision of the division superintendent.

Each division should be subdivided into districts about 100 miles in length, and each such district should be in charge of an assistant engineer.

Such a large force must be employed by the engineer department for rapid reconstruction that no provision is made herein for a maintenance department such as, on civil railways, is in charge of a **roadmaster.**

Maintenance work can be divided into water supply, track, and bridge work. Each of these departments on a 100-mile stretch will be in charge of a supervisor.

496. The **supervisor of water supply** has charge of the installation and repair of all pumping stations, including the boilers, pumps, windmills, and other structures.

The machinery that is installed should have interchangeable parts wherever practicable, and there will be a supply of extra parts on hand at all times.

**Tanks** for watering stations will be kept knocked down in the storehouses. It may be impracticable to erect the tanks with the regulation supply pipe; for watering the locomotives, a hose or pipe can be used as a siphon to take the water out of the tank. The pulsometer, referred to in par. 163, may be useful for watering stations, since they have very few parts, no wearing parts, and require no foundations.

The supervisor will have under him one foreman and from 6 to 10 mechanics. He will have a car in which is stored parts of a pumping station likely to be destroyed by an enemy.

497. The **supervisor of track** has charge of the maintenance and repair of all track and roadbed.

A large gang of trackmen will be kept together on each division, equipped with tools and supplies, ready to start on short notice to repair the track or the roadbed. When this gang moves to repair a break, they will move in a train consisting of box cars fitted with bunks, and other cars for tools, supplies, and commissary stores. One car will be fitted up as a kitchen car. A few portable forges will be carried with the outfit.

The supervisor is assisted by 1 clerk, 1 timekeeper, a commissary and quartermaster, and a surgeon. He will have 1 foreman, and 3 subforemen to every 60 men. A gang will have about 1 mechanic to every 6 laborers, and 1 cook to every 30 men, 1 for headquarters, and 1 for the foremen's mess. The above makes a flexible organization; it can be worked as a whole, or be subdivided and still retain its efficiency.

In addition to repairing breaks, the supervisor of track has charge of the normal maintenance of the division that is usually called **section work.** He will attend to this duty with his gangs during the intervals between breaks in the line.

498. **Section work.**—A section will comprise from 5 to 7 miles of single track, and where practicable, the middle of the section will lie at a station. Such a section will be in charge of a section foreman, who will have a gang of from 6 to 8 men on an old road, or 12 to 16 on a new road. The section foreman is responsible for the condition of his section under normal conditions. He will see that the rail joints are kept up, that the crossings are in repair, that the track is kept in alignment, that bad ties are replaced with good ones, and that a thorough inspection is made of his section as often as the conditions necessitate, and always once a day. He will keep sharp lookout for broken rails, fires on wooden structures, and washouts. During rainstorms he will patrol his section and immediately report any danger that may threaten, and will stop all traffic if necessary until proper repairs have been made. He will inspect for and report any break in the telegraph lines. Such section gangs will be detailed and controlled by the supervisor of track.

499. **When replacing broken rails** or making other repairs to the track, section foremen will see that the proper signals are put out to warn trains (see pars. 241 and 258). No tools or appliances will be operated or left between the rails except when necessary.

500. Each section will be supplied with the following **tools and appliances,** for which the section foreman is responsible to the supervisor of track:

| | | | |
|---|---|---|---|
| Adzes | 2 | Hammer, striking, 10-lb | 1 |
| Augers, post hole | 2 | Hoes, scuffle or weed | 4 |
| Ax, chopping | 1 | Hooks, brush | 2 |
| Ax, hand | 1 | Jacks, track | 2 |
| Bars, claw | 4 | Keg, water | 1 |
| Bars, lining | 6 | Key, switch | 1 |
| Bars, pinch | 2 | Lanterns (white), complete | 4 |
| Bars, tamping | 6 | Lanterns (red), complete | 6 |
| Board, spot | 1 | Lanterns (green), complete | 4 |
| Brace, carpenter's | 1 | Level, track | 1 |
| Brace bits | 2 | Mauls, spike | 4 |
| Brooms | 2 | Mattocks | 2 |
| Car, hand | 1 | Padlocks | 3 |
| Car, push | 1 | Picks, clay | 6 |
| Chains, lock | 2 | Pail, water | 1 |
| Can, oiler | 1 | Punch, rail | 1 |
| Chisels, track | 6 | Rakes | 2 |
| Cups, tin | 2 | Saw, hand | 1 |
| Drill, ratchet | 1 | Scythes, grass and weed | 6 |
| Drill bits | 6 | Shovels, track | 6 |
| File, large flat | 1 | Shovels, scoop | 6 |
| File, hand saw | 1 | Stretcher, wire-fence | 1 |
| Flags, white | 2 | Sledge | 1 |
| Flags, green | 2 | Spike puller | 1 |
| Flags, red | 4 | Square, steel | 1 |
| Gage, track | 1 | Tapeline | 1 |
| Grindstone, complete | 1 | Tongs, rail | 2 |
| Handle, extra ax | 1 | Torpedoes | 12 |
| Handle, extra adz | 1 | Wheelbarrow | 1 |
| Handles, extra spike maul | 2 | Whetstones | 6 |
| Handles, extra pick | 2 | Wrenches, track | 6 |
| Hammer, claw | 1 | Wrench, monkey | 1 |
| Hammers, spike | 4 | | |

501. Each section will keep on hand the following **supplies:**

| | | | |
|---|---|---|---|
| Angle bars, prs | 12 | Torpedoes | 18 |
| Nut locks | 100 | Track bolts, kegs | 1 |
| Spikes, kegs | 2 | | |

502. The quickest way to **replace a line of rails** is to string out the rail along the track, with the necessary angle bars, nuts, and bolts. The rail is replaced on one side at a time. The new rail is bolted together and laid along the outside of the rail to be taken out. The old rails are then removed, a few at a time, and the new rail slid into place and spiked. The old rail is only unspiked a short distance ahead of the new one; and when a train is due the new rail is spiked into position nearly up to the end of the old rail, and at this point a switch rail from a split switch is bolted to the old rail and spiked against the new rail. After the train passes, the switch rail is taken out, and work proceeds as before. This work should usually progress against the current of traffic on double-track work.

503. The **supervisor of bridges** will have charge of the maintenance and repair of all bridges on the section of line assigned to him. These bridges will be either steel, masonry, or wooden. The work on each class of bridge requires a different class of skilled labor, and each will be under a separate head foreman. There will be about three laborers for each skilled mechanic. The ratio of foremen, subforemen, and cooks will be as in the track gang. The common labor will be allotted to each head foreman as the necessity arises. The requirements of work may demand separate messing and camping arrangements for each class; if so, the necessary arrangements are made by the supervisor. When different gangs work together, the supervisor designates one man as head of the work. The supervisor will thoroughly acquaint himself with all the bridges on his section of line. He will have drawings and complete bills of material for all bridges, so that on notice of a break the proper repair materials can be started without delay.

504. The **organization of the bridge parties** is similar to that of the track gang. The force of assistants to the supervisor of bridges is similar to that of the supervisor of track. When the parties are working at separate points, he will arrange for separate medical attendants, commissaries, quartermasters, and clerks to suit the circumstances.

The bridge train is similar to the track train, with the addition of timbers, blocking, girders, derrick, and other tools and appliances for rapid bridge work. If conditions justify, one car may be made up as a concrete car and carry a certain amount of concrete materials. The size of the derrick will be determined by the weight of the rolling stock and the weights of the heaviest spans. The wrecking derrick, when not otherwise employed, can be used on bridge work.

### RECONSTRUCTION.

505. As the army advances along a line of railway the track and structures will usually be found more or less destroyed and until repairs are effected the line cannot be operated. Owing to the nearness to the front, civilian labor can not be counted upon, and this duty must be performed by railway troops assisted by such civilian labor or details from other troops as may be required by the extent of the damage and the necessity of speedy repair.

This work will be in charge of the **A. D. R. of reconstruction,** who is responsible to the military head of the line in question.

In special cases, where temporary repairs will involve practically as much time as permanent repairs, it may be advisable to make the permanent repairs at once. Wherever practicable, the maintenance of way gangs in rear will be called upon for assistance.

The reconstruction forces can profitably be organized in the manner described for the maintenance of way gangs of the divisions.

41421°—16——10

506. The work is carried on at the railhead from a construction train made up as follows from head to rear:

- Two flat cars with rails.
- Two flat cars with ties.
- One flat car with timbers, namely, 12 by 12, 16 by 8, and 18 by 9 ins.
- One flat car of tools and supplies.
- One box car for finer tools and stores.
- Three tourist sleepers for engineer troops.
- Three tourist sleepers for laborers.
- One combination car for office and officers.
- One box car for commissary supplies, etc.
- One dynamo car.
- One locomotive.
- One tank car.
- One gondola car for coal.

The office car will be connected by telephone and telegraph with the rear. This train should carry about six to 10 days' rations, and an electric light plant should be carried along to light up the work, especially bridge work, at night.

There will be a **derrick car** near the railhead at all times. This car will be found of the greatest use in reconstructing bridges and removing débris from wrecked structures.

507. The **construction train** will be supplied with the following tools and equipment and, in addition to these, with any other tools or appliances that will materially assist in rapid reconstruction:

| | |
|---|---|
| Adzes, carpenter's | 10 |
| Anvils and blocks | 3 |
| Augers, long and short, 3/8 to 2¼ in | 100 |
| Axes, hand and felling | 30 |
| Axes, pick, helved | 350 |
| Angle bars to suit rails | 150 |
| Bags, sand | 500 |
| Bags, waterproof, for explosives | 3 |
| Bar claw (bull's foot) | 20 |
| Barrows, wheel, wood | 12 |
| Bars, boring and tamping, 1½-in | 17 |
| Bars, crow | 60 |
| Bars, hold-up | 25 |
| Bars, pinch, track | 25 |
| Bellows, smith's, with frame | 1 |
| Bellows, tinsmith's | 2 |
| Billhooks | 29 |
| Blocks, iron, for 3½ ins, circumference rope, single and double | 3 |
| Blocks, wooden, for 3½ ins. circumference rope, single and double | 8 |
| Boards, pine, 20 ft. by 3 ins. to 16 ft. by 1 in., assorted sizes. pieces | 120 |
| Bolt ends, 7/8-in | 200 |
| Boltheads, 7/8-in | 200 |
| Boltheads, 1½-in | 100 |
| Bolts and nuts (3/4-in.), 8, 14, 20, 24, 30, and 36 ins. long . . of each | 100 |
| Bolts and nuts (½-in.), 2, 4, and 6 ins. long . . . of each | 75 |
| Bolts and nuts (½-in.), 3 and 9 ins. long . . . of each | 100 |
| Bolts and nuts (1½-in.), 30 ins. long | 24 |
| Bolts, drift (3/4-in.), 19, 22, and 26 ins. long . . . of each | 100 |
| Bolts, rail (to suit rail) | 3,000 |
| Bolts, steel, for bridge ties | 1,000 |
| Brushes, No. 8, and liners, 1 and 1½ in . . . of each | 2 |
| Brushes, paint, 6-oz | 8 |
| Buckets, galvanized iron | 20 |
| Bunting, red, white, and green . . . yards of each | 10 |
| Cans, oil, feeding | 8 |
| Canvas . . . yards | 36 |
| Car, push | 1 |
| Chests, tool, filled, U. S. Engineer Company, carpenter | 2 |

| | | |
|---|---|---|
| Chests, tool, filled, U. S. Engineer Company, blacksmith | | 4 |
| Chest, tool, filled, U. S. Engineer Company, demolition | | 1 |
| Chisels, brick, 18-in | | 12 |
| Chisels, cold | | 25 |
| Chisels, smith's, round nose and crosscut | | 25 |
| Chocks for wheels | | 6 |
| Clamps for track drills | | 14 |
| Cold sets | | 50 |
| Coupling screws | | 5 |
| Crows, jim | | 5 |
| Dogs, timber, 12, 18, and 24 ins. long | | 75 |
| Drills, 3/4 and 1 in | of each | 6 |
| Drills for ratchets, long and short, 7/8 to 2 in | | 100 |
| Drier, patent | lbs | 14 |
| Elbows and T pieces, 1-in., galvanized iron | of each | 12 |
| Files, assorted | | 40 |
| Flags, hand, red, green, and white | of each | 20 |
| Forges, smith's, round | | 2 |
| Gage, wheel | | 1 |
| Gages, track | | 14 |
| Gimlets, assorted | | 12 |
| Glue | lbs | 5 |
| Grindstone, general service | | 1 |
| Hammers, hand and claw | | 16 |
| Hammers, sledge, 4-lb. to 14-lb | | 33 |
| Hammers, spiking | | 50 |
| Hammers, stone | | 24 |
| Handles for augers | | 75 |
| Handles for axes and adzes | | 15 |
| Handles for hammers, spike and hand | | 200 |
| Handles for tamping picks and pickaxes | | 150 |
| Hinges, T and butt, assorted | pairs | 120 |
| Hose for pumps | lengths | 24 |
| Hot sets | | 20 |
| Iron, bar, round, 7/8, 1, 1 1/4, and 1 1/2 in | bars | 20 |
| Iron, bar, round, 3/8, 1/2, and 3/4 in | bars | 50 |
| Iron, bar, round, 3-in | pieces | 3 |
| Iron, bar, flat, 6 by 1 to 2 by 1/4 in., assorted | bars | 24 |
| Irons, expansion | | 40 |
| Jacks, ratchet pulling | | 2 |
| Jacks, track (Barrett's) | | 10 |
| Jacks, Pearson's | pairs | 2 |
| Jacks, traversing, 10 to 20 ton | | 10 |
| Kegs, water, with faucets | | 2 |
| Ladles, melting | | 2 |
| Lanterns, hand (red 10, green 10, white 20) | | 40 |
| Lanterns, tail | | 4 |
| Lead, bar | lbs | 200 |
| Lead, red and white | lbs | 168 |
| Levels, field | | 4 |
| Levels, spirit | | 13 |
| Locks for switches, with key | sets | 6 |
| Machines, boring, with augers | | 10 |
| Nails, wire, 5 and 6 in | cwt. of each | 3 |
| Nails, wire, 1, 1 1/2, 2, and 4 in | cwt. of each | 1 |
| Nipples, plugs, and sockets, 1-in., galvanized iron, and bibcocks, brass | of each | 6 |
| Oil, olive, castor, colza, linseed | gallons of each | 5 |
| Oil, paraffin | gallons | 30 |
| Padlocks, galvanized iron | | 6 |
| Pins, split, steel, assorted | gross | 1 |
| Piping, galvanized iron, 1-in | running ft | 340 |
| Planes, jack and smoothing | | 3 |
| Plates, fish, special junction (or angle bars) | pairs | 36 |
| Poles, iron-shod (for lights and wires) | | 30 |

| | |
|---|---|
| Pumps, lift and force | 3 |
| Punches, center | 6 |
| Rail saws (each with extra saws and a saw sharpener), "Bryant" | 2 |
| Rails cut to fit standard turnouts (frogs Nos. 8 and 10) . of each.. | 4 |
| Rails, steel, standard T pattern, 24 and 30 ft ... of each.. | 80 |
| Ratchets, track drill (Paulus or Q. & C.) | 13 |
| Ratchets, fitters | 3 |
| Replacers, Fewing's car ... sets.. | 2 |
| Rivets, iron (¾-in.), 4½ to 2½ ins., assorted lengths | 600 |
| Rivets, iron (⅞-in.), 4 to 2½ ins., assorted lengths | 700 |
| Rods, leveling, 6-ft | 5 |
| Rope, manila, 3 ins. circumference ... coils.. | 2 |
| Rope, manila, 2¼, 2½, and 4½ in ... coil of each.. | 1 |
| Rules, carpenter's | 12 |
| Saw-sets, hand and crosscut ... of each | 3 |
| Saws, 26-in., hand, crosscut, and pit | 42 |
| Screws, wood, ¾ to 5 in., assorted ... gross of each.. | 4 to 10 |
| Screws and washers, galvanized iron, for sheets ... gross.. | 2 |
| Sheets, galvanized iron, corrugated, 6 and 10 ft. long ... of each.. | 100 |
| Shovels (square-pointed 300, round-pointed 100) | 400 |
| Slings, chain (see wrecking outfit) | 4 |
| Sockets, reducing, 2 to 1 in. and 1½ to 1 in ... of each.. | 6 |
| Solder ... lbs.. | 15 |
| Spikes, hand | 6 |
| Spikes, iron, 10-in ... cwt.. | 3 |
| Spikes, iron, 8-in ... cwt.. | 1½ |
| Spikes, rail ... kegs.. | 30 |
| Spun yarn, tarred ... coils.. | 2 |
| Squares, carpenter's, 6, 9, 12, and 20 in ... of each.. | 2 to 4 |
| Steel, blister ... lbs.. | 28 |
| Steel, tool, octagonal, ½, ¾, 1, 1¼, and 1½ in. bars ... of each.. | 2 |
| Stocks and dies, 2 to 1⅜ in., 1½ to ⅜ in., and 1⅛ to ¼ in., set of each.. | 1 |
| Switches and frogs, complete, Nos. 8 and 10 ... set of each.. | 1 |
| Tallow, Russian ... lbs.. | 200 |
| Tamping picks, helved (stone ballast) | 100 |
| Tank, water, galvanized iron, 200 gallons | 1 |
| Tanks, water, galvanized iron, 50 gallons | 3 |
| Tapes, measuring, 100 and 50 ft | 12 |
| Tarpaulins | 4 |
| Theodolite, level, pair of rods, and chain ... of each.. | 1 |
| Ties, crossing | 23 |
| Ties, standard | 672 |
| Timbers, 18 by 9 ins., from 36 to 20 ft. lengths | 10 |
| Timbers, 16 by 8 ins., from 32 to 16 ft. lengths | 25 |
| Timbers, 12 by 12 ins., from 36 to 30 ft. lengths | 8 |
| Tongs for cold sets ... pair.. | 1 |
| Tongs, pipe, 1, 1½, and 2 in ... of each . | 1 |
| Tongs, rail | 40 |
| Tools, riveter's: | |
| Spanners and snaps, ¾ and ⅞ in ... of each.. | 6 |
| Hammers, with 30-in. handles | 12 |
| Tongs ... pairs.. | 4 |
| Drifts, ¾ and ⅞ in ... of each.. | 24 |
| Hammers, sledge, 8-lb., with 36-in. handles | 6 |
| Turpentine ... gallons.. | 5 |
| Twine ... balls.. | 12 |
| Vise, standing | 1 |
| Washers, iron, 1 by ¼ in | 224 |
| Waste, cotton ... lbs.. | 50 |
| Wells lights, No. 3 | 2 |
| Wicks for lamps, hand, tail, and hurricane ... per lamp.. | 4 |
| Wrenches, assorted | 22 |
| Wrenches, monkey, 12 and 15 in ... of each.. | 4 |
| Wrenches, Stillson's, 18-in | 6 |
| Wrenches, track | 50 |

508. **Construction wagon train.**—It will frequently be found that all the construction party can not work to advantage on a bridge or a single break at one time, and if there is a wagon train with the construction party that can go on ahead with a party and supplies, repairs can be made for 5 or 6 miles ahead of the train by the time that the train can advance. This wagon train ought to consist of from 30 to 40 wagons.

509. A suitable amount of **tentage and camp equipage** must be carried to protect the construction parties from inclement weather, and whenever the parties stop long enough at one point a camp will be formed. This will make the men more comfortable and healthy, both of which tend to make them work better under difficulties.

510. **Night work and lighting.**—Night work, except in bridge construction, is done at a disadvantage. For night work the lighting arrangements should be electric lights if possible. Holophane prismatic globes would be of great advantage, as they do not cast such black shadows as do the lights in ordinary globes. Acetylene lamps have reached a high stage of perfection at the present time, but if used as searchlights they throw a very black shadow. Wells lights (fig. 69) give good satisfaction for field use.

511. A large amount of railway supplies, tools, etc., must be kept in store at the advance depot and moved ahead as the depot advances. The available supply of stores and tools must be such that at no time will the work be laid out for lack of either.

512. **All army stores** arriving at the railhead station must be unloaded *immediately* and cars shipped back. If supplies can not be unloaded immediately, the loaded cars must be sent back to the nearest storehouse and the proper person disciplined for blocking the railhead.

513. **Precedence** in trains and supplies will be given to anything that pertains to the construction party, except possibly during an engagement. The temporary construction party will only be called upon to lay additional sidings under cases of great emergency.

514. The following is a **list of the supplies** that Colonel Girouard, Director of Railways in South Africa, took with him to South Africa when he assumed charge of the railways:

(*a*) STORES.

| | |
|---|---|
| Balks, 14 by 14, and 12 by 12 ins., and timbers from 16 by 8 to 9 by 7 ins. ....cu. ft.. | 152,000 |
| Bolts, $\frac{3}{4}$-in., of assorted lengths.... | 4,400 |
| Boltheads and ends, with washers.... | 5,800 |
| Spikes, timber, $\frac{5}{8}$-in., 7 to 10 ins. long.... | 12,000 |
| Piping, iron, galvanized, 2, 3, and 4 ins. diameter. running ft. | 29,000 |
| Collars, flanges, bends, sockets, elbows, tubes, connecting cocks, plugs, valves, and bibcocks for pipes as above. of each.. | 20 to 250 |
| Stocks, taps and dies, pipe tongs, spanners, and vises for pipes as above.... of each.. | 4 to 24 |

(*b*) TOOLS.

A large number of tools of various kinds was ordered, of which the following were the principal ones:

| | |
|---|---|
| Axes, pick, 5-lb.... | 200 |
| Helves for same.... | 500 |
| Shovels, universal, helved.... | 100 |
| Spades.... | 200 |
| Bars, boring, jumping, and tamping, $1\frac{1}{4}$ and $1\frac{1}{2}$ in.... | 300 |
| Dogs, sawyer's, straight and cross-ended.... | 5,000 |
| Saws, crosscut, blade 5 ft.... | 50 |
| Wire, steel, telegraph, $7\frac{1}{2}$ B. W. G., assorted.... tons.. | 20 |
| Iron, wrought, bars, round and square, assorted sizes.... tons.. | 33 |

| | | |
|---|---|---|
| Screws, iron, flat-headed, 2 to 5 in | gross.. | 225 |
| Blocks, wood, with sheaves for rope 3, 4½, and 5 ins. circumference, single, double, treble, and snatch | | 165 |
| Rope, manila, 1½ to 5 ins. circumference | ft.. | 30,000 |
| Jacks, screw, traversing, 6 to 20 ton | | 30 |
| Winches, crab, double purchase, to lift from 25 to 60 cwt | | 10 |
| Pile drivers, hand, 15-cwt | | 4 |
| Forges | | 12 |
| Well-boring tools, complete, to bore 50 ft | sets.. | 2 |
| Rope, wire, Bullivant's, 1½ to 4½ ins. circumference, | running ft.. | 11,000 |
| Clamps, shackles, thimbles, turnbuckles, nippers, and chain slings for above wire rope | each.. | 2 to 12 |
| Wells lights, with 3 extra burners | | 10 |
| Cable, interruption, 4-core | miles.. | 2 |
| Pumps, hand and steam | | 42 |
| Tanks, water, 1,500-gallon | | 60 |
| Bridges, 50-ft. span | | 10 |
| Bridges, 30-ft. span | | 30 |

515. The following is a list of the **principal stores and tools used** on the rail ways in South Africa during the first and second years of the war:

STORES.

| | | |
|---|---|---|
| Asbestos | lbs.. | 386 |
| Bolts and nuts | | 27,000 |
| Bolts, fish | | 46,500 |
| Bibcocks | | 211 |
| Bridge work | bridges.. | 40 |
| Cement | barrels.. | 335 |
| Crossings and points | | 80 |
| Coal | tons.. | 520 |
| Cocks | | 300 |
| Candles | lbs.. | 525 |
| Copper | lbs.. | 1,000 |
| Carbide of calcium | lb.. | ½ |
| Dogs, sawyer's | | 18,000 |
| Detonators | | 700 |
| Dynamite | lbs.. | 150 |
| Ends, bolt | | 864 |
| Flanges, pipe | | 200 |
| Ferrules, tube | | 500 |
| Fuse | coils.. | 52 |
| Grease | lbs.. | 1,150 |
| Glasses, gage | | 250 |
| Heads, bolt | | 6,100 |
| Iron, corrugated, galvanized, sheets | ft.. | 52,000 |
| Iron, bar, peak, etc | tons.. | 94 |
| Links, coupling | | 250 |
| Lead, red, white, and black | tons.. | 2½ |
| Lead | lbs.. | 1,896 |
| Matches | boxes.. | 432 |
| Nails | tons.. | 5 |
| Nipples | | 250 |
| Nuts | | 4,800 |
| Oil | gallons.. | 7,400 |
| Piping | running ft.. | 30,500 |
| Pipes, earthenware, etc | | 750 |
| Pins, coupling, etc | | 5,000 |
| Plates, fish | | 24,250 |
| Pitch | lbs.. | 430 |
| Rope | tons.. | 15 |
| Rails | tons.. | 3,300 |
| Rivets | tons.. | 5 |

| | | |
|---|---|---|
| Stays and washers | lbs.. | 3,750 |
| Steel | tons.. | 16 |
| Screws | gross.. | 1,030 |
| Spikes, dog | | 174,000 |
| Sleepers (ties) | | 66,000 |
| Sal ammoniac | lbs.. | 60 |
| Tubing | running ft.. | 900 |
| Tees | | 550 |
| Tallow | lbs.. | 1,500 |
| Tin | sheets.. | 110 |
| Timber | cu. ft.. | 52,000 |
| Timber | running ft.. | 833,000 |
| Valves | | 150 |
| Vises | | 27 |
| Waste | lbs.. | 3,800 |
| Washers, of sorts | | 20,000 |
| Zinc | sheets.. | 55 |

TOOLS.

| | | |
|---|---|---|
| Axes, felling and hand | | 150 |
| Augers, screw | | 950 |
| Braces, ratchet | | 76 |
| Bars, boring, etc | | 315 |
| Beaters, plate layer's (tamping picks) | | 400 |
| Bits for ratchet braces | | 100 |
| Braces, carpenter's | | 48 |
| Bits for carpenter's braces | | 53 |
| Blocks, various | | 280 |
| Buckets, various | | 370 |
| Bullivant's gear, complete | set.. | 1 |
| Belting | ft.. | 600 |
| Cans of oil | | 160 |
| Crowbars | | 200 |
| Chisels | | 1,000 |
| Drills, ratchets, clamps, etc | | 120 |
| Emery cloth | sheets.. | 430 |
| Files, various | | 1,400 |
| Forges | | 16 |
| Hammers, various | | 900 |
| Handles, various | | 5,800 |
| Hose | running ft.. | 3,200 |
| Jackscrews, etc | | 52 |
| Lamps, various | | 270 |
| Levels | | 55 |
| Lines, various | | 620 |
| Lines, log | fathoms.. | 1,200 |
| Mallets, carpenter's, etc | | 132 |
| Needles, sailmaker's, etc | | 380 |
| Pile drivers, hand and steam | | 3 |
| Picks | | 1,900 |
| Pencils, carpenter's | | 800 |
| Pumps and boilers, complete | | 7 |
| Pumps | | 30 |
| Phonophores | | 28 |
| Rules for carpenters, etc | | 340 |
| Ramps, rail | | 24 |
| Shovels | | 3,000 |
| Saws, various | | 400 |
| Spanners (bar wrenches) | | 400 |
| Stone, oil and grind | | 100 |
| Set saws, cold, etc | | 110 |
| Stocks and dies | | 40 |
| Tape measures | | 60 |

| | |
|---|---|
| Tarpaulins | 75 |
| Trolleys (small cars) | 50 |
| Tongues | 140 |
| Tools, chests of, etc | 50 |
| Wheelbarrows | 200 |
| Winches | 16 |
| Wedges, hardwood and iron | 540 |
| Wrenches | 150 |

The two foregoing lists furnish about the only available data to guide an officer in his preparation of railway supplies for a campaign. They are too indefinite in many cases to furnish more than a very general guide, but nevertheless they are extremely valuable.

516. **The issue of stores.**—Tools or supplies urgently needed can be issued on receipt of an officer by any storekeeper, who will report to the chief storekeeper. This informal issue applies principally to the advanced bases and, in cases of emergency, to storekeepers along the line in rear. Normally, a requisition should come through the proper division channels.

Storekeepers in making regulations should exercise a wise discretion between expendable and nonexpendable articles, making the amount of paper work as small as possible, and yet be consistent with the regulations.

517. The **storekeeper** of the base storehouse will be in complete charge of all stores. It is his duty to keep track of issues, receipts, and amount of stock on hand; promptly filling all requisitions and taking charge of and properly storing all articles received. Simplicity and promptness must characterize the method of accounting for stores. **Memorandum receipts** will be taken when practicable. This will make receiving officers more careful in the use of the property and will give a closer line on the disposition of property when the same is lost or expended.

518. When any considerable amount of army stores have been unloaded at the railhead, they will **not be reloaded** for shipment to the front, except under great emergency, until traffic at that point has become normal. It will be found that less delay will be caused by getting up new shipments than by reloading at or near the railhead, unless very favorable conditions exist as regards sidings, cars, etc.

519. **Demolitions.**—The constructing engineer may be called upon to make demolitions in case of retreat. The **lower chords** and **batter posts** of trusses and the abutments and piers of girder bridges are the most open to attack with explosives. **Abutments** are destroyed by sinking a shaft behind the masonry, burying a charge at this point, and exploding same by the electric exploder. **Spans** 20 to 60 ft. in length are best destroyed by placing charges at the ends of the truss. This destroys both masonry and truss.

520. **Arches** are destroyed by exploding a charge in a shaft sunk from above to the crown of the arch or to the haunches. A **tunnel** is best destroyed by sinking shafts from above and exploding charges to blow in the top of the tunnel. Two trains loaded with railroad iron or other heavy material will effectually close a tunnel if these trains are started at a high speed from opposite ends of the tunnel at the same time and allowed to collide in the middle of the same.

521. A method of **track demolition** recommended by Capt. W. D. Waghorn, R. E., is to blow up alternate joints of rails for several miles, which, he says would have been much more effective than any form of demolition used by the Boers.

522. In a report on the railroads of the Civil War, an engineer who had great experience in the repair of demolished railways states that in his opinion the most effective way to **demolish a railroad** is to build a fire every 100 ft. along the track on top of the rails. The heat expands the rails and twists them out of shape. The ends of the ties burn off and the resulting demolition is complete. **To repair it,** the twisted mass of wreckage must first be removed, and then the track laid; whereas, if the rails are taken up and bent, only half as much work must be done by the reconstruction party. See chapter on Demolitions.

## DEFENSE OF A LINE OF RAILWAY.

523. The defense of a railway against a brigade or division that may be sent against it for its systematic destruction can only be made by a force of sufficient strength to meet and defeat the raiding forces. Besides these attacks by large bodies there are the **continual depredations** against the line made by small bodies ranging from a regiment down to the lone individual who tries to burn a bridge or misplace a switch. The **greatest difficulties** in operating a road come from small bands which can operate against the line, especially in a hostile country, without great danger of apprehension, and these bands must be constantly watched for by a special railway guard.

The defense of the railway may be maintained by the combined use of **block-houses and armored trains.**

524. **Blockhouses.**—Blockhouses will be placed at points along the line within sight of one another and about 2,000 or 3,000 yds. apart on tangents, and at all important points, such as bridges, viaducts, and tunnels. The **interval on curves** depends on the radius of the curve and the destructibility of the road in the interval. These blockhouse should be of the type and construction shown elsewhere in the Engineer Field Manual. Each blockhouse will be built for a garrison of 8 or more men; each will be supplied with a good-sized water tank, and will be connected with the other blockhouses by telephone or telegraph. For every three companies of a battalion in the line of blockhouses the fourth company should be stationed at a town in the middle of such line as a support in case of attack; and for every two battalions on the line the third battalion should be held at about the middle point as a reserve. These troops belong to the Service of Defense of the Line of Communications.

The track will be **patrolled continually,** both night and day. The patrols should be doubled at night and in inclement weather.

A system of **rocket signals** will be arranged to indicate the presence of the enemy or of an attack by him during the night.

(Pars. 525 to 552, inclusive, are practically condensed from the History of Railways in the South African war, Royal Engineers' Institute, 1904, altered to suit conditions of the United States service.)

525. **Armored trains** are made up of an armored locomotive and certain armored and unarmored cars. The locomotives should be considerably stronger than the weight of the trains demand, as they are in constant use under adverse circumstances. The locomotive will be covered over its vital parts with **bullet-proof armor of sheet steel.**

The cab, tender, air pump, injector, and other parts, depending upon the make of the engine, that could be injured by bullets at close range, will be protected in like manner. The rear of the cab will be protected from reverse fire, and in the sides of the cab will be placed small hoods with slits, fore and aft, through which the engineman can observe the track in his front and watch for train signals without exposing himself. The sides of the cab will be provided with sliding steel-plate windows.

The boiler need not be armored if it is thick enough to resist rifle fire; otherwise it must be armored also.

The locomotive will be habitually in the middle of the train.

The **train from front to rear** will be as follows: (1) Gondola loaded with sand; (2) No. 1 machine-gun car; (3) dynamo car; (4) officer's car; (5) baggage car; (6) locomotive; (7) R. F. gun car; (8) such other cars as may be needed in the train; (9) dynamo car; (10) No. 2 machine-gun car.

526. **Searchlights.**—An armored train will be supplied with one, or preferably two, 12-in. searchlights. The dynamo and engine for each of these lights will occupy about half a car. The motive power for the dynamo may be either steam or gasoline. **Gasoline engines** have many advantages, the greatest of which are their independence from a steam generator and the compactness of the plant.

These **dynamo cars** will be run next to the machine-gun cars. If a gasoline engine be used, the entire lighting plant may be carried in the machine-gun car. Steam from the locomotive can not be used for the motive power, since then the light could only be operated when the locomotive was connected with the dynamo car, and the use of the searchlight when the armored train was disposed as in fig. 146 would be impossible. Steam engines and boilers take up too much space if other motive power is available. **Direct-connected units** give the best satisfaction and take up the least room. The steam turbine is most compact and noiseless, but requires a steam generator. Gasoline motive power is doubtless the best for this purpose, and will be used wherever possible. Direct-connected gasoline sets are now on the market.

527. **Glass mirrors** are commonly used in the projectors, but they are more liable to breakage than metal mirrors. On the other hand, glass mirrors can be more readily purchased, and if set in rubber will stand considerable jarring. The projector itself will be armored on all sides and will have a sliding door in front. The light can be maneuvered from inside the car by means of a hand or rope control mechanism, such as shown in figs. 143 and 144. Electrical-control apparatus is only manufactured for projectors 24 ins. or more in diameter.

FIG. 143.—PILOT-HOUSE CONTROL PROJECTOR.

FIG. 144.—ROPE-CONTROL GEAR.

For the 12-in. searchlight a dynamo of about 2 kw. is required. A 12-in. light was found to answer every purpose that was required of it in the South African war.

The searchlights will be located on top of the machine-gun cars, or on the forward machine-gun car if only one light is used. Each searchlight will be provided with a signal shutter similar to the Gibbs shutter used in the Signal Corps. The locomotive should have a searchlight on it for use when the train is disposed as in fig. 146. The turbo-generator sets for this purpose occupy hardly a cubic foot of space, and as an auxiliary light this would be invaluable.

Any extra room in the dynamo cars will be used for bunks for the enlisted men.

The sides of the dynamo car will be plated with ¼-in. steel for a height of 7 ft., and the sides will be slotted for rifle fire.

528. A combination diner and sleeper will be utilized for the **office car.** This car need not be armored unless it is intended to use it as a hospital car. One end of this car will be partitioned off and used as a kitchen for the entire force with the armored train. The telegraph office will also be in this car.

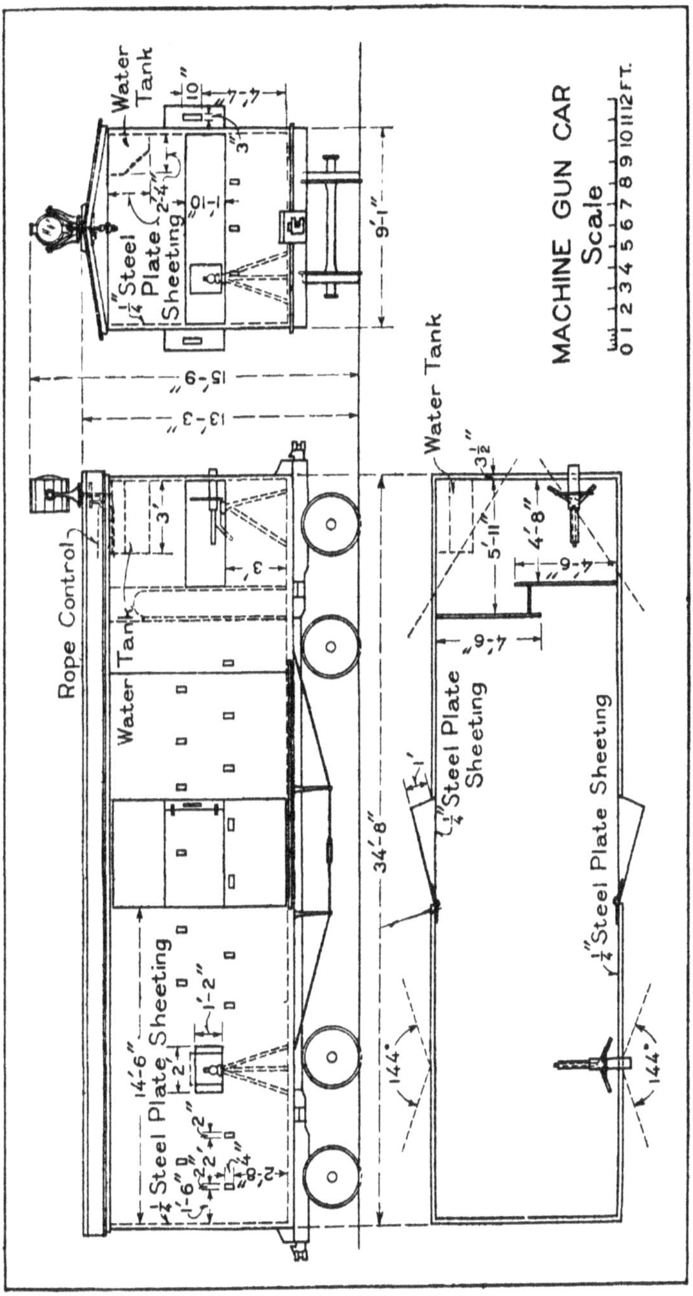
MACHINE GUN CAR
Scale
0 1 2 3 4 5 6 7 8 9 10 11 12 FT.
Rope Control
Water Tank
Water Tank
Water Tank
1/4" Steel Plate Sheeting
Steel Plate Sheeting
1/4" Steel Plate Sheeting
1/4" Steel Plate Sheeting
Steel Plate Sheeting
34'-8"
15'-9"
13'-3"
9'-1"
14'-6"
144°
144°

FIG. 145.

529. The **machine-gun cars** will be armored with 1¼-in. sheet steel for a height of 7 ft., and provided with loopholes for infantry fire. The general points of their construction are shown in fig. 145.

530. The front car of the train will be a gondola loaded with sand and rigged with a cowcatcher on its forward end. This car is the defense against contact mines.

531. Immediately behind the engine is the R. F. gun car, and at the rear of the train is machine-gun car No. 2.

532. The details of the R. F. gun car will depend upon the class of mount available and the extra width that the car can have on the line. The car can not be widened very much for fear of "side swiping" other trains. This subject should be investigated before planning the car, and no extra width provided if possible to avoid it. It does not take long to traverse the gun for reloading.

533. It will be necessary to carry a tourist sleeper for the enlisted men and a baggage car for supplies. The position of these cars in the train is shown in fig. 146. A flat car of ties, rails, spikes, etc., for slight repairs will accompany each train.

534. The **side doors** of at least two cars should be so protected that sections can be pushed out about a foot from the car to give a flank fire along the train in both directions (fig. 145).

535. **Armament.**—The main armament of the armored train is a 3-in. R. F. gun, or possibly a 6-pounder, and four machine guns of whatever type may be adopted. The R. F. gun will be placed on a pedestal mount, similar to that used in the Navy, or an adaptation of the pedestal mount with foundation ring and bolts used in our seacoast fortifications. The ammunition for this gun is carried in the car with the gun. The car will carry about 500 rounds of ammunition. This car is also designed for an infantry defense of about 12 men.

The machine guns may be of any of the approved types, on a tripod or fixed mount. Each gun will be supplied with 30,000 rounds of ammunition.

The **garrison of the armored train** should consist of 2 officers and the following enlisted men: Infantry, 8 noncommissioned officers and 42 privates; engineers, 1 sergeant and 8 privates; signal troops, 1 telegraph lineman and 1 operator; artillery, 3 noncommissioned officers and 7 men; hospital corps, 2 noncommissioned officers. Of the officers, one will be an artillery officer. There will be a double crew for the train.

536. **Communications.**—The cars must all open into one another, and must be provided with platforms to lay from one car to the next. There should be telephonic connection from between different parts of the train, and a system of bell signals arranged in case the telephone is broken. All wires should have slip connections between the cars. It is not feasible to protect all the air-brake system of the train, hence some signal should be arranged to order the release of all brakes in case the air line is cut. The engine will thereafter control the train by its own brakes, assisted by such inside hand-brake arrangements as can be made.

537. **Posts of officers when on duty.**—The artillery officer will ride in the R. F. gun car, and the other officer in the forward machine-gun car. The noncommissioned officers in the other cars will be so instructed in their duties that they can handle their men in action and carry out the intention of the commanding officer.

538. **Administration of armored trains.**—The armored trains are under the orders of the commander of the district of the line of communications in which they are stationed. They will be assigned to districts by the commander of the line of communications. They will be moved about within the district by the district commander. The commanding officer of the train being ordered to any point will communicate with the railway authorities and request orders for his train. The trains form part of the line of communications and are only temporarily a part of the district command. The trains must not be used for any other than for railway defense. When it is necessary to proceed to any point immediately, the commanding officer of the armored train is authorized to inform the train dispatcher of his desires, using the signal "21" to give him immediate right of way over the wires. The train dispatcher will, on receipt of this message, immediately issue the necessary train orders to carry out the move.

539. The commanding officer of an armored train will not make use of privileged telegrams, nor shall he interfere with the regular movement of traffic by sudden and unexpected moves except in an emergency; and he must understand that every such case will be passed upon by a higher authority and that he will be held responsible for unnecessary interference with traffic.

Any unnecessary interference with traffic by any armored train will be reported promptly by the division personnel.

540. An armored train will not be used by the commanding officer of the railway guard for **inspection purposes** unless this can be done in the course of its other duties. Unauthorized persons will not be carried on the armored trains.

When any district commander of the line of communication has reason to believe that his section of the line is to be attacked and that the use of an armored train is necessary. he will communicate his information to the Chief of Staff, Line of Communication.

541. **The garrison of an armored train**, after being detailed on this duty, is subject to the orders of the commander of the line of communication, and changes from one district to another, or changes in the garrison, should be made by him only.

542. The commanding officer of an armored train should have had some experience in railway work, so as to appreciate the traffic conditions in addition to the military conditions. He will render a weekly report showing the make-up of the train, the mileage made during the week, the points of the line covered, the condition of the train and its armament, the amount of ammunition spent during the week and the amount on hand, and any repairs that may have been made to the railroad by the engineer detachment of the armored train. After an engagement a report will be submitted showing the amount of ammunition expended, the number of the enemy, the casualties on both sides, and any damage that may have been done to the train or its armament.

543. **Larger guns.**—In case it is desired for any reason to mount larger guns on railway cars, this can be easily done. The 6-in. gun can be mounted and fired from a flat car in a direction 30° on either side of the track without danger of upsetting the car. It can be fired at right angles to the line of the track by the use of two girders or timbers, that can be carried on the car, and which before firing will be shoved under the car and blocked up tight against the floor. It is a slow process to traverse and load for every shot, but with the longer guns this must be done between 50° and 90° from the line of the track to give room for loading. The possibilities for using guns mounted on cars in the **defense of a place** are very great. The guns can be rapidly moved from point to point as needed, or to get under cover when the fire of the enemy gets too hot. It would be impossible for the enemy to locate such a "train battery," for it would have no fixed emplacement. It would also deceive the enemy as to the number of guns opposing him.

In South Africa, 6-in. guns were used on flat cars with a 3 ft. 6 in. gage, and a 9.2-in. gun was mounted and fired on a low metal car of the same gage, with no bad result to the car or track.

**Cars can be armored** by putting one thickness of rail up the sides and ends, taking precautions to fasten the rails so that they will not be moved by the motion or jar of the train. One rail left out at the proper height makes a continuous loophole for rifle fire. By thus utilizing the rails and ties that must be carried along to repair slight breaks in the line, an extra armored car is obtained without increasing the total number of cars in the train.

The commanding officer of the armored train must have **judgment and discretion,** as well as bravery and dash, in the execution of his duty.

### TACTICS OF ARMORED TRAINS.

544. **Positions of machine guns and artillery in action.**—The machine-gun cars and the R. F. gun car are self-supporting against a small force of the enemy; any one of them is practically impregnable against infantry fire alone.

The general practice to be adopted against the enemy will be to extend the line by distributing the armored cars along the track such a distance that the rear can not be turned. The cars must be within rifle range of each other, and will be about 1,000 yds. apart. As the train advances, if the enemy is at long range, the train is cut in two just ahead of the R. F. gun car and the locomotive runs on ahead, with the forward part of the train, until within an easy rifle range; here it cuts off the No. 1 machine-gun and dynamo cars, and the locomotive retires to the R. F. gun car. In case the enemy attempts to cut the railroad in rear, the rear section of the train will be backed down the line where the machine-gun car No. 2 is cut off, and the R. F. gun car and the locomotive return to their former position.

If the locomotive is in rear of the R. F. gun car, or if the train is backing up, the train will push up to within easy rifle range, cut off the machine-gun and dynamo cars at that end, and then back down the line and leave the R. F. gun car and the other machine-gun car where it is desired to use them.

The **field of fire and position** of the cars **in action** is shown in fig. 146.

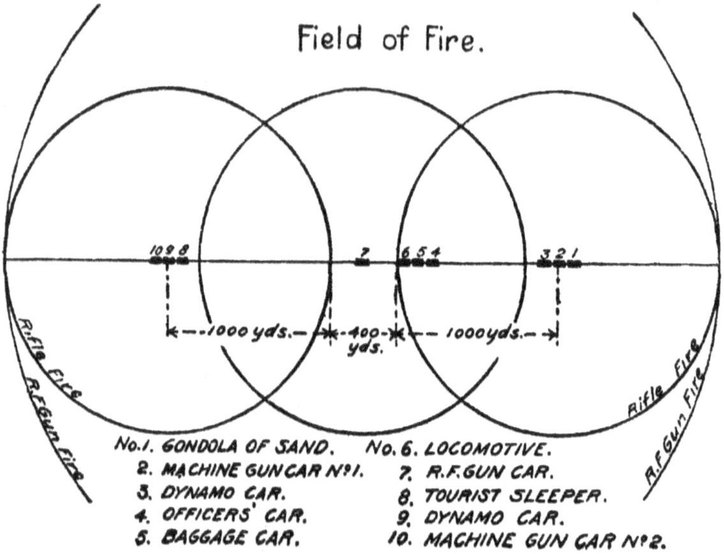


FIG. 146.

In using two or more armored trains together, each train is divided up as described for one train, thus covering a long section of line. The track to the rear is patrolled by the rear locomotive and a machine-gun car, to give notice of any turning movement and prevent the destruction of the track in the rear.

### DUTIES OF ARMORED TRAINS.

545. The chief duties of armored trains may be briefly stated as follows:

(1) To intercept and attack a retreating enemy whom the army is driving onto the railroad line.
(2) The train being well advanced, to prevent the enemy from moving around the flank of a column or a line of columns.
(3) To reenforce stations and camps that are threatened by the enemy.
(4) To escort ordinary trains.
(5) To reconnoiter.
(6) To patrol the railroad.

546. In the first two uses above mentioned, the railway must be divided into sections, each train taking care of a section. Each train should keep moving back and forth, especially at night, over its section. Foot patrols, provided with rockets or fusees, should patrol the track.

In the first use mentioned above, searchlights will not be used unless it is desired to harass the enemy by frightening him into cautious movement. In the second case they will be used to a very great extent.

547. The third use permits of **smaller garrisons** along the line, and of rapid and efficient reenforcement of same.

548. The fourth use mentioned is one of the most important duties of armored trains. On this work the ordinary trains are either run in fleets under the protection of the armored trains, or the latter remain on the threatened sections, escorting trains each way. When the threatened section is short, trains can be escorted one by one, but over a long stretch the fleet system must be adopted. Special care must be taken in the use of the fleet system to prevent collisions. This danger together with the difficulty of handling a fleet of trains in different yards and over sections of line with short sidings, makes the running rate of the trains very low. On account of this, the system will only be used when there is reasonable ground for supposing that the trains would be in imminent danger.

549. The **position of an armored train** is, normally, behind the first ordinary train, as in this position it has the ordinary train constantly in view and can protect it correspondingly better. When it is desired to give the enginemen confidence, the armored train may be run ahead. If ordinary trains are provided with escort cars, these escort cars of the whole fleet should be run together in the last train, except possibly one car, which might be run in advance of the leading engine.

550. In using an armored train for **reconnoitering purposes**, the train should under no circumstances be sent so far ahead of the troops that the track in the rear can be broken beyond supporting distance of the troops and the train thus captured. The proper use of the armored train in reconnoitering toward a large force of the enemy is in conjunction with mounted troops, whose principal duty is to assure the safety of the railway behind the train and to scout on the flanks, the armored train keeping well in advance of the horsemen. Deep cuts, however, should be reconnoitered by the cavalry before the train enters them.

551. **Patrolling by day** is not a very important duty, especially if the railway is protected by a line of blockhouses. A certain amount of day patroling, however, is advantageous. Good work is done and important information can be frequently obtained by dropping scouts from the armored train at one point with instructions to join it later at the same or some other point. No information should be given out relative to the position of an armored train at any future hour.

**Patrolling by night** is one of the most frequent duties of armored trains, for night is the time when the enemy will most frequently attempt to cross or destroy the railway. In patrolling at night, if ordinary traffic is stopped, information should be sent ahead to the stations, ordering switches to be set so that the train can pass through without whistling. Every precaution should be taken to prevent any more noise and light than is absolutely necessary in running the train at a fair rate of speed.

The searchlights should be ready for work at all times. The train need not be on the move all the time in patrolling, as much information can be obtained by lying in a cut or behind a hill and sending out scouts on foot.

The night work just described presupposes that ordinary traffic is suspended during the hours that the armored trains are patrolling the line.

Where **blockhouses** are used in conjunction with the armored trains, the system of signals will notify the armored trains in that vicinity of the presence of the enemy. Armored trains should halt at certain prearranged hours, not over 2½ hours apart, and establish telegraphic communication with other armored trains, and with neighboring stations, to give information and receive orders for further movements.

552. The use of armored trains on single-track road is of doubtful value when the consequent interference with traffic is considered. If the capacity of the road is fully taxed by the requirements of transportation it will doubtless be best to depend upon the defense by troops and block houses; if it is not fully occupied, armored trains may advantageously supplement the other means of defense. On double-track road the interference is far less marked.

## TABLE XVII.—Curve formulæ.*

| | Given. | Sought. | Formulæ. |
|---|---|---|---|
| 1 | D | R | $R = \frac{50}{\sin \frac{1}{2} D}$ |
| 2 | R | D | $\sin \frac{1}{2} D = \frac{50}{R}$ |
| 3 | $\Delta$, D | L | $L = 100 \frac{\Delta}{D}$ |
| 4 | D, L | $\Delta$ | $\Delta = \frac{DL}{100}$ |
| 5 | $\Delta$, L | D | $D = 100 \frac{\Delta}{L}$ |
| 6 | R, $\Delta$ | T | $T = R \tan \frac{1}{2} \Delta$ |
| 7 | " | C | $C = 2R \sin \frac{1}{2} \Delta$ |
| 8 | " | M | $M = R \text{ vers } \frac{1}{2} \Delta$ |
| 9 | " | E | $E = R \text{ exsec } \frac{1}{2} \Delta$ |
| 10 | T, $\Delta$ | R | $R = T \cot \frac{1}{2} \Delta$ |
| 11 | " | E | $E = T \tan \frac{1}{4} \Delta$ |
| 12 | " | C | $C = 2T \cos \frac{1}{2} \Delta$ |
| 13 | " | M | $M = T \cot \frac{1}{2} \Delta \cdot \text{vers } \frac{1}{2} \Delta$ |
| 14 | E, $\Delta$ | R | $R = \frac{E}{\text{exsec } \frac{1}{2} \Delta}$ |
| 15 | " | T | $T = E \cot \frac{1}{4} \Delta$ |
| 16 | " | C | $C = 2E \frac{\sin \frac{1}{2} \Delta}{\text{exsec } \frac{1}{2} \Delta}$ |
| 17 | " | M | $M = E \cos \frac{1}{2} \Delta$ |
| 18 | C, $\Delta$ | R | $R = \frac{C}{2 \sin \frac{1}{2} \Delta}$ |
| 19 | " | M | $M = \frac{1}{2} C \tan \frac{1}{4} \Delta$ |
| 20 | " | T | $T = \frac{C}{2 \cos \frac{1}{2} \Delta}$ |
| 21 | " | E | $E = \frac{1}{2} C \frac{\text{exsec } \frac{1}{2} \Delta}{\sin \frac{1}{2} \Delta}$ |
| 22 | M, $\Delta$ | R | $R = \frac{M}{\text{vers } \frac{1}{2} \Delta}$ |
| 23 | " | C | $C = 2M \cot \frac{1}{4} \Delta$ |
| 24 | " | T | $T = M \frac{\tan \frac{1}{2} \Delta}{\text{vers } \frac{1}{2} \Delta}$ |
| 25 | " | E | $E = \frac{M}{\cos \frac{1}{2} \Delta}$ |

*See par. 16 for meaning of letters.

TABLE XVII.—**Curve formulæ**—*Continued.*

| | Given. | Sought. | Formulæ. |
|---|---|---|---|
| 26 | R, T | $\triangle$ | $\tan \frac{1}{2} \triangle = \frac{T}{R}$ |
| 27 | " | " | $\sin \frac{1}{2} \triangle = \frac{T}{\sqrt{T^2 + R^2}}$ |
| 28 | R, C | $\triangle$ | $\sin \frac{1}{2} \triangle = \frac{C}{2R}$ |
| 29 | " | " | $\cos \frac{1}{2} \triangle = \frac{1}{R}\sqrt{\left(R + \frac{C}{2}\right)\left(R - \frac{C}{2}\right)}$ |
| 30 | R, M | $\triangle$ | $\text{vers} \frac{1}{2} \triangle = \frac{M}{R}$ |
| 31 | " | " | $\cos \frac{1}{2} \triangle = \frac{R - M}{R}$ |
| 32 | R, E | $\triangle$ | $\text{exsec} \frac{1}{2} \triangle = \frac{E}{R}$ |
| 33 | " | " | $\cos \frac{1}{2} \triangle = \frac{R}{R + E}$ |
| 34 | T, C | $\triangle$ | $\cos \frac{1}{2} \triangle = \frac{C}{2T}$ |
| 35 | " | " | $\tan \frac{1}{4} \triangle = \sqrt{\frac{2T - C}{2T + C}}$ |
| 36 | T, E | $\triangle$ | $\tan \frac{1}{4} \triangle = \frac{E}{T}$ |
| 37 | " | " | $\cos \frac{1}{2} \triangle = \frac{T^2 - E^2}{T^2 + E^2}$ |
| 38 | C, M | $\triangle$ | $\tan \frac{1}{4} \triangle = \frac{2M}{C}$ |
| 39 | " | " | $\cos \frac{1}{2} \triangle = \frac{C^2 - 4M^2}{C^2 + 4M^2}$ |
| 40 | M, E | $\triangle$ | $\cos \frac{1}{2} \triangle = \frac{M}{E}$ |
| 41 | " | " | $\tan \frac{1}{4} \triangle = \sqrt{\frac{E - M}{E + M}}$ |
| 42 | R, T | C | $C = \frac{2TR}{\sqrt{T^2 + R^2}}$ |
| 43 | " | M | $M = R - \frac{R^2}{\sqrt{T^2 + R^2}}$ |
| 44 | " | E | $E = \sqrt{T^2 + R^2} - R$ |
| 45 | R, C | T | $T = \frac{CR}{2\sqrt{\left(R + \frac{C}{2}\right)\left(R - \frac{C}{2}\right)}}$ |
| 46 | " | M | $M = R - \sqrt{(R + \frac{1}{2}C)(R - \frac{1}{2}C)}$ |
| 47 | " | E | $E = \frac{R^2}{\sqrt{(R + \frac{1}{2}C)(R - \frac{1}{2}C)}} - R$ |

TABLE XVII.—**Curve formulæ**—*Continued.*

| | Given. | Sought. | Formulæ. |
|---|---|---|---|
| 48 | R, M | T | $T = \frac{R\sqrt{M(2R - M)}}{R - M}$ |
| 49 | " | C | $C = 2\sqrt{M(2R - M)}$ |
| 50 | " | E | $E = \frac{RM}{R - M}$ |
| 51 | R, E | T | $T = \sqrt{E(2R + E)}$ |
| 52 | " | C | $C = \frac{2R\sqrt{E(2R + E)}}{R + E}$ |
| 53 | " | M | $M = \frac{RE}{R + E}$ |
| 54 | T, C | R | $R = \frac{CT}{\sqrt{(2T + C)(2T - C)}}$ |
| 55 | " | M | $M = \frac{1}{2}C\sqrt{\frac{2T - C}{2T + C}}$ |
| 56 | " | E | $E = T\sqrt{\frac{2T - C}{2T + C}}$ |
| 57 | T, E | R | $R = \frac{(T + E)(T - E)}{2E}$ |
| 58 | " | C | $C = \frac{2T(T^2 - E^2)}{T^2 + E^2}$ |
| 59 | " | M | $M = \frac{E(T^2 - E^2)}{T^2 + E^2}$ |
| 60 | C, M | R | $R = \frac{M^2 + (\frac{1}{2}C)^2}{2M}$ |
| 61 | " | T | $T = \frac{C(C^2 + 4M^2)}{2(C^2 - 4M^2)}$ |
| 62 | " | E | $E = M\frac{C^2 + 4M^2}{C^2 - 4M^2}$ |
| 63 | M, E | R | $R = \frac{EM}{E - M}$ |
| 64 | " | T | $T = E\sqrt{\frac{E + M}{E - M}}$ |
| 65 | " | C | $C = 2M\sqrt{\frac{E + M}{E - M}}$ |
| 66 | T, M | R | $R^3 - R^2\frac{M^2 + T^2}{2M} + RT^2 - \frac{1}{2}MT^2 = 0$ |
| 67 | " | E | $E^3 + E^2M - ET^2 + MT^2 = 0$ |
| 68 | " | C | $C^3 + 2TC^2 + 4M^2C - 8M^2T = 0$ |
| 69 | C, E | R | $R^3 + R^2\frac{4E^2 - C^2}{8E} - R\frac{C^2}{4} - \frac{C^2E}{8} = 0$ |
| 70 | " | T | $2T^3 - T^2C - 2TE^2 - CE^2 = 0$ |
| 71 | " | M | $M^3 + M^2E + M\frac{C^2}{4} - \frac{C^2E}{4} = 0$ |

TABLE XVIII.—Natural versed sines and external secants.

| 0°-10 | | | | | 10°-20° | | | | |
|---|---|---|---|---|---|---|---|---|---|
| ° ′ | Vers. | d. | Exsec. | d. | ° ′ | Vers. | d. | Exsec. | d. |
| 0 0 | .00000 | 0 | .00000 | 0 | 10 0 | .01519 | 51 | .01542 | 52 |
| 10 | .00000 | 1 | .00000 | 1 | 10 | .01570 | 52 | .01595 | 53 |
| 20 | .00001 | 2 | .00001 | 2 | 20 | .01622 | 52 | .01648 | 54 |
| 30 | .00004 | 3 | .00004 | 3 | 30 | .01674 | 53 | .01703 | 55 |
| 40 | .00007 | 3 | .00007 | 3 | 40 | .01728 | 54 | .01758 | 56 |
| 50 | .00010 | 4 | .00010 | 4 | 50 | .01782 | 55 | .01814 | 57 |
| 1 0 | .00015 | 5 | 00015 | 5 | 11 0 | 01837 | 55 | 01871 | 58 |
| 10 | .00020 | 6 | .00020 | 6 | 10 | .01893 | 57 | .01929 | 59 |
| 20 | .00027 | 7 | .00027 | 7 | 20 | .01950 | 57 | .01988 | 60 |
| 30 | .00034 | 8 | .00034 | 8 | 30 | .02007 | 58 | .02048 | 61 |
| 40 | .00042 | 8 | .00042 | 8 | 40 | .02066 | 59 | .02109 | 62 |
| 50 | .00051 | 10 | .00051 | 10 | 50 | .02125 | 60 | .02171 | 62 |
| 2 0 | 00061 | 10 | 00061 | 10 | 12 0 | 02185 | 61 | .02234 | 63 |
| 10 | .00071 | 11 | .00071 | 11 | 10 | .02246 | 62 | .02297 | 65 |
| 20 | .00083 | 12 | .00083 | 12 | 20 | .02308 | 62 | .02362 | 65 |
| 30 | .00095 | 13 | .00095 | 13 | 30 | .02370 | 63 | .02428 | 66 |
| 40 | .00108 | 13 | .00108 | 14 | 40 | .02434 | 64 | .02494 | 67 |
| 50 | .00122 | 15 | .00122 | 14 | 50 | .02498 | 65 | .02562 | 68 |
| 3 0 | .00137 | 15 | .00137 | 16 | 13 0 | .02563 | 66 | .02630 | 69 |
| 10 | .00152 | 16 | .00153 | 16 | 10 | .02629 | 66 | .02700 | 70 |
| 20 | .00169 | 17 | .00169 | 17 | 20 | .02695 | 67 | .02770 | 71 |
| 30 | .00186 | 18 | .00187 | 18 | 30 | .02763 | 68 | .02841 | 72 |
| 40 | .00204 | 19 | .00205 | 19 | 40 | .02831 | 69 | .02914 | 73 |
| 50 | .00223 | 20 | .00224 | 20 | 50 | .02900 | 70 | 02987 | 74 |
| 4 0 | .00243 | 21 | .00244 | 21 | 14 0 | .02970 | 70 | .03061 | 75 |
| 10 | .00264 | 21 | 00265 | 21 | 10 | .03041 | 72 | .03136 | 76 |
| 20 | 00286 | 22 | .00286 | 22 | 20 | .03113 | 72 | .03213 | 77 |
| 30 | .00308 | 23 | 00309 | 23 | 30 | .03185 | 72 | .03290 | 78 |
| 40 | .00331 | 24 | 00332 | 24 | 40 | .03258 | 74 | .03368 | 79 |
| 50 | .00355 | 25 | .00357 | 25 | 50 | 03332 | 75 | .03447 | 80 |
| 5 0 | .00380 | 26 | .00382 | 26 | 15 0 | .03407 | 75 | .03527 | 81 |
| 10 | .00406 | 26 | .00408 | 27 | 10 | .03483 | 76 | .03609 | 82 |
| 20 | .00433 | 27 | .00435 | 27 | 20 | .03559 | 77 | .03691 | 83 |
| 30 | .00460 | 28 | .00462 | 28 | 30 | .03637 | 78 | .03774 | 84 |
| 40 | .00488 | 29 | 00491 | 29 | 40 | .03715 | 79 | .03858 | 85 |
| 50 | .00518 | 30 | 00520 | 30 | 50 | .03794 | 80 | .03943 | 86 |
| 6 0 | 00548 | 30 | .00551 | 31 | 16 0 | .03874 | 80 | .04030 | 87 |
| 10 | .00578 | 32 | .00582 | 32 | 10 | .03954 | 81 | .04117 | 88 |
| 20 | .00610 | 32 | .00614 | 33 | 20 | .04036 | 82 | .04205 | 89 |
| 30 | .00643 | 33 | .00647 | 34 | 30 | .04118 | 83 | .04295 | 90 |
| 40 | .00676 | 33 | .00681 | 34 | 40 | .04201 | 84 | .04385 | 91 |
| 50 | .00710 | 35 | .00715 | 35 | 50 | .04285 | 84 | 04476 | 92 |
| 7 0 | 00745 | 36 | .00751 | 36 | 17 0 | .04369 | 85 | .04569 | 93 |
| 10 | .00781 | 36 | .00787 | 37 | 10 | .04455 | 86 | .04662 | 95 |
| 20 | .00818 | 37 | .00824 | 38 | 20 | .04541 | 87 | .04757 | 95 |
| 30 | .00855 | 38 | .00863 | 39 | 30 | .04628 | 87 | .04853 | 96 |
| 40 | .00894 | 39 | .00902 | 40 | 40 | .04716 | 89 | .04949 | 98 |
| 50 | .00933 | 40 | .00942 | 41 | 50 | .04805 | 89 | .05047 | 98 |
| 8 0 | .00973 | 41 | 00983 | 41 | 18 0 | 04894 | 90 | 05146 | 100 |
| 10 | .01014 | 42 | 01024 | 42 | 10 | .04984 | 91 | .05246 | 101 |
| 20 | .01056 | 42 | .01067 | 43 | 20 | .05075 | 92 | .05347 | 102 |
| 30 | .01098 | 43 | .01110 | 44 | 30 | .05167 | 93 | .05449 | 103 |
| 40 | .01142 | 44 | .01155 | 45 | 40 | .05260 | 93 | .05552 | 104 |
| 50 | .01186 | 45 | .01200 | 46 | 50 | .05354 | 94 | .05656 | 105 |
| 9 0 | .01231 | 46 | .01246 | 47 | 19 0 | .05448 | 95 | .05762 | 106 |
| 10 | .01277 | 47 | .01293 | 48 | 10 | .05543 | 96 | .05868 | 107 |
| 20 | .01324 | 47 | .01341 | 49 | 20 | .05639 | 97 | .05976 | 109 |
| 30 | .01371 | 48 | .01390 | 50 | 30 | .05736 | 97 | .06085 | 109 |
| 40 | .01420 | 49 | .01440 | 50 | 40 | .05833 | 98 | .06194 | 111 |
| 50 | .01469 | 50 | .01491 | 51 | 50 | .05931 | 99 | .06305 | 112 |
| 10 0 | .01519 | | .01542 | | 20 0 | .06030 | | 06418 | |
| ° ′ | Vers. | d. | Exsec. | d. | ° ′ | Vers. | d. | Exsec. | d. |

P. P.

| | 110 | 100 | 90 | 80 | 70 |
|---|---|---|---|---|---|
| 1 | 11 | 10 | 9 | 8 | 7 |
| 2 | 22 | 20 | 18 | 16 | 14 |
| 3 | 33 | 30 | 27 | 24 | 21 |
| 4 | 44 | 40 | 36 | 32 | 28 |
| 5 | 55 | 50 | 45 | 40 | 35 |
| 6 | 66 | 60 | 54 | 48 | 42 |
| 7 | 77 | 70 | 63 | 56 | 49 |
| 8 | 88 | 80 | 72 | 64 | 56 |
| 9 | 99 | 90 | 81 | 72 | 63 |

| | 60 | 50 | 40 | 30 | 20 |
|---|---|---|---|---|---|
| 1 | 6 | 5 | 4 | 3 | 2 |
| 2 | 12 | 10 | 8 | 6 | 4 |
| 3 | 18 | 15 | 12 | 9 | 6 |
| 4 | 24 | 20 | 16 | 12 | 8 |
| 5 | 30 | 25 | 20 | 15 | 10 |
| 6 | 36 | 30 | 24 | 18 | 12 |
| 7 | 42 | 35 | 28 | 21 | 14 |
| 8 | 48 | 40 | 32 | 24 | 16 |
| 9 | 54 | 45 | 36 | 27 | 18 |

| | 10 | 9 | 9 | 8 | 8 |
|---|---|---|---|---|---|
| 1 | 1 | 0 9 | 0.9 | 0.8 | 0 8 |
| 2 | 2 | 1 9 | 1.8 | 1.7 | 1.6 |
| 3 | 3 | 2 8 | 2.7 | 2.5 | 2.4 |
| 4 | 4 | 3.8 | 3.6 | 3.4 | 3.2 |
| 5 | 5 | 4.7 | 4.5 | 4.2 | 4.0 |
| 6 | 6 | 5.7 | 5.4 | 5.1 | 4.8 |
| 7 | 7 | 6 6 | 6.3 | 5 9 | 5.6 |
| 8 | 8 | 7.6 | 7.2 | 6.8 | 6.4 |
| 9 | 9 | 8.5 | 8.1 | 7.6 | 7.2 |

| | 7 | 7 | 6 | 6 | 5 |
|---|---|---|---|---|---|
| 1 | 0.7 | 0.7 | 0.6 | 0 6 | 0.5 |
| 2 | 1.5 | 1.4 | 1.3 | 1 2 | 1.1 |
| 3 | 2.2 | 2.1 | 1.9 | 1.8 | 1.6 |
| 4 | 3.0 | 2.8 | 2.6 | 2 4 | 2.2 |
| 5 | 3.7 | 3.5 | 3.2 | 3 0 | 2.7 |
| 6 | 4.5 | 4.2 | 3.9 | 3 6 | 3.3 |
| 7 | 5.2 | 4.9 | 4.5 | 4.2 | 3.8 |
| 8 | 6.0 | 5.6 | 5.2 | 4.8 | 4.4 |
| 9 | 6.7 | 6.3 | 5.8 | 5.4 | 4.9 |

| | 5 | 4 | 4 | 3 | 3 |
|---|---|---|---|---|---|
| 1 | 0.5 | 0.4 | 0.4 | 0.3 | 0.3 |
| 2 | 1.0 | 0.9 | 0.8 | 0.7 | 0.6 |
| 3 | 1.5 | 1.3 | 1.2 | 1.0 | 0.9 |
| 4 | 2.0 | 1.8 | 1.6 | 1.4 | 1.2 |
| 5 | 2.5 | 2.2 | 2.0 | 1.7 | 1.5 |
| 6 | 3.0 | 2.7 | 2.4 | 2.1 | 1.8 |
| 7 | 3.5 | 3.1 | 2 8 | 2.4 | 2.1 |
| 8 | 4.0 | 3 6 | 3.2 | 2.8 | 2.4 |
| 9 | 4.5 | 4.0 | 3.6 | 3.1 | 2.7 |

| | 2 | 2 | 1 | 1 | 0 |
|---|---|---|---|---|---|
| 1 | 0.2 | 0.2 | 0.1 | 0.1 | 0.0 |
| 2 | 0.5 | 0.4 | 0.3 | 0.2 | 0.1 |
| 3 | 0.7 | 0.6 | 0.4 | 0.3 | 0.1 |
| 4 | 1.0 | 0.8 | 0.6 | 0.4 | 0.2 |
| 5 | 1.2 | 1.0 | 0.7 | 0.5 | 0.2 |
| 6 | 1.5 | 1.2 | 0.9 | 0.6 | 0.3 |
| 7 | 1.7 | 1.4 | 1.0 | 0.7 | 0.3 |
| 8 | 2.0 | 1.6 | 1.2 | 0.8 | 0.4 |
| 9 | 2.2 | 1.8 | 1.3 | 0.9 | 0.4 |

P. P.

TABLE XVIII.—Natural versed sines and external secants—*Continued.*

| ° ′ (20°-30°) | Vers. | d. | Exsec. | d. | ° ′ (30°-40°) | Vers. | d. | Exsec. | d. |
|---|---|---|---|---|---|---|---|---|---|
| 20 0 | .0603 | 10 | .0642 | 11 | 30 0 | .1339 | 15 | .1547 | 19 |
| 10 | .0613 | 10 | .0653 | 11 | 10 | .1354 | 14 | .1566 | 19 |
| 20 | .0623 | 10 | .0664 | 11 | 20 | .1369 | 14 | .1586 | 20 |
| 30 | .0633 | 10 | .0676 | 12 | 30 | .1383 | 15 | .1606 | 20 |
| 40 | .0643 | 10 | .0688 | 11 | 40 | .1398 | 15 | .1626 | 20 |
| 50 | .0654 | 10 | .0699 | 12 | 50 | .1413 | 15 | .1646 | 20 |
| 21 0 | .0664 | 10 | .0711 | 12 | 31 0 | .1428 | 15 | .1666 | 20 |
| 10 | .0674 | 10 | .0723 | 12 | 10 | .1443 | 15 | .1687 | 20 |
| 20 | .0685 | 11 | .0735 | 12 | 20 | .1458 | 15 | .1707 | 21 |
| 30 | .0696 | 10 | .0748 | 12 | 30 | .1473 | 15 | .1728 | 21 |
| 40 | .0706 | 11 | .0760 | 12 | 40 | .1489 | 15 | .1749 | 21 |
| 50 | .0717 | 10 | .0772 | 13 | 50 | .1504 | 15 | .1770 | 21 |
| 22 0 | .0728 | 11 | .0785 | 12 | 32 0 | .1519 | 15 | .1792 | 21 |
| 10 | .0739 | 11 | .0798 | 13 | 10 | .1535 | 15 | .1813 | 21 |
| 20 | .0750 | 11 | .0811 | 13 | 20 | .1550 | 15 | .1835 | 22 |
| 30 | .0761 | 11 | .0824 | 13 | 30 | .1566 | 16 | .1857 | 22 |
| 40 | .0772 | 11 | .0837 | 13 | 40 | .1582 | 15 | .1879 | 22 |
| 50 | .0783 | 11 | .0850 | 13 | 50 | .1597 | 16 | .1901 | 22 |
| 23 0 | .0795 | 11 | .0863 | 13 | 33 0 | .1613 | 15 | .1923 | 23 |
| 10 | .0806 | 11 | .0877 | 13 | 10 | .1629 | 16 | .1946 | 22 |
| 20 | .0818 | 11 | .0890 | 14 | 20 | .1645 | 16 | .1969 | 23 |
| 30 | .0829 | 11 | .0904 | 14 | 30 | .1661 | 16 | .1992 | 23 |
| 40 | .0841 | 12 | .0918 | 14 | 40 | .1677 | 16 | .2015 | 23 |
| 50 | .0853 | 11 | .0932 | 14 | 50 | .1693 | 16 | .2038 | 23 |
| 24 0 | .0864 | 12 | .0946 | 14 | 34 0 | .1709 | 16 | .2062 | 24 |
| 10 | .0876 | 12 | .0960 | 14 | 10 | .1726 | 16 | .2086 | 24 |
| 20 | .0888 | 12 | .0975 | 14 | 20 | .1742 | 16 | .2110 | 24 |
| 30 | .0900 | 12 | .0989 | 14 | 30 | .1758 | 16 | .2134 | 24 |
| 40 | .0912 | 12 | .1004 | 15 | 40 | .1775 | 17 | .2158 | 24 |
| 50 | .0924 | 12 | .1019 | 15 | 50 | .1792 | 16 | .2183 | 24 |
| 25 0 | .0937 | 12 | .1034 | 15 | 35 0 | .1808 | 16 | .2207 | 25 |
| 10 | .0949 | 12 | .1049 | 15 | 10 | .1825 | 17 | .2232 | 25 |
| 20 | .0961 | 12 | .1064 | 15 | 20 | .1842 | 17 | .2258 | 25 |
| 30 | .0974 | 12 | .1079 | 15 | 30 | .1859 | 17 | .2283 | 25 |
| 40 | .0986 | 13 | .1094 | 16 | 40 | .1876 | 17 | .2309 | 25 |
| 50 | .0999 | 12 | .1110 | 15 | 50 | .1893 | 17 | .2334 | 26 |
| 26 0 | .1012 | 13 | .1126 | 16 | 36 0 | .1910 | 17 | .2360 | 26 |
| 10 | .1025 | 12 | .1142 | 16 | 10 | .1927 | 17 | .2387 | 26 |
| 20 | .1037 | 13 | .1158 | 16 | 20 | .1944 | 17 | .2413 | 26 |
| 30 | .1050 | 13 | .1174 | 16 | 30 | .1961 | 17 | .2440 | 27 |
| 40 | .1063 | 13 | .1190 | 16 | 40 | .1979 | 17 | .2467 | 27 |
| 50 | .1077 | 13 | .1206 | 17 | 50 | .1996 | 17 | .2494 | 27 |
| 27 0 | .1090 | 13 | .1223 | 16 | 37 0 | .2013 | 17 | .2521 | 27 |
| 10 | .1103 | 13 | .1240 | 17 | 10 | .2031 | 18 | .2549 | 27 |
| 20 | .1116 | 13 | .1257 | 17 | 20 | .2049 | 17 | .2576 | 28 |
| 30 | .1130 | 13 | .1274 | 17 | 30 | .2066 | 17 | .2604 | 28 |
| 40 | .1143 | 13 | .1291 | 17 | 40 | .2084 | 18 | .2633 | 28 |
| 50 | .1157 | 13 | .1308 | 17 | 50 | .2102 | 18 | .2661 | 28 |
| 28 0 | .1170 | 14 | .1325 | 18 | 38 0 | .2120 | 18 | .2690 | 29 |
| 10 | .1184 | 14 | .1343 | 17 | 10 | .2138 | 18 | .2719 | 29 |
| 20 | .1198 | 13 | .1361 | 18 | 20 | .2156 | 18 | .2748 | 29 |
| 30 | .1212 | 14 | .1379 | 18 | 30 | .2174 | 18 | .2778 | 29 |
| 40 | .1225 | 14 | .1397 | 18 | 40 | .2192 | 18 | .2807 | 30 |
| 50 | .1239 | 14 | .1415 | 18 | 50 | .2210 | 18 | .2837 | 30 |
| 29 0 | .1254 | 14 | .1433 | 18 | 39 0 | .2228 | 18 | .2867 | 30 |
| 10 | .1268 | 14 | .1452 | 18 | 10 | .2247 | 18 | .2898 | 30 |
| 20 | .1282 | 14 | .1470 | 19 | 20 | .2265 | 18 | .2928 | 31 |
| 30 | .1296 | 14 | .1489 | 19 | 30 | .2284 | 18 | .2959 | 31 |
| 40 | .1311 | 14 | .1508 | 19 | 40 | .2302 | 18 | .2991 | 31 |
| 50 | .1325 | 14 | .1527 | 19 | 50 | .2321 | 18 | .3022 | 31 |
| 30 0 | .1339 | | .1547 | | 40 0 | .2339 | | .3054 | |
| ° ′ | Vers. | d. | Exsec. | d. | ° ′ | Vers. | d. | Exsec. | d. |

P. P.

| | 31 | 30 | 29 | 28 |
|---|---|---|---|---|
| 1 | 3.1 | 3.0 | 2.9 | 2.8 |
| 2 | 6.2 | 6.0 | 5.8 | 5.6 |
| 3 | 9.3 | 9.0 | 8.7 | 8.4 |
| 4 | 12.4 | 12.0 | 11.6 | 11.2 |
| 5 | 15.5 | 15.0 | 14.5 | 14.0 |
| 6 | 18.6 | 18.0 | 17.4 | 16.8 |
| 7 | 21.7 | 21.0 | 20.3 | 19.6 |
| 8 | 24.8 | 24.0 | 23.2 | 22.4 |
| 9 | 27.9 | 27.0 | 26.1 | 25.2 |

| | 27 | 26 | 25 | 24 |
|---|---|---|---|---|
| 1 | 2.7 | 2.6 | 2.5 | 2.4 |
| 2 | 5.4 | 5.2 | 5.0 | 4.8 |
| 3 | 8.1 | 7.8 | 7.5 | 7.2 |
| 4 | 10.8 | 10.4 | 10.0 | 9.6 |
| 5 | 13.5 | 13.0 | 12.5 | 12.0 |
| 6 | 16.2 | 15.6 | 15.0 | 14.4 |
| 7 | 18.9 | 18.2 | 17.5 | 16.8 |
| 8 | 21.6 | 20.8 | 20.0 | 19.2 |
| 9 | 24.3 | 23.4 | 22.5 | 21.6 |

| | 23 | 22 | 21 | 20 |
|---|---|---|---|---|
| 1 | 2.3 | 2.2 | 2.1 | 2.0 |
| 2 | 4.6 | 4.4 | 4.2 | 4.0 |
| 3 | 6.9 | 6.6 | 6.3 | 6.0 |
| 4 | 9.2 | 8.8 | 8.4 | 8.0 |
| 5 | 11.5 | 11.0 | 10.5 | 10.0 |
| 6 | 13.8 | 13.2 | 12.6 | 12.0 |
| 7 | 16.1 | 15.4 | 14.7 | 14.0 |
| 8 | 18.4 | 17.6 | 16.8 | 16.0 |
| 9 | 20.7 | 19.8 | 18.9 | 18.0 |

| | 19 | 18 | 17 | 16 |
|---|---|---|---|---|
| 1 | 1.9 | 1.8 | 1.7 | 1.6 |
| 2 | 3.8 | 3.6 | 3.4 | 3.2 |
| 3 | 5.7 | 5.4 | 5.1 | 4.8 |
| 4 | 7.6 | 7.2 | 6.8 | 6.4 |
| 5 | 9.5 | 9.0 | 8.5 | 8.0 |
| 6 | 11.4 | 10.8 | 10.2 | 9.6 |
| 7 | 13.3 | 12.6 | 11.9 | 11.2 |
| 8 | 15.2 | 14.4 | 13.6 | 12.8 |
| 9 | 17.1 | 16.2 | 15.3 | 14.4 |

| | 15 | 14 | 13 | 12 |
|---|---|---|---|---|
| 1 | 1.5 | 1.4 | 1.3 | 1.2 |
| 2 | 3.0 | 2.8 | 2.6 | 2.4 |
| 3 | 4.5 | 4.2 | 3.9 | 3.6 |
| 4 | 6.0 | 5.6 | 5.2 | 4.8 |
| 5 | 7.5 | 7.0 | 6.5 | 6.0 |
| 6 | 9.0 | 8.4 | 7.8 | 7.2 |
| 7 | 10.5 | 9.8 | 9.1 | 8.4 |
| 8 | 12.0 | 11.2 | 10.4 | 9.6 |
| 9 | 13.5 | 12.6 | 11.7 | 10.8 |

| | 11 | 10 | 0̄ |
|---|---|---|---|
| 1 | 1.1 | 1.0 | 0.0 |
| 2 | 2.2 | 2.0 | 0.1 |
| 3 | 3.3 | 3.0 | 0.1 |
| 4 | 4.4 | 4.0 | 0.2 |
| 5 | 5.5 | 5.0 | 0.2 |
| 6 | 6.6 | 6.0 | 0.3 |
| 7 | 7.7 | 7.0 | 0.3 |
| 8 | 8.8 | 8.0 | 0.4 |
| 9 | 9.9 | 9.0 | 0.4 |

P. P.

TABLE XVIII.—**Natural versed sines and external secants**—*Continued.*

| 40°-50° | | | | | 50°-60° | | | | |
|---|---|---|---|---|---|---|---|---|---|
| ° ′ | Vers. | d. | Exsec. | d. | ° ′ | Vers. | d. | Exsec. | d. |
| 40 0 | .2339 | 19 | .3054 | 32 | 50 0 | .3572 | 22 | .5557 | 53 |
| 10 | .2358 | 18 | .3086 | 32 | 10 | .3594 | 22 | .5611 | 54 |
| 20 | .2377 | 19 | .3118 | 32 | 20 | .3617 | 22 | .5666 | 54 |
| 30 | .2396 | 19 | .3151 | 32 | 30 | .3639 | 22 | .5721 | 55 |
| 40 | .2415 | 19 | .3183 | 33 | 40 | .3661 | 22 | .5777 | 56 |
| 50 | .2434 | 19 | .3217 | 33 | 50 | .3684 | 23 | .5833 | 56 |
| 41 0 | .2453 | 19 | .3250 | 34 | 51 0 | .3707 | 22 | .5890 | 57 |
| 10 | .2472 | 19 | .3284 | 33 | 10 | .3729 | 22 | .5947 | 58 |
| 20 | .2491 | 19 | .3317 | 34 | 20 | .3752 | 23 | .6005 | 58 |
| 30 | .2510 | 19 | .3352 | 34 | 30 | .3775 | 22 | .6064 | 59 |
| 40 | .2529 | 19 | .3386 | 34 | 40 | .3797 | 23 | .6123 | 59 |
| 50 | .2549 | 19 | .3421 | 35 | 50 | .3820 | 23 | .6182 | 60 |
| 42 0 | .2568 | 19 | .3456 | 35 | 52 0 | .3843 | 23 | .6242 | 61 |
| 10 | .2588 | 19 | .3491 | 36 | 10 | .3866 | 23 | .6303 | 61 |
| 20 | .2607 | 19 | .3527 | 36 | 20 | .3889 | 23 | .6365 | 62 |
| 30 | .2627 | 20 | .3563 | 36 | 30 | .3912 | 23 | .6427 | 62 |
| 40 | .2647 | 19 | .3599 | 37 | 40 | .3935 | 23 | .6489 | 63 |
| 50 | .2666 | 20 | .3636 | 37 | 50 | .3958 | 23 | .6552 | 64 |
| 43 0 | .2686 | 20 | .3673 | 37 | 53 0 | .3982 | 23 | .6616 | 64 |
| 10 | .2706 | 20 | .3710 | 37 | 10 | .4005 | 23 | .6681 | 65 |
| 20 | .2726 | 20 | .3748 | 38 | 20 | .4028 | 23 | .6746 | 65 |
| 30 | .2746 | 20 | .3786 | 38 | 30 | .4052 | 23 | .6811 | 66 |
| 40 | .2766 | 20 | .3824 | 39 | 40 | .4075 | 23 | .6878 | 67 |
| 50 | .2786 | 20 | .3863 | 38 | 50 | .4098 | 23 | .6945 | 68 |
| 44 0 | .2806 | 20 | .3901 | 39 | 54 0 | .4122 | 23 | .7013 | 68 |
| 10 | .2827 | 20 | .3941 | 39 | 10 | .4145 | 24 | .7081 | 69 |
| 20 | .2847 | 20 | .3980 | 40 | 20 | .4169 | 23 | .7150 | 70 |
| 30 | .2867 | 20 | .4020 | 40 | 30 | .4193 | 23 | .7220 | 70 |
| 40 | .2888 | 20 | .4060 | 40 | 40 | .4216 | 24 | .7291 | 71 |
| 50 | .2908 | 20 | .4101 | 41 | 50 | .4240 | 23 | .7362 | 72 |
| 45 0 | .2929 | 20 | .4142 | 41 | 55 0 | .4264 | 24 | .7434 | 73 |
| 10 | .2949 | 20 | .4183 | 41 | 10 | .4288 | 24 | .7507 | 73 |
| 20 | .2970 | 21 | .4225 | 42 | 20 | .4312 | 24 | .7581 | 74 |
| 30 | .2991 | 20 | .4267 | 42 | 30 | .4336 | 24 | .7655 | 75 |
| 40 | .3011 | 21 | .4309 | 43 | 40 | .4360 | 24 | .7730 | 75 |
| 50 | .3032 | 21 | .4352 | 43 | 50 | .4384 | 24 | .7806 | 77 |
| 46 0 | .3053 | 21 | .4395 | 43 | 56 0 | .4408 | 24 | .7883 | 77 |
| 10 | .3074 | 21 | .4439 | 44 | 10 | .4432 | 24 | .7960 | 78 |
| 20 | .3095 | 21 | .4483 | 44 | 20 | .4456 | 24 | .8039 | 79 |
| 30 | .3116 | 21 | .4527 | 44 | 30 | .4480 | 24 | .8118 | 80 |
| 40 | .3137 | 21 | .4572 | 45 | 40 | .4505 | 24 | .8198 | 81 |
| 50 | .3159 | 21 | .4617 | 45 | 50 | .4529 | 24 | .8279 | 82 |
| 47 0 | .3180 | 21 | .4663 | 45 | 57 0 | .4553 | 24 | .8361 | 82 |
| 10 | .3201 | 21 | .4708 | 46 | 10 | .4578 | 24 | .8443 | 83 |
| 20 | .3222 | 21 | .4755 | 47 | 20 | .4602 | 24 | .8527 | 84 |
| 30 | .3244 | 21 | .4802 | 47 | 30 | .4627 | 24 | .8611 | 85 |
| 40 | .3265 | 21 | .4849 | 47 | 40 | .4651 | 24 | .8697 | 86 |
| 50 | .3287 | 21 | .4896 | 48 | 50 | .4676 | 25 | .8783 | 87 |
| 48 0 | .3308 | 22 | .4945 | 48 | 58 0 | .4701 | 24 | .8871 | 88 |
| 10 | .3330 | 21 | .4993 | 48 | 10 | .4725 | 24 | .8959 | 89 |
| 20 | .3352 | 22 | .5042 | 49 | 20 | .4750 | 25 | .9048 | 90 |
| 30 | .3374 | 21 | .5091 | 50 | 30 | .4775 | 25 | .9139 | 91 |
| 40 | .3395 | 22 | .5141 | 50 | 40 | .4800 | 24 | .9230 | 92 |
| 50 | .3417 | 22 | .5192 | 50 | 50 | .4824 | 25 | .9322 | 93 |
| 49 0 | .3439 | 22 | .5242 | 51 | 59 0 | .4849 | 25 | .9416 | 94 |
| 10 | .3461 | 22 | .5294 | 51 | 10 | .4874 | 25 | .9510 | 95 |
| 20 | .3483 | 22 | .5345 | 52 | 20 | .4899 | 25 | .9606 | 97 |
| 30 | .3505 | 22 | .5397 | 53 | 30 | .4924 | 25 | .9703 | 98 |
| 40 | .3527 | 22 | .5450 | 53 | 40 | .4949 | 25 | .9801 | 99 |
| 50 | .3550 | 22 | .5503 | 53 | 50 | .4975 | 25 | .9900 | 100 |
| 50 0 | .3572 | | .5557 | | 60 0 | .5000 | | 1.0000 | |
| ° ′ | Vers. | d. | Exsec. | d. | ° ′ | Vers. | d. | Exsec. | d. |

P. P.

| | 9 | 8 | 7 | 6 | 5 | 4 |
|---|---|---|---|---|---|---|
| 1 | 0.9 | 0.8 | 0.7 | 0.6 | 0.5 | 0.4 |
| 2 | 1.8 | 1.6 | 1.4 | 1.2 | 1.0 | 0.8 |
| 3 | 2.7 | 2.4 | 2.1 | 1.8 | 1.5 | 1.2 |
| 4 | 3.6 | 3.2 | 2.8 | 2.4 | 2.0 | 1.6 |
| 5 | 4.5 | 4.0 | 3.5 | 3.0 | 2.5 | 2.0 |
| 6 | 5.4 | 4.8 | 4.2 | 3.6 | 3.0 | 2.4 |
| 7 | 6.3 | 5.6 | 4.9 | 4.2 | 3.5 | 2.8 |
| 8 | 7.2 | 6.4 | 5.6 | 4.8 | 4.0 | 3.2 |
| 9 | 8.1 | 7.2 | 6.3 | 5.4 | 4.5 | 3.6 |

| | 3 | 2 | 1 | 9 | 8 | 7 |
|---|---|---|---|---|---|---|
| 1 | 0.3 | 0.2 | 0.1 | 0.9 | 0.8 | 0.7 |
| 2 | 0.6 | 0.4 | 0.2 | 1.9 | 1.7 | 1.5 |
| 3 | 0.9 | 0.6 | 0.3 | 2.8 | 2.5 | 2.2 |
| 4 | 1.2 | 0.8 | 0.4 | 3.8 | 3.4 | 3.0 |
| 5 | 1.5 | 1.0 | 0.5 | 4.7 | 4.2 | 3.7 |
| 6 | 1.8 | 1.2 | 0.6 | 5.7 | 5.1 | 4.5 |
| 7 | 2.1 | 1.4 | 0.7 | 6.6 | 5.9 | 5.2 |
| 8 | 2.4 | 1.6 | 0.8 | 7.6 | 6.8 | 6.0 |
| 9 | 2.7 | 1.8 | 0.9 | 8.5 | 7.6 | 6.7 |

| | 6 | 5 | 4 | 3 | 2 | 1 |
|---|---|---|---|---|---|---|
| 1 | 0.6 | 0.5 | 0.4 | 0.3 | 0.2 | 0.1 |
| 2 | 1.3 | 1.1 | 0.9 | 0.7 | 0.5 | 0.3 |
| 3 | 1.9 | 1.6 | 1.3 | 1.0 | 0.7 | 0.4 |
| 4 | 2.6 | 2.2 | 1.8 | 1.4 | 1.0 | 0.6 |
| 5 | 3.2 | 2.7 | 2.2 | 1.7 | 1.2 | 0.7 |
| 6 | 3.9 | 3.3 | 2.7 | 2.1 | 1.5 | 0.9 |
| 7 | 4.5 | 3.8 | 3.1 | 2.4 | 1.7 | 1.0 |
| 8 | 5.2 | 4.4 | 3.6 | 2.8 | 2.0 | 1.2 |
| 9 | 5.8 | 4.9 | 4.0 | 3.1 | 2.2 | 1.3 |

| | 25 | 25 | 24 | 24 | 23 |
|---|---|---|---|---|---|
| 1 | 2.5 | 2.5 | 2.4 | 2.4 | 2.3 |
| 2 | 5.1 | 5.0 | 4.9 | 4.8 | 4.7 |
| 3 | 7.6 | 7.5 | 7.3 | 7.2 | 7.0 |
| 4 | 10.2 | 10.0 | 9.8 | 9.6 | 9.4 |
| 5 | 12.7 | 12.5 | 12.2 | 12.0 | 11.7 |
| 6 | 15.3 | 15.0 | 14.7 | 14.4 | 14.1 |
| 7 | 17.8 | 17.5 | 17.1 | 16.8 | 16.4 |
| 8 | 20.4 | 20.0 | 19.6 | 19.2 | 18.8 |
| 9 | 22.9 | 22.5 | 22.0 | 21.6 | 21.1 |

| | 23 | 22 | 22 | 21 | 21 |
|---|---|---|---|---|---|
| 1 | 2.3 | 2.2 | 2.2 | 2.1 | 2.1 |
| 2 | 4.6 | 4.5 | 4.4 | 4.3 | 4.2 |
| 3 | 6.9 | 6.7 | 6.6 | 6.4 | 6.3 |
| 4 | 9.2 | 9.0 | 8.8 | 8.6 | 8.4 |
| 5 | 11.5 | 11.2 | 11.0 | 10.7 | 10.5 |
| 6 | 13.8 | 13.5 | 13.2 | 12.9 | 12.6 |
| 7 | 16.1 | 15.7 | 15.4 | 15.0 | 14.7 |
| 8 | 18.4 | 18.0 | 17.6 | 17.2 | 16.8 |
| 9 | 20.7 | 20.2 | 19.8 | 19.3 | 18.9 |

| | 20 | 20 | 19 | 19 | 18 |
|---|---|---|---|---|---|
| 1 | 2.0 | 2.0 | 1.9 | 1.9 | 1.8 |
| 2 | 4.1 | 4.0 | 3.9 | 3.8 | 3.7 |
| 3 | 6.1 | 6.0 | 5.8 | 5.7 | 5.5 |
| 4 | 8.2 | 8.0 | 7.8 | 7.6 | 7.4 |
| 5 | 10.2 | 10.0 | 9.7 | 9.5 | 9.2 |
| 6 | 12.3 | 12.0 | 11.7 | 11.4 | 11.1 |
| 7 | 14.3 | 14.0 | 13.6 | 13.3 | 12.9 |
| 8 | 16.4 | 16.0 | 15.6 | 15.2 | 14.8 |
| 9 | 18.4 | 18.0 | 17.5 | 17.1 | 16.6 |

P. P.

TABLE XVIII.—**Natural versed sines and external secants**—*Continued.*

| ° ′ | Vers. | d. | Exsec. | d. | ° ′ | Vers. | d. | Exsec. | d. |
|---|---|---|---|---|---|---|---|---|---|
| | 60°-70° | | | | | 70°-80° | | | |
| 60 0 | .5000 | 25 | 1.0000 | 101 | 70 0 | .6580 | 27 | 1.9238 | 235 |
| 10 | .5025 | 25 | 1.0101 | 102 | 10 | .6607 | 27 | 1.9473 | 240 |
| 20 | .5050 | 25 | 1.0204 | 103 | 20 | .6634 | 27 | 1.9713 | 244 |
| 30 | .5076 | 25 | 1.0307 | 105 | 30 | .6662 | 27 | 1.9957 | 248 |
| 40 | .5101 | 25 | 1.0413 | 106 | 40 | .6689 | 27 | 2.0205 | 253 |
| 50 | .5126 | 25 | 1.0519 | 107 | 50 | .6717 | 27 | 2.0458 | 257 |
| 61 0 | .5152 | 25 | 1.0626 | 109 | 71 0 | .6744 | 27 | 2.0715 | 262 |
| 10 | .5177 | 25 | 1.0735 | 110 | 10 | .6772 | 27 | 2.0977 | 266 |
| 20 | .5203 | 25 | 1.0846 | 111 | 20 | .6799 | 27 | 2.1244 | 271 |
| 30 | .5228 | 25 | 1.0957 | 113 | 30 | .6827 | 27 | 2.1515 | 276 |
| 40 | .5254 | 25 | 1.1070 | 114 | 40 | .6854 | 27 | 2.1792 | 281 |
| 50 | .5279 | 26 | 1.1184 | 116 | 50 | .6882 | 28 | 2.2073 | 287 |
| 62 0 | .5305 | 25 | 1.1300 | 117 | 72 0 | .6910 | 27 | 2.2360 | 292 |
| 10 | .5331 | 25 | 1.1418 | 118 | 10 | .6937 | 27 | 2.2653 | 298 |
| 20 | .5356 | 26 | 1.1536 | 120 | 20 | .6965 | 28 | 2.2951 | 304 |
| 30 | .5382 | 26 | 1.1657 | 121 | 30 | .6993 | 27 | 2.3255 | 310 |
| 40 | .5408 | 25 | 1.1778 | 123 | 40 | .7020 | 28 | 2.3565 | 316 |
| 50 | .5434 | 26 | 1.1902 | 125 | 50 | .7048 | 28 | 2.3881 | 322 |
| 63 0 | .5460 | 26 | 1.2027 | 126 | 73 0 | .7076 | 27 | 2.4203 | 328 |
| 10 | .5486 | 26 | 1.2153 | 128 | 10 | .7104 | 28 | 2.4531 | 335 |
| 20 | .5512 | 26 | 1.2281 | 130 | 20 | .7132 | 28 | 2.4867 | 342 |
| 30 | .5538 | 26 | 1.2411 | 131 | 30 | .7160 | 27 | 2.5209 | 349 |
| 40 | .5564 | 26 | 1.2543 | 133 | 40 | .7187 | 28 | 2.5558 | 356 |
| 50 | .5590 | 26 | 1.2676 | 135 | 50 | .7215 | 28 | 2.5915 | 364 |
| 64 0 | .5616 | 26 | 1.2811 | 137 | 74 0 | .7243 | 28 | 2.6279 | 372 |
| 10 | .5642 | 26 | 1.2948 | 139 | 10 | .7271 | 28 | 2.6651 | 380 |
| 20 | .5668 | 26 | 1.3087 | 140 | 20 | .7299 | 28 | 2.7031 | 388 |
| 30 | .5695 | 26 | 1.3228 | 143 | 30 | .7327 | 28 | 2.7420 | 396 |
| 40 | .5721 | 26 | 1.3371 | 144 | 40 | .7355 | 28 | 2.7816 | 406 |
| 50 | .5747 | 26 | 1.3515 | 146 | 50 | .7383 | 28 | 2.8222 | 414 |
| 65 0 | .5774 | 26 | 1.3662 | 148 | 75 0 | .7412 | 28 | 2.8637 | 424 |
| 10 | .5800 | 26 | 1.3810 | 151 | 10 | .7440 | 28 | 2.9061 | 434 |
| 20 | .5826 | 26 | 1.3961 | 152 | 20 | .7468 | 28 | 2.9495 | 444 |
| 30 | .5853 | 26 | 1.4114 | 155 | 30 | .7496 | 28 | 2.9939 | 454 |
| 40 | .5879 | 26 | 1.4269 | 157 | 40 | .7524 | 28 | 3.0394 | 465 |
| 50 | .5906 | 26 | 1.4426 | 159 | 50 | .7552 | 28 | 3.0859 | 476 |
| 66 0 | .5932 | 26 | 1.4586 | 161 | 76 0 | .7581 | 28 | 3.1335 | 488 |
| 10 | .5959 | 27 | 1.4747 | 164 | 10 | .7609 | 28 | 3.1824 | 500 |
| 20 | .5986 | 26 | 1.4912 | 166 | 20 | .7637 | 28 | 3.2324 | 512 |
| 30 | .6012 | 26 | 1.5078 | 169 | 30 | .7665 | 28 | 3.2836 | 525 |
| 40 | .6039 | 27 | 1.5247 | 171 | 40 | .7694 | 28 | 3.3362 | 539 |
| 50 | .6066 | 26 | 1.5419 | 174 | 50 | .7722 | 28 | 3.3901 | 553 |
| 67 0 | .6092 | 27 | 1.5593 | 177 | 77 0 | .7750 | 28 | 3.4454 | 567 |
| 10 | .6119 | 27 | 1.5770 | 179 | 10 | .7779 | 28 | 3.5021 | 582 |
| 20 | .6146 | 26 | 1.5949 | 182 | 20 | .7807 | 28 | 3.5604 | 598 |
| 30 | .6173 | 27 | 1.6131 | 184 | 30 | .7835 | 28 | 3.6202 | 614 |
| 40 | .6200 | 27 | 1.6316 | 188 | 40 | .7864 | 28 | 3.6816 | 631 |
| 50 | .6227 | 27 | 1.6504 | 190 | 50 | .7892 | 28 | 3.7448 | 649 |
| 68 0 | .6254 | 27 | 1.6694 | 194 | 78 0 | .7921 | 28 | 3.8097 | 667 |
| 10 | .6281 | 27 | 1.6888 | 196 | 10 | .7949 | 28 | 3.8765 | 686 |
| 20 | .6308 | 27 | 1.7085 | 200 | 20 | .7978 | 28 | 3.9451 | 707 |
| 30 | .6335 | 27 | 1.7285 | 203 | 30 | .8006 | 28 | 4.0158 | 728 |
| 40 | .6362 | 27 | 1.7488 | 206 | 40 | .8035 | 28 | 4.0886 | 749 |
| 50 | .6389 | 27 | 1.7694 | 210 | 50 | .8063 | 28 | 4.1636 | 772 |
| 69 0 | .6416 | 27 | 1.7904 | 213 | 79 0 | .8092 | 28 | 4.2408 | 796 |
| 10 | .6443 | 27 | 1.8117 | 216 | 10 | .8120 | 28 | 4.3205 | 821 |
| 20 | .6470 | 27 | 1.8334 | 220 | 20 | .8149 | 28 | 4.4026 | 847 |
| 30 | .6498 | 27 | 1.8554 | 224 | 30 | .8177 | 29 | 4.4874 | 875 |
| 40 | .6525 | 27 | 1.8778 | 228 | 40 | .8206 | 28 | 4.5749 | 904 |
| 50 | .6552 | 27 | 1.9006 | 231 | 50 | .8235 | 28 | 4.6653 | 934 |
| 70 0 | .6580 | | 1.9238 | | 80 0 | .8263 | | 4.7587 | |
| ° ′ | Vers. | d. | Exsec. | d. | ° ′ | Vers. | d. | Exsec. | d. |

P. P.

| | 9 | 8 | 7 | 6 | 5 |
|---|---|---|---|---|---|
| 1 | 0.9 | 0.8 | 0.7 | 0.6 | 0.5 |
| 2 | 1.8 | 1.6 | 1.4 | 1.2 | 1.0 |
| 3 | 2.7 | 2.4 | 2.1 | 1.8 | 1.5 |
| 4 | 3.6 | 3.2 | 2.8 | 2.4 | 2.0 |
| 5 | 4.5 | 4.0 | 3.5 | 3.0 | 2.5 |
| 6 | 5.4 | 4.8 | 4.2 | 3.6 | 3.0 |
| 7 | 6.3 | 5.6 | 4.9 | 4.2 | 3.5 |
| 8 | 7.2 | 6.4 | 5.6 | 4.8 | 4.0 |
| 9 | 8.1 | 7.2 | 6.3 | 5.4 | 4.5 |

| | 4 | 3 | 2 | 1 | $\bar{9}$ |
|---|---|---|---|---|---|
| 1 | 0.4 | 0.3 | 0.2 | 0.1 | 0.9 |
| 2 | 0.8 | 0.6 | 0.4 | 0.2 | 1.9 |
| 3 | 1.2 | 0.9 | 0.6 | 0.3 | 2.8 |
| 4 | 1.6 | 1.2 | 0.8 | 0.4 | 3.8 |
| 5 | 2.0 | 1.5 | 1.0 | 0.5 | 4.7 |
| 6 | 2.4 | 1.8 | 1.2 | 0.6 | 5.7 |
| 7 | 2.8 | 2.1 | 1.4 | 0.7 | 6.6 |
| 8 | 3.2 | 2.4 | 1.6 | 0.8 | 7.6 |
| 9 | 3.6 | 2.7 | 1.8 | 0.9 | 8.5 |

| | $\bar{8}$ | $\bar{7}$ | $\bar{6}$ | $\bar{5}$ | $\bar{4}$ |
|---|---|---|---|---|---|
| 1 | 0.8 | 0.7 | 0.6 | 0.5 | 0.4 |
| 2 | 1.7 | 1.5 | 1.3 | 1.1 | 0.9 |
| 3 | 2.5 | 2.2 | 1.9 | 1.6 | 1.3 |
| 4 | 3.4 | 3.0 | 2.6 | 2.2 | 1.8 |
| 5 | 4.2 | 3.7 | 3.2 | 2.7 | 2.2 |
| 6 | 5.1 | 4.5 | 3.9 | 3.3 | 2.7 |
| 7 | 5.9 | 5.2 | 4.5 | 3.8 | 3.1 |
| 8 | 6.8 | 6.0 | 5.2 | 4.4 | 3.6 |
| 9 | 7.6 | 6.7 | 5.8 | 4.9 | 4.0 |

| | $\bar{3}$ | $\bar{2}$ | $\bar{1}$ |
|---|---|---|---|
| 1 | 0.3 | 0.2 | 0.1 |
| 2 | 0.7 | 0.5 | 0.3 |
| 3 | 1.0 | 0.7 | 0.4 |
| 4 | 1.4 | 1.0 | 0.6 |
| 5 | 1.7 | 1.2 | 0.7 |
| 6 | 2.1 | 1.5 | 0.9 |
| 7 | 2.4 | 1.7 | 1.0 |
| 8 | 2.8 | 2.0 | 1.2 |
| 9 | 3.1 | 2.2 | 1.3 |

| | 29 | $2\bar{8}$ | 28 | $2\bar{7}$ |
|---|---|---|---|---|
| 1 | 2.9 | 2.8 | 2.8 | 2.7 |
| 2 | 5.8 | 5.7 | 5.6 | 5.5 |
| 3 | 8.7 | 8.5 | 8.4 | 8.2 |
| 4 | 11.6 | 11.4 | 11.2 | 11.0 |
| 5 | 14.5 | 14.2 | 14.0 | 13.7 |
| 6 | 17.4 | 17.1 | 16.8 | 16.5 |
| 7 | 20.3 | 19.9 | 19.6 | 19.2 |
| 8 | 23.2 | 22.8 | 22.4 | 22.0 |
| 9 | 26.1 | 25.6 | 25.2 | 24.7 |

| | 27 | $2\bar{6}$ | 26 | $2\bar{5}$ |
|---|---|---|---|---|
| 1 | 2.7 | 2.6 | 2.6 | 2.5 |
| 2 | 5.4 | 5.3 | 5.2 | 5.1 |
| 3 | 8.1 | 7.9 | 7.8 | 7.6 |
| 4 | 10.8 | 10.6 | 10.4 | 10.2 |
| 5 | 13.5 | 13.2 | 13.0 | 12.7 |
| 6 | 16.2 | 15.9 | 15.6 | 15.3 |
| 7 | 18.9 | 18.5 | 18.2 | 17.8 |
| 8 | 21.6 | 21.2 | 20.8 | 20.4 |
| 9 | 24.3 | 23.8 | 23.4 | 22.9 |

P. P.

TABLE XVIII.—**Natural versed sines and external secants**—*Continued.*

**80°–85°**

| ° ′ | Vers. | d. | Exsec. | d. |
|---|---|---|---|---|
| 80 0 | ·8263 | 28 | 4·7587 | 966 |
| 10 | ·8292 | 29 | 4·8554 | 999 |
| 20 | ·8321 | 28 | 4·9553 | 1035 |
| 30 | ·8349 | 28 | 5·0588 | 1072 |
| 40 | ·8378 | 29 | 5·1660 | 1111 |
| 50 | ·8407 | 28 | 5·2772 | 1152 |
| 81 0 | ·8435 | 29 | 5·3924 | 1196 |
| 10 | ·8464 | 28 | 5·5121 | 1242 |
| 20 | ·8493 | 29 | 5·6363 | 1291 |
| 30 | ·8522 | 28 | 5·7654 | 1343 |
| 40 | ·8550 | 29 | 5·8998 | 1398 |
| 50 | ·8579 | 29 | 6·0396 | 1456 |
| 82 0 | ·8608 | 28 | 6·1853 | 1519 |
| 10 | ·8637 | 29 | 6·3372 | 1585 |
| 20 | ·8666 | 28 | 6·4957 | 1656 |
| 30 | ·8694 | 29 | 6·6613 | 1731 |
| 40 | ·8723 | 29 | 6·8344 | 1812 |
| 50 | ·8752 | 29 | 7·0156 | 1898 |
| 83 0 | ·8781 | 28 | 7 2055 | 1991 |
| 10 | ·8810 | 29 | 7·4046 | 2091 |
| 20 | ·8839 | 29 | 7·6138 | 2198 |
| 30 | ·8868 | 29 | 7·8336 | 2315 |
| 40 | ·8897 | 29 | 8·0651 | 2440 |
| 50 | ·8926 | 28 | 8·3091 | 2576 |
| 84 0 | ·8954 | 29 | 8·5667 | 2723 |
| 10 | ·8983 | 29 | 8·8391 | 2884 |
| 20 | ·9012 | 29 | 9·1275 | 3059 |
| 30 | ·9041 | 29 | 9 4334 | 3250 |
| 40 | ·9070 | 29 | 9·7585 | 3460 |
| 50 | ·9099 | 29 | 10·1045 | 3691 |
| 85 0 | ·9128 | | 10 4737 | |
| ° ′ | Vers. | d. | Exsec. | d. |

**85°–90°**

| ° ′ | Vers. | d. | Exsec. | d. |
|---|---|---|---|---|
| 85 0 | ·9128 | 29 | 10·4737 | ·3946 |
| 10 | ·9157 | 29 | 10·8683 | ·4229 |
| 20 | ·9186 | 29 | 11·2912 | ·4542 |
| 30 | ·9215 | 29 | 11·7455 | ·4892 |
| 40 | ·9244 | 29 | 12·2347 | ·5284 |
| 50 | ·9273 | 29 | 12 7631 | ·5725 |
| 86 0 | ·9302 | 29 | 13·3356 | ·6223 |
| 10 | ·9331 | 29 | 13·9579 | ·6789 |
| 20 | ·9360 | 29 | 14·6368 | ·7436 |
| 30 | ·9389 | 29 | 15·3804 | ·8180 |
| 40 | ·9418 | 29 | 16·1984 | ·9041 |
| 50 | ·9447 | 29 | 17·1026 | 1·0047 |
| 87 0 | ·9476 | 29 | 18·1073 | 1·1230 |
| 10 | ·9505 | 29 | 19·2303 | 1·2634 |
| 20 | ·9534 | 29 | 20·4937 | 1·4319 |
| 30 | ·9564 | 29 | 21·9256 | 1·6365 |
| 40 | ·9593 | 29 | 23·5621 | 1·8884 |
| 50 | ·9622 | 29 | 25·4505 | 2·2082 |
| 88 0 | ·9651 | 29 | 27·6537 | 2·6039 |
| 10 | ·9680 | 29 | 30·2576 | 3·1247 |
| 20 | ·9709 | 29 | 33·3823 | 3·8192 |
| 30 | ·9738 | 29 | 37·2015 | 4·7741 |
| 40 | ·9767 | 29 | 41·9757 | 6·1383 |
| 50 | ·9796 | 29 | 48 1140 | 8·1846 |
| 89 0 | ·9825 | 29 | 56·2987 | |
| 10 | ·9854 | 29 | 67·7573 | |
| 20 | ·9883 | 29 | 84·9456 | |
| 30 | ·9912 | 29 | 113·5930 | |
| 40 | ·9942 | 29 | 170·8883 | |
| 50 | ·9971 | 29 | 342 7752 | |
| 90 0 | 1·0000 | | ∞ | |
| ° ′ | Vers. | d. | Exsec. | d. |

**P. P.**

| | 29 | 29 |
|---|---|---|
| 1 | 2·9 | 2·9 |
| 2 | 5·9 | 5·8 |
| 3 | 8·8 | 8·7 |
| 4 | 11·8 | 11·6 |
| 5 | 14·7 | 14·5 |
| 6 | 17·7 | 17·4 |
| 7 | 20·6 | 20·3 |
| 8 | 23·6 | 23·2 |
| 9 | 26·5 | 26·1 |

| | 28 |
|---|---|
| 1 | 2·8 |
| 2 | 5·7 |
| 3 | 8·5 |
| 4 | 11·4 |
| 5 | 14·2 |
| 6 | 17·1 |
| 7 | 19·9 |
| 8 | 22·8 |
| 9 | 25·6 |

TABLE XIX.—**Elements of a circular curve** of 1° **curvature**, 5,730 ft. radius.

| Δ | Tang., T. | Ext. dist., E. | Long chord, L. C. | Δ | Tang., T. | Ext. dist., E. | Long chord, L. C. |
|---|---|---|---|---|---|---|---|
| ° ′ | | | | ° ′ | | | |
| 1 00 | 50.00 | 0.218 | 100.00 | 9 00 | 450.93 | 17.717 | 899.09 |
| 10 | 58.34 | 0.297 | 116.67 | 10 | 459.32 | 18.381 | 915.70 |
| 20 | 66.67 | 0.388 | 133.33 | 20 | 467.71 | 19 058 | 932.31 |
| 30 | 75.01 | 0.491 | 150.00 | 30 | 476.10 | 19.746 | 948.92 |
| 40 | 83.34 | 0.606 | 166.66 | 40 | 484.49 | 20.447 | 965.53 |
| 50 | 91.68 | 0.733 | 183.33 | 50 | 492.88 | 21.161 | 982.14 |
| 2 00 | 100.01 | 0.873 | 199.99 | 10 00 | 501.28 | 21.886 | 998.74 |
| 10 | 108.35 | 1.024 | 216.66 | 10 | 509.68 | 22.624 | 1015.35 |
| 20 | 116.68 | 1.188 | 233.32 | 20 | 518.08 | 23.375 | 1031.95 |
| 30 | 125.02 | 1.364 | 249.98 | 30 | 526.48 | 24.138 | 1048.54 |
| 40 | 133.36 | 1.552 | 266.65 | 40 | 534.89 | 24.913 | 1065.14 |
| 50 | 141.70 | 1.752 | 283.31 | 50 | 543.29 | 25.700 | 1081.73 |
| 3 00 | 150.04 | 1.964 | 299.97 | 11 00 | 551.70 | 26.500 | 1098.3 |
| 10 | 158.38 | 2.188 | 316.63 | 10 | 560.11 | 27.313 | 1114.9 |
| 20 | 166.72 | 2.425 | 333.29 | 20 | 568.53 | 28.137 | 1131.5 |
| 30 | 175.06 | 2.674 | 349.95 | 30 | 576.95 | 28.974 | 1148.1 |
| 40 | 183.40 | 2.934 | 366.61 | 40 | 585.36 | 29.824 | 1164.7 |
| 50 | 191.74 | 3.207 | 383.27 | 50 | 593.79 | 30.686 | 1181.2 |
| 4 00 | 200.08 | 3.492 | 399.92 | 12 00 | 602.21 | 31.561 | 1197.8 |
| 10 | 208.43 | 3.790 | 416.58 | 10 | 610.64 | 32.447 | 1214.4 |
| 20 | 216.77 | 4.099 | 433 24 | 20 | 619.07 | 33.347 | 1231.0 |
| 30 | 225.12 | 4.421 | 449.89 | 30 | 627.50 | 34.259 | 1247.5 |
| 40 | 233.47 | 4.755 | 466.54 | 40 | 635.93 | 35.183 | 1264.1 |
| 50 | 241.81 | 5.100 | 483.20 | 50 | 644.37 | 36.120 | 1280.7 |
| 5 00 | 250.16 | 5.459 | 499.85 | 13 00 | 652.81 | 37.069 | 1297.2 |
| 10 | 258.51 | 5.829 | 516.50 | 10 | 661.25 | 38.031 | 1313.8 |
| 20 | 266.86 | 6.211 | 533.15 | 20 | 669.70 | 39.006 | 1330.3 |
| 30 | 275.21 | 6.606 | 549.80 | 30 | 678.15 | 39.993 | 1346 9 |
| 40 | 283.57 | 7.013 | 566.44 | 40 | 686.60 | 40.992 | 1363.4 |
| 50 | 291.92 | 7.432 | 583.09 | 50 | 695.06 | 42.004 | 1380.0 |
| 6 00 | 300.28 | 7.863 | 599.73 | 14 00 | 703.51 | 43.029 | 1396.5 |
| 10 | 308.64 | 8.307 | 616.38 | 10 | 711.97 | 44.066 | 1413.1 |
| 20 | 316 99 | 8.762 | 633.02 | 20 | 720.44 | 45.116 | 1429.6 |
| 30 | 325.35 | 9.230 | 649.66 | 30 | 728.90 | 46.178 | 1446.2 |
| 40 | 333.71 | 9.710 | 666.30 | 40 | 737.37 | 47.253 | 1462.7 |
| 50 | 342.08 | 10.202 | 682.94 | 50 | 745.85 | 48.341 | 1479.2 |
| 7 00 | 350.44 | 10.707 | 699.57 | 15 00 | 754.32 | 49.441 | 1495.7 |
| 10 | 358.81 | 11.224 | 716.21 | 10 | 762.80 | 50.554 | 1512.3 |
| 20 | 367.17 | 11.753 | 732.84 | 20 | 771.29 | 51.679 | 1528.8 |
| 30 | 375.54 | 12.294 | 749.47 | 30 | 779.77 | 52.818 | 1545.3 |
| 40 | 383.91 | 12.847 | 766.10 | 40 | 788.26 | 53.969 | 1561.8 |
| 50 | 392.28 | 13.413 | 782.73 | 50 | 796.75 | 55.132 | 1578.3 |
| 8 00 | 400.66 | 13.991 | 799.36 | 16 00 | 805.25 | 56.309 | 1594.8 |
| 10 | 409.03 | 14.582 | 815 99 | 10 | 813.75 | 57.498 | 1611.3 |
| 20 | 417.41 | 15.184 | 832 61 | 20 | 822 25 | 58.699 | 1627.8 |
| 30 | 425.79 | 15.799 | 849.23 | 30 | 830.76 | 59.914 | 1644.3 |
| 40 | 434.17 | 16.426 | 865.85 | 40 | 839.27 | 61.141 | 1660.8 |
| 50 | 442.55 | 17.066 | 882.47 | 50 | 847.78 | 62.381 | 1677.3 |

TABLE XIX.—**Elements of a circular curve of 1° curvature, 5,730 ft. radius—*Continued.***

| Δ | | Tang., T. | Ext. dist., E. | Long chord, L. C. | Δ | | Tang., T. | Ext. dist., E. | Long chord, L. C. |
|---|---|---|---|---|---|---|---|---|---|
| ° | ′ | | | | ° | ′ | | | |
| 17 | 00 | 856.30 | 63.634 | 1693.8 | 25 | 00 | 1270.2 | 139.11 | 2480.2 |
| | 10 | 864.82 | 64.900 | 1710.3 | | 10 | 1279.0 | 141.01 | 2496.5 |
| | 20 | 873.35 | 66.178 | 1726.8 | | 20 | 1287.7 | 142.93 | 2512.8 |
| | 30 | 881.88 | 67.470 | 1743.2 | | 30 | 1296.5 | 144.85 | 2529.0 |
| | 40 | 890.41 | 68.774 | 1759.7 | | 40 | 1305.3 | 146.79 | 2545.3 |
| | 50 | 898.95 | 70.091 | 1776.2 | | 50 | 1314.0 | 148.75 | 2561.5 |
| 18 | 00 | 907.49 | 71.421 | 1792.6 | 26 | 00 | 1322.8 | 150.71 | 2577.8 |
| | 10 | 916.03 | 72.764 | 1809.1 | | 10 | 1331.6 | 152.69 | 2594.0 |
| | 20 | 924.58 | 74.119 | 1825.5 | | 20 | 1340.4 | 154.69 | 2610.3 |
| | 30 | 933.13 | 75.488 | 1842.0 | | 30 | 1349.2 | 156.70 | 2626.5 |
| | 40 | 941.69 | 76.869 | 1858.4 | | 40 | 1358.0 | 158.72 | 2642.7 |
| | 50 | 950.25 | 78.261 | 1874.9 | | 50 | 1366.8 | 160.76 | 2658.9 |
| 19 | 00 | 958.81 | 79.671 | 1891.3 | 27 | 00 | 1375.6 | 162.81 | 2675.1 |
| | 10 | 967.38 | 81.092 | 1907.8 | | 10 | 1384.4 | 164.87 | 2691.3 |
| | 20 | 975.96 | 82.525 | 1924.2 | | 20 | 1393.2 | 166.95 | 2707.5 |
| | 30 | 984.53 | 83.972 | 1940.6 | | 30 | 1402.0 | 169.04 | 2723.7 |
| | 40 | 993.12 | 85.431 | 1957.1 | | 40 | 1410.9 | 171.15 | 2739.9 |
| | 50 | 1001.70 | 86.904 | 1973.5 | | 50 | 1419.7 | 173.27 | 2756.1 |
| 20 | 00 | 1010.29 | 88.389 | 1989.9 | 28 | 00 | 1428.6 | 175.41 | 2772.3 |
| | 10 | 1018.89 | 89.888 | 2006 3 | | 10 | 1437.4 | 177.55 | 2788.4 |
| | 20 | 1027.49 | 91.399 | 2022.7 | | 20 | 1446.3 | 179.72 | 2804.6 |
| | 30 | 1036.09 | 92.924 | 2039.1 | | 30 | 1455.1 | 181.89 | 2820.7 |
| | 40 | 1044.70 | 94.462 | 2055.5 | | 40 | 1464.0 | 184.08 | 2836.9 |
| | 50 | 1053.31 | 96.013 | 2071.9 | | 50 | 1472.9 | 186.29 | 2853.0 |
| 21 | 00 | 1061.9 | 97.58 | 2088.3 | 29 | 00 | 1481.8 | 188.51 | 2869.2 |
| | 10 | 1070.6 | 99.15 | 2104.7 | | 10 | 1490.7 | 190.74 | 2885.3 |
| | 20 | 1079.2 | 100.75 | 2121.1 | | 20 | 1499.6 | 192.99 | 2901.4 |
| | 30 | 1087.8 | 102.35 | 2137.4 | | 30 | 1508.5 | 195.25 | 2917.6 |
| | 40 | 1096.4 | 103.97 | 2153.8 | | 40 | 1517.4 | 197.53 | 2933.7 |
| | 50 | 1105.1 | 105.60 | 2170.2 | | 50 | 1526.3 | 199.82 | 2949.8 |
| 22 | 00 | 1113.7 | 107.24 | 2186.5 | 30 | 00 | 1535.3 | 202.12 | 2965.9 |
| | 10 | 1122.4 | 108.90 | 2202.9 | | 10 | 1544.2 | 204.44 | 2982.0 |
| | 20 | 1131.0 | 110.57 | 2219 2 | | 20 | 1553.1 | 206.77 | 2998.1 |
| | 30 | 1139.7 | 112.25 | 2235.6 | | 30 | 1562.1 | 209.12 | 3014.2 |
| | 40 | 1148.4 | 113.95 | 2251.9 | | 40 | 1571.0 | 211.48 | 3030.2 |
| | 50 | 1157.0 | 115.66 | 2268.3 | | 50 | 1580.0 | 213.86 | 3046.3 |
| 23 | 00 | 1165.7 | 117.38 | 2284.6 | 31 | 00 | 1589.0 | 216.25 | 3062.4 |
| | 10 | 1174.4 | 119.12 | 2301.0 | | 10 | 1598.0 | 218.66 | 3078.4 |
| | 20 | 1183.1 | 120.87 | 2317.3 | | 20 | 1606.9 | 221.08 | 3094.5 |
| | 30 | 1191.8 | 122.63 | 2333.6 | | 30 | 1615.9 | 223.51 | 3110.5 |
| | 40 | 1200.5 | 124.41 | 2349.9 | | 40 | 1624.9 | 225.96 | 3126.6 |
| | 50 | 1209.2 | 126.20 | 2366.2 | | 50 | 1633.9 | 228.42 | 3142.6 |
| 24 | 00 | 1217.9 | 128.00 | 2382.5 | 32 | 00 | 1643.0 | 230.90 | 3158.6 |
| | 10 | 1226.6 | 129.82 | 2398.8 | | 10 | 1652.0 | 233.39 | 3174.6 |
| | 20 | 1235.3 | 131.65 | 2415.1 | | 20 | 1661.0 | 235.90 | 3190.6 |
| | 30 | 1244.0 | 133.50 | 2431.4 | | 30 | 1670.0 | 238.43 | 3206.6 |
| | 40 | 1252.8 | 135.36 | 2447.7 | | 40 | 1679.1 | 240.96 | 3222.6 |
| | 50 | 1261.5 | 137.23 | 2464.0 | | 50 | 1688.1 | 243.52 | 3238.6 |

TABLE XIX.—**Elements of a circular curve** of 1° **curvature, 5,730 ft. radius**-*Continued.*

| Δ | Tang., T. | Ext. dist., E. | Long chord, L. C. | Δ | Tang., T. | Ext. dist., E. | Long chord, L. C. |
|---|---|---|---|---|---|---|---|
| ° ′ | | | | ° ′ | | | |
| 33 00 | 1697.2 | 246.08 | 3254.6 | 41 00 | 2142.2 | 387.38 | 4013.1 |
| 10 | 1706.3 | 248.66 | 3270.6 | 10 | 2151.7 | 390.71 | 4028.7 |
| 20 | 1715.3 | 251.26 | 3286.6 | 20 | 2161.2 | 394.06 | 4044.3 |
| 30 | 1724.4 | 253.87 | 3302.5 | 30 | 2170.8 | 397.43 | 4059.9 |
| 40 | 1733.5 | 256 50 | 3318.5 | 40 | 2180 3 | 400.82 | 4075.5 |
| 50 | 1742.6 | 259.14 | 3334 4 | 50 | 2189.9 | 404.22 | 4091.1 |
| 34 00 | 1751.7 | 261.80 | 3350 4 | 42 00 | 2199.4 | 407.64 | 4106.6 |
| 10 | 1760.8 | 264.47 | 3366 3 | 10 | 2209.0 | 411.07 | 4122.2 |
| 20 | 1770.0 | 267.16 | 3382.2 | 20 | 2218.6 | 414.52 | 4137.7 |
| 30 | 1779.1 | 269.86 | 3398.2 | 30 | 2228.1 | 417.99 | 4153.3 |
| 40 | 1788.2 | 272.58 | 3414 1 | 40 | 2237.7 | 421.48 | 4168.8 |
| 50 | 1797.4 | 275.31 | 3430.0 | 50 | 2247.3 | 424.98 | 4184.3 |
| 35 00 | 1806.6 | 278.05 | 3445.9 | 43 00 | 2257.0 | 428.50 | 4199.8 |
| 10 | 1815.7 | 280.82 | 3461.8 | 10 | 2266.6 | 432.04 | 4215.3 |
| 20 | 1824.9 | 283.60 | 3477.7 | 20 | 2276.2 | 435.59 | 4230.8 |
| 30 | 1834.1 | 286 39 | 3493.5 | 30 | 2285.9 | 439.16 | 4246.3 |
| 40 | 1843.3 | 289.20 | 3509.4 | 40 | 2295.6 | 442.75 | 4261.8 |
| 50 | 1852.5 | 292.02 | 3525.3 | 50 | 2305.2 | 446.35 | 4277.3 |
| 36 00 | 1861.7 | 294.86 | 3541 1 | 44 00 | 2314.9 | 449.98 | 4292.7 |
| 10 | 1870.9 | 297.72 | 3557.0 | 10 | 2324.6 | 453.62 | 4308.2 |
| 20 | 1880.1 | 300.59 | 3572 8 | 20 | 2334.3 | 457.27 | 4323.6 |
| 30 | 1889.4 | 303.47 | 3588.6 | 30 | 2344.1 | 460.95 | 4339.0 |
| 40 | 1898.6 | 306.37 | 3604.5 | 40 | 2353.8 | 464.64 | 4354.5 |
| 50 | 1907.9 | 309.29 | 3620.3 | 50 | 2363.5 | 468.35 | 4369.9 |
| 37 00 | 1917.1 | 312.22 | 3636.1 | 45 00 | 2373.3 | 472.08 | 4385.3 |
| 10 | 1926.4 | 315.17 | 3651.9 | 10 | 2383.1 | 475.82 | 4400.7 |
| 20 | 1935.7 | 318.13 | 3667.7 | 20 | 2392.8 | 479.59 | 4416.1 |
| 30 | 1945.0 | 321.11 | 3683.5 | 30 | 2402.6 | 483.37 | 4431.4 |
| 40 | 1954.3 | 324.11 | 3699.3 | 40 | 2412.4 | 487.16 | 4446.8 |
| 50 | 1963.6 | 327.12 | 3715.0 | 50 | 2422.3 | 490.98 | 4462.2 |
| 38 00 | 1972.9 | 330.15 | 3730.8 | 46 00 | 2432.1 | 494.82 | 4477.5 |
| 10 | 1982.2 | 333.19 | 3746.5 | 10 | 2441.9 | 498.67 | 4492.8 |
| 20 | 1991.5 | 336.25 | 3762.3 | 20 | 2451.8 | 502.54 | 4508.2 |
| 30 | 2000.9 | 339.32 | 3778.0 | 30 | 2461.7 | 506.42 | 4523.5 |
| 40 | 2010.2 | 342.41 | 3793.8 | 40 | 2471.5 | 510.33 | 4538.8 |
| 50 | 2019.6 | 345.52 | 3809.5 | 50 | 2481.4 | 514.25 | 4554.1 |
| 39 00 | 2029.0 | 348.64 | 3825.2 | 47 00 | 2491.3 | 518.20 | 4569.4 |
| 10 | 2038.4 | 351.78 | 3840.9 | 10 | 2501.2 | 522.16 | 4584.7 |
| 20 | 2047.8 | 354.94 | 3856.6 | 20 | 2511.2 | 526.13 | 4599.9 |
| 30 | 2057.2 | 358.11 | 3872.3 | 30 | 2521.1 | 530.13 | 4615.2 |
| 40 | 2066.6 | 361.29 | 3888.0 | 40 | 2531.1 | 534.15 | 4630 4 |
| 50 | 2076.0 | 364.50 | 3903.6 | 50 | 2541.0 | 538.18 | 4645.7 |
| 40 00 | 2085.4 | 367.72 | 3919.3 | 48 00 | 2551.0 | 542.23 | 4660.9 |
| 10 | 2094.9 | 370.95 | 3935.0 | 10 | 2561.0 | 546.30 | 4676.1 |
| 20 | 2104.3 | 374.20 | 3950.6 | 20 | 2571.0 | 550.39 | 4691.3 |
| 30 | 2113.8 | 377.47 | 3966.3 | 30 | 2581.0 | 554.50 | 4706.5 |
| 40 | 2123.3 | 380.76 | 3981.9 | 40 | 2591.1 | 558.63 | 4721.7 |
| 50 | 2132.7 | 384.06 | 3997.5 | 50 | 2601.1 | 562.77 | 4736.9 |

TABLE XIX.—Elements of a circular curve of 1° curvature, 5,730 ft. radius—*Continued.*

| Δ | | Tang., T. | Ext. dist., E. | Long chord, L. C. | Δ | | Tang., T. | Ext. dist., E. | Long chord, L. C. |
|---|---|---|---|---|---|---|---|---|---|
| ° | ′ | | | | ° | ′ | | | |
| 49 | 00 | 2611.2 | 566.94 | 4752.1 | 57 | 00 | 3110.9 | 790.08 | 5467.9 |
| | 10 | 2621.2 | 571.12 | 4767.3 | | 10 | 3121.7 | 795.24 | 5482.5 |
| | 20 | 2631.3 | 575.32 | 4782.4 | | 20 | 3132.6 | 800.42 | 5497.2 |
| | 30 | 2641.4 | 579.54 | 4797.5 | | 30 | 3143.4 | 805.62 | 5511.8 |
| | 40 | 2651.5 | 583.78 | 4812.7 | | 40 | 3154.2 | 810.85 | 5526.4 |
| | 50 | 2661.6 | 588.04 | 4827.8 | | 50 | 3165.1 | 816.10 | 5541.0 |
| 50 | 00 | 2671.8 | 592.32 | 4842.9 | 58 | 00 | 3176.0 | 821.37 | 5555.6 |
| | 10 | 2681.9 | 596.62 | 4858.0 | | 10 | 3186.9 | 826.66 | 5570.2 |
| | 20 | 2692.1 | 600.93 | 4873.1 | | 20 | 3197.8 | 831.98 | 5584.7 |
| | 30 | 2702.3 | 605.27 | 4888.2 | | 30 | 3208.8 | 837.31 | 5599.3 |
| | 40 | 2712.5 | 609.62 | 4903.2 | | 40 | 3219.7 | 842.67 | 5613.8 |
| | 50 | 2722.7 | 614.00 | 4918.3 | | 50 | 3230.7 | 848.06 | 5628.3 |
| 51 | 00 | 2732.9 | 618.39 | 4933.4 | 59 | 00 | 3241.7 | 853.46 | 5642.8 |
| | 10 | 2743.1 | 622.81 | 4948.4 | | 10 | 3252.7 | 858.89 | 5657.3 |
| | 20 | 2753.4 | 627.24 | 4963.4 | | 20 | 3263.7 | 864.34 | 5671.8 |
| | 30 | 2763.7 | 631.69 | 4978.4 | | 30 | 3274.8 | 869.82 | 5686.3 |
| | 40 | 2773.9 | 636.16 | 4993.4 | | 40 | 3285.8 | 875.32 | 5700.8 |
| | 50 | 2784.2 | 640.66 | 5008.4 | | 50 | 3296.9 | 880.84 | 5715.2 |
| 52 | 00 | 2794.5 | 645.17 | 5023.4 | 60 | 00 | 3308.0 | 886.38 | 5729.7 |
| | 10 | 2804.9 | 649.70 | 5038.4 | | 10 | 3319.1 | 891.95 | 5744.1 |
| | 20 | 2815.2 | 654.25 | 5053.4 | | 20 | 3330.3 | 897.54 | 5758.5 |
| | 30 | 2825.6 | 658.83 | 5068.3 | | 30 | 3341.4 | 903.15 | 5772.9 |
| | 40 | 2835.9 | 663.42 | 5083.3 | | 40 | 3352.6 | 908.79 | 5787.3 |
| | 50 | 2846.3 | 668.03 | 5098.2 | | 50 | 3363.8 | 914.45 | 5801.7 |
| 53 | 00 | 2856.7 | 672.66 | 5113.1 | 61 | 00 | 3375.0 | 920.14 | 5816.0 |
| | 10 | 2867.1 | 677.32 | 5128.0 | | 10 | 3386.3 | 925.85 | 5830.4 |
| | 20 | 2877.5 | 681.99 | 5142.9 | | 20 | 3397.5 | 931.58 | 5844.7 |
| | 30 | 2888.0 | 686.68 | 5157.8 | | 30 | 3408.8 | 937.34 | 5859.1 |
| | 40 | 2898.4 | 691.40 | 5172.7 | | 40 | 3420.1 | 943.12 | 5873.4 |
| | 50 | 2908.9 | 696.13 | 5187.6 | | 50 | 3431.4 | 948.92 | 5887.7 |
| 54 | 00 | 2919.4 | 700.89 | 5202.4 | 62 | 00 | 3442.7 | 954.75 | 5902.0 |
| | 10 | 2929.9 | 705.66 | 5217.3 | | 10 | 3454.1 | 960.60 | 5916.3 |
| | 20 | 2940.4 | 710.46 | 5232.1 | | 20 | 3465.4 | 966.48 | 5930.5 |
| | 30 | 2951.0 | 715.28 | 5246.9 | | 30 | 3476.8 | 972.39 | 5944.8 |
| | 40 | 2961.5 | 720.11 | 5261.7 | | 40 | 3488.2 | 978.31 | 5959.0 |
| | 50 | 2972.1 | 724.97 | 5276.5 | | 50 | 3499.7 | 984.27 | 5973.3 |
| 55 | 00 | 2982.7 | 729.85 | 5291.8 | 63 | 00 | 3511.1 | 990.24 | 5987.5 |
| | 10 | 2993.3 | 734.76 | 5306.1 | | 10 | 3522.6 | 996.24 | 6001.7 |
| | 20 | 3003.9 | 739.68 | 5320.9 | | 20 | 3534.1 | 1002.3 | 6015.9 |
| | 30 | 3014.5 | 744.62 | 5335.6 | | 30 | 3545.6 | 1008.3 | 6030.0 |
| | 40 | 3025.2 | 749.59 | 5350.4 | | 40 | 3557.2 | 1014.4 | 6044.2 |
| | 50 | 3035.8 | 754.57 | 5365.1 | | 50 | 3568.7 | 1020.5 | 6058.4 |
| 56 | 00 | 3046.5 | 759.58 | 5379.8 | 64 | 00 | 3580.3 | 1026.6 | 6072.5 |
| | 10 | 3057.2 | 764.61 | 5394.5 | | 10 | 3591.9 | 1032.8 | 6086.6 |
| | 20 | 3067.9 | 769.66 | 5409.2 | | 20 | 3603.5 | 1039.0 | 6100.7 |
| | 30 | 3078.7 | 774.73 | 5423.9 | | 30 | 3615.1 | 1045.2 | 6114.8 |
| | 40 | 3089.4 | 779.83 | 5438.6 | | 40 | 3626.8 | 1051.4 | 6128.9 |
| | 50 | 3100.2 | 784.94 | 5453.3 | | 50 | 3638.5 | 1057.7 | 6143.0 |

TABLE XIX.—**Elements of a circular curve of 1° curvature, 5,730 ft. radius—** *Continued.*

| Δ | Tang., T. | Ext. dist., E. | Long chord, L. C. | Δ | Tang., T. | Ext. dist., E. | Long chord, L. C. |
|---|---|---|---|---|---|---|---|
| ° ′ | | | | ° ′ | | | |
| 65 00 | 3650.2 | 1063.9 | 6157.1 | 73 00 | 4239.7 | 1398.0 | 6816.3 |
| 10 | 3661.9 | 1070.2 | 6171.1 | 10 | 4252.6 | 1405.7 | 6829.6 |
| 20 | 3673.7 | 1076.6 | 6185.2 | 20 | 4265.6 | 1413.5 | 6843.0 |
| 30 | 3685.4 | 1082.9 | 6199.2 | 30 | 4278.5 | 1421.2 | 6856.4 |
| 40 | 3697.2 | 1089.3 | 6213.2 | 40 | 4291.5 | 1429.0 | 6869.7 |
| 50 | 3709.0 | 1095.7 | 6227.2 | 50 | 4304.6 | 1436.8 | 6883.1 |
| 66 00 | 3720.9 | 1102.2 | 6241.2 | 74 00 | 4317.6 | 1444.6 | 6896.4 |
| 10 | 3732.7 | 1108.6 | 6255.2 | 10 | 4330.7 | 1452.5 | 6909.7 |
| 20 | 3744.6 | 1115.1 | 6269.1 | 20 | 4343.8 | 1460.4 | 6923.0 |
| 30 | 3756.5 | 1121.7 | 6283.1 | 30 | 4356.9 | 1468.4 | 6936.2 |
| 40 | 3768.5 | 1128.2 | 6297 0 | 40 | 4370.1 | 1476.4 | 6949.5 |
| 50 | 3780.4 | 1134.8 | 6310.9 | 50 | 4383.3 | 1484.4 | 6962.8 |
| 67 00 | 3792.4 | 1141.4 | 6324.8 | 75 00 | 4396.5 | 1492.4 | 6976.0 |
| 10 | 3804.4 | 1148.0 | 6338.7 | 10 | 4409.8 | 1500.5 | 6989.2 |
| 20 | 3816.4 | 1154.7 | 6352.6 | 20 | 4423.1 | 1508.6 | 7002.4 |
| 30 | 3828.4 | 1161.3 | 6366.4 | 30 | 4436.4 | 1516.7 | 7015.6 |
| 40 | 3840.5 | 1168.1 | 6380.3 | 40 | 4449.7 | 1524.9 | 7028.8 |
| 50 | 3852.6 | 1174.8 | 6394.1 | 50 | 4463.1 | 1533.1 | 7041.9 |
| 68 00 | 3864.7 | 1181.6 | 6408.0 | 76 00 | 4476.5 | 1541.4 | 7055.0 |
| 10 | 3876.8 | 1188.4 | 6421.8 | 10 | 4489.9 | 1549.7 | 7068.2 |
| 20 | 3889.0 | 1195.2 | 6435.6 | 20 | 4503.4 | 1558.0 | 7081.3 |
| 30 | 3901.2 | 1202.0 | 6449.4 | 30 | 4 16.9 | 1566.3 | 7094.4 |
| 40 | 3913.4 | 1208.9 | 6463.1 | 40 | 4530.4 | 1574.7 | 7107.5 |
| 50 | 3925.6 | 1215.8 | 6476.9 | 50 | 4544.0 | 1583.1 | 7120.5 |
| 69 00 | 3937.9 | 1222.7 | 6490.6 | 77 00 | 4557.6 | 1591.6 | 7133.6 |
| 10 | 3950.2 | 1229.7 | 6504.4 | 10 | 4571.2 | 1600.1 | 7146.6 |
| 20 | 3962 5 | 1236.7 | 6518.1 | 20 | 4584.8 | 1608.6 | 7159.6 |
| 30 | 3974.8 | 1243.7 | 6531.8 | 30 | 4598.5 | 1617.1 | 7172.6 |
| 70 | 3987.2 | 1250.8 | 6545.5 | 40 | 461 .2 | 1625.7 | 7185.6 |
| 50 | 3999.5 | 1257.9 | 6559.1 | 50 | 4626.0 | 1634.4 | 7198.6 |
| 70 00 | 4011.9 | 1265.0 | 6572.8 | 78 00 | 4639.8 | 1643.0 | 7211.6 |
| 10 | 4024.4 | 1272.1 | 6586.4 | 10 | 4653.6 | 1651.7 | 7224.5 |
| 20 | 4036.8 | 1279.3 | 6600.1 | 20 | 4667.4 | 1660.5 | 7237.4 |
| 30 | 4049.3 | 1286.5 | 6613.7 | 30 | 4681.3 | 1669.2 | 7250.4 |
| 40 | 4061.8 | 1293.7 | 6627.3 | 40 | 4695.2 | 1678.1 | 7263.3 |
| 50 | 4074.4 | 1300.9 | 6640.9 | 50 | 4709.2 | 1686.9 | 7276.1 |
| 71 00 | 4086.9 | 1308.2 | 6654.4 | 79 00 | 4723.2 | 1695.8 | 7289.0 |
| 10 | 4099.5 | 1315.5 | 6668.0 | 10 | 4737.2 | 1704.7 | 7301.9 |
| 20 | 4112.1 | 1322.9 | 6681.6 | 20 | 4751.2 | 1713.7 | 7314.7 |
| 30 | 4124.8 | 1330.3 | 6695.1 | 30 | 4765.3 | 1722.7 | 7327.5 |
| 40 | 4137.4 | 1337.7 | 6708.6 | 40 | 4779.4 | 1731.7 | 7340.3 |
| 50 | 4150.1 | 1345.1 | 6722.1 | 50 | 4793.6 | 1740.8 | 7353.1 |
| 72 00 | 4162.8 | 1352.6 | 6735.6 | 80 00 | 4808.7 | 1749.9 | 7365.9 |
| 10 | 4175.6 | 1360.1 | 6749.1 | 10 | 4822.0 | 1759.0 | 7378.7 |
| 20 | 4188.4 | 1367.6 | 6762.5 | 20 | 4836.2 | 1768.2 | 7391.4 |
| 30 | 4201.2 | 1375.2 | 6776.0 | 30 | 4850.5 | 1777.4 | 7404.1 |
| 40 | 4214.0 | 1382.8 | 6789.4 | 40 | 4864.8 | 1786.7 | 7416.8 |
| 50 | 4226.8 | 1390.4 | 6802.8 | 50 | 4879.2 | 1796.0 | 7429.5 |

TABLE XIX.—**Elements of a circular curve** of 1° **curvature, 5,730 ft. radius**—*Concluded.*

| Δ ° | Δ ′ | **Tang., T.** | **Ext. dist., E.** | Long chord, L. C. | Δ ° | Δ ′ | **Tang., T.** | **Ext. dist., E.** | **Long chord, L. C.** |
|---|---|---|---|---|---|---|---|---|---|
| 81 | 00 | 4893.6 | 1805.3 | 7442.2 | 86 | 00 | 5343.0 | 2104.7 | 7815.2 |
| | 10 | 4908.0 | 1814.7 | 7454.9 | | 10 | 5358.6 | 2115.3 | 7827.4 |
| | 20 | 4922.5 | 1824.1 | 7467.5 | | 20 | 5374.2 | 2126.0 | 7839.6 |
| | 30 | 4937.0 | 1833.6 | 7480.2 | | 30 | 5389.9 | 2136.7 | 7851.7 |
| | 40 | 4951.5 | 1843.1 | 7492.8 | | 40 | 5405.6 | 2147.5 | 7863.8 |
| | 50 | 4966.1 | 1852.6 | 7505.4 | | 50 | 5421.4 | 2158.4 | 7876.0 |
| 82 | 00 | 4980.7 | 1862.2 | 7518.0 | 87 | 00 | 5437.2 | 2169.2 | 7888.1 |
| | 10 | 4995.4 | 1871.8 | 7530.5 | | 10 | 5453.1 | 2180.2 | 7900.1 |
| | 20 | 5010.0 | 1881.5 | 7543.1 | | 20 | 5469.0 | 2191.1 | 7912.2 |
| | 30 | 5024.8 | 1891.2 | 7555.6 | | 30 | 5484.9 | 2202.2 | 7924.3 |
| | 40 | 5039.5 | 1900.9 | 7568.2 | | 40 | 5500.9 | 2213.2 | 7936.3 |
| | 50 | 5054.3 | 1910.7 | 7580.7 | | 50 | 5517.0 | 2224.3 | 7948.3 |
| 83 | 00 | 5069.2 | 1920.5 | 7593.2 | 88 | 00 | 5533.1 | 2235.5 | 7960.3 |
| | 10 | 5084.0 | 1930.4 | 7605.6 | | 10 | 5549.2 | 2246.7 | 7972.3 |
| | 20 | 5099.0 | 1940.3 | 7618.1 | | 20 | 5565.4 | 2258.0 | 7984.2 |
| | 30 | 5113.9 | 1950.3 | 7630.5 | | 30 | 5581.6 | 2269.3 | 7996.2 |
| | 40 | 5128.9 | 1960.2 | 7643.0 | | 40 | 5597.8 | 2280.6 | 8008.1 |
| | 50 | 5143.9 | 1970.3 | 7655.4 | | 50 | 5614.2 | 2292.0 | 8020.0 |
| 84 | 00 | 5159.0 | 1980.4 | 7667.8 | 89 | 00 | 5630.5 | 2303.5 | 8031.9 |
| | 10 | 5174.1 | 1990.5 | 7680.1 | | 10 | 5646.9 | 2315.0 | 8043.8 |
| | 20 | 5189.3 | 2000.6 | 7692.5 | | 20 | 5663.4 | 2326.6 | 8055.7 |
| | 30 | 5204.4 | 2010.8 | 7704.9 | | 30 | 5679.9 | 2338.2 | 8067.5 |
| | 40 | 5219.7 | 2021.1 | 7717.2 | | 40 | 5696.4 | 2349.8 | 8079.3 |
| | 50 | 5234.9 | 2031.4 | 7729.5 | | 50 | 5713.0 | 2361.5 | 8091.2 |
| 85 | 00 | 5250.3 | 2041.7 | 7741.8 | 90 | 00 | 5729.7 | 2373.3 | 8103.0 |
| | 10 | 5265.6 | 2052.1 | 7754.1 | | 10 | 5746.3 | 2385.1 | 8114.7 |
| | 20 | 5281.0 | 2062.5 | 7766.3 | | 20 | 5763.1 | 2397.0 | 8126.5 |
| | 30 | 5296.4 | 2073.0 | 7778.6 | | 30 | 5779.9 | 2408.9 | 8138.2 |
| | 40 | 5311.9 | 2083.5 | 7790.8 | | 40 | 5796.7 | 2420.9 | 8150.0 |
| | 50 | 5327.4 | 2094.1 | 7803.0 | | 50 | 5813.6 | 2432.9 | 8161.7 |

**Note.**—If $\Delta \times D$ is less than 600, the error in **tang. dist.** of the above table is less than 0.4 ft. If $\Delta \times D$ is less than 400, the error in tang. dist. is less than 0.25 ft. If $\Delta \times D$ is less than 200, the error in tang. dist. is less than 0.1 ft.

TABLE XX.—**Middle ordinates** for curving rails (feet).

| Radius (feet). | Length of rail chords. | | | | | | | | | | | |
|---|---|---|---|---|---|---|---|---|---|---|---|---|
| | 32 | 30 | 28 | 26 | 24 | 22 | 20 | 18 | 16 | 14 | 12 | 10 |
| 5,730 | 0.022 | 0.020 | 0.017 | 0.015 | 0.013 | 0.011 | 0.009 | 0.007 | 0.006 | 0.004 | 0.003 | 0.002 |
| 2,865 | .045 | .039 | .034 | .030 | .025 | .021 | .017 | .014 | .011 | .009 | .006 | .004 |
| 1,910 | .067 | .059 | .051 | .044 | .038 | .032 | .026 | .021 | .017 | .013 | .009 | .007 |
| 1,432 | .089 | .079 | .068 | .059 | .050 | .042 | .035 | .028 | .022 | .017 | .013 | .009 |
| 1,146 | .112 | .098 | .086 | .074 | .063 | .053 | .044 | .035 | .028 | .021 | .016 | .011 |
| 955 | .134 | .118 | .103 | .088 | .075 | .063 | .052 | .042 | .034 | .026 | .019 | .013 |
| 819 | .156 | .137 | .120 | .103 | .088 | .074 | .061 | .049 | .039 | .030 | .022 | .015 |
| 716 | .179 | .157 | .137 | .118 | .100 | .084 | .070 | .057 | .045 | .034 | .025 | .017 |
| 637 | .201 | .177 | .154 | .133 | .113 | .095 | .078 | .064 | .050 | .038 | .028 | .020 |
| 573 | .223 | .196 | .171 | .147 | .126 | .105 | .087 | .071 | .056 | .043 | .031 | .022 |
| 521 | .245 | .216 | .188 | .162 | .138 | .116 | .096 | .078 | .061 | .047 | .035 | .024 |
| 477 | .268 | .235 | .205 | .177 | .151 | .127 | .105 | .085 | .067 | .051 | .038 | .026 |
| 409 | .312 | .274 | .238 | .206 | .175 | .147 | .122 | .099 | .078 | .060 | .044 | .030 |
| 357 | .356 | .313 | .273 | .235 | .200 | .168 | .139 | .113 | .089 | .068 | .050 | .035 |
| 318 | .400 | .352 | .307 | .264 | .225 | .189 | .156 | .127 | .100 | .077 | .056 | .039 |
| 286 | .445 | .391 | .340 | .293 | .250 | .210 | .174 | .141 | .111 | .085 | .063 | .043 |
| 225 | .57 | .50 | .44 | .38 | .32 | .27 | .22 | .18 | .14 | .11 | .08 | .05 |
| 200 | .64 | .56 | .49 | .42 | .36 | .30 | .25 | .20 | .16 | .12 | .09 | .06 |
| 175 | .73 | .64 | .56 | .49 | .41 | .35 | .29 | .24 | .18 | .13 | .10 | .08 |
| 150 | .86 | .75 | .65 | .56 | .48 | .40 | .33 | .27 | .21 | .16 | .12 | .09 |
| 125 | 1.03 | .90 | .79 | .68 | .58 | .49 | .40 | .32 | .26 | .20 | .15 | .10 |
| 100 | 1.31 | 1.13 | .98 | .85 | .73 | .61 | .51 | .41 | .33 | .25 | .18 | .13 |
| 80 | 1.62 | 1.42 | 1.28 | 1.06 | .91 | .76 | .63 | .51 | .41 | .32 | .23 | .16 |
| 60 | 2.17 | 1.91 | 1.74 | 1.42 | 1.21 | 1.09 | .84 | .68 | .54 | .41 | .30 | .21 |
| 50 | 2.63 | 2.31 | 2.00 | 1.73 | 1.46 | 1.23 | 1.01 | .82 | .73 | .49 | .36 | .25 |
| 30 | 4.62 | 4.02 | 3.47 | 2.96 | 2.51 | 2.09 | 1.72 | 1.38 | 1.09 | .83 | .61 | .42 |

TABLE XXI.—Bill of **material** for **standard pile bridges.**

| Details. | 16-ft. span. | | | | | | | | | | | | | | | | | | | | |
|---|---|---|---|---|---|---|---|---|---|---|---|---|---|---|---|---|---|---|---|---|---|
| | For 1 span. | For 2 spans. | For 3 spans. | For 4 spans. | For 5 spans. | For 6 spans. | For 7 spans. | For 8 spans. | For 9 spans. | For 10 spans. | For 11 spans. | For 12 spans. | For 13 spans. | For 14 spans. | For 15 spans. | For 16 spans. | For 17 spans. | For 18 spans. | For 19 spans. | For 20 spans. | For each addl. span. |
| **Piles:** | | | | | | | | | | | | | | | | | | | | | |
| **End bents** | 8 | 8 | 8 | 8 | 8 | 8 | 8 | 8 | 8 | 8 | 8 | 8 | 8 | 8 | 8 | 8 | 8 | 8 | 8 | 8 | ---- |
| **Int. bents** | ---- | 5 | 10 | 15 | 20 | 25 | 30 | 35 | 40 | 45 | 50 | 55 | 60 | 65 | 70 | 75 | 80 | 85 | 90 | 95 | 5 |
| **Caps, white pine, 14 by 14 ins., 14 ft. long** | 2 | 3 | 4 | 5 | 6 | 7 | 8 | 9 | 10 | 11 | 12 | 13 | 14 | 15 | 16 | 17 | 18 | 19 | 20 | 21 | 1 |
| **Sway braces, white pine, 4 by 10 ins*** | ---- | 2 | 4 | 6 | 8 | 10 | 12 | 14 | 16 | 18 | 20 | 22 | 24 | 26 | 28 | 30 | 32 | 34 | 36 | 38 | 2 |
| **Stringers, Douglas fir, 8 by 16 ins.:** | | | | | | | | | | | | | | | | | | | | | |
| 16 ft. long | 6 | ---- | 6 | 6 | 6 | 6 | 6 | 6 | 6 | 6 | 6 | 6 | 6 | 6 | 6 | 6 | 6 | 6 | 6 | 6 | ---- |
| 32 ft. long | ---- | 6 | 6 | 9 | 12 | 15 | 18 | 21 | 24 | 27 | 30 | 33 | 36 | 39 | 42 | 45 | 48 | 51 | 54 | 57 | 3 |
| **Ties, white pine, S 1 S, 8 by 8 ins., 10 ft. long** | 15 | 29 | 43 | 57 | 71 | 85 | 99 | 113 | 127 | 141 | 155 | 169 | 183 | 197 | 211 | 225 | 239 | 253 | 267 | 281 | 14 |
| **Guard rails, white pine, S 1 S, 4 by 10 ins., 16 ft. long** | 2 | 5 | 7 | 9 | 11 | 14 | 16 | 18 | 20 | 22 | 25 | 27 | 29 | 31 | 33 | 36 | 38 | 40 | 42 | 45 | 2 |
| **Stringer bolts (square heads and nuts), ¾ in. diameter, 3 ins. threaded, 35 ins. long** | 4 | 8 | 20 | 28 | 36 | 44 | 52 | 60 | 68 | 76 | 84 | 92 | 100 | 108 | 116 | 124 | 132 | 140 | 148 | 156 | 8 |
| **Floor bolts (square heads and nuts), ¾ in. diameter, 3 ins. threaded, 44½ ins. long** | 4 | 6 | 8 | 10 | 12 | 14 | 16 | 18 | 20 | 22 | 24 | 26 | 28 | 30 | 32 | 34 | 36 | 38 | 40 | 42 | 2 |
| **Sway-brace bolts (square heads and nuts), ¾ in. diameter, 3½ ins. threaded:** | | | | | | | | | | | | | | | | | | | | | |
| 21 ins. long | ---- | 10 | 20 | 30 | 40 | 50 | 60 | 70 | 80 | 90 | 100 | 110 | 120 | 130 | 140 | 150 | 160 | 170 | 180 | 190 | 10 |
| 25 ins. long | ---- | 1 | 2 | 3 | 4 | 5 | 6 | 7 | 8 | 9 | 10 | 11 | 12 | 13 | 14 | 15 | 16 | 17 | 18 | 19 | 1 |
| **Packing spools** | 8 | 16 | 40 | 56 | 72 | 88 | 104 | 120 | 136 | 152 | 168 | 184 | 200 | 216 | 232 | 248 | 264 | 280 | 296 | 312 | 16 |
| **Standard cast slot washers for ¾-in. bolts** | 16 | 50 | 100 | 142 | 184 | 226 | 268 | 310 | 352 | 394 | 436 | 478 | 520 | 562 | 604 | 646 | 688 | 730 | 772 | 814 | 42 |

TABLE XXI.—Bill of **material** for **standard pile bridges**—*Continued.*

| Details. | 16-ft. span. | | | | | | | | | | | | | | | | | | | | |
|---|---|---|---|---|---|---|---|---|---|---|---|---|---|---|---|---|---|---|---|---|---|
| | For 1 span. | For 2 spans. | For 3 spans. | For 4 spans. | For 5 spans. | For 6 spans. | For 7 spans. | For 8 spans. | For 9 spans. | For 10 spans. | For 11 spans. | For 12 spans. | For 13 spans. | For 14 spans. | For 15 spans. | For 16 spans. | For 17 spans. | For 18 spans. | For 19 spans. | For 20 spans. | For each addl. span. |
| Driftbolts, ¾ in. diameter, 22 ins. long | 8 | 13 | 18 | 23 | 28 | 33 | 38 | 43 | 48 | 53 | 58 | 63 | 68 | 73 | 78 | 83 | 88 | 93 | 98 | 103 | 5 |
| Spikes: | | | | | | | | | | | | | | | | | | | | | |
| ⅝ in. by 14 ins. long | 13 | 22 | 31 | 40 | 49 | 58 | 67 | 76 | 85 | 94 | 103 | 112 | 121 | 130 | 139 | 148 | 157 | 166 | 175 | 184 | 9 |
| ½ in. by 10 ins. long | 28 | 56 | 84 | 112 | 140 | 168 | 196 | 224 | 252 | 280 | 308 | 336 | 364 | 392 | 420 | 448 | 476 | 504 | 532 | 560 | 28 |
| BULKHEADS. | | | | | | | | | | | | | | | | | | | | | |
| Furring strips, 2 by 4 ins., 3 ft. 4 ins. long (cut from four 10-ft. lengths) | 12 | Alike for all bridges. | | | | | | | | | | | | | | | | | | | |
| Planks, 3 by 10 ins.: | | | | | | | | | | | | | | | | | | | | | |
| 14 ft. long | 2 | | | | | | | | | | | | | | | | | | | | |
| 16 ft. long | 6 | | | | | | | | | | | | | | | | | | | | |
| Spikes, 10 ins. long (planks to bents) | 48 | | | | | | | | | | | | | | | | | | | | |
| Nails, 4½ ins. long (strips to bents) | 24 | | | | | | | | | | | | | | | | | | | | |

| | | | | |
|---|---|---|---|---|
| * Height of bridge ft. | 10 to 12 | 13 to 15 | 16 to 18 | 19 to 20 |
| * Length of brace ft. | 16 | 18 | 20 | 22 |

TABLE XXII.—Grades and grade angles.

| Ft. per station. | Ft. per mile. | Inclination. | Ft. per station. | Ft. per mile. | Inclination. | Ft. per station. | Ft. per mile. | Inclination. |
|---|---|---|---|---|---|---|---|---|
| | | ° ′ ″ | | | ° ′ ″ | | | ° ′ ″ |
| 0.02 | 1.056 | 0 00 41 | 0.52 | 27.456 | 0 17 53 | 1.02 | 53.856 | 0 35 04 |
| .04 | 2.112 | 1 23 | .54 | 28.512 | 18 34 | 1.04 | 54.912 | 35 45 |
| .06 | 3.168 | 2 04 | .56 | 29.568 | 19 15 | 1.06 | 55.968 | 36 26 |
| .08 | 4.224 | 2 45 | .58 | 30.624 | 19 56 | 1.08 | 57.024 | 37 08 |
| .10 | 5.280 | 3 26 | .60 | 31.680 | 20 38 | 1.10 | 58.080 | 37 49 |
| .12 | 6.336 | 4 08 | .62 | 32.736 | 21 19 | 1.12 | 59.136 | 38 30 |
| .14 | 7.392 | 4 49 | .64 | 33.792 | 22 00 | 1.14 | 60.192 | 39 11 |
| .16 | 8.448 | 5 30 | .66 | 34.848 | 22 41 | 1.16 | 61.248 | 39 53 |
| .18 | 9.504 | 6 11 | .68 | 35.904 | 23 23 | 1.18 | 62.304 | 40 34 |
| .20 | 10.560 | 6 53 | .70 | 36.960 | 24 04 | 1.20 | 63.360 | 41 15 |
| .22 | 11.616 | 7 34 | .72 | 38.016 | 24 45 | 1.22 | 64.416 | 41 56 |
| .24 | 12.672 | 8 15 | .74 | 39.072 | 25 26 | 1.24 | 65.472 | 42 38 |
| .26 | 13.728 | 8 56 | .76 | 40.128 | 26 08 | 1.26 | 66.528 | 43 19 |
| .28 | 14.784 | 9 38 | .78 | 41.184 | 26 49 | 1.28 | 67.584 | 44 00 |
| .30 | 15.840 | 10 19 | .80 | 42.240 | 27 30 | 1.30 | 68.640 | 44 41 |
| .32 | 16.896 | 11 00 | .82 | 43.296 | 28 11 | 1.32 | 69.696 | 45 23 |
| .34 | 17.952 | 11 41 | .84 | 44.352 | 28 53 | 1.34 | 70.752 | 46 04 |
| .36 | 19.008 | 12 23 | .86 | 45.408 | 29 34 | 1.36 | 71.808 | 46 45 |
| .38 | 20.064 | 13 04 | .88 | 46.464 | 30 15 | 1.38 | 72.864 | 47 26 |
| .40 | 21.120 | 13 45 | .90 | 47.520 | 30 57 | 1.40 | 73.920 | 48 08 |
| .42 | 22.176 | 14 26 | .92 | 48.576 | 31 38 | 1.42 | 74.976 | 48 49 |
| .44 | 23.232 | 15 08 | .94 | 49.632 | 32 19 | 1.44 | 76.032 | 49 30 |
| .46 | 24.288 | 15 49 | .96 | 50.688 | 33 00 | 1.46 | 77.088 | 50 11 |
| .48 | 25.344 | 16 30 | .98 | 51.744 | 33 41 | 1.48 | 78.144 | 50 52 |
| .50 | 26.400 | 17 11 | 1.00 | 52.800 | 34 23 | 1.50 | 79.200 | 51 34 |
| 1.52 | 80.256 | 52 15 | 2.10 | 110.880 | 1 12 11 | 5.20 | 274.560 | 2 58 36 |
| 1.54 | 81.312 | 52 56 | 2.20 | 116.160 | 1 15 37 | 5.40 | 285.120 | 3 05 27 |
| 1.56 | 82.368 | 53 37 | 2.30 | 121.440 | 1 19 03 | 5.60 | 295.680 | 3 12 19 |
| 1.58 | 83.424 | 54 19 | 2.40 | 126.720 | 1 22 29 | 5.80 | 306.240 | 3 19 10 |
| 1.60 | 84.480 | 55 00 | 2.50 | 132.000 | 1 25 56 | 6.00 | 316.800 | 3 26 01 |
| 1.62 | 85.536 | 55 41 | 2.60 | 137.280 | 1 29 22 | 6.20 | 327.360 | 3 32 52 |
| 1.64 | 86.592 | 56 22 | 2.70 | 142.560 | 1 32 48 | 6.40 | 337.920 | 3 39 43 |
| 1.66 | 87.648 | 57. 04 | 2.80 | 147.840 | 1 36 14 | 6.60 | 348.480 | 3 46 34 |
| 1.68 | 88.704 | 57 45 | 2.90 | 153.120 | 1 39 40 | 6.80 | 359.040 | 3 53 24 |
| 1.70 | 89.760 | 58 26 | 3.00 | 158.400 | 1 43 06 | 7.00 | 369.600 | 4 00 15 |
| 1.72 | 90.816 | 59 07 | 3.10 | 163.680 | 1 46 32 | 7.20 | 380.160 | 4 07 06 |
| 1.74 | 91.872 | 59 49 | 3.20 | 168.960 | 1 49 58 | 7.40 | 390.720 | 4 13 56 |
| 1.76 | 92.928 | 1 00 30 | 3.30 | 174.240 | 1 53 24 | 7.60 | 401.280 | 4 20 46 |
| 1.78 | 93.984 | 1 01 11 | 3.40 | 179.520 | 1 56 50 | 7.80 | 411.840 | 4 27 36 |
| 1.80 | 95.040 | 1 01 52 | 3.50 | 184.800 | 2 00 16 | 8.00 | 422.400 | 4 34 26 |
| 1.82 | 96.096 | 1 02 34 | 3.60 | 190.080 | 2 03 42 | 8.20 | 432.960 | 4 41 16 |
| 1.84 | 97.152 | 1 03 15 | 3.70 | 195.360 | 2 07 08 | 8.40 | 443.520 | 4 48 06 |
| 1.86 | 98.208 | 1 03 56 | 3.80 | 200.640 | 2 10 34 | 8.60 | 454.080 | 4 54 55 |
| 1.88 | 99.264 | 1 04 37 | 3.90 | 205.920 | 2 14 00 | 8.80 | 464.640 | 5 01 44 |
| 1.90 | 100.320 | 1 05 19 | 4.00 | 211.200 | 2 17 26 | 9.00 | 475.200 | 5 08 34 |
| 1.92 | 101.376 | 1 06 00 | 4.20 | 221.760 | 2 24 18 | 9.20 | 485.760 | 5 15 23 |
| 1.94 | 102.432 | 1 06 41 | 4.40 | 232.320 | 2 31 10 | 9.40 | 496.320 | 5 22 12 |
| 1.96 | 103.488 | 1 07 22 | 4.60 | 242.880 | 2 38 01 | 9.60 | 506.880 | 5 29 01 |
| 1.98 | 104.544 | 1 08 04 | 4.80 | 253.440 | 2 44 53 | 9.80 | 517.440 | 5 35 50 |
| 2.00 | 105.600 | 1 08 45 | 5.00 | 264.000 | 2 51 45 | 10.00 | 528.000 | 5 42 38 |

41421°—16——12

TABLE XXIII.—Inches in decimals of a foot.

| 1/16 | 3/32 | 1/8 | 3/16 | 1/4 | 5/16 | 3/8 | 1/2 | 5/8 | 3/4 | 7/8 |
|---|---|---|---|---|---|---|---|---|---|---|
| .0052 | .0078 | .0104 | .0156 | .0208 | .0260 | .0313 | .0417 | .0521 | .0625 | .0729 |
| 1 | 2 | 3 | 4 | 5 | 6 | 7 | 8 | 9 | 10 | 11 |
| .0833 | .1667 | .2500 | .3333 | .4167 | .5000 | .5833 | .6667 | .7500 | .8333 | .9167 |

TABLE XXIV.—Radii and deflections.

| Deg. of curve. | | Radius. | Tan. Def. 100 ft. | Chd. Def. 100 ft. | Def. for 1 ft. | Deg. of curve. | | Radius. | Tan Def. 100 ft. | Chd. Def. 100 ft. | Def. for 1 ft. |
|---|---|---|---|---|---|---|---|---|---|---|---|
| ° | ′ | Ft. | Ft. | Ft. | Minutes. | ° | ′ | Ft. | Ft. | Ft. | Minutes. |
| 0 | 10 | 34377 | .145 | .291 | 0.05 | 7 | | 819.0 | 6.105 | 12.21 | 2.10 |
| | 20 | 17189 | .291 | .582 | 0.10 | | 20 | 781.8 | 6.395 | 12.79 | 2.20 |
| | 30 | 11459 | .436 | .873 | 0.15 | | 30 | 764.5 | 6.540 | 13.08 | 2.25 |
| | 40 | 8594.4 | .582 | 1.164 | 0.20 | | 40 | 747.9 | 6.685 | 13.37 | 2.30 |
| | 50 | 6875.5 | .727 | 1.454 | 0.25 | 8 | | 716.8 | 6.976 | 13.95 | 2.40 |
| 1 | | 5729.6 | .873 | 1.745 | 0.30 | | 20 | 688.2 | 7.266 | 14.53 | 2.50 |
| | 10 | 4911.2 | 1.018 | 2.036 | 0.35 | | 30 | 674.7 | 7.411 | 14.82 | 2.55 |
| | 20 | 4297.3 | 1.164 | 2.327 | 0.40 | | 40 | 661.7 | 7.556 | 15.11 | 2.60 |
| | 30 | 3819.8 | 1.309 | 2.618 | 0.45 | 9 | | 637.3 | 7.846 | 15.69 | 2.70 |
| | 40 | 3437.9 | 1.454 | 2.909 | 0.50 | | 20 | 614.6 | 8.136 | 16.27 | 2.80 |
| | 50 | 3125.4 | 1.600 | 3.200 | 0.55 | | 30 | 603.8 | 8.281 | 16.56 | 2.85 |
| 2 | | 2864.9 | 1.745 | 3.490 | 0.60 | | 40 | 593.4 | 8.426 | 16.85 | 2.90 |
| | 10 | 2644.6 | 1.891 | 3.781 | 0.65 | 10 | | 573.7 | 8.716 | 17.43 | 3.00 |
| | 20 | 2455.7 | 2.036 | 4.072 | 0.70 | | 30 | 546.4 | 9.150 | 18.30 | 3.15 |
| | 30 | 2292.0 | 2.181 | 4.363 | 0.75 | 11 | | 521.7 | 9.585 | 19.16 | 3.30 |
| | 40 | 2148.8 | 2.327 | 4.654 | 0.80 | | 30 | 499.1 | 10.02 | 20.04 | 3.45 |
| | 50 | 2022.4 | 2.472 | 4.945 | 0.85 | 12 | | 478.3 | 10.45 | 20.91 | 3.60 |
| 3 | | 1910.1 | 2.618 | 5.235 | 0.90 | | 30 | 459.3 | 10.89 | 21.77 | 3.75 |
| | 10 | 1809.6 | 2.763 | 5.526 | 0.95 | 13 | | 441.7 | 11.32 | 22.64 | 3.90 |
| | 20 | 1719.1 | 2.908 | 5.817 | 1.00 | | 30 | 425.4 | 11.75 | 23.51 | 4.05 |
| | 30 | 1637.3 | 3.054 | 6.108 | 1.05 | 14 | | 410.3 | 12.18 | 24.37 | 4.20 |
| | 40 | 1562.9 | 3.199 | 6.398 | 1.10 | | 30 | 396.2 | 12.62 | 25.24 | 4.35 |
| | 50 | 1495.0 | 3.345 | 6.689 | 1.15 | 15 | | 383.1 | 13.05 | 26.11 | 4.50 |
| 4 | | 1432.7 | 3.490 | 6.980 | 1.20 | | 30 | 370.8 | 13.49 | 26.97 | 4.65 |
| | 10 | 1375.4 | 3.635 | 7.271 | 1.25 | 16 | | 359.3 | 13.92 | 27.84 | 4.80 |
| | 20 | 1322.5 | 3.718 | 7.561 | 1.30 | | 30 | 348.5 | 14.35 | 28.70 | 4.95 |
| | 30 | 1273.6 | 3.926 | 7.852 | 1.35 | 17 | | 338.3 | 14.78 | 29.56 | 5.10 |
| | 40 | 1228.1 | 4.071 | 8.143 | 1.40 | 18 | | 319.6 | 15.64 | 31.29 | 5.40 |
| | 50 | 1185.8 | 4.217 | 8.433 | 1.45 | 19 | | 302.9 | 16.51 | 33.01 | 5.70 |
| 5 | | 1146.3 | 4.362 | 8.724 | 1.50 | 20 | | 287.9 | 17.37 | 34.73 | 6.00 |
| | 10 | 1109.3 | 4.507 | 9.014 | 1.55 | 21 | | 274.4 | 18.22 | 36.44 | 6.30 |
| | 20 | 1074.7 | 4.653 | 9.305 | 1.60 | 22 | | 262.0 | 19.08 | 38.16 | 6.60 |
| | 30 | 1042.1 | 4.798 | 9.596 | 1.65 | 23 | | 250.8 | 19.94 | 39.87 | 6.90 |
| | 40 | 1011.5 | 4.943 | 9.886 | 1.70 | 24 | | 240.5 | 20.79 | 41.58 | 7.20 |
| | 50 | 982.6 | 5.088 | 10.18 | 1.75 | 25 | | 231.0 | 21.64 | 43.28 | 7.50 |
| 6 | | 955.4 | 5.234 | 10.47 | 1.80 | 26 | | 222.3 | 22.50 | 44.99 | 7.80 |
| | 10 | 929.6 | 5.379 | 10.76 | 1.85 | 27 | | 214.2 | 23.35 | 46.69 | 8.10 |
| | 20 | 905.1 | 5.524 | 11.05 | 1.90 | 28 | | 206.7 | 24.19 | 48.38 | 8.40 |
| | 30 | 881.9 | 5.669 | 11.34 | 1.95 | 29 | | 199.7 | 25.04 | 50.07 | 8.70 |
| | 40 | 859.9 | 5.814 | 11.63 | 2.00 | 30 | | 193.2 | 25.88 | 51.76 | 9.00 |

TABLE XXV.—DATA CONCERNING **standard gage cars.**

| Class. | Length. | Width. | Height. | Approx. weight (empty in tons). | Capacity. Cu. ft. | Capacity. Tons. |
|---|---|---|---|---|---|---|
| | ′ ″ | ′ ″ | ′ ″ | | | |
| Box cars | 33 6 | 8 3 | 7 0 | 14 to 20 | 1,934.6 | 20 to 30 |
| | [1] 36 0 | 8 6 | 8 0 | 16 to 22 | 2,448.0 | 30 to 40 |
| | [1] 40 0 | 8 6 | 8 0 | 18 to 25 | 2,720.0 | 40 to 50 |
| Furniture cars | [1] 40 0 | 9 0 | 10 0 | 18 to 24 | 3,600.0 | 25 to 40 |
| | 44 5 | 8 4 | 8 6 | 20 to 24 | 3,146.1 | 30 to 40 |
| | [1] 50 0 | 8 8 | 10 0 | 22 to 24 | 4,333.5 | 30 to 40 |
| Refrigerator cars | [2] 29 0 | 8 1 | 7 1 | 20 to 25 | 1,660.4 | 20 to 30 |
| | [1] 30 0 | 8 4 | 7 4 | 20 to 25 | 1,833.3 | 20 to 30 |
| | [2,3] 34 0 | 8 3 | 7 5 | 20 to 28 | 2,080.5 | 25 to 45 |
| Stock cars, single deck | 34 0 | 8 8 | 7 0 | 15 to 18 | 2,062.7 | 20 to 25 |
| | [1] 36 0 | 8 8 | 7 0 | 15 to 18 | 2,184.1 | 25 to 30 |
| | 40 0 | 8 8 | 8 0 | 18 to 21 | 2,773.4 | 35 to 40 |
| Stock cars, double deck | 34 0 | 8 8 | 7 6 | 15 to 18 | 2,210.1 | 20 to 25 |
| | [1] 36 0 | 8 8 | 7 2 | 15 to 18 | 2,236.2 | 25 to 30 |
| Flat cars | [1] 36 0 | 8 6 | ......... | 12 to 15 | .......... | 20 to 40 |
| | [1] 40 0 | 8 8 | ......... | 15 to 20 | .......... | 30 to 50 |
| | 44 0 | 8 8 | ......... | 15 to 20 | .......... | 30 to 50 |
| Gondola cars | 32 0 | 8 3 | 3 7 | 13 to 15 | 945.9 | 20 to 30 |
| | 34 0 | 8 4 | 3 8 | 15 to 18 | 1,038.9 | 30 to 40 |
| | [1] 38 0 | 9 2 | 3 9 | 18 to 20 | 1,306.3 | 40 to 50 |
| | 40 0 | 8 9 | 4 8 | 19 to 24 | 1,633.5 | 40 to 50 |
| Caboose | 30′ to 36′ long | | | 15 to 18 | .......... | .......... |
| Baggage, express, and mail | 60′ to 70′ long | | | 25 to 45 | .......... | .......... |
| Coach | 60′ to 75′ long | | | 28 to 48 | .......... | .......... |
| Dining cars | 60′ to 70′ long | | | 40 to 60 | .......... | .......... |
| Sleeping cars | 60′ to 70′ long | | | 36 to 55 | .......... | .......... |

[1] Seem to be most usual sizes.
[2] Length between ice tanks, outside length about 8′ greater.
[3] Refrigerator cars carry from 4 to 5 tons of ice.

# INDEX.

A.



B.

S.

T.

Y.



O

www.ingramcontent.com/pod-product-compliance
Lightning Source LLC
Chambersburg PA
CBHW030733250426
43671CB00034B/205
* 9 7 8 1 5 8 9 6 3 8 7 8 5 *